OER: A Field Guide for Academic Librarians

OER: A Field Guide for Academic Librarians

Andrew Wesolek, Jonathan Lashley, & Anne Langley

To
Lauren

Don't read
it in
one sitting!
HA!

PACIFIC
UNIVERSITY
PRESS

PACIFIC UNIVERSITY PRESS
2043 College Way
Forest Grove, Oregon 97116

Cover design by Alex Bell
ISBN (pbk) 978-1-945398-79-7
ISBN (epub) 978-1-945398-00-1
ISBN (PDF) 978-1-945398-01-8

Published in the United States

Errata / Version Statement: All formats (print, PDF, epub) corrected 12/04/2018 to reflect editorial corrections not captured in initial publication. Substantive revisions made to Reed & Turner (chapter and bios).

Table of Contents

Introduction   1

Section 1: The Case for OER   15

Stakes and Stakeholders: Open Educational   17
Resources—Framing the Issues
Brady Yano & Carla Myers

What Does the Research Say About OER?   41
John Hilton III

Section 2: The Pedagogical Implications of OER   49

From Textbook Affordability to Transformative Pedagogy: 51
Growing an OER Community
Jean Amaral

Creating Learning Opportunities in Open Education: An   73
Exploration of the Intersections of Information Literacy and
Scholarly Communication
Michelle Reed

Experiential Learning and Open Education: Partnering with   93
Students to Evaluate OER Accessibility
Michelle Reed & Ciara Turner

Course Material Decisions and Factors: Unpacking the   115
Opaque Box
Anita Walz

An Open Athenaeum: Creating an Institutional Home for   141
Open Pedagogy
Rajiv S. Jhangiani & Arthur G. Green

Section 3: OER Advocacy, Partnerships, Sustainability, and   163
Student Engagement

Open Partnerships: Identifying and Recruiting Allies for   165
Open Educational Resources Initiatives
Rebel Cummings-Sauls, Matt Ruen, Sarah Beaubien, &
Jeremy Smith

Getting to Know You: How We Turned Community   193
Knowledge into Open Advocacy
Lillian Rigling & William Cross

Advancing Access for First-Generation College Students: 213
OER Advocacy at UT San Antonio
DeeAnn Ivie & Carolyn Ellis

Student-Driven OER: Championing the Student Voice in   239
Campus-Wide Efforts
Alesha Baker & Cinthya Ippoliti

From Conversation to Cultural Change: Strategies for   253
Connecting with Students and Faculty to Promote OER
Adoption
Kirsten N. Dean

Making the Connections: The Role of Professional   273
Development in Advocating for OER
Michael LaMagna

Advocacy in OER: A Statewide Strategy for Building a   291
Sustainable Library Effort
Emily Frank & Teri Gallaway

Interinstitutional Collaborations to Forge Intracampus   309
Connections: A Case Study from the Duke Endowment
Libraries
Sarah Hare, Andrea Wright, Christy Allen, Geneen E.
Clinkscales, & Julie Reed

Section 4: Library-Supported Adoption and Creation Programs   331

Seeking Alternatives to High-Cost Textbooks: Six Years of The Open Education Initiative at the University of Massachusetts Amherst   333
Jeremy Smith

From Start-Up to Adolescence: University of Oklahoma's OER Efforts   351
Jen Waller, Cody Taylor, & Stacy Zemke

A Grassroots Approach to OER Adoption: The University of Saskatchewan Experience   381
Heather M. Ross, Shannon Lucky, & David Francis

Bringing OER to the Liberal Arts: An Innovative Grant Program   399
Jonathan Miller

Transforming Publishing with a Little Help From Our Friends: Supporting an Open Textbook Pilot Project with Friends of the Libraries Grant Funding   415
Chelle Batchelor

Closing Reflections   433
Nicole Allen

About the Authors   439

Index   449

Introduction

OER: A Mechanism for Educational Change

Jonathan Lashley, Andrew Wesolek, & Anne Langley

For many of us, the drive to effect positive change—however vague or idiosyncratic our sense of this might be—has guided our work in higher education. We champion the pursuit of a college degree because few endeavors can match it in terms of advancing a person's economic mobility (Chetty, Friedman, Saez, Turner, & Yagan, 2017). Despite recent debates about the value of a college degree (Pew Research Center, 2017), the opportunities and financial stability awarded to those with college degrees remain apparent when they are compared to peers who have only graduated high school (National Center for Education Statistics, 2017). And while more Americans have a college degree than ever before (Ryan & Bauman, 2016), access to a formal, post-secondary education continues to be elusive for some.

Indeed, over the last 10 years, analysts have projected that the cost of attending college would keep 2.4 million low-to-moderate income, college-qualified high school graduates from completing a college degree (Advisory Committee on Student Financial Assistance, 2006). During that same period, college students in the United States saw expenses related to tuition and fees increase by 63 percent, school housing costs (excluding board) increase by 51 percent, and textbook prices increase by 88 percent (Bureau of Labor, 2016). Because few students can afford a college education through salary alone, 44.2 million Americans have sought financial aid via student loans. As a result, total student loan debt is now topping $1.45 trillion in the United States (Board of Governors of the Federal Reserve System, 2017), and student loan delinquency rates are averaging 11.2 percent (Federal Reserve Bank of New York, 2017). The burden of a student's financial decisions extends beyond the mere individual: society will inevitably carry the weight of this debt for years to come.

As a means of making college more affordable and promoting access to educational content, many of us look to open educational resources (OER) as a catalyst for positive, tangible change. Residing in the public domain or licensed in such a way that they are made free for use and repurposing by others (Hewlett Foundation, n.d.), these open teaching, learning, and research resources not only serve as alternatives to commercial educational products, they promote new relationships between academic communities and educational content. Take, for instance, the *Project Management for Instructional Designers (PM4ID)* (2016) project that David Wiley undertook with instructional design students at Brigham Young University. Though open project management textbooks existed, none addressed the work of instructional designers in particular. Rather than make do with a general textbook, the affordances of openly licensed content engendered Wiley's students to work as co-authors and -editors on the content of a new, specialized open textbook that is still widely distributed and updated regularly. Thanks to OER, students became consumers and producers of increasingly valuable content while Wiley's assignments and course materials became only more relevant to the context of his class.

The Basics of OER

Open textbooks like *PM4ID* may arguably be the best-known form of OER, but the potential implementation of OER extends well beyond the textbook format. Definitions of OER account for a plethora of education-related assets including "full courses, materials, modules, textbooks, streaming videos, tests, software, and any other tools, materials, or techniques used to support access to knowledge" (Hewlett Foundation, n.d.). While any such content that exists in the public domain is free to (re)use and may play a valuable role in the development of OER, because copyright protection does or will not apply to such authored work (United States Copyright Office, n.d.), it is the affordances to retain, reuse, revise, remix, and redistribute (the 5 Rs) of open licensing that promote OER adoption as worthwhile. Coined by Wiley (Open Content, n.d.), the 5 Rs describe the ways in which openly licensed content may be transformed while still celebrating the work of the original author. Under open permissions, anyone might responsibly copy, keep, combine, edit, and share the original author's IP:

1. Retain: the right to make, own, and control copies of the content (e.g., download, duplicate, store, and manage)
2. **Reuse**: the right to use the content in a wide range of ways (e.g., in a class, in a study group, on a website, in a video)
3. **Revise**: the right to adapt, adjust, modify, or alter the content itself (e.g., translate the content into another language)
4. **Remix**: the right to combine the original or revised content with other material to create something new (e.g., incorporate the content into a mashup)
5. Redistribute: the right to share copies of the original content, your revisions, or your remixes with others (e.g., give a copy of the content to a friend) (Open Content, n.d.).

Thus, by way of the 5R permissions, users may transform openly licensed content under new, more fitting applications across myriad creative and educational contexts.

Organizations like Creative Commons (CC) exist to provide standardized, alternative means of licensing content so as to support original content creators and the 5R permissions alike. CC—a nonprofit organization that is the perhaps the most prominent platform for open licensing—maintains six licenses (BY, BY-ShareAlike, BY-NoDerivative, BY-NonCommercial, BY-NonCommercial-ShareAlike, BY-NonCommercial-NoDerivative). Through these licenses, authors may easily redefine the terms of copyright that are otherwise automatically applied to creative work, allowing materials to be shared broadly, reused flexibly, and modified legally (Creative Commons, n.d.). While any of the CC licenses may accompany OER, the least restrictive, CC-BY, is the one that we, the authors of this book, most heartily endorse (note that this book is licensed CC-BY). This particular license ensures that any resulting application of a work will provide attribution to its original authors without discouraging the transformative activities of others. A license that fully protects ownership and guides the open improvement of materials by all original and potential authors thus becomes a mechanism for great change in the development and distribution of resources to aid teaching, learning, and research.

This Book: A Guide

The production of new scholarly material is not without costs. While the end product may be free to read and free of most copyright restrictions, the production of OER requires substantial institutional investment—primarily in labor—for services such as peer review management, copy editing, typesetting, and the like. These up-front costs, combined with the lack of a clear revenue stream for OER, pose a challenge. Further complicating things, the possible implementations of OER may vary significantly as OER initiatives span departments, institutions, and systems. As is the case with other initiatives in higher education, research, assessment, and evaluation activities become necessary to support and sustain OER. Whether it is identifying milestones and stakeholders, surveying technical infrastructure and support, designing success criteria and evaluation, or shepherding training and curriculum changes, OER initiatives beg for collaboration among the various departments of our institutions. Some, including the editors of this book, look to academic librarians as uniquely qualified to lead such efforts (Bell & Salem, 2017). Simply, academic librarians are already well versed in managing content and working with others across disciplinary, professional, and geographic lines.

While faculty members and academic departments ultimately determine which educational materials are most appropriate for their courses, faculty, educators and academic leaders are not always aware of affordable or open alternatives to publisher content. Librarians, on the other hand, have a rich history of discovering educational materials broadly defined, ensuring access to such resources, and educating others about their use. This professional perspective encourages librarians to take a comprehensive view of educational resources. The greater the complexity of OER in form, the more we see a need for such wide gaze in coordinating the community-driven approaches modeled by cases covered in the following chapters. It takes a village to adopt, modify, create, and share content well.

Structure of this Book

We intend this book to act as a guide writ large for would-be champions of OER, that anyone—called to action by the example set by our chapter authors—might serve as guides themselves. The following chapters tap into the deep experience of practitioners who represent a meaningful cross section of higher education institutions in North America. It is our hope that the examples and discussions presented by our authors will facilitate connections among practitioners, foster the development of best practices for OER adoption and creation, and more importantly, lay a foundation for novel, educational excellence.

The openly licensed content of this book is organized into four sections: (1) an introduction to OER, (2) discussions of how OER transforms teaching and learning, (3) examples of how librarians advocate for OER across campus, and (4) models of library-supported adoption and creation of OER. We encourage readers who are new to OER to read through this volume linearly, beginning with the introductory material. Seasoned practitioners may wish to pick and choose among the case studies that most closely relate to the contexts of their particular institutions. The open education movement is made up of passionate professionals who are willing to share their experience with others (as evidenced by this open access collection of case studies). Readers will find brief biographies for all of our contributing authors, and we suggest that you reach out to those figures who seem most compelling or whose work most closely aligns with your own.

Section 1: The Case for OER

In Section 1, our authors describe the interdepartmental and transdisciplinary stakes, strategies, and opportunities that exist as the academic community endeavors to support OER in higher education.

Throughout "**Stakes and Stakeholders: Open Educational Resources—Framing the Issues**," Yano and Myers offer a broad survey of the ways in which OER is uniquely equipped to address the political, economic, and cultural conditions at play in modern education contexts. The authors further elaborate on how the escalating price tag for a college education relates to changes in the commercial publishing market, and identify the ways in which publishers' "digital direct" and "inclusive access" models are attempting to confound and cannibalize non-commercial technology like OER. As Yano and Myers explain, however, government entities, nonprofit organizations, and grassroots organizing have proven helpful in launching OER initiatives and keeping them open. Finally, this chapter puts forward a shared discourse for OER by highlighting the terms, actions, and responsibilities that we might share when working with others.

Hilton, in "**What Does the Research Say About OER?**," reviews the empirical research proving the efficacy of OER as an intervention. He situates the rise of OER as a means of combating the otherwise unchecked rise in textbook prices that has negatively affected students, taxpayers, and institutions financially. Perhaps even more important than securing financial equity, however, are the ways in which OER facilitates effective teaching and learning. By tracing how studies about cost savings, student outcomes, OER use, and user perception have proliferated over the last decade, Hilton paints a lucid picture of the meaningful relationships that exists between student success and open access to educational materials.

Section 2: The Pedagogical Implications of OER

In Section 2, our authors dive deeper into how OER-based interventions transform educational experiences for students and instructors alike.

Drilling down into the specific opportunities that OER initiatives might provide for academic librarians, Amaral's chapter, "**From Textbook Affordability to Transformative Pedagogy: Growing an OER Community**," situates support of OER as inherently complementary to the mission, resources, and priorities found at many libraries. Celebrating the top-down leadership of the City University of New York (CUNY) subsidizing library leadership in promoting low- and no-cost course materials, Amaral accounts for the hurdles, milestones, and opportunities that have helped position CUNY OER initiatives as some of the most compelling, scalable, and library-centric in the nation. At Borough of Manhattan Community College (BMCC), Amaral's home institution, success with OER has come through a variety of approaches that are measurable for impact and, in turn, reveal a clear picture of positive outcomes around OER. As a result, the chapter highlights the ways in which an active and engaged culture may emerge from librarians setting clear goals and working with others in the greater pursuit of reclaiming knowledge as public good.

When it comes to supporting OER, Reed recognizes a need for increased collaboration between information literacy and scholarly communication librarians. In her chapter, "**An Exploration of the Intersections of Information Literacy and Scholarly Communication**," Reed reflects on recommendations put forward by the Association of College & Research Libraries (ACRL) white paper for how these two areas of librarianship might intersect in significant ways. For librarians who are serving in one of these two contexts, or for non-librarian readers who seek to better connect with their library counterparts, this chapter underscores the importance of not neglecting one's own department when forming OER partnerships. Further, under the diversity of roles that occupy modern librarianship, Reed makes a case for why academic libraries are so perfectly positioned to initiate, innovate and support OER.

Reed and Turner, both of University of Texas at Arlington, in their chapter, "**Experiential Learning and Open Education: Partnering with Students to Evaluate OER Accessibility**," provide us with a description of their work with a student intern on evaluating OER for accessibility with disabled students. This chapter describes how they created a student internship program that designed guidelines, criteria, and standards for accessibility evaluation. The chapter includes the methods they used, the key resources they used to design their evaluation, and describes in detail how to evaluate OER for accessibility. They looked at content organization, how images are presented, tables, hyperlinks and multimedia, formulas, fonts, and color contrast. They also describe how the internship worked.

In her chapter, "**Course Material Decisions and Factors: Unpacking the Opaque Box**," Walz helps us consider the many factors that accompany course material selection and adoption. Though powerful forces like academic culture, tradition, and training might stymie the work of librarians, instructional designers, and others in cultivating a more purposeful relationship between instructors and the course materials they use, Walz observes an opportunity for open education advocates to break through these barriers and create more transparent, deliberate practices when evaluating and selecting required materials. Emphasizing how openness may inspire an ethic of understanding in those of us who work closely with faculty, this chapter offers insight as to how an individual librarian or other academic staff member might spark new and powerful conversations about course content by establishing shared values through a culture of trust and understanding.

In the final chapter of this section, Jhangiani and Green propose unity between librarians and others under the imperative of openly sharing practices and resources to support pedagogical innovation. "**An Open Athenaeum: Creating an Institutional Home for Open Pedagogy**" promotes contemporary conversations about how OER empower pedagogy in transformative ways, and illuminates the ways in which academic librarians and library resources might support these innovations. Jhangiani and Green provide multiple, tangible examples of open pedagogical practice across several disciplines and offer suggestions for how pedagogy, not tools or texts, is at the heart of our efforts when we advocate for OER. For the authors of this chapter, there is no better locale in which to cultivate the pedagogical efforts of an individual than among the resources and staff of an academic library.

Section 3: OER Advocacy, Partnerships, Sustainability, and Student Engagement

Section 3 provides a series of case studies about the practical, collaborative, and renewable aspects of supporting OER. Many strategies thus emerge for engaging instructors/students, finding and evaluating existing OER, and partnering with other units to support adoption/modification/creation initiatives.

In "**Open Partnerships: Identifying and Recruiting Allies for Open Educational Resources Initiatives**," Cummings-Sauls, Ruen, Beaubien, and Smith extend conversations about OER-enabled partnerships by exhaustively describing the roles and responsibilities harbored by potential stakeholders in OER initiatives and highlighting the ways in which librarians might instigate partnerships between these groups. By clearly identifying the stakes of library, faculty, student, administrative, instructional design, information technology, and bookstore partnerships, the authors promote a sort of inventory for how and why we might meaningfully engage these local audiences in support of OER. Looking beyond our institutions to the broader external communities, legislation, and services related to OER, this chapter introduces the importance of considering how conversations might (and ultimately should) scale to include metrics that are worth sharing outside of our respective institutions.

"**Getting to Know You: How We Turned Community Knowledge into Open Advocacy**," by Lillian Rigling and William Cross is about how North Carolina State University (NCSU) Libraries assessed their OER work and outreach strategies with students. NCSU implemented an Alt-Textbook program to fund the creation of free or low-cost learning materials in 2014. While the program had success in the specific areas where it was adopted, the library wanted to work through their students to support wider advocacy for the program. This chapter describes how they designed and conducted targeted outreach to students and how they assessed their outreach work.

DeeAnn Ivie and Carolyn Ellis's chapter, "**Advancing Access for First-Generation College Students: OER Advocacy at UT San Antonio**," describes in detail how they worked through campus partnerships and multiple student groups for OER advocacy with major campus stakeholders. This university with a large population of Hispanic first-generation students had strong economic drivers for OER, and the library took advantage of this unique population to lead the way. This chapter discusses integration with the registrar, the campus bookstore, and partnering with the Provost and the teaching and learning center; describes how they worked with the student government and various student organizations to not only market but assess progress; describes the metrics they used to measure the program's strengths and weaknesses; and finally talks about their future directions and how they will use strategic indicators to assess outcomes.

Alesha Baker and Cinthya Ippoliti, in their case study, "**Student-Driven OER: Championing the Student Voice in Campus-Wide Efforts**," focus on the adoption of OER through working closely with students in multiple ways. These authors describe how they engaged students at Oklahoma State University to become advocates for OER adoption, how they worked closely with student groups, student government, and through the creation of a committee that included students. They talk about how they obtained a development grant to get the work started, and how they provided supporting grants to faculty to design resources; and finally, they describe how students designed OER.

Dean's chapter, "**From Conversation to Cultural Change: Strategies for Connecting with Students and Faculty to Promote OER Adoption**," describes how Clemson University supported OER adoption through a multi-pronged effort. Because they wanted to change their culture, they used a variety of outreach and advocacy efforts. The library led the process through in-depth analysis of the environment, and extensive assessment of the existing culture in order to implement a variety of communication strategies. The process is described in detail, as well as the relationship building that is needed for successful implementation. Dean addresses the sustainability of the program and talks about future planning.

In the case study "**Making the Connections: The Role of Professional Development in Advocating for Open Educational Resources**," Michael LaMagna describes and presents a novel approach that uses training in professional development as a pathway to supporting future OER design and implementation. At Delaware County Community College, faculty librarians led the way serving as advocates and trainers to offer faculty in-service presentations about various aspects of OER. LaMagna describes the various sessions: OER writ large, an open discussion about campus adoption of OER, how to build alternative course content, and copyright and OER. Particulars about how they created the program, the funding sources, and the design of the curriculum are included in the case study.

"**Advocacy in OER: A Statewide Strategy for Building a Sustainable Library Effort**," by Emily Frank and Teri Gallaway, outlines how Lousiana's state library consortium, LOUIS, advanced OER initiatives across an entire state. Frank and Gallaway include discussion about OER for cost savings at the state level, how they used grants to subsidize library faculty work, and how state legislation supported their work to reach statewide adoption. In particular, they describe their train-the-trainer approach, how they used training efforts to increase outreach, and how the libraries served as leaders throughout the process. They talk about how their advocacy changed the culture in the state.

Five authors, Sarah Hare, Andrea Wright, Christy Allen, Geneen E. Clinkscales, and Julie Reed, in the chapter, "**Interinstitutional Collaborations to Forge Intracampus Connections: A Case Study From the**

Duke Endowment Libraries," provide a study on how different institutions can work together to implement open education programs in a variety of different settings and campus cultures. This chapter talks about endowment support, assessment and analysis of their work together, advocacy, implementation and training, program customization, and using a train-the-trainer approach, and discusses how they engaged faculty. The institutions involved include: Duke University, Davidson College, Furman University, and Johnson C. Smith University.

Section 4: Library-Supported Adoption and Creation Programs

The final section of this book offers case studies in which library staff and operations successfully lead the development, sharing, and adoption of OER at a variety of institutions.

In "**Seeking Alternatives to High-Cost Textbooks**," Smith outlines the growth OER initiatives at the University of Massachusetts, Amherst. With a focus on improvisation, developing partnerships and transitioning from textbook affordability to true open education, Smith details grant funding opportunities offered through U. Mass. Amherst while wrestling with the questions of what exactly libraries support when they support "open education" and how can that support be provided sustainably.

Waller, Taylor, and Zemke, writing about the University of Oklahoma, present a chapter all about the multiple aspects of implementing their open education program. "**From Start-Up to Adolescence: University of Oklahoma's OER Efforts**," maps out their route to deep OER implementation. This chapter describes a top-down approach that included faculty support grants, creation of an OER Librarian position, the program design, how they put together an OER planning committee, an assessment of OER technologies, and OER course assessment design. They include a thorough description of their outreach strategies, and an assessment of those strategies.

Ross and Francis describe a unique bottom-up approach to adopting OER in "**A Grassroots Approach to OER Adoption: The University of Saskatchewan Experience**." They talk about how outreach builds awareness, and describe their multiple projects and partnerships across the university. Ross and Francis describe how individual champions can be terrific instruments for change, and how even a single faculty adoption can start changing campus opinions. They tell how they used their institutional repository to support their adoption efforts and describe the library as the leader for OER.

In "**Bringing OER to the Liberal Arts: An Innovative Grant Program**," Miller discusses at length the work at Rollins College, a small liberal arts college in Florida, to use faculty grants to inspire and initiate the creation of OER. Their program focused on full-time, tenure-track faculty, and designed an iterative grant process with clearly defined criteria that mapped to their program goals. Miller describes their experience with an art and art history professor, a political science professor, and a physics professor. The unique challenges each professor faced are discussed, as well as some of the lessons they learned throughout the process.

Finally, In "**Transforming Publishing with a Little Help From our Friends**," Batchelor offers a case study in OER textbook publishing through the University of Washington and the Rebus Foundation. Specifically, she offers an example of what the Reebus Foundation could look like in the future, while calling on librarians to serve as catalysts and connectors in a broader faculty-driven OER publishing community.

A Call to Action

Though this book cannot fully account for all of the considerations that are necessary for supporting the OER movement, we have volunteered a common understanding for you to consult and reuse regarding the stakes, stakeholders, strategies, and opportunities worth anticipating in your work. Whether institutional or individual in scope, participation in the OER movement sponsors meaningful change for education. Those of us who work as academic librarians, however, are fortunate to harbor many of the relevant resources and skill sets that have proven invaluable to shaping the open education movement for broadest, most sustainable impact. Librarians have a long and rich history of connecting researchers with relevant information, preserving material, and facilitating access to that material. There are themes that run through many of the case studies, including the library and librarians as both catalysts and community leaders in awareness building, adoption oversight, and implementation project management. In short, we are certain you will be able to find potential solutions and a new network of colleagues to help you address the role of OER at your institution.

References

Advisory Committee on Student Financial Assistance. (2006). *Mortgaging our future: How financial barriers to college undercut America's global competitiveness.* Retrieved from ERIC Institute of Education Sciences website: https://eric.ed.gov/?id=ED529499.

Bell, S. J., & Salem, J. J. (2017). It's up to the librarians: Establishing a statewide OER initiative. *Pennsylvania Libraries: Research & Practice, 5*(2), 77-82. doi:10.5195/palrap.2017.166

Board of Governors of the Federal Reserve System. (2017). Consumer credit—G.19 [Online data set]. Retrieved from https://www.federalreserve.gov/releases/g19/current/default.htm

Bureau of Labor and Statistics. (2016, August 30). College tuition and fees increase 63 percent since January 2006 [Blog post]. Retrieved from https://www.bls.gov/opub/ted/2016/college-tuition-and-fees-increase-63-percent-since-january-2006.htm

Chetty, R., Friedman, J., Saez, E., Turner, N., & Yagan, D. (2017). *Mobility report cards: The* role of colleges in intergenerational mobility (NBER Working Paper No. 23618). doi:10.3386/w23618

Creative Commons. (n.d.). FAQ. Retrieved from https://creativecommons.org/faq/#what-is-creative-commons-and-what-do-you-do

Federal Reserve Bank of New York. (2017). *Quarterly report on household debt and credit.* Retrieved from https://www.newyorkfed.org/medialibrary/interactives/householdcredit/data/pd/HHDC_2016Q4.pdf

Hewlett Foundation. (n.d.). Open educational resources. Retrieved from http://www.hewlett.org/strategy/open-educational-resources

National Center for Education Statistics. (2017). *The condition of education 2017* (NCES 2017-144). Retrieved from https://nces.ed.gov/programs/coe/pdf/Indicator_CBA/coe_cba_2017_05.pdf

Open Content. (n.d.). Defining the "open" in open content and open educational resources. Retrieved from http://opencontent.org/definition

Pew Research Center. (2017). Sharp partisan divisions in views of national institutions. Retrieved from http://www.people-press.org/2017/07/10/sharp-partisan-divisions-in-views-of-national-institutions

Ryan, C. L., & Bauman, K. (2016). *Educational attainment in the United States: 2015.* Retrieved from United States Census Bureau website: https://www.census.gov/content/dam/Census/library/publications/2016/demo/p20-578.pdf.

United States Copyright Office. (n.d.) Definitions. Retrieved from https://www.copyright.gov/help/faq-definitions.html.

Wiley, D. et al. (2016). Project management for instructional designers. Retrieved from https://pm4id.org/.

Section 1:

The Case for OER

Readers of this brief introductory section will find a broad overview of current political and economic contexts affecting higher education affordability, and a survey of literature proposing OER as one potential solution. Those readers new to OER will benefit from succinct explanations of what OER are, the problems they are meant to solve, and some documented solutions.

First, Yano and Myers introduce us to a shared discourse surrounding OER, highlighting the terms, actions, and responsibilities of OER practice. Learning this shared language is significant in the OER space when one considers that government entities, nonprofit organizations, and grassroots efforts have all contributed to the advancement of OER, in comparison to the language established publishers employ in related ventures, i.e. "digital direct" and "inclusive access" models. In order to move toward truly open resources, it is imperative that practitioners agree on the terminology surrounding the movement.

In the following chapter John Hilton then offers compelling evidence of the efficacy of OER in the classroom. Through his thorough review of studies about cost savings, student outcomes, OER use, and user perceptions have proliferated over the last decade, Hilton makes clear the strength of the relationships between student success and open access to educational materials.

Stakes and Stakeholders: Open Educational Resources—Framing the Issues

Brady Yano & Carla Myers

College is still valuable, but more students are enrolling than graduating. According to a 2014 study by Complete College America that investigated the length of time for college graduation, the four-year degree is simply no longer the reality for most undergraduate students (Complete College America, 2014). The vast majority of students at U.S. public universities are completing their bachelor's degree in six years, and for students completing two-year associate's degrees at community colleges the average graduation rate is three years. On-time graduation rates account for only 36 percent of students completing four-year bachelor's degrees at flagship institutions.[1] This number drops to 19 percent for students completing four-year bachelor's degrees at non-flagship institutions, and drops as low as 5 percent for students completing a two-year associate's degree at non-flagship institutions. The same report also found that only 50 of the more than 580 public four-year institutions have graduation rates above 50 percent. This has resulted in more than 31 million students in the past two decades having attended a U.S. college but never earning a degree. The reality is that higher education costs too much, takes too long, and graduates far too few.

The rising cost of higher education poses a significant challenge to those who are interested in pursuing a degree, as students cannot access what they cannot afford. There has been a consistent increase in the cost

---

[1] The phrase flagship institution may be applied to an individual school or campus within each state system. A flagship institution is the best-known institution in the state, often the first to be established, and frequently the largest and most selective, as well as the most research-intensive public universities.

of tuition in both the U.S.[2] and Canada,[3] and textbook costs have surpassed that rate of growth. According to a report conducted by the U.S. Government Accountability Office (2013), from 2002 to 2012, textbook prices rose on average 6 percent per year. The same report revealed that new textbook prices increased by a total of 82 percent during that same time period. This increase is significant, especially when compared to the 28 percent increase in overall consumer prices during the same time period.

When it comes to recommended student budgets versus actual student spending, a large discrepancy exists. The College Board (www.collegeboard.org) releases an annual report detailing a breakdown of student budgets for the academic year based on information received by their member institutions. According to their 2016 report, the U.S. average annual undergraduate student budget for books and supplies falls between $1,200 and $1,400.[4] The Financial Consumer Agency of Canada (n.d.) recommends that students should budget between $800 and $1,000 per year for textbooks and other course materials. However, according to the National Association of College Stores (NACS) (2016), average student spending on course materials is $602, which represents a 14 percent decrease since 2007. This discrepancy is problematic as it indicates students are not purchasing the materials they are expected to. While one could conclude that students are finding cheaper ways to access their required materials, studies lead us to believe otherwise. A survey of 22,000 Florida students conducted by Florida Virtual Campus (2016) found that high textbook prices have a negative impact on academic behavior. Two thirds of students did not purchase the required textbook, more than one

---

[2] The College Board has been documenting trends in higher education, including tuition and fees. More information on their findings is available here:
https://trends.collegeboard.org/sites/default/files/2017-trends-in-college-pricing_1.pdf

[3] In the past decade, Statistics Canada has reported a tuition increase of 40 percent. More information on their findings is available here:
http://globalnews.ca/news/2924898/university-tuition-fees-rise-40-percent-in-a-decade/

[4] The College Board has a membership of over 6,000 institutions and organizations in the United States and around the world.

third earned a poor grade as a result of not purchasing the textbook, and nearly one fifth failed a course as a result of not having access to the textbook. The same survey also showed that nearly half of students took fewer courses due to textbook costs while over one-in-four had dropped a course because of the associated textbook costs. The results of this survey are alarming, as they indicate that cost barriers are forcing students into making decisions that have negative impacts on their academic success.

Textbook Affordability—Issues and Solutions

Market Changes

It is important to understand how the textbook market operates to gain an understanding of why textbook costs have spiraled out of control. Unlike other markets where a product is desired and consumers may select which option they prefer, the textbook market is similar to the prescription drug market. Much like the relationship between a doctor and their patient, students are obliged to purchase the specific textbook(s) assigned by their instructor; regardless of how widespread the alternatives may be, students are expected to use a certain edition of the material. The burden on consumers is compounded by the fact that there are five major publishers that hold nearly 90 percent of the market; together they have the ability to regulate the price point at which textbooks are sold (Koch, 2013). Data published by the Bureau of Labor Statistics (BLS) has shown that textbook prices rose at over three times the rate of inflation from January 1977 to June 2015—a 1,041 percent increase (Popken, 2015). Publishers are effectively abusing the market and as a result, students are being priced out.

Another reason for escalating costs is the periodic release of new editions. Publishers have relied on producing newer editions to reduce the reuse of a specific text and effectively eliminate the resale market. With publisher representatives leading with the newest versions of materials when approaching faculty, these revised editions are typically the ones sought. In a discipline like mathematics where the content does not change frequently, it begs the question of how different the content between the two editions really is, as updated images and tables should not be justification for significantly increasing the cost of a resource. Additionally, for a faculty member faced with both time and resource constraints, a publisher's offer of a textbook coupled with lecture slides and test banks is incredibly compelling.

The bundling of learning resources is yet another tactic used by publishers to increase costs. New textbooks are often accompanied with an assortment of additional digital resources including study guides, homework assignments, and quizzes. These resources can be "unlocked" by students using an access code included in their textbook bundle. Instructors may recommend that students use these resources as supplemental learning materials, or assign their students online homework assignments and quizzes that contribute to their final grades. The inclusion of these online resources is used as justification for inflating prices, regardless of whether they are used by the student or not. Like many software licenses, these codes are tied to a single user and therefore have no resale value. Students purchasing used textbooks are obligated to purchase a new access code from the publisher to access the digital content, thereby negating much of the cost savings normally associated with purchasing used copies.

Going Digital

As student spending on textbooks has decreased, publishers have felt the hit directly. In 2014, Brian Kibb, president of McGraw-Hill stunned many when he said, "Textbooks are dead. They're dinosaurs" (Smith, 2014). In 2016 the world's largest education publisher, Pearson, garnered a pre-tax loss of £2.6 billion (US$3.3 billion), primarily due to the collapse of their U.S. higher education business (Sweney, 2017). With a decline in print textbook sales—which is consistent with the NACS finding—there has been a major push from publishers to expand their digital offerings. Electronic versions of textbooks (eTextbooks) can be sold at a cheaper price point as this online delivery model allows publishers to save significant amounts of money on printing and distribution. The rental market for eTextbooks is another option put forward by publishers in an attempt to increase sales to students. Students are offered access to materials at a recognizably lower price; however, the catch is that students only have access to that resource for a limited period of time—usually the duration of the semester—eliminating any opportunity for retention while simultaneously eliminating contributions to the used textbook market.

Another popular approach has been through automatic purchasing programs that publishers are marketing as "Digital Direct" or "Inclusive

Access" (Straumsheim, 2017).[5] In these automatic purchasing programs, every student pays a mandatory course materials fee lower than the cost of a new hardbound version of the same text. While publishers collect less revenue per student, a consistent revenue stream is guaranteed for the duration of time outlined in the contract signed between the publisher and institution. The fee is charged directly to a student's account, and an electronic version of the textbook and any supplementary materials is made available on a digital delivery platform. Depending on the contract, students may have the option to opt out, but the terms often used are restrictive and aimed at minimizing these numbers.[6] In other cases, students are charged directly regardless of their consent. This model holds numerous similarities to the access codes mentioned previously and hold the same concerns from both a 5Rs,[7] and a copyright and usage data perspective. Under these models, students are restricted from exercising the 5R permissions and it is also unclear who owns the copyright to the content created within the platform. While the student should retain ownership over the works they create, copyright may ultimately fall to the publisher. Further concerns surround publishers' unfettered access to tracking student usage data on their platforms. While publishers may argue that this data will help build stronger platforms, this data could also be used to justify changes to the offerings that may hurt students.

The promise of more affordable textbooks and greater access may appeal to a higher education audience concerned about students lacking access to the resources necessary for academic success. But while digital content is currently being offered at a lower price point than print ver-

---

[5] As this initiative is fairly new there has not been much published on the topic yet. This article is, currently, one of the most notable pieces available: https://www.insidehighered.com/news/2017/01/31/textbook-publishers-contemplate-inclusive-access-business-model-future

[6] In the United States, federal law stipulates that students must have the ability to opt out of such programs, however no such stipulations exist in Canada. Algonquin College, the first Canadian institution to pilot the eTexts model, does not allow students to opt out: http://www.algonquincollege.com/etexts/texidium-faq/#optout

[7] The 5 Rs are reuse, revise, remix, redistribute and retain. More information about the 5 Rs can be found here: http://opencontent.org/definition/

sions, publishers have been clear in their intent to transition towards digital;[8] and without the print textbook market helping with price regulation, the digital market would only be in competition with itself. As academic librarians have experienced the escalation of prices in the subscription journal market,[9] it could be assumed the same would happen in a textbook market dominated by a few major publishers.

While automatic purchasing programs may be one solution toward textbook affordability, open educational resources (OER) are freely available learning materials that have proven to be effective in serving students. Hilton (2016) explored the results of nine studies that examined the impact of OER on student learning outcomes in higher education settings. Across the studies, only one showed that the use of OER was connected with lower learning outcomes in more instances than it was with positive outcomes, and another showed that the majority of the classes analyzed had non-significant differences. Though these freely available materials that can be used, adapted, and shared to better serve all students exist in the marketplace, their use and adoption are not guaranteed. The intervention of larger government and civil society organizations may be necessary to shape market trends in favor of students.

The Role of Government

Affordability issues in higher education have not gone unnoticed by the federal and state governments in the U.S. A growing number of government initiatives have encouraged and promoted the growth of OER as a means to curb textbook prices while also ensuring access to high-quality educational content. The 113th (2013–2014) and 114th Congress (2015–2016) introduced the Affordable College Textbook Act in an effort

---

[8] Pearson's chief executive, John Fallon, was quoted saying "Education like every other sector and sphere of life is going through this digital transformation. There is going to be a big winner in the transformation in education. We are absolutely determined to make Pearson that winner." https://www.theguardian.com/business/2017/feb/24/education-publisher-pearson-loss-us-penguin-random-house

[9] The prices for many journal and database subscriptions has also been rising beyond the rate of inflation. Library Journal (http://www.libraryjournal.com/) publishes an annual Periodicals Price Survey that explores how the rising costs of periodicals impacts library budgets.

"to expand the use of open textbooks in order to achieve savings for students" (H.R.3721, 2015–2016). Language in the Act calls for new grant funding to support the creation of OER, especially for use in large-enrollment courses that have high textbook costs. It would also require that textbook publishers unbundle educational materials students are required to purchase (e.g. textbooks, lab manuals, online access codes) to help facilitate cost savings. The bill did not advance in the 113th and 114th Congress, but was reintroduced in the 115th Congress (H.R. 3840, 2017–2019) with hopes that it could reinvigorate discussion on these important issues.[10]

State legislation and initiatives addressing similar issues have been passed, including:

- Oregon House Bills 2871 (2015) and 2729 (2017), which provided "legislative investment" in addressing textbook affordability by creating a grant program for OER development, standardizing interinstitutional evaluation of student savings that resulted from OER, and formalizing collaborations between the stakeholders (e.g., faculty, staff, librarians, etc.) across Oregon (Oregon.gov, n.d.).
- Executive Order 2015-01K, signed by Ohio Governor John Kasich in 2015, established the Ohio Task Force on Affordability and Efficiency in Higher Education, which was charged with making recommendations on the ways that "state-sponsored institutions of higher education … can be more efficient, offering an education of equal or higher quality while at the same time decreasing their costs" (Ohio-HigherEd.org, n.d.).
- SHB 6117, passed by the Connecticut Legislature in 2015, which charged the Board of Regents for Higher Education and the University of Connecticut to develop a pilot program for the development and promotion of open-source textbooks. It also established a task force charged with identifying ways to incentivize the creation and adoption of OER "that will significantly reduce the cost to students of course materials, including, but not limited to, offering financial or academic

---

[10] The progress of bills through Congress can be tracked here: https://www.govtrack.us/congress/bills/

or professional credit to faculty to create open educational resources"
(SHB 6117, 2015).

These Bills have been seen by many campus stakeholders as a step in the
right direction to address textbook affordability issues. Because these government initiatives may not provide all of the funding needed to successfully
pursue these goals, support has also been sought from the private sector.

Foundational Support

Foundations have played a key role in supporting the creation, adoption
and adaptation of OER. Since 2001, the William and Flora Hewlett
Foundation has donated over $170 million to support the development
and expansion of the open movement (Jhangiani & Biswas-Diener,
2017). With a specific emphasis on OER, the Hewlett Foundation has
played a crucial role in backing early initiatives such as MIT Open-
CourseWare, the Institute for the Study of Knowledge Management
in Education (ISKME) (http://www.iskme.org/), OER Commons
(https://www.oercommons.org/), and supported the development of
Creative Commons (CC). Other foundations that have provided financial
support for the development and promotion of OER include (but are
not limited to) the Laura and John Arnold Foundation
(http://www.arnoldfoundation.org/), the Shuttleworth Foundation
(https://www.shuttleworthfoundation.org/), and the Bill and Melinda
Gates Foundation (https://www.gatesfoundation.org/).

Funding provided by these organizations has gone beyond supporting
the creation of OER to include financial support for organizations and
their projects such as the Open Textbook Network
(http://research.cehd.umn.edu/otn/), Achieving the Dream's OER Degree Initiative (http://achievingthedream.org/resources/initiatives/
open-educational-resources-oer-degree-initiative), and the Scholarly
Publishing and Academic Resources Coalition's (SPARC) Open Education
program (https://sparcopen.org/open-education/). Collectively, these organizations provide a variety of valuable services to the community, including education, leadership development, community-building, policy
work, and large-scale OER adoption.

Grassroots Action by Users

On campuses across the U.S. and Canada, student groups have been in-spired to take action and advocate for OER. The U.S.-based Student Public Interest Research Groups (PIRG) (http://www.studentpirgs.org/) sparked the textbook affordability conversation back in 2003 and started advocating for open textbooks in 2008. Through the utilization of their grassroots organizing network and campus chapters, the Student PIRG has coordinated a number of successful education and advocacy campaigns surrounding open textbooks. At U.S. universities, student groups have organized educational events on OER and have been the driving force behind the creation of multiple OER grant programs.[11] Students at Cana-dian universities have played key roles in influencing institutional OER commitments, including the creation of an OER grant program,[12] the es-tablishment of a university-wide OER network,[13] and the recognition of OER contributions in faculty tenure and promotion.[14] Student leaders have recognized that their peers cannot learn from textbooks that they cannot afford, and have therefore been advocating for greater adoption of OER that are high quality, well aligned with the content they are evalu-ated on, and are accessible at low or no cost.

Other members of the higher educational community, including fac-ulty, librarians, and administrators, have also worked to raise awareness on textbook affordability issues and the use of OER.[15] Faculty and early career academics have been critical in producing OER research through

---

[11] Information on the Rutgers University Library Open and Affordable Textbooks Project can be found here: http://www.libraries.rutgers.edu/open-textbooks; and the University of Connecticut Open and Affordable Initiative here: http://open.uconn.edu/faculty-incentives-2/

[12] Information on the Simon Fraser University Library OER Grants pro-gram can be found here: https://www.sfu.ca/oergrants.html

[13] More information can be found here: https://www.ucalgary.ca/open/.

[14] The University of British Columbia's Guide to Reappointment, Pro-motion and Tenure Procedures at UBC can be found here: http://www.hr.ubc.ca/faculty-relations/files/SAC-Guide.pdf

[15] The SPARC website provides a tool that allows users to search for OER educational efforts being offered in North America: https://connect.sparcopen.org/filter/events/

their involvement in OER fellowship programs.[16, 17] Their research has ranged from assessing OER perception and efficacy to sustainability and student success. Librarians often provide guidance and support to faculty looking to learn about, find, and integrate OER into their classrooms.[18] Administrators have provided financial support to develop grant programs that support faculty in replacing their commercial textbooks with OER and in championing OER degree programs at their institutions.[19]

While many steps still need to be taken in raising OER awareness, grassroots action led by students, librarians, faculty, and campus administrators have laid a strong foundation to build upon.

OER Repositories and Open Textbook Libraries

OER are only useful if they can be found by those looking to use them. Over the years, various repositories that boast diverse collections of learning materials have been developed to allow for the collection and curation of OER and to help facilitate their ease of discovery by faculty. One of the largest of these OER repositories is the Multimedia Educational Resource for Learning and Online Teaching (MERLOT) (https://www.merlot.org/merlot/index.htm), a California State University program dating back to 1997. The MERLOT collection comprises over 40,000 OER spanning over 22 different material types.[20] Ranging in both size and scope, MERLOT includes everything from entire online courses to a single animation. OER Commons—a project of ISKME—is another large repository that consists of a digital public library and collaboration platform. Built with the intent to assist knowledge management and educational innovation,

---

[17] The Open Education Group recruits faculty members and early career academics to produce research on OER. More information on the program can be found here: http://openedgroup.org/people

[18] Examples of these efforts include but are not limited to workshops, one-on-one consultations, and informational websites.

[19] Dr. Daniel T. DeMarte, Vice President for Academic Affairs and Chief Academic Officer at Tidewater Community College, is recognized as having been a principal lead in the implementation of their Z-Degree initiative. More information is available here: https://www.tcc.edu/academics/degrees/textbook-free

[20] A full listing of materials types with definitions can be found here: http://info.merlot.org/merlothelp/index.htm#merlot_collection.htm

OER Commons offers a comprehensive infrastructure for curriculum experts and instructors at all educational levels, though especially those teaching K–12, to identify high-quality OER and collaborate around their adaptation, evaluation, and use.

Open textbook libraries, on the other hand, host an array of ready-to-adopt resources that can be seamlessly used in place of a traditional textbook. There are multiple OER repositories and open textbook libraries that boast diverse collections of learning materials. Arguably the most recognized materials come from OpenStax (https://openstax.org/), a nonprofit open textbook publisher based out of Rice University. OpenStax began as Connexions—a platform that provides authors and scholars with an open space where they can share and freely adapt educational materials such as courses, books, and reports. Now known as OpenStax CNX, this platform has developed into a dynamic nonprofit digital ecosystem, serving millions of users per month in the delivery of educational content to improve learning outcomes. The platform hosts tens of thousands of learning objects in a host of disciplines. Meanwhile, OpenStax has developed 27 peer-reviewed open textbooks for the most-attended college courses and several AP courses. Since 2012, OpenStax has saved nearly 3.5 million students an estimated $340 million and is on track to meet or beat its goal of saving students $500 million by 2020 (OpenStax, 2017). They've also started developing their own research-based learning technology, OpenStax Tutor.

The University of Minnesota Open Textbook Library (https://open.umn.edu/opentextbooks/), the BCcampus Open Textbook Project (https://open.bccampus.ca/find-open-textbooks/), Lumen Learning's Catalog (https://courses.lumenlearning.com/catalog/lumen), and eCampus Ontario's Open Textbook Project (https://openlibrary.ecampusontario.ca/find-open-textbooks/) are other well-known open textbook libraries hosting hundreds of open textbooks that can be integrated into instruction. The majority of materials from these collections have been peer-reviewed and are already in use at numerous higher education institutions.

Perspectives on the Current State of OER

The OER movement has been shaped by the evolving higher education landscape, including textbook market changes, governmental directives, foundational support, and grassroots advocacy efforts. These factors also influence the current state of the movement, which can be interpreted from the perspective of various users, including librarians, faculty, students, and administrators.

Librarian Perspectives on OER

Key action areas identified by the American Library Association (ALA) (American Library Association, n.d.) include (but are not limited to):

- Education and lifelong learning;
- Equitable access to information;
- Intellectual freedom; and
- Literacy.

It should therefore come as no surprise that librarians have emerged as key leaders in the OER movement, as many of the defining characteristics of OER directly address these action areas. The retention of OER allows a user the ability to utilize the material in the present, but also reference it in the future, making OER a tool to support lifelong learning. Because OER are made freely available to the public, they help promote equitable access to information: cost no longer acts as a barrier. Being able to revise and customize an OER resource to address specific learning needs helps support intellectual freedom and literacy.

Academic librarians have taken on a large role in promoting OER to faculty and students on their campuses. Examples of these efforts include but are not limited to:

- Providing workshops and other educational activities that help raise awareness of OER.
- Creating and maintaining websites that include information about OER and links to OER repositories and libraries.
- Helping to coordinate and administer grant programs that promote the integration of OER into class instruction.
- Providing faculty and students with assistance in finding quality resources such as magazine and newspaper articles, scholarly publications, and video recordings that supplement OER.

Some academic libraries have created OER Librarian positions that focus on promoting the creation, use, and adoption of OER on their campuses. However, these responsibilities often fall on librarians who are also teaching, providing reference services, or working in other library departments, who need to balance these new responsibilities with their current job duties. At some small institutions with few librarians on staff, this can be especially challenging. However, this challenge provides an opportunity for librarians to partner with other groups on campus to provide information about OER to faculty and students. Libraries often house writing and tutoring centers or liaise with other academic departments, providing research guidance and support to faculty and bibliographic instruction sessions for students. Librarians can utilize their relationships with these groups to help promote OER to their campus community, and are also well situated on campus to coordinate group efforts aimed at supporting teaching and learning.

Faculty Perspectives on OER

When it comes to OER adoption, faculty awareness is critical. According to a 2016 study conducted by the members of the Babson Survey Research Group, when faculty members were asked to self-report their level of awareness of OER, a majority (58%) said that they were generally unaware of OER, while only a quarter (26%) of respondents identified themselves as being aware or very aware (Allen et al. 2016). This is comparable to the 2015 results, where the number of faculty reporting no awareness was two thirds (66%) of respondents, while those who identified as being aware or very aware sat at one fifth (20%) (Allen et al. 2014). Therefore, there has been an increase in awareness. The 2016 study also asked about faculty members' awareness of open textbooks. The results showed that 34 percent of faculty claimed some level of awareness of open textbooks, while 15 percent of faculty reported that they were only somewhat aware, and nearly two thirds of faculty (66%) reported that they were generally unaware of open textbooks (Allen et al. 2016). Increased discoverability may prove useful as people become more aware of OER, but some positive developments have already been found in high-impact courses. Open textbook publishers like OpenStax and BCcampus have built collections aimed at achieving the highest return on investment and as such, these ready-to-adopt resources continue to gain traction across high-enrollment first- and second-year courses.

In a 2013 study in which researchers examined student and instructor perceptions of open textbook adoption at eight post-secondary institutions in the U.S., Bliss et al. found that 90 percent of instructors indicated that their students were equally (60%) or more prepared (30%), compared to students taught in previous semesters. This may be due to the fact that OER are available at no cost to the student and can be accessed immediately. Another possible reason is that the material has been better curated to meet their learning needs. The same study also found that of the 490 students surveyed, 90 percent indicated that the open textbooks used in their courses were of the same quality as traditional materials (50%) or better (40%). Interested in observing whether or not student perception, use, and impact of open textbooks was similar in the Canadian context, Jhangiani and Jhangiani (2017) surveyed 320 post-secondary students enrolled in courses that used an open textbook. Their study found that 63 percent of students judged the open textbook to be above average (36%) or excellent (27%), while an additional 33 percent of students found it average. Less than 4 percent of students surveyed indicated that the open textbook was below average. In recognition of the fact that the overwhelming majority of students were satisfied with the quality of their open textbooks, and that each of these students were able to save money that would have otherwise been spent on course materials, it should come as no surprise that students are increasingly drawn to the promise of OER.

One area of interest for faculty exploring the teaching and learning opportunities associated with OER is open pedagogy. Conversation surrounding open pedagogy (as understood in this context) began with a blog post[21] written by David Wiley in 2013. In this post he wrote about open pedagogy and his distaste for the "disposable assignment".[22] Looking for

---

[21] This post covers the basic concepts of the open pedagogy movement: https://opencontent.org/blog/archives/2975

[22] A "disposable assignment" can be understood as a closed homework process in which the content created is only viewed by a student author and faculty grader. Wiley argues that these types of assignments "suck value out of the world". More information is available here: https://opencontent.org/blog/archives/2975

an alternative approach to assigning coursework which incorporated his desire to have students' assignments add value to the world, Wiley proposed examples of open pedagogy. While open pedagogy lacks a universal definition, DeRosa et al. (2017) understand the term as "a site of praxis, a place where theories about learning, teaching, technology and social justice enter into a conversation with each other and inform the development of educational practices and structures". The application of the term 'open' as understood in 'open licenses' has given way to a dynamic and innovative approach to teaching and learning. Leaders in this space such as DeRosa and Robinson (2015) stress the value of having students interacting with OER as part of course instruction:

If we think of OER as just free digital stuff, as product, we can surely lower costs for students; we might even help them pass more courses because they will have reliable, free access to their learning materials. But we largely miss out on the opportunity to empower our students, to help them see content as something they can curate and create, and to help them see themselves as contributing members to the public marketplace of ideas. Essentially, this is a move from thinking about [OER] as finished products to thinking about them as dynamic components of our pedagogical processes. When we think about OER as something we do rather than something we find/adopt/acquire, we begin to tap its full potential for learning.

With new programming[23] and resources[24] to explore digital pedagogy being developed and a greater number of educators understanding the broad ranging benefits of open pedagogy, including the learning benefits for students, knowledge reception and creation is venturing down an exciting path.

Student Perspectives on OER

Students may find cost savings and immediate access to be obvious benefits of OER. According to Jhangiani and Jhangiani (2017), when students were asked to rate the importance of the features of their open textbook, 68 per-

---

[23] The Digital Pedagogy Lab hosted two Digital Pedagogy Labs in 2017. More information is available here: http://www.digitalpedagogylab.com/

[24] The Rebus Community has produced a new resource exploring how to make open textbooks with students available here: https://press.rebus.community/makingopentextbookswithstudents/

cent rated cost savings as being very important (30%) or absolutely essential (38%), while nearly 70 percent indicated that immediate access was very important (36%) or absolutely essential (34%). Students face a number of barriers to accessing a quality education and with OER, textbook costs are not one of them. The prospect of textbook costs no longer contributing to rising student debt is incredibly compelling, especially considering that the average U.S. class of 2016 graduate finished their degree with a debt of $37,172 (U.S. Student Loan Debt Statistics for 2017, 2017). Beyond cost savings, students are also able to retain these materials forever. Whether students can benefit from using a specific text for multiple courses throughout their education or are interested in referring to a text far into the future, OER grant students this flexibility.

Administrator Perspectives on OER

Recognizing that many colleges and universities are under immense pressure to maintain their enrollment numbers amidst declining state funding, rising criticism, and stiff competition, administrators at a handful of institutions have begun to recognize OER as a means to their desired ends. When it comes to the learning materials being used in the classroom, all stakeholders, especially institutional administrators, want the resources used by teachers and students to meet their needs. A 2015 study conducted by Fischer, Hilton, Robinson, and Wiley analyzed whether the adoption of digital open textbooks significantly predicted students' completion of courses, class achievement, and enrollment intensity during and after semesters in which OER were used. When analyzing course grades, the study found that students using OER did the same or better when compared to those using traditional materials. The same study also found that students in courses using OER enrolled in a significantly higher number of credits in the next semester, meaning that OER propelled students closer to graduation. From the perspective of an administrator concerned with enrollment and graduation rates, the value of greater OER adoption is clear.

Challenges and Opportunities

Challenges

While the challenge of the publishing industry has already been addressed, there are other practical barriers limiting the widespread adoption of OER including their creation, adaptation, and adoption. These challenges span both those within and beyond the institution.

OER Development and Maintenance. Creating an OER is a time-intensive undertaking. Knowledgeable and reputable authors must be identified, and be available to commit to the development of an OER. Some OER are developed by groups, including classes, programs, and professional organizations. This option may help facilitate the speed with which an OER is created, but requires greater oversight in quality control. While OER are marketed as being free of cost to the consumer, it is important to recognize that there are costs associated with their creation. These costs can include but are not limited to honoraria for authors, "buyouts" of faculty time for writing and compiling OER, and accessing platforms. To date, OER creation has primarily been funded by private foundations and government agencies. However, there is no guarantee that this funding will continue in perpetuity. Like any textbook or learning resource, OER must be updated on a regular basis to ensure its relevance. If sustainability is not considered during the creation of the resource, it may become outdated. Fortunately, because of the open license applied to the work, the work's revision and therefore future relevance is not solely reliant on the initial creator.

Adoption of OER Resources. In addition to the faculty awareness issues covered previously, the actual adoption of OER can also pose challenges. Bliss, Hilton, Wiley, and Thanos (2013) found that the time spent by an instructor using the material for the first time is one cost often not calculated into the use of open textbooks. Their report indicated that 82 percent of surveyed faculty spent somewhat more or much more time preparing to teach in that semester compared to others. This is a finding worth noting, as adopting an OER may not be as easy as selecting a traditional textbook bundled with ancillary materials. While open textbook publishers are working to proactively address this issue, not all open textbooks have easily identifiable ancillaries.

Access to Digital **OER.** As most OER are digital, a device and a stable internet connection are required to access them. However, there is a disparity in North America among those who have access to the technology and infrastructure needed to access the internet and those who do not. Often referred to as the "digital divide," many factors can impact who is able to access the internet in the U.S., including income,[25] race,[26] and geographical location.[27] Challenges associated with the digital divide are not unique to the United States. According to a 2016 report published by the Canadian Radio-television and Telecommunications Commission (CRTC), there is a disparity in the speed of service offered in rural and urban environments, and "urban households generally [pay] lower Internet service prices and [have] a greater number of Internet service providers to choose from than rural households" (Canadian Radio-television and Telecommunications Commission, 2016). OER that are highly functional in print format, such as OpenStax materials, provide a solution, but not a fix, to these digital divide issues. However, providing access to OER materials could be used as an argument to help advocate for the resolutions of the digital divide in North America.

Accessibility Considerations. According to the World Bank (2017) "one billion people, or 15% of the world's population, experience some form of disability, and one-fifth of the estimated global total, or between 110 million and 190 million people, experience significant disabilities." Those with visual, hearing, mobility, and learning disabilities can have trouble accessing the internet in general. Even with tools and technology that help facilitate internet access, if the resources they find online, including OER, do not have accessible design components they may be unable to use them. "Accessible design is a design process in which the needs of people with disabilities are specifically considered" (Center for Universal

---

[25] Those living in poverty often finding it difficult to pay for internet services and the technology needed to access the internet. "Americans with family incomes between $75,000 and $99,999 per year adopted the Internet at an 83 percent rate, compared to 80 percent of those reporting income between $50,000 and $74,999, and 70 percent of those in the $25,000 to $49,999 range" (Carlson, 2016).

[26] Carlson (2016), citing U.S. National Telecommunications and Information Administration (NTIA) research, reports that "78 percent of Whites nationally used the Internet in 2015, compared to 68 percent of African Americans and 66 percent of Hispanics. In rural areas, 70 percent of White Americans had adopted the Internet, compared to 59 percent of African Americans and 61 percent of Hispanics."

[27] According to research performed by NTIA, "in 2015, 69 percent of rural residents [reported] using the Internet, versus 75 percent of urban residents" (Carlson, 2016).

Design in Education, 2015). Common examples of accessible design include captioning videos and formatting text documents so that they can be read by screen readers. Some creators have considered accessible design practices when developing OER and, as a result, their works can be readily utilized by those with visual, hearing, and learning disabilities. While OER do not universally possess accessible design components, the open license applied to the work allows for them to be revised to better serve all students.

Openwashing. With the increase in popularity of OER, openwashing is a problem that is on the rise.[28] Similar to the rise of greenwashing as a response to the environmental movement,[29] publishers and other education companies are moving forward with practices that appear or are marketed as "open" or "OER" but fail to adhere to the free plus 5R permissions we expect. These practices confuse people's understanding of open and OER, and reinforce the need for the OER community to better communicate open.

Opportunities

While challenges persist, the OER community has done a terrific job building the foundation necessary to support emerging projects and initiatives. Recognizing the massive success of the "Z-Degree" program at Tidewater Community College, in 2016 Achieving the Dream announced their OER Degree Initiative, which seeks to establish zero textbook cost degree programs at 38 community colleges across 13 U.S. states over the next three years. In the same year, the California Governor's office also announced $5 million in funding to support Z-degrees within the state and in 2017 BCcampus opened their call for proposals for Canada's first "Zed Cred". With community colleges serving student populations from lower income backgrounds, we can see firsthand how OER is being used as a tool to address important issues of equity in education.

---

[28] The term openwashing originates from a blog post written by Audrey Watters. The post is available here: http://hackeducation.com/2015/01/16/what-do-we-mean-by-open-education

[29] More information on greenwashing is available here: http://www.investopedia.com/terms/g/greenwashing.asp

Advances in the OER movement have not been restricted to the community college level. In 2017, New York Governor Cuomo announced a commitment of $8 million to expand OER use at the City University of New York and State University of New York systems.[30] Supported by organizations across the OER community, the impacts of New York's leadership on OER will not be confined to state borders. Another 2017 announcement came from Lumen Learning and Follett, who announced a partnership aimed at increasing faculty access to OER at over 1,200 U.S. institutions.[31]

Noticing the pace at which the OER community has grown, key organizations have been collaboratively developing programming to respond to the needs of the community. Creative Commons is developing a professional development opportunity aimed at providing a thorough CC education through their Certificate program (https://certificates.creativecommons.org/). Offering four learning pathways including a specialized track for academic librarians, these open courses are being built to be adaptable to any delivery mode. In an effort to share and discover information about OER activities at campuses across North America, SPARC has developed Connect OER (https://connect.sparcopen.org). Through Connect OER, academic libraries can sign up to maintain a profile page about their institution's efforts on OER, with the data used to populate a searchable directory and annual report identifying best practices and highlight collective impact being achieved. Connect OER is aimed at supporting campus action, regardless of an institution's familiarity with OER. Yet another notable initiative is the Peer Review Working Group (https://about.rebus.community/category/working-groups/) led by the Rebus Community. Identifying the need to establish a standardized process for reviewing open textbooks, Re-

---

[30] An overview and commentary on this announcement published by Carl Straumsheim, writing for Inside Higher Ed, can be found here: https://www.insidehighered.com/news/2017/04/14/cuny-suny-plan-major-expansion-oer-efforts

[31] Carl Straumsheim, writing for Inside Higher Ed, offers his summary and thoughts on this announcement here: https://www.insidehighered.com/news/2017/04/18/follett-lumen-learning-announce-oer-partnership

bus has brought together stakeholders across the OER community to help develop a collaborative and clear approach for open textbook review.

Other opportunities for promoting and expanding the use of OER can be found in increased education and advocacy efforts on campus. Providing forums for librarians, faculty, students, and administrators to discuss textbook affordability issues can help in formulating individual and collective action. Providing learning opportunities, including where to find OER, and how they can enable innovative pedagogy, can also help increase awareness and adoption of OER. Librarians, faculty, students, and campus administrators should continue to work with members of state and federal government to help pass legislation that promotes and funds the creation of OER. Foundational partnerships can also continue to provide opportunities to advance OER issues and initiatives. The current relationships the educational community has with funding organizations like the Hewlett Foundation will hopefully serve as an inspiration to others to help support the OER movement.

Conclusion

OER improves teaching and learning through practices enabled by content that is freely available to download, edit, and share. Stakeholders ranging from the individual to institutional level have recognized the tremendous potential of OER and have committed to a series of robust policies and practices to increase their adoption, adaptation, and creation. Although it is difficult to predict the future of the OER movement, there are plenty of reasons to be optimistic. Much will depend on how the OER community—including stakeholders from within higher education institutions, government, and civil society organizations—respond to the challenges and opportunities that present themselves. While stakeholders from a range of different backgrounds have stepped up to the plate, academic librarians perhaps have the greatest potential to emerge as leaders in this space. Supported by organizations like SPARC and the Open Textbook Network, and informed by their experiences interacting with publishers, faculty, teaching and learning centers, and students, librarians are in a strong position to help grow this movement. Combined with their knowledge of digital rights management and copyright, the potential for librarians to both lead and work alongside fellow impassioned stakeholders is undeniable. As OER are on a trend towards mainstream adoption levels across first- and second-year courses in higher education,[32] we are beginning to see the degree to which OER can improve higher education. With an expansive network of libraries, institutions, and civil society organizations championing OER across the continent, together we can ensure that the future of OER remains bright.

References

Affordable College Textbook Act, H.R. 3538, 113th Cong., 1st Sess. (2013–2014).

Affordable College Textbook Act, H.R. 3721, 114th Cong., 1st Sess. (2015–2016).

Affordable College Textbook Act, H.R. 3840, 115th Cong., 1st Sess. (2016–2017).

Allen, I. E., Seaman, J. (2014) *Opening the Textbook: Educational Resources in U.S. Higher Education, 2014.* Babson Park, Massachusetts: Babson Survey Research Group. Retrieved from https://www.onlinelearningsurvey.com/reports/openingthecurriculum2014.pdf

Allen, I. E., Seaman, J. (2016) *Opening the Textbook: Educational Resources in U.S. Higher Education, 2015-16.* Babson Park, Massachusetts: Babson Survey Research Group. Retrieved from https://www.onlinelearningsurvey.com/reports/openingthetextbook2016.pdf

American Library Association. (n.d.). About ALA. Retrieved from http://www.ala.org/aboutala/.

Bliss, T., Hilton J., III, Wiley, D., & Thanos, K. (2013). The cost and quality of online open textbooks: Perceptions of community college faculty and students. *First Monday, 18*(1). doi: http://dx.doi.org/10.5210/fm.v18i1.3972

Canadian Radio-television and Telecommunications Commission (2016). Communications Monitoring Report. Retrieved from https://crtc.gc.ca/eng/publications/reports/PolicyMonitoring/2016/cmr.pdf.

Carlson, E. (2016). *The state of the urban/rural digital divide.* Retrieved from https://www.ntia.doc.gov/blog/2016/state-urbanrural-digital-divide

Center for Universal Design in Education. (2015). *What is the difference between accessible, usable, and universal design?* Retrieved from http://www.washington.edu/doit/what-difference-between-accessible-usable-and-universal-design

College Board. (2016). *Trends in college pricing 2016.* Retrieved from https://trends.collegeboard.org/sites/default/files/2016-trends-college-pricing-web_1.pdf

Complete College America. (2014). *Four-year myth.* Retrieved from https://completecollege.org/wp-content/uploads/2017/05/4-Year-Myth.pdf

---

[32] In the US alone, 1.5 million college students are expected to save an estimated $145 million in the 2017–2018 academic year by using materials from the OpenStax collection. More information available here: http://news.rice.edu/2017/08/10/nearly-1-5-million-college-students-to-use-free-textbooks-this-school-year/

Conn. H.R. H.B. 06177. *An act concerning the use of digital open-source textbooks in higher education, 2015.* Retrieved from https://www.cga.ct.gov/2015/fc/ 2015HB-06117-R000823-FC.htm

DeRosa, R. & Jhangiani, R. (n.d.). *Open Pedagogy.* Retrieved from http://openpedagogy.org/open-pedagogy/

DeRosa, R. & Robinson, S. (2015). Pedagogy, technology, and the example of open educational resources. *EDUCAUSEreview.* Retrieved from http://er.educause.edu/ articles/2015/11/ pedagogy-technology-and-the-example-of-open-educational-resources

Financial Consumer Agency of Canada. (n.d.). *Budgeting for student life.* https://www.canada.ca/en/financial-consumer-agency/services/ budget-student-life.html

Fischer, L., Hilton, J., III, Robinson, T.J., and Wiley, D. (2015). A multi-institutional study of the impact of open textbook adoption on the learning outcomes of post-secondary students. *Journal of Computing in Higher Education 27*:159. doi:10.1007/s12528-015-9101-x

Florida Virtual Campus. (2016). *2016 student textbook and course materials survey.* Retrieved from: https://dlss.flvc.org/documents/210036/361552/ 2016+Student+Textbook+Survey.pdf/fa58795e-f2d3-4fc7-9f07-a7e1b31fbbcd

Hilton, J., III. (2016). Open educational resources and college textbook choices: a review of research on efficacy and perceptions. *Educational Technology Research and Development, 64*(4), 573–590. Retrieved from https://link.springer.com/article/ 10.1007/s11423-016-9434-9

Jhangiani, R., & Biswas-Diener, R. (2017*). Open: The philosophy and practices that are revolutionizing education and science.* London: Ubiquity Press.

Jhangiani, R. S., & Jhangiani, S. (2017). Investigating the perceptions, use, and impact of open textbooks: A survey of post-secondary students in British Columbia. *The International Review of Research in Open and Distributed Learning, 18*(4).

Koch, J. V. (2013). *Turning the page.* Lumina Foundation.

National Association of College Stores. (2016). Cost sensitive students are spending less on course materials. Retrieved from https://www.nacs.org/advocacynewsmedia/ pressreleases/tabid/1579/ArticleID/463/ Cost-Sensitive-Students-are-Spending-Less-on-Course-Materials.aspx

OhioHigherEd.org. (n.d.). Affordability & efficiency. Retrieved from https://www.ohiohighered.org/affordability-efficiency/task-force

OpenStax. (2017). Retrieved from http://news.rice.edu/2017/08/10/ nearly-1-5-million-college-students-to-use-free-textbooks-this-school-year/

Oregon.gov. (n.d.) *Open educational resources.* Retrieved from https://www.oregon.gov/ HigherEd/Pages/oer.aspx

Popken, B. (2015, August 6). College textbook prices have risen 1,041 percent since 1977. *NBC News.* Retrieved from http://www.nbcnews.com/feature/freshman-year/ college-textbook-prices-have-risen-812-percent-1978-n399926

Smith, F. D. (2014). EDUCAUSE 2014: Publisher says 'textbooks are dead,' and adaptive learning is rising from the ashes. *EdTech.* Retrieved from https://edtechmagazine.com/higher/article/2014/10/educause-2014- publisher-says-textbooks-are-dead-and-adaptive-learning-rising-ashes

Straumsheim, C. (2017). Is 'inclusive access' the future for publishers? *Inside Higher Ed.*
    Retrieved from https://www.insidehighered.com/news/2017/01/31/
    textbook-publishers-contemplate-inclusive-access-business-model-future
Sweney, M. (2017). Education publisher Pearson reports biggest loss in its history. *The
    Guardian.* Retrieved from https://www.theguardian.com/business/2017/feb/24/
    education-publisher-pearson-loss-us-penguin-random-house
U.S. Government Accountability Office. (2013). *COLLEGE TEXTBOOKS: Students have
    greater access to textbook information* (GAO-13-368). Retrieved from
    http://www.gao.gov/assets/660/655066.pdf
U.S. Student Loan Debt Statistics for 2017. (2017, May 17). Retrieved June 15, 2017, from
    https://studentloanhero.com/wp-content/uploads/
    Student-Loan-Hero-2017-Student-Loan-Statistics.pdf.
Wiley, D. (2013, October 21). What is open pedagogy? [Blog post]. Retrieved from
    https://opencontent.org/blog/archives/2975
World Bank. (2017). Disability inclusion. Retrieved from www.worldbank.org/en/topic/
    disability

What Does the Research Say About OER?

John Hilton III

The high cost of textbooks is a substantial challenge in America's higher education. A survey of 22,906 post-secondary students in Florida reported that 67 percent of students went without a required textbook because of high prices. Severe academic consequences are often a direct result of limited access to the necessary resources; this same study noted that deficiency of learning materials caused 37.6 percent of students to earn a poor grade, and 19.8 percent to fail a course. High textbook prices also lengthen the time to graduation. Approximately half the students surveyed stated that they take fewer courses because of the high cost of materials; moreover, textbook prices cause one quarter of students to drop classes (Florida Virtual Campus, 2016).

While college students may be thought to be the only audience affected by these high costs, expensive educational materials also affect taxpayers. Some student loans costs, as well as money used to purchase textbooks for public elementary and secondary schools, pull from the pockets of taxpayers. Furthermore, high textbook costs can keep schools from purchasing new materials, leaving many students learning from outdated books, and classrooms lacking a sufficient number of textbooks.

Open educational resources (OER) are one solution to the problem of high textbook costs. The term "open educational resources" was developed in the 2002 UNESCO Forum on the Impact of Open Courseware for Higher Education in Developing Countries. OER are educational resources that are (1) freely available to all people, and (2) openly licensed in such a way that authorize reuse, and in many instances, remix and redistribution.

Over the past 15 years, there has been extensive growth and development of OER (Wiley, Bliss, & McEwen, 2014). A large variety of OER have been generated, many of which are high quality and contain sufficiently robust content to replace traditional textbooks. Creative Commons licenses provide the required legal clearances to freely share, modify, and reuse OER (Bissell, 2009; D'Antoni, 2009; Hewlett, 2013). Several sources, such as the Minnesota Open Textbook Library (open.umn.edu/opentextbooks/) provide links to and insightful reviews of open materials. The utilization of OER is becoming more widespread. These resources have been used in hundreds of colleges and universities internationally, including Harvard University, Ohio State University, University of Illinois (Urbana-Champaign), Purdue University, University of British Columbia, and the University of Calgary.[1]

Despite the widespread belief that freely available educational materials must be less effective or of lower quality than expensive, published materials, research demonstrates otherwise. Between 2002 and 2015 there were only 16 efficacy and perceptions studies related to OER. Hilton (2016) synthesized these 16 reports to investigate the usefulness and/or perceptions of OER. Since that time, as of August 2017, 17 additional peer-reviewed studies have been published regarding higher education OER efficacy and/or perceptions. This illustrates a rapid rise in research related to OER efficacy and perceptions, with more published studies in the past two years than the previous 15. I next summarize the research that has been done to date.

Research Between 2002 and 2015

Of the studies reviewed in Hilton (2016), nine investigated OER efficacy and the relation of OER influence to learning outcomes, providing a collective 46,149 student participants. Only one of these nine studies conveyed that the OER use was associated with lower learning outcomes at a higher rate than with positive outcomes; however, even this study illustrated that in general, OER use resulted in non-significant differences.

---

[1] A list of colleges that have adopted open textbooks published by Rice University is provided at https://openstax.org/adopters. Note that these textbooks are only a small fraction of the total number of open textbooks that are currently available.

Three of the nine studies had results that significantly favored OER over traditional textbooks, another three revealed no significant difference and two did not discuss the statistical significance of their findings.

Hilton (2016) investigates the opinions of 4,510 students and faculty members surveyed across nine studies regarding perceptions of OER. Not once did students or faculty state that OER were less likely than commercial textbooks to aid student learning. Overall, roughly half of students and faculty noted OER to be analogous to traditional resources, a sizeable minority considered them to be superior, and a smaller minority found them to be inferior.

Efficacy Research Between 2015 and 2017

In addition to the research just summarized, there were eight OER efficacy studies published between late 2015 and August 2017, containing a total of 108,809 students. The number of participants, in some respects, is deceptively large, as some of the studies (e.g., Hilton, Fischer, Wiley, and Williams, 2016; Wiley, Williams, DeMarte, and Hilton, 2016) contained large student populations but only a small portion of students in these studies used OER. Regardless, the overall results across these eight studies imply that students do as well, or better, when utilizing OER.

Wiley et al. (2016) observed that students at Tidewater Community College (n=23,985) were less likely to drop courses when utilizing OER. Although the difference was small (0.8%), it was statistically significant. Similarly, Hilton et al. (2016), who reviewed two later semesters of OER adoption at Tidewater Community College (n=45,237) found that when considering drop, withdrawal, and passing rates, students who used OER were 6 percent more likely to complete the class with credit than their peers who did not use OER.

Ozdemir and Hendricks (2017) examined 51 e-portfolios written by faculty in the state of California about their use of open textbooks. For the 55 percent of the 51 faculty who assessed the impact of adopting an open textbook on student learning outcomes, all reported that the outcomes remained the same or were enriched. Chiorescu (2017) studied 606 students at a university in Georgia across four semesters and noted that students were either as or more likely to pass the class when OER was used; furthermore, significantly fewer students withdrew when OER were implemented.

Croteau (2017) surveyed 24 separate data sets involving 3,847 college students in Georgia and found no significant differences in student pass rates, completion rates, or final exam scores before and after implementing OER. Hendricks, Reinsberg, and Rieger (2017) found that students in a physics course at the University of British Columbia (n=811) performed equivalently well in terms of final exams scores and grade distributions whether they used OER or commercial textbooks. Grewe and Davis (2017) studied 146 students who attended Northern Virginia Community College. They found a moderate correlation between OER use and student achievement. Winitzky-Stephens and Pickavance (2017) assessed a large-scale OER adoption across 37 different courses in several different general education subjects at Salt Lake Community College (n=34,126). The multilevel models used by the authors revealed no significant difference between courses using OER and traditional textbooks for continuing students, and a small benefit for new students.

Perceptions Research Between 2015 and 2017

There were 12 OER perceptions studies published between late 2015 and August 2017, involving 2,160 students and faculty. Two of these studies also included efficacy data, and thus were also included as efficacy studies in the previous section.

Five studies investigated faculty perceptions of OER. Ozdemir and Hendricks' (2017) study of 51 e-portfolios written by faculty in the state of California who used open textbooks found that a strong majority reported that the quality of the open textbooks was as good or better than that of traditional textbooks. Moreover, 40 of the 51 portfolios contained data about students' attitudes towards the open textbooks; only 15 percent of these e-portfolios reported any negative student comments. Pitt (2015) surveyed 126 educators who utilized OER. Roughly two thirds reported that using OER facilitated meeting diverse learners' needs and perceived greater pupil satisfaction using OER. Jung, Bauer, and Heaps (2017) surveyed faculty members who used OpenStax textbooks and found that 81 percent believed OpenStax textbooks are of the same or higher quality as commercial textbooks. Fischer, Ernst, and Mason (2017) examined 416 online reviews of 121 open textbooks and observed that reviewers commonly gave open textbooks high ratings (a median of 4.5/5 overall rating).

Delimont, Turtle, Bennett, Adhikari, and Lindshield (2016) surveyed 524 learners in 13 different courses at Kansas State University concerning their use of OER, as well as 13 teachers. Students regarded the OER as high quality and favored OER over purchasing textbooks. Of the 13 faculty members interviewed, 12 preferred teaching with OER.

Furthermore, several studies directly questioned students how their experience with OER compared with commercial textbooks. Hendricks, Reinsberg, and Rieger (2017) considered survey answers from 143 students who used OER in a physics course at the University of British Columbia and noted that 93 percent of respondents reported their open textbook was the same or better than textbooks in other courses. Similarly, Illowsky, Hilton, Whiting, and Ackerman (2016) surveyed 325 students in California who used two versions of an open statistics textbook. They found that 90 percent of students rated the OER as good or better than the textbooks in their other courses. Jhangiani and Jhangiani (2017) surveyed 320 college students in British Columbia registered in courses with an open textbook. These students positively rated open textbooks, with 96 percent of survey participants stating that they were at or above average. Cooney (2017) studied 67 individuals enrolled in health courses at New York City College of Technology. She found that over 80 percent of 67 students surveyed rated the OER as being better than a traditional textbook, with an additional 16 percent saying it was similar quality. Coleman-Prisco (2017) surveyed 16 students, five of whom were later interviewed regarding their experiences with OER. She found that 25 percent of participants felt OER were worse than traditional learning materials; 37.5 percent stated they were equal, and 37.5 percent said they were better.

Vojtech and Grissett (2017) explored a novel approach to student perceptions by examining how students perceive hypothetical faculty members who use open textbooks. They find that students rated faculty who assign an open textbook to be kinder, as well as more encouraging and creative. Although the study was intended to have open textbooks be the only difference between the hypothetical professors that students rated, only 14 percent students attributed their belief that the professor who used OER was kinder, more creative, etc. to the prices of textbooks.

Watson, Domizi, and Clouser (2017) surveyed 1,299 students at the University of Georgia who used the OpenStax biology textbook (an open textbook). These students were directly asked to "rate the quality of the OpenStax textbook as compared to other textbooks they had used." The majority of students (64%) reported that the OpenStax book had approximately the same quality as traditional books and 22 percent said it had higher quality. Only 14 percent of students who used the OpenStax book deemed it to have a lower quality than traditional textbooks.

Research Between 2002 and 2017: A Summary

To date, a total of 17 peer-reviewed studies that examine the efficacy of OER have been published; these studies involve 154,958 students. While there certainly are limitations in individual studies, collectively, there is a robust finding that utilizing OER in the classroom does not appear to decrease learning outcomes and saves considerable funds.

In terms of perceptions, at the time of this writing, 21 peer-reviewed studies of student and faculty perceptions of OER have been published. These studies involve 7,969 students or faculty members. While people may debate whether students are biased towards free books, or the extent to which they are good judges of what constitutes quality, it is clear that a strong majority of both faculty and students who have used OER prefer them to commercial textbooks.

Based on the increasingly extensive research on the efficacy and perceptions of OER, policy makers and faculty may need to judiciously examine the rationale for obliging students to purchase commercial textbook when excellent, free, openly licensed textbooks are an option. But significant questions remain. How can OER be more extensively utilized on college campuses? To what extent should administrators encourage the use of OER? What are the roles of libraries in increasing faculty awareness of OER? Are there additional pedagogies that become available when OER are the primary learning resources? As will be described in the following pages, these are important questions, and this book provides the beginnings of some very meaningful answers.

References

Bissell, A. (2009). Permission granted: Open licensing for educational resources. *Open Learning, The Journal of Open and Distance Learning, 24*, 97–106.

Chiorescu, M. (2017). Exploring Open Educational Resources for College Algebra. *The International Review of Research in Open and Distributed Learning, 18*(4). Retrieved from http://www.irrodl.org/index.php/irrodl/article/view/3003/4223

Coleman-Prisco, V. (2017). Factors influencing faculty innovation and adoption of open educational resources in United States higher education. *International Journal of Education and Human Developments, 3*(4), 1–12. Retrieved from http://ijehd.cgrd.org/images/vol3no4/1.pdf

Cooney, C. (2017). What impacts do OER have on students? Students share their experiences with a health psychology OER at New York City College of Technology. *The International Review of Research in Open and Distributed Learning, 18*(4). Retrieved from http://www.irrodl.org/index.php/irrodl/article/view/3111/4216

Croteau, E. (2017). Measures of student success with textbook transformations: The Affordable Learning Georgia Initiative. *Open Praxis, 9*(1), 93–108. Retrieved from https://openpraxis.org/index.php/OpenPraxis/article/view/505/251

D'Antoni, S. (2009). Open educational resources: Reviewing initiatives and issues. *Open Learning, The Journal of Open and Distance Learning, 24*, 3–10.

Delimont, N., Turtle, E. C., Bennett, A., Adhikari, K., & Lindshield, B. L. (2016). University students and faculty have positive perceptions of open/alternative resources and their utilization in a textbook replacement initiative. *Research in Learning Technology, 24*.

Fischer, L., Ernst, D., & Mason, S. L. (2017). Rating the quality of open textbooks: How reviewer and text characteristics predict ratings. *The International Review of Research in Open and Distributed Learning, 18*(4). Retrieved from http://www.irrodl.org/index.php/irrodl/article/view/2985/4217

Florida Virtual Campus. (2016). *2016 student textbook and course materials survey*. Retrieved from https://florida.theorangegrove.org/og/items/3a65c507-2510-42d7-814c-ffdefd394b6c/1/

Grewe, K. E., and Davis, W. P. (2017). The impact of enrollment in an OER course on student learning outcomes. *The International Review of Research in Open and Distributed Learning, 18*(4).

Hendricks, C., Reinsberg, S. A., & Rieger, G. W. (2017). The adoption of an open textbook in a large physics course: An analysis of cost, outcomes, use, and perceptions. *The International Review of Research in Open and Distributed Learning, 18*(4). Retrieved from http://www.irrodl.org/index.php/irrodl/article/view/3006/4220

Hewlett (2013). Open educational resources. Retrieved from http://www.hewlett.org/programs/education-program/open-educational-resources

Hilton, J., III. (2016). Open educational resources and college textbook choices: a review of research on efficacy and perceptions. *Educational Technology Research and Development 64*(4), 573–590.

Hilton, J., III, Fischer, L., Wiley, D., and Williams, L. (2016). Maintaining momentum toward graduation: OER and the course throughput rate. *The International Review of Research in Open and Distance Learning, 17*(6). Retrieved from http://www.irrodl.org/index.php/irrodl/article/view/2686/3967

Illowsky, B. S., Hilton, J., III, Whiting, J., & Ackerman, J. D. (2016). Examining student perception of an open statistics book. *Open Praxis, 8*(3), 265–276. Retrieved from https://openpraxis.org/index.php/OpenPraxis/article/view/304/218

Jhangiani, R. S., & Jhangiani, S. (2017). Investigating the perceptions, use, and impact of open textbooks: A survey of post-secondary students in British Columbia. *The International Review of Research in Open and Distributed Learning, 18*(4). Retrieved from http://www.irrodl.org/index.php/irrodl/article/view/3012/4214

Jung, E., Bauer, C., & Heaps, A. (2017). Higher education faculty perceptions of open textbook adoption. *The International Review of Research in Open and Distributed Learning, 18*(4). Retrieved from http://www.irrodl.org/index.php/irrodl/article/view/3120/4218

Ozdemir, O., & Hendricks, C. (2017). Instructor and student experiences with open textbooks, from the California open online library for education (Cool4Ed). *Journal of Computing in Higher Education, 29*(1), 98–113. Retrieved from https://link.springer.com/article/10.1007/s12528-017-9138-0

Pitt, R. (2015). Mainstreaming open textbooks: Educator perspectives on the impact of OpenStax College open textbooks. *International Review of Research on Open and Distributed Learning, 16*(4). Retrieved from http://www.irrodl.org/index.php/irrodl/article/view/2381/3497

Vojtech, G., & Grissett, J. (2017) Student perceptions of college faculty who use OER. *The International Review of Research in Open and Distributed Learning, 18*(4). Retrieved from http://www.irrodl.org/index.php/irrodl/article/view/3032

Watson, C., Domizi, D., & Clouser, S. (2017). Student and faculty perceptions of OpenStax in high enrollment courses. *The International Review Of Research In Open And Distributed Learning, 18*(5). doi: http://dx.doi.org/10.19173/irrodl.v18i5.2462

Wiley, D., Bliss, T. J., & McEwen, M. (2014). Open educational resources: A review of the literature. In J. M. Spector, M. D. Merrill, J. Elen, & M. J. Bishop. (Eds.), *Handbook of research on educational communications and technology* (pp. 781–789). New York: Springer. doi:10.1007/978-1-4614-3185-5_63

Wiley, D., Williams, L., DeMarte, D., and Hilton, J., III. (2016). The Tidewater Z-Degree and the INTRO model for sustaining OER adoption. *Education Policy Analysis Archives, 24*(41), 1–12. Retrieved from https://epaa.asu.edu/ojs/article/view/1828

Winitzky-Stephens, J. R., & Pickavance, J. (2017). Open educational resources and student course outcomes: A multilevel analysis. *The International Review of Research in Open and Distributed Learning, 18*(4). Retrieved from http://www.irrodl.org/index.php/irrodl/article/view/3118/4224

Section 2:
The Pedagogical Implications of OER

Selection of course materials is one of the few ways in which faculty have complete control over one of the costs of higher education. The role of OER in reducing these costs cannot be understated. However, OER also have the power to enable new forms of open pedagogy. Course materials that are free from most copyright restrictions allow faculty to design and implement innovative teaching methods which can engage students in new and exciting ways. This section showcases the potential of open pedagogy, and describes the role of the academic librarian within it.

First, Amaral explores the complementary alignment of the OER community and academic libraries. Through the lens of OER initiatives supported by the City University of New York (CUNY) and implemented at Borough of Manhattan Community College (BMCC), Amaral describes how an active and engaged culture can emerge when librarians set clear goals and work collaboratively for the public good.

In a similar vein, Reed talks about collaboration between scholarly communication librarians and information literacy librarians in support of OER initiatives, and underscores the importance of partnering with colleges and departments in the development and use of OER and open pedagogy.

Reed and Turner share that there are experiential learning opportunities inherent in OER initiatives. Specifically, the authors describe a student internship program focused on designing guidelines, criteria, and standards for evaluating OER for accessibility for disabled students and their use in the classroom.

Decisions on the adoption of course materials into open resources can be based on more than cost and accessibility. These decisions are often complex and influenced by existing cultures, policies, and other consid-erations. Walz explains an opportunity for open education advocates to overcome these obstacles to create more transparent, deliberate practices when evaluating and selecting required materials.

Finally, through multiple examples of open pedagogical practice across several disciplines, Jhangiani and Green explore how pedagogy, not tools or texts, is at the heart of OER advocacy efforts. For these authors, the resources and staff of an academic library provide the optimal locale to cultivate an individual's pedagogical efforts.

From Textbook Affordability to Transformative Pedagogy: Growing an OER Community

Librarians as Community Leaders in Open Knowledge

Similar to the potential for open access initiatives to position librarians as campus leaders, the open educational resources (OER) movement provides an ideal opportunity for librarians to lead in their communities. OER and libraries reside at the convergence of academic affairs and student affairs, faculty development and student learning. Leading OER initiatives taps librarians' unique expertise in instructional design, copyright and licensing, collection development and management, and needs assessment. As one of the few institutional entities serving both students and faculty, libraries are perfectly positioned to lead our institutions' OER programs, with the potential to establish or cement the library as integral to student success initiatives and as an important partner in faculty and curriculum development.

There are many high-visibility library-led programs at R1 universities and prestigious colleges (Salem, 2017) and a growing cadre of community college librarians doing this work (Community College Consortium for Open Educational Resources, n.d.). At Borough of Manhattan Community College (BMCC), our Open/Alternative Textbook Program has received the attention of our president, as well as favorable press within and without the college. Similar to OER initiatives at colleges nationwide (Yano, 2017), the BMCC library is leading our community in this effort.

The BMCC Community

The community that the BMCC library serves is both large and diverse. BMCC is one of 24 colleges in the City University of New York (CUNY) system and the largest of the system's seven community colleges, with over 26,000 undergraduate students enrolled in fall 2016. We are a majority minority college, with students self-identifying as Asian (15%), Black (31%), Hispanic (41%), and White (13%). As well, 54 percent self-identify as first-generation college students; many are immigrants, and some are undocumented (CUNY Office of Institutional Research and Assessment, 2017).

The college is located in lower Manhattan, three blocks from the World Trade Center and not far from Wall Street. While BMCC is part of Tribeca, one of the most affluent Manhattan neighborhoods minutes away from the seat of unimaginable wealth, in contrast our students mainly come from low socioeconomic status households throughout all five New York City boroughs: 65 percent have an annual household income of less than $25,000, and 83 percent less than $40,000; approximately 65 percent are eligible for Pell grants, a federal income-based student aid, and just under 90 percent are eligible for Tuition Assistance Program (TAP), New York's income-based aid (BMCC Office of Institutional Effectiveness and Analytics, 2017; CUNY Office of Institutional Research and Assessment, 2017).

But our students are not numbers. Each is a person facing their own challenges, often making difficult decisions and balancing tough choices, including sometimes, "If I buy my textbooks, will I have enough money for groceries?" As might be expected, the BMCC community, along with the larger CUNY community, is very concerned about and committed to addressing textbook affordability. BMCC faculty make accommodations in classrooms where many students have not purchased the textbook; administrators create programs to address the effects of high-priced course materials on retention and persistence among other barriers, and BMCC librarians maintain textbook reserve programs. None of which gets to the heart of the issue: high-priced textbooks, whether purchased by students, the library, or the institution. Led by the library, the BMCC community has come together, across academic affairs and student affairs, across departments and disciplines, to pursue what we consider a sounder, more sustainable solution with OER. At BMCC this solution involves growing a strong, vibrant OER initiative focused on transformative pedagogy, equity, and student success.

Growing an OER Community

From the Top Down

Several events in the CUNY system contributed to a growing open culture prior to BMCC launching an OER initiative. In 2013, CUNY established a Textbook Savings Committee to explore avenues for lowering textbook costs for students. In these initial discussions, OER was not the focus but one of many options for reducing costs, as described by CUNY's Associate Vice Chancellor and Chief Information Officer in testimony before a hearing of the New York City Council's Committee on Higher Education in fall 2014 (New York City Council, 2014). The University had for several years provided students with information through a textbook savings flyer and website, which listed various options for reducing costs. The Textbook Savings Committee also investigated and made recommendations for moving from brick and mortar bookstores to online bookstores that offered reduced pricing models; four CUNY colleges have implemented this since, with several others to follow even though students have expressed dissatisfaction with the online option (Inderjeit, 2016) and preference for a physical bookstore ("York reacts," 2017).

While replacing one bookstore with another and more expensive textbooks with less can reduce costs for students in the short term, more helpful solutions seek zero cost to students; any cost for materials, even low cost, can be a barrier to learning as evidenced by recent research on food and housing insecurity for students across the country (Goldrick-Rab, 2017). At the committee hearing, the Vice Chancellor for Budget and Finance described CUNY's efforts to mitigate the impact of textbook costs through financial assistance programs, including funding for library textbook reserves through CUNY's Student Financial Assistance Initiative, and student retention and success programs, such as Accelerated Studies in Associate Programs (ASAP), which provide students with textbook vouchers (New York City Council, 2014).

Also at the Committee on Higher Education hearing, CUNY's Dean for Libraries and Information Services testified about the efforts by CUNY Libraries which, similar to the financial assistance programs, focused on eliminating textbook costs for students rather than merely reducing them. CUNY Libraries oversaw the funding to procure textbooks for reserve, purchasing over 30,000 textbooks in 2013–14 which were borrowed more than 380,000 times (New York City Council, 2014). During the 2014–15 academic year, the CUNY Office of Library Services also offered an online OER 101 course to faculty and librarians across the system.[1] The first faculty cohort to participate received a $500 stipend, and the second $250; librarians were not remunerated due to contractual constraints. Thirty faculty, two of whom were from BMCC, and 13 librarians completed the course.

The administration's emphasis has been on reducing textbook costs, while the libraries are committed to ensuring the primary option is to provide no-cost materials. This focus on no-cost specifically includes textbook reserves and OER, but we envision that within the next five to ten years textbook reserves will be eliminated, or at least significantly reduced, as the use of OER for course materials continues to grow. More generally, another important source of no-cost materials is the library's digital collection, from articles to ebooks to streaming videos. No-cost materials are better understood as no additional cost to students beyond existing tuition and fees. To achieve no cost, BMCC has reallocated funds, such as those used on reserve textbooks, investing them in resources and materials that are available beyond an individual course to the community as a whole (library subscriptions) and globally (OER).

From the Ground Up

While BMCC faculty were for the most part unaware of these CUNY-wide efforts, there were concurrent activities shining light on textbook affordability and open culture on our campus, including a textbook affordability event co-sponsored and co-facilitated by the library and the New York Public Interest Research Group (NYPIRG) in fall 2014 and a faculty development day on OER and open access in spring 2015. The fall event, entitled "Campus Conversation: Addressing Textbook Affordability," drew about 40 students, faculty, and staff, providing participants the space for a lively discussion exploring perspectives, frustrations, and possible solutions.

---

[1] See: https://canvas.instructure.com/courses/815700/pages/class-introduction

At this event, students quickly framed textbook affordability as a social justice issue relating to access to education generally, not just to textbooks. They also described the catch-22 of not being able to afford books, doing poorly or perhaps failing courses, then having to repeat courses at additional cost. Students wanted faculty to consider their struggles when they were selecting course materials, avoiding options such as bundled books and media or choosing every new edition that comes out. Many students were concerned about the impact on their grades. And the students told poignant stories about worrying that their instructors would think they were less invested in their education when they weren't able to purchase the textbooks, as well as the difficulty of admitting that they didn't have the money to buy books.

BMCC Public Affairs highlighted this event in its reporting of campus activities, which provided a visible statement in support of students and faculty looking to address textbook affordability and its impact on learning. It was clear from this event that there was fertile ground for continuing the conversation within the community, especially among faculty who hold the key to transitioning from expensive commercial textbooks to no-cost options.

The faculty development event the following spring, entitled "The Power of Open: Unlocking Your Research and Course Materials for Maximum Impact," included presentations by librarians and faculty highlighting the benefits and acknowledging the challenges of open, elucidated through their own personal experiences. The presentations were followed by robust group discussions and a Q&A which surfaced faculty concerns, as well as enthusiasm for growing an open culture on campus. The library built on this momentum with an OER presentation at BMCC's spring 2015 Technology Day. These efforts and events at both CUNY and BMCC were the foundation on which we built our Open/Alternative Textbook Program, beginning with a proposal for a pilot presented to the Provost and Senior Vice President for Academic Affairs that was approved in fall 2014.

Initiated and developed by the library, BMCC's Open/Alternative Textbook pilot was launched with funding from the library's textbook reserves budget, the use of which had been encouraged and supported by CUNY's Dean for Libraries and Information Services. The pilot was led by BMCC's open knowledge librarian in collaboration with the director for the Center for Excellence in Teaching, Learning and Scholarship (CETLS). Faculty were recruited through an application process in fall 2014, participated in training workshops in spring 2015, and piloted their zero textbook cost courses the following semester. While the emphasis of the program was on OER, the goal for the program was zero cost to students, which faculty achieved using OER and alternative no-cost materials available through the library and on the Web, or what is often called zero textbook cost (ZTC).

Faculty responded overwhelmingly positively to the pilot in an evaluation, with all of the respondents indicating they would recommend the workshops to colleagues and most indicating they would redesign additional courses using OER. Given this evidence of the pilot's success with faculty, BMCC's Provost and Senior Vice President for Academic Affairs established the Open/Alternative Textbook Program with the continued leadership of the library and CETLS. The program now receives $30,000/academic year, which funds faculty stipends.

At the end of spring 2017, 75 faculty from 15 of BMCC's 17 departments had completed training workshops and redesigned at least one section of one course (but often more sections and more courses) replacing commercial textbooks with OER or alternative no-cost materials. As of fall 2017, we estimate that students have saved approximately $1 million. In questionnaire responses, faculty who completed the training described feeling "happier," "excited," "energized," "confident," and "liberated," among other positive characterizations, which they shared with colleagues. Enthusiastic word-of-mouth promotion generated much interest in the program, and faculty have been turned away each semester as there are more applications than can be accommodated. As the community continues to grow, we know that we will eventually need to successfully recruit faculty who are significantly skeptical of OER. When we do, we have some confidence that the growing research evidence in support of positive outcomes combined with their colleagues' often transformative experiences will be convincing and compelling.

The growth of OER at BMCC and CUNY is due in large part to these simultaneous efforts occurring from the ground up and top down. At both the city and state levels, Student PIRGs have been advocating for textbook affordability (New York City Council, 2014; Senack & Donoghue, 2016; Senack, Donoghue, Grant, & Steen, 2016), and their efforts have kept the issue in the forefront. At the same time as this grassroots advocacy, CUNY's administration continued to be concerned with and address unsustainable textbook costs through cost-reduction tactics. Similarly, at BMCC from the ground up, faculty enthusiastically embraced OER, with crucial program support from the administration and CUNY Office of Library Services. Local funding has since been complemented and exceeded by the investment of foundations and New York State. These myriad stakeholders working on the issue from both the ground up and top down contribute significantly to our continuing success at BMCC, which has led to the inclusion of the OER initiative as one of the strategies in BMCC's college-wide retention and completion agenda under the category of improving teaching and learning.

Key Community Partnerships

As BMCC's OER community grows, several key partnerships have been and continue to be fostered. Foremost is the collaboration between the library and CETLS. This synergistic partnership leverages the strengths of each unit. At BMCC prior to the OER program, the library was not well known for faculty development programs, while this is the main focus of CETLS. The OER program has been strengthened by the different perspectives and expertise brought to the planning, implementation, and ongoing improvement by the CETLS director and open knowledge librarian. There is also a natural complement between OER and e-learning, and we are exploring ways to cross-pollinate the training for each of these programs. While other logical partners include instructional design and user experience staff, BMCC does not currently have personnel in these areas.

We also believe there is fruitful potential in partnerships with cohort programs aimed at student retention and success. We've begun conversations with ASAP, which provides students with substantial and targeted academic, financial, and personal support. Currently, ASAP provides textbook vouchers that do not always cover the entire cost of required materials; the vouchers are also costly and complicated to manage. OER has the potential to provide a more sustainable and pedagogically innovative alternative. A second cohort program, the BMCC Learning Academy, does not provide vouchers and needs incentives to attract students to the program. If all of their cohort courses were ZTC, this could be used to recruit and retain students.

Partnerships with Student Affairs and Student Government Association are also in their infancy. We know that advisors are instrumental in educating students about ZTC courses, and at BMCC they fully support the program, given that they are the front line for counseling students who are considering dropping out of courses or who are doing poorly because they haven't been able to access expensive course materials. Continually educating and updating staff and faculty about important initiatives is always a challenge at an institution the size of BMCC, so efforts are ongoing and new strategies are always being considered. Every fall, we also reach out to the incoming members of our Student Government Association encouraging their voice and advocacy for OER, especially with faculty who have not yet embraced ZTC courses. Finally, we are partnering with our Office of Institutional Effectiveness and Analytics (IEA) to assess the impact of ZTC courses and the effectiveness of the Open/Alternative Textbook Program. IEA will examine a number of indicators, including drop-fail-withdraw (DFW) rates, persistence, and time to graduation, among others. All of these partnerships are crucial to the success of the program and to the success of our students.

Moving from Opportunistic to Systematic Growth

When we launched the Open/Alternative Textbook Program at BMCC, we made a strategic decision to focus on zero textbook cost with an emphasis on OER. With 27,000 students, our community needs the largest number of courses possible that do not require purchase of course materials. We found that the most effective way to achieve this goal in terms of recruiting faculty and redesigning courses was through using OER along with other no-cost materials. While growing our OER community from spring 2015 through spring 2017, we welcomed any faculty members who expressed interest in redesigning their courses to achieve zero cost to students. We chose not to focus on specific departments or courses in order to promote as widespread adoption as possible and a campus culture of open. Because of this opportunistic approach and because the number of ZTC courses is currently less than 20 percent of the total number of courses, students may not be able to find a ZTC course that fulfills needed requirements and fits their schedule. With our current program, it would take 15 years to convert 75 percent of the approximately 450 courses offered at BMCC.

Beginning in summer 2016, two additional funding sources have facilitated a concurrent effort that moves us from course by course development to a more systematic approach. The first opportunity to make this shift came with BMCC's participation in Achieving the Dream's Open Educational Resources (OER) Degree Initiative,[2] which launched in summer 2016. This initiative has the ambitious and laudable goal of boosting "college access and completion, particularly for underserved students, by engaging faculty in the redesign of courses and degree programs through the replacement of proprietary textbooks with open educational resources. Over the next three years, the Open Educational Resources Degree Initiative will lay the groundwork for nationwide adoption of OER Degrees" (Achieving the Dream, n.d.). Through spring 2019, Achieving the Dream is working with 38 community colleges nationwide to create OER degrees that can be adopted and adapted by other colleges across the country. The initiative includes a research component that will assess the program's goals to reduce student textbook costs and positively impact student success.

CUNY Office of Library Services took the lead on the proposal for the Achieving the Dream grant, which includes two other CUNY campuses, Hostos Community College and Bronx Community College, and is coordinating efforts across the three campuses. BMCC is converting its Criminal Justice Associate in Arts degree, Hostos its Early Childhood Education, and Bronx its General Education with a concentration in history. The criminal justice degree program is BMCC's second largest after liberal arts, with 2,865 students enrolled in fall 2016. There are 20 courses required for the degree, six within the major. As of fall 2017, all six criminal justice courses will include at least one OER section, with 24 sections being offered across the six courses. The department plans to increase the

---

[2] See: http://achievingthedream.org/resources/initiatives/open-educational-resources-oer-degree-initiative

number of OER sections in each course in the following semesters. The remaining 14 courses across several departments are in the works and will all have OER sections offered by fall 2018. While we expect that the majority of criminal justice course sections will be ZTC by 2020, giving students the possibility of finding sections that fit their schedules, the goal of adequate course sections for meaningful schedule choices will be much more challenging to achieve with general education requirements, given the large number of courses that fulfill these.

Achieving the Dream has taken a holistic approach in working with participants focusing on developing the capacity of the institution to implement and sustain OER degrees. The participating colleges received a framework for working across college units, including student affairs and academic affairs, and with advisors and administrators, as well as faculty. As an example, BMCC worked with our registrar and CUNY Office of Library Services to implement a zero textbook cost course designation that allows students to search for these courses when registering.

To ensure that the degrees created under this initiative can be adopted seamlessly at other institutions, the participating colleges are required to use only materials that carry a Creative Commons or other open license. While similar degrees have been called zero textbook cost or Z-degrees in the past, this is an important distinction as OER degrees do not use library resources, which differ college to college, nor other no-cost materials on the Web, such as YouTube videos, which usually do not adhere to the 5 Rs (retain, reuse, revise, remix and redistribute). Without being able to retain a copy of this material, it may disappear at any time, as faculty are well aware, rendering its use unstable.

Given that our Open/Alternative Textbook Program provided a foundation off which to build, we have experienced one unanticipated challenge as we develop our OER degree. Because BMCC's efforts to achieve zero textbook cost embraced OER and alternative no-cost materials, some BMCC faculty have been stretched by the requirement to use solely OER. Our faculty have found that often there are texts and films accessed through the library that achieve learning outcomes in ways not matched by available OER. There are also quality, no-cost options on the Web that are not OER, such as Stanford Encyclopedia of Philosophy and The Marshall Project, that faculty value and struggle to find adequate OER replacements for. The faculty participating in the grant have embraced this challenge and are creating OER courses, but some faculty have chosen not to participate in the OER degree even though they are offering zero textbook cost courses.

As mentioned earlier, another challenge that has become clear as we work to create the Criminal Justice OER degree is having enough sections of OER courses to make it possible for most students to find sections that fit into their schedules. Achieving the Dream's preliminary report on the OER Degree Initiative identified a concern with this "thin line" pathway of just a few sections of OER courses, which many participating colleges are encountering (Griffiths et al., 2017). The key moving forward will be to combine programs that develop Z-degrees with initiatives that support the redesign with OER of all or the majority of sections for general education courses.

The Achieving the Dream OER Degree grant received by CUNY has been the catalyst for additional funding from New York State, which is making it possible for us to address this challenge of thin lines for OER offerings within the degree and the need for more sections of general education courses. After strong advocacy by Student PIRGs for the past few years and coverage of CUNY's involvement in the OER Degree Initiative, the New York State Education Department contacted CUNY's Office of Academic Affairs in spring 2017 to express interest in supporting OER efforts on CUNY campuses. CUNY Academic Affairs together with the Office of Library Services submitted a funding proposal in response to the Education Department's enquiry. This led to New York State including $4 million in funding for CUNY and another $4 million for the State University of New York (SUNY) in its budget for 2017–18. Before the State's funding, about eight of the CUNY colleges had active OER programs; now all 24 campuses have applied to CUNY Office of Library Services, who is administering the funds, to begin or grow OER programs.

As part of this initiative, approximately 100 BMCC faculty will redesign 45 courses, 25 of which are in the top 30 in enrollment, using OER and alternative materials. This funding begins to address the need for more sections of general education courses in order to make OER degrees viable for most students. Some of the funds will also be used for assessment, conducting similar studies to those that have examined student success indicators in relation to OER (Feldstein et al., 2012; Fischer, Hilton, Robinson, & Wiley, 2015; Hilton, Fischer, Wiley, & William, 2016; Ozdemir & Hendricks, 2017). While cost savings is a compelling argument for redesigning courses, for faculty who are hesitant the research indicating positive impacts can be persuasive, as well as for administrators who often focus on student success and retention as strategic priorities.

Moving from Cost Savings to Transformative Pedagogy

Most OER programs estimate what they have saved their students in aggregate; at BMCC, we estimate that in the first four semesters of running the Open/Alternative Textbook Program we saved students $1 million, that a student who takes all 20 OER courses as part of the Criminal Justice OER degree will save $2,500, and that the ZTC courses created under the state funding will save students over $1.5 million each year. For individual students, savings vary depending on availability of zero textbook cost courses that fit their schedule. When an Achieving the Dream representative visited our campus recently, we recruited a group of five students to talk about their experiences with textbooks. They candidly responded to a question about how textbook cost impacts their choice of classes, indicating that it was minimal. For this group of students, the first criteria for choosing a class was whether it fit their schedule, and the second was the professor's rating on various websites. Sometimes, after considering those two criteria, they might consider the cost of the textbook.

These students were resourceful, and one reason they gave for cost being a lower priority was the ability to take advantage of "free" sources, some legal and some not, such as library textbook reserves, a friend's or classmate's copy, and torrent or other document sharing sites. Of course, there are no similar options when access codes for online publisher sites are required. We also know that students may enroll in a class regardless of textbook cost but end up dropping out because of those costs if they cannot get consistent and reliable access to the text, among other negative impacts (Florida Virtual Campus, 2016). In questionnaire responses, BMCC students recognize the positive impact of OER on their learning. Beyond cost savings, they note that immediate and 24/7 access throughout the semester means they don't have an excuse not to do their work and they are able to keep pace with coursework and complete assignments and reading on time. While cost savings are important, it is the affordances of OER and their positive impact on learning that we focus on in our Open/ Alternative Textbook Program.

For participating in the program, faculty receive $1,000 stipends and complete four two-and-a-half-hour workshops which provide the foundation for redesigning their courses around open and alternative materials. As might be expected, this redesign takes hours well beyond the training time allotted. Workshops are run seminar style, encouraging conversation and building a community of practice. They are also designed with active learning, including group discussion of scenarios, think-pair-share activities, and reflective exercises. In program evaluations, faculty expressed appreciation for this cross-disciplinary, collegial model, as the discussion-based format promotes connections across the departments. With over 1,500 faculty at BMCC, participants often meet for the first time, and conversations have sparked cross-department collaborations. For example, during one of the workshops, a faculty member in English and another in Speech, Communications and Theatre Arts discovered that they had a shared interest in conflict resolution and non-violent activism with both incorporating related material and lessons in their courses. The two are planning to teach connected courses in a learning community, allowing them to collaborate on resources and assignments. With few, but increasing, opportunities to discuss pedagogy on campus, faculty relish these conversations.

The curriculum for the four workshops was designed to give faculty a foundation for completing their course redesigns. In the first workshop, faculty are introduced to learner-centered teaching through two articles, one on creating a learner-centered syllabus (Fulmer, 2017) and the other on backward design (Wiggins & McTighe, 2006). The syllabus article situates the conversation in learner-centered design, providing examples of syllabus items before and after being rewritten with the learner in mind and modeling learner-centered language that can be used when explaining why the faculty chose to create a ZTC course. For backward design, participants read an article describing and assessing the process applied to a class session (Reynolds & Kearns, 2017). The authors provide a worksheet that guides faculty through key backward design steps, including identifying learning outcomes that will be addressed and the assessments of the learning outcomes, then considering content and activities that will help the students achieve the learning outcomes and be successful on the assessments. This model provides participants with a process and structure for thinking about, searching for, and finding appropriate OER for their courses.

Building on this learner-centered focus, the faculty also read articles on culturally relevant and culturally sustaining pedagogy (Milner, 2011; Paris, 2012). With the readings as prompts, faculty discuss how they currently enact culturally relevant and culturally sustaining pedagogy in their classes, as well as brainstorming ideas for activities and assignments that would frame the course from the first day or first week within this pedagogical space. The last pedagogical framework faculty explore is open pedagogy; in groups, the faculty create assignments that engage students as knowledge producers rather than just knowledge consumers, often having the students adapt or create OER. It is during this initial session that faculty first begin to see the pedagogical opportunities afforded by using open and other no-cost materials.

The second workshop covers OER context and definitions, situating faculty in the global open movement, and familiarizing them with the 5 Rs. Faculty are also given hands-on time to explore OER repositories and sites. Because the program also includes using alternative no-cost materials available through the library and on the Web, copyright and fair use are also covered, with an emphasis on "reclaiming fair use" (Aufderheide & Jaszi, 2011) which has the potential for broad application in higher education. Faculty are introduced to Columbia's fair use checklist, as well as three questions recommended by Aufderheide and Jaszi focusing on transformative purpose, appropriate amount, and reasonableness within field or discipline. This second session also presents Creative Commons licensing to participants.

The third workshop addresses course and materials delivery, looking at examples in the learning management system (LMS) and alternatives including WordPress, Facebook, and LibGuides. Many BMCC faculty are satisfied with the LMS, while recognizing and to some extent making peace with its issues, while others find they are ready to move to a more user-friendly online space, such as WordPress. After considering delivery options, this session looks at creating OER, with examples from faculty colleagues. Participants are encouraged to start small, thinking of materials they have already created, including assignments, lecture slides, and handouts. Lastly, the participants discuss assessment. In the first semester that faculty teach with OER, they are asked to administer a questionnaire addressing students' experiences in the course and with OER. Participants are encouraged to think about what they would like to explore and learn about the experience of teaching OER, and to use the questionnaire or other assessment to write an article within the scholarship of teaching and learning.

The last workshop focuses on the importance of community, both the OER community of practice at BMCC, as well as the larger communities within faculty disciplines and higher education in general. Listservs such as that hosted by CCCOER (the Community College Consortium for Open Educational Resources) and SPARC (the Scholarly Publishing and Academic Resources Coalition) are recommended to extend and expand the community of practice beyond BMCC and CUNY. On the listservs, faculty can connect with others in their discipline as well as across disciplines, solicit assistance, and contribute to the growing national community of practice. Faculty also complete an assignment in which they upload an OER they have created to CUNY's institutional repository, Academic Works, as well as review OER in one of the repositories, such as MERLOT (the Multimedia Educational Resource for Learning and Online Teaching). Concluding the workshop series, faculty present whatever portion of the course redesign they have completed, sharing the resources they found and how they were using them in their courses. This sharing reinforces the community of practice and provides the opportunity for participants to receive feedback and suggestions on their redesigned course.

The focus on pedagogy in the BMCC Open/Alternative Textbook Program has been an important contributing factor to its success. While BMCC faculty are committed to the social justice issue of textbook affordability, the opportunity to redesign their courses in innovative ways made possible by OER and other no-cost materials energized faculty going through the workshops and attracted others to join them, as was made clear in the faculty questionnaire responses mentioned earlier. Some faculty were able to ditch the textbook altogether, while others who used open textbooks often supplemented with videos and other sources that transformed their courses. The costs savings are undeniably important to our students and part of this program's success, but even more so is the pedagogical transformation that we see taking place.

Sustaining and Scaling OER

At BMCC there are several issues that need to be addressed to sustain OER initiatives at meaningful scale. Increasing general education OER course offerings requires us to work within, around, or through departmental constraints, which vary by discipline. For example, some departments encourage and support adjunct participation while others actively discourage it, which is problematic given that two thirds of our faculty are part-time. In our science department, the faculty in each discipline (biology, chemistry, physics, and astronomy) vote on the textbook that will be adopted for all sections of their courses. For OER to be used by our science faculty there needs to be consensus, which we are working toward. Science faculty who have gone through the Open/Alternative Textbook Program are able to act as OER champions, and this can be particularly effective if the OER champion is the course coordinator.

On the other hand, in the humanities and social sciences, there is more independence in course material selection, and often faculty use different frames or lenses for the same course. This most often requires us to work course section by course section with individual faculty members. Within the OER Degree and New York State funding initiatives, we are beginning to use communities of practice to encourage more sharing of resources between these independent faculty members, which would help with scaling beyond one or two sections. Within the humanities, after we announced the zero textbook cost attribute in our registration system, we heard from some English instructors who were using zero cost resources before the launch of the Open/Alternative Textbook Program, with more taking up the option after participating. Contemporary literature courses understandably remain out of reach due to the appropriate materials remaining under copyright, though many faculty seek out the lowest cost options and the library purchases ebooks whenever possible to support faculty efforts.

Another discipline-specific barrier is the loss of publisher ancillaries when courses are redesigned with OER. This is a barrier in STEM disciplines (science, technology, engineering, and math) as well as social sciences, even though faculty in the latter are more likely to individually choose their textbooks. Most faculty have neither the time nor the expertise to develop valid and reliable test questions. To address this, BMCC will be exploring various options available for personalized learning systems, also known as adaptive learning, that use OER (e.g., Carnegie Mellon OLI). Most personalized learning systems are produced by commercial publishers, and their use of OER for the content on which the ancillary material is based may reduce the cost, at least initially. As stated earlier though, even low-cost materials may prove a barrier to many students. At BMCC, there is an effort to incorporate any costs for personalized learning systems into already existing programs and fees to avoid passing the cost along to students in new fees thus maintaining courses as zero textbook cost.

CUNY Office of Library Services also received a grant from the Bill and Melinda Gates Foundation to test one system, Lumen Learning's Waymaker platform, which combines OER with adaptive or personalized learning. Several CUNY schools are participating, and BMCC's psychology faculty will be using the platform for several sections of Introduction to Psychology. This project is part of a larger three-year research study that will evaluate impact on student success, persistence, and retention. BMCC math faculty, who are probably the furthest along in moving their courses to OER, are also exploring open source alternatives, including My Open Math and WeBWorK, as possible solutions for developing homework assignments and practice tests, rather than using publishers' online sites. These homework systems and personalized learning platforms address the reservation raised by many faculty who hesitate to move to OER because they lose publisher test banks and other ancillaries.

Along with these department and disciplinary challenges, faculty are on the whole concerned with how OER will count toward tenure and promotion. At BMCC, while participating in OER initiatives is generally viewed favorably by most departments in tenure and promotion reviews, the adoption, adaptation, and creation of OER in redesigning courses is not officially included in the evaluation of teaching, service, or scholarship. This is one reason that in the Open/Alternative Textbook Program we spend time discussing assessment and encourage faculty to publish about OER within the scholarship of teaching and learning, as currently any peer-reviewed publications would count toward tenure and promotion in our current tenure system. BMCC's Associate Dean of Faculty has suggested that OER could fall under Boyer's "scholarship of integration," and we'll be exploring this avenue going forward (Boggs, 2017). Tenure and promotion is a particularly complex issue to address as policies and procedures can have many layers, including disciplinary, departmental, college, and system, but without valuing this work in tenure and promotion, it will be extremely difficult to sustain and scale our efforts.

Another important challenge both locally and beyond is developing a viable funding model that values faculty expertise and the labor required in redesigning courses with OER. At BMCC, the $1,000 stipend we offer faculty is the equivalent of approximately 22 hours at a non-adjunct teaching rate. The faculty are in workshops for 10 hours, leaving 12 hours to significantly redesign their courses around these new materials and within this new pedagogical framework. To date none of our faculty have chosen to adopt available OER courses as a whole from third party providers. Although this type of adoption is often touted as the answer to issues of sustainability and scalability, even this takes some labor, with faculty needing to become familiar with the materials and flow of the course. But the potential for pedagogical transformation we have demonstrated in BMCC's Open/Alternative Textbook Program comes from faculty rethinking and redesigning their courses, which takes substantially more time. Ideally, to adequately value this creative and innovative work, we would provide our faculty, who labor under 5/4 teaching loads (5 courses in fall, 4 in spring), with a course release. Counting toward tenure as scholarship of integration would also allow faculty to choose how they spend their time in fulfilling the scholarship requirement. Both of these changes would help in recruiting faculty who have stated that the undervaluing of this work is a barrier to their embracing OER.

The Importance of the Commons

For the library, we want to take our success with OER and solidify our role in leading campus-wide initiatives that contribute significantly to our university's strategic goals, as the Open/Alternative Textbook Program has on our campus. Librarians also have the opportunity to lead a public dialog about OER, as we have with open access (OA), which often focuses on economics and monetary costs in particular: high prices for journals, high prices for textbooks, large profits for the companies producing them. Librarians are well positioned to expand this discussion to include the knowledge commons (Hess & Ostrom, 2011), which speaks to social justice issues often inherent in the work at community colleges specifically and higher education generally. At BMCC, some faculty and librarians believe in fighting against what Bollier terms "enclosures of commons—in which corporate interests appropriate our shared wealth [or information and knowledge] and turn it into expensive private commodities" (Bollier, 2014, p. 3). This should sound familiar, as it's what we've seen happen in both scholarly publishing and textbook publishing, and just as scholarly publishing behemoths have entered the OA sphere, publishers and vendors are moving into OER. Recently, librarians have authored important critiques (Almeida, 2017), and Crissinger (2015) urges us "to be cognizant of our position within increasingly corporatized institutions and consider how we might be furthering the goals of those institutions, to think seriously about how we can be actively dismantling power structures instead of perpetuating them, and to remind ourselves why we think open is worth fighting for in the first place." With librarians leading OER initiatives, we have the opportunity to reclaim knowledge as a public good, if we choose to heed the call.

References

Achieving the Dream. (n.d.). Open Educational Resources (OER) Degree Initiative. Retrieved from http://achievingthedream.org/resources/initiatives/open-educational-resources-oer-degree-initiative

Almeida, N. (2017). Open educational resources and rhetorical paradox in the neoliberal univers(ity). *Journal of Critical Library and Information Studies, 1*(1). Retrieved from http://libraryjuicepress.com/journals/index.php/jclis/article/view/16

Aufderheide, P., & Jaszi, P. (2011). *Reclaiming fair use: How to put balance back in copyright.* Chicago, IL: The University of Chicago Press.

BMCC Office of Institutional Effectiveness and Analytics. (2017). Borough of Manhattan Community College: Factsheet fall 2016.

Boggs, G. R. (2017). *Encouraging scholarship in the community college* (NISOD Papers 7). Retrieved from http://www.nisod.org/archive_files/nisod-papers/The%20NISOD%20Papers-April2017.pdf?x14288

Bollier, D. (2014). *Think like a commoner: A short introduction to the life of the commons.* Gabriola, British Columbia: New Society Publishers.

Community College Consortium for Open Educational Resources. (n.d.). About us. Retrieved from https://www.cccoer.org/about/about-cccoer/

Crissinger, S. (2015). A critical take on OER practices: Interrogating commercialization, colonialism, and content. *In the Library with the Lead Pipe*. Retrieved from http://www.inthelibrarywiththeleadpipe.org/2015/a-critical-take-on-oer-practices-interrogating-commercialization-colonialism-and-content/

CUNY Office of Institutional Research and Assessment. (2017). 2016 student experience survey. Retrieved from https://public.tableau.com/views/2016StudentExperienceSurvey/MainMenu?%3Aembed=y&%3AshowVizHome=no&%3Adispla_count=y&%3Adisplay_static_image=y&%3AbootstrapWhen Notified=true

Feldstein, A., Martin, M., Hudson, A., Warren, K., Hilton, J., III, & Wiley, D. (2012). Open textbooks and increased student access and outcomes. *European Journal of Open, Distance and E-Learning, 2*, 1–9.

Fischer, L., Hilton, J., III, Robinson, T. J., & Wiley, D. A. (2015). A multi-institutional study of the impact of open textbook adoption on the learning outcomes of post-secondary students. *Journal of Computing in Higher Education, 27*(3), 159–172. doi: https://doi.org/10.1007/s12528-015-9101-x

Florida Virtual Campus. (2016). *2016 student textbook and course materials survey*. Retrieved from https://florida.theorangegrove.org/og/items/3a65c507-2510-42d7-814c-ffdefd394b6c/1/

Fulmer, S. (2017, June 18). Weekly digest #64: Preparing a learning-focused syllabus [Blog post]. Retrieved from http://www.learningscientists.org/blog/2017/6/18/weekly-digest-64

Goldrick-Rab, S. (2017). *Paying the price: College costs, financial aid, and the betrayal of the American dream*. Chicago, IL: University of Chicago Press.

Griffiths, R., Mislevy, J., Wang, S., Shear, L., Mitchell, N., Bloom, M., ... Desrochers, D. (2017). *Launching OER degree pathways: An early snapshot of Achieving the Dream's OER Degree Initiative and emerging lessons*. Menlo Park, CA: SRI International.

Hess, C., & Ostrom, E. (Eds.). (2011). *Understanding knowledge as a commons: From theory to practice*. Cambridge, MA: MIT Press.

Hilton, J., III, Fischer, L., Wiley, D., & William, L. (2016). Maintaining momentum toward graduation: OER and the course throughput rate. *The International Review of Research in Open and Distributed Learning, 17*(6). Retrieved from http://www.irrodl.org/index.php/irrodl/article/view/2686

Inderjeit, A. (2016, October 19). Online bookstore causes problems for some students. *The Knight News*. Retrieved from https://theknightnews.com/2016/10/19/online-bookstore-causes-problems-for-some-students/

Milner, H. R. (2011). Culturally relevant pedagogy in a diverse urban classroom. *The Urban Review, 43*(1), 66–89. https://doi.org/10.1007/s11256-009-0143-0

New York City Council. (2014). Oversight—Reducing the cost of college textbooks. The New York City Council—File #: T2014-1782, Hearing testimony. Retrieved from http://legistar.council.nyc.gov/LegislationDetail.aspx?ID=1909591&GUID=5849FC13-9E5E-4117-BF41-0A738FC7F784&Options=&Search=

Ozdemir, O., & Hendricks, C. (2017). Instructor and student experiences with open textbooks, from the California open online library for education (Cool4Ed). *Journal of Computing in Higher Education, 29*(1), 98–113.

Paris, D. (2012). Culturally sustaining pedagogy: A needed change in stance, terminology, and practice. *Educational Researcher, 41*(3), 93–97. https://doi.org/10.3102/0013189X12441244

Reynolds, H. L., & Kearns, K. D. (2017). A planning tool for incorporating backward design, active learning, and authentic assessment in the college classroom. *College Teaching, 65*(1), 17–27. https://doi.org/10.1080/87567555.2016.1222575

Salem, J. A. (2017). Open pathways to student success: Academic library partnerships for open educational resource and affordable course content creation and adoption. *The Journal of Academic Librarianship, 43*(1), 34–38.

Senack, E., & Donoghue, R. (2016, February). *Covering the cost: Why we can no longer afford to ignore textbook prices.* Student PIRGs. Retrieved from http://www.studentpirgs.org/sites/student/files/reports/National%20-%20COVERING%20THE%20COST.pdf

Senack, E., Donoghue, R., Grant, K. O., & Steen, K. (2016, September). *Access denied: The new face of the textbook monopoly.* Student PIRGs. Retrieved from http://www.studentpirgs.org/sites/student/files/reports/Access%20Denied%20-%20Final%20Report.pdf

Wiggins, G. P., & McTighe, J. (2006). *Understanding by design* (Expanded 2nd ed.). Upper Saddle River, NJ: Pearson.

Yano, B. (2017). *Connect OER annual report, 2016–2017.* Washington, DC: SPARC. Retrieved from https://sparcopen.org/our-work/connect-oer/reports

York reacts: Barnes and Nobel replaced by online based book store fall semester 2017. (2017, March 28). *Pandora's Box.* Retrieved from http://yorkpbnews.net/campus/york-reacts-barnes-and-nobel-replaced-by-online-based-book-store-fall-semester-2017/

Creating Learning Opportunities in Open Education: An Exploration of the Intersections of Information Literacy and Scholarly Communication

Michelle Reed

Introduction

In many academic libraries, scholarly communication and information literacy are considered distinct areas of librarianship that are typically managed by separate units within an organization. Those who practice in the realm of scholarly communication tend to emphasize support for faculty and sometimes graduate students, focusing on the topics of copyright, access, visibility, and data management as they relate to research and scholarly publishing. Information literacy librarians, on the other hand, prioritize undergraduate students and focus on information-seeking behavior, information evaluation, and ethical use of information. The practice of information literacy librarians has been deeply impacted by educational theory, instructional design, and the scholarship of teaching and learning, resulting in a growing emphasis on learning outcomes and assessment, while that of scholarly communication librarians shifts in confluence with case law, public policy, and commercial publishing practices.

In 2013, the Association of College & Research Libraries (ACRL) published *Intersections of Scholarly Communication and Information Literacy: Creating Strategic Collaborations for a Changing Academic Environment,* a white paper that defined three important connections between these two critical areas of librarianship and proposed a variety of strategic actions that librarians can take to capitalize on the potential of the *Intersections.* Recommendations included developing integrated educational programs for librarians, redesigning information literacy curricula for all audiences to include topics of scholarly communication, discussing organizational models that break down silos, and advocating for the value of libraries in disseminating scholarship and contributing to student learning.

Since then, a number of books, articles, and presentations have been published on topics central to the *Intersections*. A bibliography of relevant readings is available on ACRL's website (ACRL, n.d.-a), and the organization has since developed a licensed workshop, "Two Paths Converge: Designing Educational Opportunities on the Intersections of Scholarly Communication and Information Literacy," to continue outreach and advocacy around the *Intersections* (ACRL, n.d.-b). Though librarians have produced scholarship related to open education for over a decade, little has been written about the connection between open education (frequently housed within scholarly communication units) and information literacy. This chapter expands the *Intersections* discussion to include open educational resources (OER) and open pedagogy. It presents a case for the intersectional nature of open education and provides examples of how practitioners and advocates can leverage the common ground between scholarly communication and information literacy to create meaningful learning opportunities for a variety of audiences.

Background

ACRL's 2013 *Intersections* white paper grew from the recognition that our information ecosystem, and library roles within it, is changing at a rapid pace and that such dynamic change requires agility and strategic realignment of our traditional roles and responsibilities. It emphasized collaboration, both within and outside of libraries, as a mechanism for responding to the three intersections highlighted in the paper. Those intersections are the economics of the distribution of scholarship, digital literacies, and changing roles for librarians (p. 1). The paper's authors noted the publication was intended to spark further conversation and the recommendations they put forth were only a small selection of possibilities for capitalizing on the interconnectedness of our work.

Another ACRL publication, *Common Ground at the Nexus of Information Literacy and Scholarly Communication*, edited by Stephanie Davis-Kahl and Merinda Kaye Hensley (2013), followed the white paper's release and presented early examples of librarianship at the intersections. In the foreword, Joyce Ogborn wrote that information literacy and scholarly communication developed quite naturally without intersecting, though our changing landscape now requires that we think critically about the connections (p. v). Some of these connections are explored in the book's 16 chapters. Though many chapters focus on including an undergraduate audience in scholarly communication education and outreach, audiences comprised of graduate students, faculty, and librarians are also discussed. In "Teaching Our Faculty: Developing Copyright and Scholarly Communication Outreach Programs," for example, the chapter's authors discuss the formation of a campus-wide copyright committee and its approach to developing an outreach program on the topic (Duncan, Clement, & Rozum, 2013). Similarly, a chapter about ACRL's Scholarly Communication Roadshow describes how the group's approach to professional development evolved over time to support the changing needs of librarians (Kirchner & Malenfant, 2013).

ACRL's adoption of the *Framework for Information Literacy for Higher Education* in 2016 bolstered the connection between scholarly communication and information literacy by directly referencing topics central to scholarly communication when defining information literacy. The *Framework* was born out of recognition that information literacy is complex and nuanced, and it offers a set of interconnected core concepts to guide our conversations with students, faculty, and other stakeholders. It presents six frames, each with a set of example knowledge practices and dispositions that are intended to be integrated into academic programs at a variety of levels. Though the *Framework* uses student-centric language to discuss information literacy, much of the document can also apply to teachable moments with faculty and administrators; this is particularly true through the example knowledge practices and dispositions that bleed into topics of scholarly communication. Areas of overlap include the production and commodification of information ("Information Creation as a Process" and "Information Has Value"), the value of collaboration in advancing knowledge ("Research as Inquiry"), the importance of access to information ("Searching as Strategic Exploration"), the significance of how authority is established and realized in different contexts ("Authority Is Constructed and Contextual"), and the recognition that systems of communication can enforce or dismantle information privilege ("Scholarship as Conversation").

The growing body of literature around the *Intersections* and the *Framework* aren't the only movements within libraries that advocate for exploring a deeper and more thoughtful connection between information literacy and scholarly communication. Practitioners of "critical information literacy" and, more broadly, "critical librarianship" aim to interrogate the role libraries play in reinforcing systems of oppression and to address how librarians can proactively shift practices to challenge existing power structures, inequities, and biases related to information seeking and construction in our work. Examples range from examining Library of Congress subject headings and identifying problematic patterns of classification (Drabinski, 2008) to reframing our approach to the "reference interview" as a dialog, as opposed to a transaction, that enables "student-generated transformative action" (Adler, 2013, p. 4). Critical information literacy is at its heart about social justice.

A popular example of critical information literacy and the *Intersections* comes from Scott Warren and Kim Duckett, who present strategies for introducing undergraduate students to complex issues of information access and commodification by deconstructing subscription and public resources and leading a conversation about the economics of information (2010). The authors describe how they experimented over time with integrating topics central to scholarly communication into information literacy instruction. Many of their instructional strategies were tested, revised, and improved within the context of an elective English course that typically attracts junior and senior science majors. The library session for the course is divided into two parts—the first focusing on active discussion of the scholarly communication cycle and issues inherent in it, and the second focusing on hands-on discovery of peer-reviewed information. Each instructional strategy is presented with discussion questions and learning resources. Together, the two build on these strategies in a later publication that more fully defines two intertwined but distinct frames of reference that inform their praxis (2013). The sociocultural frame of reference is useful for guiding conversations related to social constructs and norms within academic communities (e.g., peer review), and the economic frame of reference allows us to explore the business side of information exchange as we bridge discovery and access (e.g., toll access journals).

The Warren and Duckett example is an excellent illustration of how information literacy can prod the politics of knowledge production. This interrogation of knowledge production, and associated issues of information ownership and commodification, is also an area of emphasis for practitioners and advocates of open education, which is why incorporating information literacy and collaborating with those who work in this realm is crucial when designing outreach around OER and open pedagogy. Librarians are increasingly involved with coordinating and leading open education efforts on college and university campuses, as evidenced by contributions to the chapters in this field guide. This expansion of our roles warrants a deeper exploration of open education's connection to information literacy and librarians' long history of teaching within higher education.

Librarians as Teachers

A foundational principle presented in *Intersections* is that all academic librarians are teachers. Beyond that, the authors assert, "All roles in an academic library are impacted and altered by the changing nature of scholarly communication and the evolution of the dissemination of knowledge. Therefore, every librarian has a role in teaching, whether formally or informally, about scholarly communication issues" (p.4). Teaching in the context of academic libraries can take many forms, from providing in-person and online reference services to introducing patrons to archives and special collections. Librarians frequently hold consultations with faculty and students, offer workshops and seminars, and share expertise with other campus units. However, teaching is most closely associated with formal, course-integrated instruction targeting a student audience.

Evidence collected during ACRL's Assessment in Action project, a three-year program that investigated how libraries impact student learning at over 200 post-secondary institutions from across North America, shows that libraries contribute to student success in four key ways (Brown, 2016). The group's research suggests students benefit from (1) using the library and (2) collaborative partnerships between the library and other academic programs and services. The other key findings are related to library instruction. Specifically, students benefit from (3) library instruction during the early stages of their academic careers and (4) library integration into general education.

When we consider how library-led learning happens on college and university campuses, our focus tends to revolve around instruction occurring in a traditional classroom. Librarians have a long history of delivering formal instruction to groups of students, as noted by Barbara Fister in a collection of essays on new roles for librarians (2015). Instruction most frequently takes the form of the "one-shot" (that is, a single session delivered to students enrolled in a course offered by another department), though librarians may also be embedded in courses, providing an opportunity for interacting with students for the duration of a course, and sometimes teach credit-bearing classes. This focus on teaching and learning through instructional design and information literacy is not a new trend, nor does it appear to be reversing course anytime soon.

The 2016 Ithaka S+R survey of library deans and directors shows that positions and resource allocations that support teaching and research are expected to grow in the coming years, as was the case in the 2013 survey (Wolff-Eisenberg, 2017). It may not be surprising, then, that many of the early examples of librarianship at the intersections of scholarly communication and information literacy focused on integrating scholarly communication concepts into formal undergraduate instruction. Intersections literature provides examples of plagiarism and copyright curriculum implemented in a first-year-seminar program (Clement & Brenenson, 2013), development of a credit-bearing course on scholarly publishing (Gilman, 2013), and library integration into courses offered by an undergraduate research program (Hensley, 2013), among others. Such approaches provide valuable opportunities to engage students in higher-order thinking about information authorship, ownership, and privilege.

Still, the types of learning opportunities created by librarians are not limited to the classroom. Librarians commonly develop guides and tutorials in order to extend learning outside the walls of a classroom, though such resources are frequently connected to course-integrated instruction. Likewise, stand-alone workshops, such as those on copyright offered to faculty and graduate students by scholarly communication librarians, tend to mimic classroom settings. Although these types of learning opportunities are important, a growing number of librarians have written and presented on less formal strategies for approaching learning. Amy Buckland, for example, offers an elegant description of opportunities for engaging with students as creators of information by making student work available through institutional repositories and supporting student-run scholarly publishing (2015). This demonstrates a change in approach that positions the library as a partner rather than a resource and is an important distinction in our interactions with all members of our university communities.

Later in this chapter we'll explore the intersectional nature of open education and related partnerships in more detail. First, we must briefly address the mechanics of learning. In How Learning Works, seven distinct yet interconnected principles of learning are presented, along with strategies for integrating each principle into teaching practices (Ambrose, Bridges, DiPietro, Lovett, & Norman, 2010). The principles, listed below, are based on the premise that learning is a process undertaken by the learner that results in lasting change and is influenced by prior experiences and knowledge:

1. Students' prior knowledge can help or hinder learning.
2. How students organize knowledge influences how they learn and apply what they know.
3. Students' motivation determines, directs, and sustains what they do to learn.
4. To develop mastery, students must acquire component skills, practice integrating them, and know when to apply what they have learned.
5. Goal-directed practice coupled with targeted feedback enhances the quality of students' learning.
6. Students' current level of development interacts with the social, emotional, and intellectual climate of the course to impact learning.
7. To become self-directed learners, students must learn to monitor and adjust their approaches to learning. (pp. 4-6).

Though the book presents a variety of evidence-based strategies for facilitating learning, a recurring theme is the importance of collecting data to better understand learners' needs and progress. It is worth noting that, like in the *Framework*, the language used in *How Learning Works* is student-centric; however, the authors do the important work of applying the principles to instructors in the book's conclusion, recognizing that teaching is a complex and dynamic activity. The principles are applied specifically to self-directed reflection and learning about teaching, which is often voluntary and, particularly at research institutions, underemphasized. However, they are just as relevant to more formal situations in which faculty assume the role of students, such as in copyright, visibility, and publishing workshops led by librarians. As such, the seven principles provide a helpful frame for librarians to evaluate these types of learning opportunities.

Learning at the Intersections

Librarians most frequently emphasize students as the beneficiaries of our teaching and learning initiatives. However, the intersections present significant learning opportunities for faculty and administrators as well. To better understand this potential, it is useful to think critically about how our profession defines both information literacy and scholarly communication. In the *Framework*, ACRL defines information literacy as "the set of integrated abilities encompassing the reflective discovery of information, the understanding of how information is produced and valued, and the use of information in creating new knowledge and participating ethically in communities of learning." Writing in *Common Ground at the Nexus*, Julia Gelfand and Catherine Palmer offer a helpful way of defining scholarly communication:

> Information-literate members of the academy should understand how knowledge is created, evaluated, shared, and preserved. If we define scholarly communication as the ways in which subject knowledge is created (research methodology), evaluated (peer review), shared (through scholarly journal articles, monographs, conference proceedings, and research reports), and preserved (repositories writ large), then it is clear that an information-literate individual is one who understands both the issues *and* processes of scholarly communication. (2013, pp. 9–10).

Sarah Crissinger, reflecting on her work at the intersections on ACRL's blog, takes this connection one step further and captures the essence of librarianship from an intersectional perspective:

> I find the ways that scholarly communication is being infused with information literacy even more interesting and exciting, partly because I believe that IL can make scholarly communication outreach more holistic and approachable. One of the

> best examples of this is librarians' outreach on altmetrics and
> impact factor. Asking faculty and graduate students to think
> critically about how we evaluate scholarship and what impact
> really means to them as scholars and information consumers *is*
> *information literacy.* (2015, italics in original)

The importance of such a holistic approach is emphasized by Shan Sutton in his review of the *Intersections* white paper, in which he advised libraries to "approach the integration process as an opportunity to rethink their faculty, as well as student, engagement across the entire spectrum of scholarly communications activities" (2013, p. 2). This focus on faculty engagement through an information literacy lens is an area of scholarship that deserves further exploration.

Numerous studies reveal gaps in faculty understanding of the issues and processes related to scholarly communication. A 2007 report from the University of California Office of Scholarly Communication and the California Digital Library eScholarship Program suggests that faculty are "under-informed" and disengaged with a range of topics central to scholarly communication (p. 3). A report on scholarly communication by the Center for Studies in Higher Education noted low recognition by faculty of the economic impact of scholarly publishing practices on libraries (i.e., the "serials crisis"), and by extension the communities they serve; beyond that, the report documented "quite a few" outright rejections of this impact (Harley, Acord, Earl-Novell, Lawrence, & King, 2010, p. 11), despite compelling evidence to the contrary (Suber, 2012; SQW Limited, 2003). Low awareness of institutional repositories has been reported by librarians investigating scholarly communication perceptions in their local contexts (Mischo & Schlembach, 2011; Odell, Dill, & Palmer, 2014; Yang & Li, 2015). Similarly, a survey of faculty members from 17 universities across the United States found that the majority of faculty were unaware of their institution's repository (Kim, 2011, p. 249). Copyright, too, remains a challenge. Both anecdotal (Duncan et al., 2013) and empirical (Smith et al., 2006) evidence suggest faculty have limited familiarity with the complexities of copyright law and how it applies to their research and teaching practices. Such low awareness among faculty could cause concern for librarians interested in broaching similar topics with students.

However, teachable moments frequently arise, particularly in course-integrated instruction, for deepening the understanding of both audiences simultaneously.

Opportunities in Open Education

Open education, with its emphasis on intellectual property rights and sharing, is fertile ground for exploring the competencies of the communities we serve through an information literacy lens. Low awareness of OER among faculty, as reported by the Babson Survey Research Group, shows there is much room for growth in this area (Allen & Seaman, 2016, p. 12). At the same time, library leaders continue to seek meaningful ways to demonstrate the value of the library and its impact on the organizational mission. It is becoming increasingly important for librarians at all levels to consider how our work aligns with these strategic priorities.

In some cases, the task of connecting learning opportunities to strategic priorities is straightforward and relatively effortless. In others, the task can be more problematic, often the result of outdated or nonexistent documentation. Still, our ability to clearly demonstrate connections between our efforts and the university's priorities is essential, especially for new initiatives like those surrounding OER outreach and education. Natural connections between open education and institutional goals frequently include increasing affordability, supporting student success, fostering innovation, and producing impactful scholarship. Finally, though outreach about open education frequently occurs in one-on-one conversations and group discussions, the practice of drafting learning outcomes and assessment strategies can prove useful in guiding and focusing conversation in these and other informal teaching scenarios.

When designing learning experiences around open education, it is critical to consider the purpose of the learning experience alongside the audience for whom it is intended, as well as a method for assessing the success of the learning experience. Deb Gilchrist offers a popular formula for learning outcomes that sandwiches "in order to" between an action and an intention. Gilchrist recommends beginning each outcome with a strong, measurable action verb, such as those listed in Bloom's Taxonomy. The way in which each verb is connected to a cognitive process should be considered, and verbs that are not measurable (e.g., understanding and knowing) should be avoided. The clause following "in order to" should describe the intention of the learning experience. That is, what should the learner be able to do as a result of the learning? Assessment of learning outcomes can take myriad forms—formal or informal and summative or formative—and should always be approached with the learner (not the teacher) at the forefront of the experience. In ACRL's Intersections Workshop, which presents strategies for crafting outcomes for learning experiences, librarians are encouraged to ask themselves a series of simple questions to form the foundation for learning: Who is your audience? What is your purpose? How will you know if the learning happened? With these basic components defined, we can begin connecting learning opportunities for specific audiences to the strategic priorities of our libraries and institutions.

For example, most open education advocates have firsthand experience with faculty and administrators who have a fundamentally flawed understanding of how open licensing integrates with traditional copyright protections. Such misunderstandings of information ownership and transfer can derail conversations and pose significant challenges for advancing open initiatives, even when those initiatives are firmly connected to institutional priorities. It can be helpful to spend time in advance of important meetings and discussions brainstorming specific learning outcomes to guide these informal learning experiences. An outcome such as "evaluate information ownership and transfer in open vs. proprietary contexts" can increase agility in responding to questions and comments that demonstrate low understanding of information ownership, a concept essential to information literacy. Considering the specific action expected following the intervention can inform the second half of the outcome. For example, learning in this context may be planned in order to increase adoption of OER, increase the creation of open scholarship, or develop stronger communication channels about OER between university administrators and instructors.

Outreach within libraries is as crucial to the success of open education initiatives as it is with stakeholders outside of libraries. As new open education initiatives emerge within academic libraries, we need to guard against the tendency to develop programming within silos. Cheryl Middleton, ACRL president, suggested that all academic librarians must be competent in scholarly communication and warned against the trend of developing scholarly communication services in isolation from the work of subject librarians, many of whom are responsible for delivering information literacy instruction and working with faculty in their designated departments (2017). This is particularly important considering that open education efforts are most frequently oriented in scholarly communication units (Walz, Jensen, & Salem, 2016; Yano, 2017), though librarians responsible for information literacy have significant expertise in working with faculty to improve their courses and design better learning experiences.

The potential here is nicely illustrated in a Twitter thread by Zoe Fisher, a librarian who specializes in information literacy instruction (2017). Fisher described a dialog with first-year students in a one-shot session that demonstrates how naturally OER integrates into instructional scenarios with undergraduate students. Fisher reports that she received the question, "How does the library help students with textbooks?" The question, along with multiple follow-up questions from the students, provided an opportunity to introduce the freshmen to course reserves, the limited purchasing power of libraries and related shift to open resources, and existing options, such as buy-back and rental programs, intended to lower costs for students. The posts are an important reminder that opportunities to engage with students about OER will arise in our information literacy work whether we plan them or not. Advance, collaborative planning by open education advocates and information literacy and subject librarians to identify talking points and connections between open education and information literacy will allow us to reframe extemporaneous responses into teachable moments that deepen our students' understanding of how information production and consumption impact our daily lives, both in academia and beyond.

Open education leaders can, of course, face numerous challenges getting librarians on board. Time constraints are a common barrier. Quill West, Amy Hofer, and Dale Coleman explore this and other findings in their report on the grant-funded Librarians as Open Education Leaders project (2017). The project website includes instructional videos and templates that can be used to ready subject librarians for supporting faculty interested in transitioning to OER. The resources serve as an important reminder that OER support is strikingly similar to any other reference consultation librarians provide. Focusing on these similarities—and emphasizing that OER consultations are guided by identifying and responding to an instructor's information need—can help time-strapped librarians understand that supporting OER isn't as foreign as it may otherwise seem and can be a very natural extension of services they already provide. Empowering our communities to understand and meet information needs *is information literacy.*

Numerous scholars both within and outside of libraries have argued that librarians cannot and should not fully own responsibility for information literacy, and the same is true when applying information literacy to open education. An exciting example of the convergence of open education and information literacy was presented by Billy Meinke, OER technologist at the University of Hawai i at Manoa, at the Open Education 2017 conference. Meinke presented on a workflow and support system intended to empower faculty by demystifying the OER design process. In planning the training to support the adaptation and creation of OER, Meinke mapped learning outcomes for faculty creators to the six frames described in the ACRL *Framework*. Foundational principles of OER, such as the significance of intellectual property rights, found natural homes in the "Authority Is Constructed and Contextual" and "Information Has Value" frames, while abilities related to OER creation and adaptation were better reflected in the "Information Creation as Process" frame. Technical skills, such as evaluating the technical adaptability of an OER and downloading a resource from a repository, were not mapped to a frame. In a paper submitted for the Open Education Global Conference in 2018, Meinke joined Reed in exploring the connections between each frame and topics related to open education, including the frames omitted from the original mapping. The paper merges technologist and librarian perspectives and probes issues of OER quality, collaboration, and student privacy.

Writing on the Open Oregon blog, Silvia Lin Hanick and Hofer argue that librarians should incorporate open practices into information literacy instruction rather than approaching them as distinct areas of focus (2017). They recommend opening our own teaching practices in order to model pedagogy for faculty. Additionally, they present connections between open education and the *Framework* that can guide scaffolding information literacy competencies into open assignments. For example, in exploring open education through the "Information Has Value" frame, the authors note that textbook costs make the commodification of information a "real-life problem" for students. OER is an excellent solution; however, oversimplifying OER by focusing on cost at the exclusion of effort and labor, which are not always compensated, does little to deepen students' understanding of how information functions in a networked society.

There is, of course, potential for student involvement beyond classroom settings, which serves as an important reminder to think broadly about collaborative opportunities within our institutional contexts. Partners who can assist in developing, distributing, or otherwise augmenting learning experiences can be found within our library, across campus, and at external organizations, such as professional societies, nonprofits, advocacy groups, and government agencies. It is in the development of these partnerships that the greatest advances in open education are achieved. Take, for example, the success of BCcampus, a government-funded organization that supports teaching and learning in British Columbia's public post-secondary education system. Since beginning an open textbook project in 2012, BCcampus has created over 160 textbooks, facilitated OER adoption in over 700 courses, and saved students over CA$2 million. Executive Director Mary Burgess attributes this success to multi-institutional collaboration, financial support from government agencies, student advocacy, an engaged staff, supportive campus partners, and strong relationships with international leaders in open education (2017).

In the United States, a growing number of state legislatures are drafting legislation that elevates open education in the public discourse and presents open education advocates with additional opportunities for partnerships that drive culture change and advance the values of open education. For example, in 2017 the Texas State Legislature signed into a law a bill that added OER to an existing textbook disclosure law and established a statewide grant program to support the adoption and creation of OER. The law requires that institutions of higher education provide searchable information allowing students to filter by courses that use only OER. Similar policies were implemented in Washington, Oregon, and California; these and other state-level activities impacting open education are tracked and curated by the Scholarly Publishing and Academic Resources Coalition (SPARC) on the OER State Policy Tracker.[1] Such top-down initiatives, such as OER disclosure mandates, present a need for open education advocates to carefully consider strategic options for creating learning experiences that educate faculty and administrators about OER. Proactive and thoughtful outreach in this area can reduce the backlash of "unfunded mandates" that could otherwise pollute growth and result in concerns over academic freedom.

The heightened attention on OER can also catalyze pedagogical change, particularly at institutions that have adopted experiential learning (learning by doing) or collaboration as a strategic priority. Though the definition of "open pedagogy" is contested, it is broadly conceived as a practice that empowers students as content creators by giving them the opportunity to demonstrate mastery through the act of creation. In the introduction to *Critical Library Instruction*, the editors describe their praxis as one that "respects what each student brings to the classroom" (Accardi, Drabinski, & Kumbier, 2010, p. x), which is how practitioners of open pedagogy often describe their work. Open pedagogy hinges on student agency within an authentic and collaborative learning environment. It challenges traditional roles of teacher and student and has the potential to transform the educational experience. However, there are significant concerns that demand sensitivity when transitioning to open practices. Robin DeRosa explores some of these considerations in writing about her experiences collaborating with students in the open (2016); she touches on concerns related to access (considering students without or new to technology), production (considering privilege and the hidden costs of labor), and privacy and safety (considering trolling and digital identities). When thoughtfully approached, however, this style of pedagogy offers an excellent opportunity for faculty to work collaboratively with both scholarly communication librarians, leveraging their expertise in copyright and visibility, and information literacy librarians, leveraging their expertise in assignment design and classroom management. The result is often elevated levels of student engagement

---

[1] OER State Policy Tracker: https://sparcopen.org/our-work/state-policy-tracking/

and motivation, deeper connections with content and collaborators, and higher levels of satisfaction with outputs of the learning experience.

Conclusion

Libraries are experiencing a number of pressures that require innovative thinking, flexibility, and critical reflection. Responding to this pressure, ACRL's publication of the *Intersections* white paper has resulted in a growing interest and energy around the common ground between information literacy and scholarly communication. Librarians writing on the intersections have introduced multiple ways that topics of scholarly communication can be integrated into undergraduate outreach and education.

Less has been written about applying the lessons learned from information literacy initiatives to outreach with faculty or connecting libraries' extensive experience with information literacy to our work in open education. The strategy presented in this chapter— of focusing on learning experiences and tailoring each to a specific audience and purpose— is one method for approaching those connections. The examples included in this chapter, such as mapping open education learning outcomes to the *Framework*, leveraging undergraduate instruction to introduce students to course resource options, and collaborating with other librarians to scale support for OER, are only a starting point for developing meaningful outreach and education about open educational practices. There is significant room for further exploration.

As libraries are faced with dwindling budgets and increasing demand to demonstrate the value of our contributions to the university community, it is important to consider the ways in which we can collaborate with partners both within and outside our libraries to advance work in support of institutional priorities. Framing our work within open education in the context of information literacy can be a useful anchor and a persistent reminder that we are almost always acting in a teaching capacity, even when we are not working directly with students in a classroom. Such an approach fosters greater intentionality, improved outcomes, and stronger partnerships.

References

Accardi, M. T., Drabinski, E., & Kumbier, A. (2010). Introduction. In M. T. Accardi, E. Drabinski, & A Kumbier (Eds.), *Critical library instruction: Theories and methods.* Duluth, MN: Library Juice Press.

Adler, K. (2013). Radical purpose: The critical reference dialogue at a progressive urban college. *Urban Library Journal, 19*(1). Retrieved from http://academicworks.cuny.edu/ulj/vol19/iss1/9

Allen, I. E., & Seaman, J. (2016). *Opening the textbook: Educational resources in U.S. higher education, 2015–16.* Babson Survey Research Group. Retrieved from https://www.onlinelearningsurvey.com/reports/openingthetextbook2016.pdf

Ambrose, S. A., Bridges, M. W., DiPietro, M., Lovett, M. C., & Norman, M. K. (2010). *How learning works: Seven research-based principles for smart teaching.* San Francisco, CA: Jossey-Bass.

Association of College and Research Libraries. (n.d.-a). *Intersections of scholarly communication and information literacy bibliography.* Retrieved from http://www.ala.org/acrl/issues/scholcomm/intersectionsbib

Association of College and Research Libraries. (n.d.-b). Two paths converge: Designing educational opportunities on the intersections of scholarly communication and information literacy [workshop overview]. Retrieved from http://www.ala.org/acrl/intersections

Association of College and Research Libraries. (2013). *Intersections of scholarly communication and information literacy: Creating strategic collaborations for a changing academic environment.* Retrieved from http://acrl.ala.org/intersections/

Association of College and Research Libraries. (2016). *Framework for information literacy for higher education.* Retrieved from http://www.ala.org/acrl/standards/ilframework

Brown, K. (2016). *Documented library contributions to student learning and success: Building evidence with team-based Assessment in Action campus projects.* Chicago, IL: ACRL.

Buckland, A. (2015). More than consumers: Students as content creators. In M. Bonn & M. Furlough (Eds.), *Getting the word out: Academic libraries as scholarly publishers* (pp. 193–202). Retrieved from http://wiki.lib.sun.ac.za/images/1/1e/2015-acrl-libraries-as-publishers.pdf#page=206

Burgess, M. (2017). The BC open textbook project. In R. Biswas-Diener & R. Jhangiani (Eds.), *Open: The philosophy and practices that are revolutionizing education and science* (pp. 227–236). Retrieved from https://www.ubiquitypress.com/site/books/10.5334/bbc/

Clement, G., & Brenenson, S. (2013). Theft of the mind: An innovative approach to plagiarism and copyright education. In S. Davis-Kahl & M.K. Hensley (Eds.), *Common ground at the nexus of information literacy & scholarly communication* (pp. 45–74). Chicago, IL: ACRL.

Crissinger, S. (2015, December 7). The best work I do is at the intersections [Blog post]. Retrieved from http://acrlog.org/2015/12/07/intersections/

Davis-Kahl, S., & Hensley, M. K. (Eds.). (2013). *Common ground at the nexus of information literacy & scholarly communication.* Chicago, IL: ACRL.

DeRosa, R. (2016, May 18). My open textbook: Pedagogy and practice [Blog post]. Retrieved from http://robinderosa.net/uncategorized/my-open-textbook-pedagogy-and-practice/

Drabinski, E. (2008). Teaching the radical catalog. In K.R. Roberto (ed.), *Radical cataloging: Essays at the front* (pp. 198–205). Jefferson, N.C.: McFarland.

Duckett, K. & Warren, S. (2013). Exploring the intersections of information literacy and scholarly communication. In S. Davis-Kahl & M. K. Hensley (Eds.), *Common ground at the nexus of information literacy & scholarly communication* (pp. 25–44). Chicago, IL: ACRL.

Duncan, J., Clement, S.K., & Rozum, B. (2013). Teaching our faculty: Developing copyright and scholarly communication outreach programs. In S. Davis-Kahl & M. K. Hensley (Eds.), *Common ground at the nexus of information literacy & scholarly communication* (pp. 269–285). Chicago, IL: ACRL.

Fisher, Z. (26 Jun 2017). Question from first-year student during #infolit instruction session: "How does the library help students with textbooks?" #oer [Twitter thread] https://twitter.com/zoh_zoh/status/879438097699811328

Fister, B. (2015). Student learning, lifelong learning, and partner in pedagogy. In S. Bell, L. Dempsey, & B. Fister (Eds.), *New roles for the road ahead: Essays commissioned for ACRL's 75th anniversary* (pp. 58–62). Chicago, IL: ACRL.

Gelfand, J. & Palmer, C. (2013). Weaving scholarly communication and information literacy: Strategies for incorporating both threads in academic library outreach. In S. Davis-Kahl & M. K. Hensley (Eds.), *Common ground at the nexus of information literacy & scholarly communication* (pp. 1–24). Chicago, IL: ACRL.

Gilman, I. (2013). Scholarly communication for credit: Integrating publishing education into undergraduate curriculum. In S. Davis-Kahl & M.K. Hensley (Eds.), *Common ground at the nexus of information literacy & scholarly communication* (pp. 75–92). Chicago, IL: ACRL.

Hanick, S. L. & Hofer, A. (2017, May 31). Opening the framework: Connecting open education practices and information literacy [Blog post]. Retrieved from http://openoregon.org/opening-the-framework/

Harley, D., Acord, S. K., Earl-Novell, S., Lawrence, S., & King, J. (2010). Assessing the future landscape of scholarly communication: An exploration of faculty values and needs in seven disciplines. Retrieved from http://escholarship.org/uc/cshe_fsc

Hensley, M. K. (2013). The poster session as a vehicle for teaching the scholarly communication process. In S. Davis-Kahl & M. K. Hensley (Eds.), *Common ground at the nexus of information literacy & scholarly communication* (pp. 113–133). Chicago, IL: ACRL.

Kim, J. (2011). Motivations of faculty self-archiving in institutional repositories. *The Journal of Academic Librarianship, 37*(3), 246–254. https://doi.org/10.1016/j.acalib.2011.02.017

Kirchner, J. & Malenfant, K.J. (2013). ACRL's Scholarly Communications Roadshow: Bellwether for a changing profession. In S. Davis-Kahl & M. K. Hensley (Eds.), *Common ground at the nexus of information literacy & scholarly communication* (pp. 299–319). Chicago, IL: ACRL.

Libraries as Leaders. (2017). Retrieved August 20, 2018, from https://libraryasleader.org/

Meinke, B. (2017, October). *Empowering faculty and staff to use OER at the University of Hawaiʻi*. Presented at the 14th Annual Open Education Conference, Anaheim, CA. Abstract retrieved from https://openeducation2017.sched.com/

Middleton, C. (2017). Closing the divide: Subject librarians and scholarly communication librarians can work together to reach common goals. *College & Research Libraries News, 78*(10), p. 552. https://doi.org/10.5860/crln.78.10.552

Mischo, W. H., & Schlembach, M. C. (2011). Open access issues and engineering faculty attitudes and practices. *Journal of Library Administration, 51*(5–6), 432–454. http://dx.doi.org/10.1080/01930826.2011.589349

Odell, J., Dill, E., & Palmer, K. (2014). *Open access policies: a survey of IUPUI faculty attitudes.* Invited paper presented at IUPUI University Library and DLIS Joint Conference on Research, Scholarship, and Practice 2014. Indianapolis, IN. Retrieved from https://scholarworks.iupui.edu/handle/1805/5933

Ogburn, J. (2013). Closing the gap between information literacy and scholarly communication. In S. Davis-Kahl & M. K. Hensley (Eds.), *Common ground at the nexus of information literacy & scholarly communication* (pp. v–viii). Chicago, IL: ACRL.

Reed, M. & Meinke, B. (2018). *Beyond open connections: Leveraging information literacy to increase impact of open education.* Presented at Open Education Global Conference 2018, Delft, Netherlands. Paper presentation retrieved from http://hdl.handle.net/10106/27285

Smith, K. H., Tobia, R. C., Plutchak, T. S., Howell, L. M., Pfeiffer, S. J., & Fitts, M. S. (2006). Copyright knowledge of faculty at two academic health science campuses: Results of a survey. *Serials Review, 32*(2), 59–67. doi:10.1016/j.serrev.2006.03.001

SQW Limited. (2003). *Economic analysis of scientific research publishing: A report commissioned by the Wellcome Trust.* Retrieved from https://wellcome.ac.uk/sites/default/files/wtd003182_0.pdf

Suber, P. (2012). *Open access.* Cambridge, MA: MIT Press.

Sutton, S. C. (2013). Time to step on the gas in approaching the *Intersections of Scholarly Communication and Information Literacy. Journal of Librarianship and Scholarly Communication 1*(3), p. eP1076. http://dx.doi.org/10.7710/2162-3309.1076

University of California Office of Scholarly Communication and the California Digital Library eScholarship Program. (2007). *Faculty attitudes and behaviors regarding scholarly communication: Survey findings from the University of California.* Retrieved from https://osc.universityofcalifornia.edu/2007/08/report-on-faculty-attitudes-and-behaviors-regarding-scholarly-communication/

Walz, A., Jensen, K., & Salem, J. A. (2016). *SPEC Kit 351: Affordable Course Content and Open Educational Resources.* Washington, D.C.: Association of Research Libraries. Retrieved from http://publications.arl.org/Affordable-Course-Content-Open-Educational-Resources-SPEC-Kit-351/

Warren, S. & Duckett, K. (2010). "Why does Google Scholar sometimes ask for money?" Engaging science students in scholarly communication and the economics of information. *Journal of Library Administration 50*(4), 349–372. https://doi.org/10.1080/01930821003667021

Wolff-Eisenberg, C. (2017). US library survey 2016. https://doi.org/10.18665/sr.303066

Yang, Z. Y. & Li, Y. (2015). University faculty awareness and attitudes towards open access publishing and the institutional repository: A case study. *Journal of Librarianship and Scholarly Communication, 3*(1), p. eP1210. Retrieved from https://jlsc-pub.org/articles/abstract/10.7710/2162-3309.1210/

Yano, B. (2017). *Connect OER Annual Report, 2016–2017*. Washington, DC: SPARC. Retrieved from https://sparcopen.org/our-work/connect-oer/reports

Experiential Learning and Open Education: Partnering with Students to Evaluate OER Accessibility

Michelle Reed & Ciara Turner

Introduction

Providing internship opportunities to students is a high-impact practice that can positively impact student retention and engagement (Kuh, 2008). In Spring 2017, the University of Texas at Arlington (UTA) Libraries partnered with administrators of the university's Minor in Disabilities Studies to initiate a series of experiential learning opportunities for undergraduate students pursuing the minor. The partnership established UTA Libraries as an internship site for Disabilities Studies students who express interest in education and/or publishing.

This form of experiential learning, which is defined as learning by doing, also supports the Maverick Advantage, a campus-wide initiative that encourages students to participate in experiential learning via five "distinguishing activities." The activities focus on career development, community engagement, global connections, leadership, and undergraduate research. The internship described in this chapter advances career development goals defined in the Maverick Advantage by providing real-world opportunities for disability studies students to apply knowledge gained during their coursework.

Our chapter focuses on an open textbook evaluation project completed by the first intern to work with the Libraries on open education initiatives. The results highlight accessibility strengths, expose problematic exclusion of students with disabilities in higher education, and demonstrate the ways in which some open textbooks, intended to be "open" for all, fall short of that promise. We will outline best practices for designing accessible, open textbooks and describe the process used to evaluate the accessibility of existing resources. We will also discuss the engagement of the student intern with open education on our campus and the potential for future projects.

Background

UTA is a four-year public research university located in northeast Texas. Total global enrollment for the 2016–17 academic year was 58,664, making it the largest institution in the University of Texas System. Established in 1895 as Arlington College, UTA was designated a Hispanic-Serving Institution by the U.S. Department of Education in 2014. The university is frequently recognized for its diverse student population and for its affordability. *U.S. News & World Report* ranked UTA as fifth in the nation for undergraduate diversity, third largest destination for transfer students, and second for lowest average student debt among U.S. universities. Additionally, the university is frequently ranked as a top school for veterans.

The Minor in Disability Studies, started by Dr. Sarah Rose in Fall 2013, is offered through the university's Department of History. Since the 1980s, UTA has been an exemplary university for accessibility, the disability community, and equal educational opportunities. Since the creation of the minor, the disability presence at UTA has increased. Disability awareness has spread as the minor has attracted over 85 students from nearly every discipline represented at UTA. Students on campus also have the opportunity to explore disability history and learn about the disability experience through events on campus, such as panel speakers, film viewings, and lectures on disability history and culture.

Students wishing to complete the Minor in Disability Studies must take several disability studies courses and ultimately undertake a 117-hour internship. In these courses, students learn about important disability studies concepts, such as the social and medical model of disability, disability identity and culture, and the intersection of disability with race, gender, and ethnicity. In these courses, students form a better understanding of the role of disability in history and in their current culture. The minor leaves students with a new perspective on the human body and ability, and the final internship and capstone assignments allow students to practice applying the concepts in a real-world professional setting. Students partner with nonprofit organizations or related business sites and use the insight gleaned during their coursework to complete projects with these organizations.[1]

In early 2017, UTA Libraries' Open Education Librarian partnered with Dr. Rose to provide such an opportunity to an undergraduate student enrolled in the minor. The Libraries began developing outreach and educational programming focused on open education with the hire of an Open Education Librarian, a new position, in Fall 2016. The position was created as the result of a library reorganization initiated in 2015. As the Libraries reassigned over one third of its staff to work within its Scholarly Communication Division, it also began seeking new opportunities to promote and support open systems for sharing information. The Open Education Librarian was tasked with developing programming to support the university's strategic goal of increasing affordability while advocating for open practices. To this end, the Libraries joined the Open Textbook Network (OTN) and hosted an Open Textbook Workshop in February 2017. Approximately 25 teaching faculty and staff were recruited to attend the workshop, where they were introduced to open educational resources (OER) and encouraged to review an open textbook indexed in the Open Textbook Library (OTL). Attendees who completed a review of an open textbook received a $200 stipend. During the signup process, workshop attendees were encouraged to identify at least one open textbook relevant to their discipline that they might be interested in reviewing.

The resulting list of resources was given to the disability studies intern for the textbook evaluation project. In addition to providing a hands-on learning experience for the student, the evaluation project identified the strengths and weaknesses of existing open textbooks being considered for adoption by teachers at UTA and informed the Libraries' long-term goal of creating high-quality, accessible OER. The Open Education Librarian, who served as internship supervisor, drafted the following objectives to guide the intern's work on the project over the course of the Spring 2017 semester:

- Investigate accessibility standards for electronic books (ebooks); this may involve communicating via email or in person with local experts.

---

[1] For more information, see: https://utadisabilitystudies.wordpress.com/

- Investigate accessibility guidelines and best practices used by established OER publishers (e.g., OpenStax, BCcampus, University of Minnesota Libraries Publishing, Open SUNY Textbooks).
- Identify or create an assessment rubric based on common accessibility standards.
- Evaluate a prioritized list of OTL resources using the rubric, draft a statement about each resource to accompany rubric evaluation, and identify areas for improvement.
- Maintain formal notes in Google project folder about the process of identifying and applying evaluation criteria.
- Draft accessibility guidelines and best practices for OER creation at UTA.

Methods

Researching Best Practices

The primary goal of the project was to evaluate the accessibility of open textbooks being considered for adoption by UTA faculty and staff and to determine whether these texts aligned with critical accessibility standards. To accomplish this goal, the project team conducted research on online publishing, accessibility, universal design, and OER. Additionally, the intern interviewed students on campus about the struggles they faced when reading textbooks online. Through the semester, the team experienced firsthand the issues students with disabilities face when using open textbooks and discovered the pressing need for a focus on accessibility in discussions about OER.

The student intern made efficient and educated contributions to the project by building on foundational knowledge derived from her coursework (specifically from courses on universal design and the history of disability). However, the intern's previous exposure to OER and publishing was limited. Therefore, readings and training around the purpose, goals, and role of OER in higher education were integrated into the research process. The intern learned about OER and Creative Commons licensing using resources such as "Models of OER" (Margulies, Sinou, & Thille, 2005) and "7 Things you should know about OER" (EDUCAUSE Learning Initiative, 2010). Although resources about OER tend to note the importance of achieving openness by proactively communicating "5R" permissions to users (i.e., revise, remix, reuse, redistribute, and retain), many do not mention accessibility or accommodation of OER. This common omission highlighted the importance of the project team's work in raising awareness of accessibility problems in open textbooks.

Research on the application of universal design principles to create inclusive OER also informed our work. Universal design is a disability studies and design concept that advocates for the conscious design of products that have equitable use for all people. Seven basic principles of universal design guide the creation of products and spaces to ensure they are universally usable (Burgstahler, 2012):

- Equitable use
- Flexibility in use
- Simple and intuitive use
- Perceptible information
- Tolerance for error
- Low physical effort
- Size and space for approach and use

When creating OER one goal should be usability by all students, and these seven principles help ensure that resources created benefit a wide range of students with varying mental and physical abilities. We used the principles to guide our approach to the evaluation process, as they go hand-in-hand with best practices in accessible design. OER created with these principles in mind tend to be the most accessible to all students.

Key Resources

Numerous resources provide useful overviews about designing with a focus on accessibility. The following resources were particularly helpful in guiding our work:

BCcampus Open Education Accessibility Toolkit: Originally published as BC Open Textbook Accessibility Toolkit, this is a valuable resource for those learning about accessibility and its role in OER. The Toolkit walks readers through BCcampus' best practices for accessibility and explains why various accessibility standards are important. The Toolkit identifies several ebook elements that demand special consideration (e.g., images, color contrast, and multimedia) and teaches readers how to design these elements so they are accessible to all students. It also suggests different methods of testing for accessibility in these areas. The Toolkit can be accessed at https://opentextbc.ca/accessibilitytoolkit/ (Coolidge, Doner, & Robertson, 2015).

Flexible Learning for Open Education (Floe): Floe is a grant-funded project managed by the Inclusive Design Research Centre at OCAD University. The website lists recommended practices for online publishing and offers tools for developers that show what accessible and inaccessible publications and sites look like. The resource is available at https://floeproject.org/ (Treviranus, Mitchell, & Clark, n.d.).

WAVE Web Accessibility Evaluation Tool: WAVE is an online accessibility checker that helps complete accurate accessibility evaluations by analyzing webpages for inaccessible content. The tool came in handy when evaluating HTML versions of texts and can scan for missing headers, missing alternative text on pictures, and inaccessible buttons on the webpage that can be easily overlooked during manual evaluations. We used the accessibility checker to perform an initial scan of each OER for formatting and textual errors. The WAVE accessibility checker can be found at http://wave.webaim.org (Web Accessibility In Mind, n.d.).

Web Content Accessibility Guidelines (WCAG): WCAG served as a master list of requirements and accessibility references during the evaluations. These guidelines outline the current accessibility standards in online publications and informed the creation of our evaluation rubric. WCAG should be considered when conducting accessibility evaluation on HTML versions of ebooks. It can be accessed at https://www.w3.org/WAI/intro/wcag (Henry, 2017).

Developing a Rubric

To assess the accessibility of the open textbooks in our sample, we created an evaluation rubric with eight accessibility standards. We evaluated each of the textbooks based on the eight standards listed below and gave them a passing or failing score based on their adherence to each accessibility standard. We found that most failed to meet the accessibility standards for images and tables whereas other standards, such as color contrast and content organization, almost universally passed. Below is a discussion of the eight standards we evaluated and an explanation of how we tested them.

1. **Content organization:** Evaluating the open textbooks for clear organization and structure ensures the text is usable by a variety of students. When checking the books for content organization, evaluate headings and titles, the table of contents, chapter and page numbers, and general reading layout and order.

    A. Heading and titles: Open textbooks are generally organized into sections and chapters. These should be created with specific markup (header 1, header 2, title 1, title 2) and should always be distinct from body and footnote text. Chapter titles and section headers that are in bold or in larger font are not distinguishable by VoiceOver and other assistive technology (AT). All chapter headers and titles should remain in their correct location during text reflow, which is when a document's contents change shape and shift position on a screen (e.g., following magnification).

    B. Table of contents with navigation: A table of contents should be present and functioning in the ebook. Students using open textbooks should be able to "flip" to certain chapters and specific page numbers as they would if reading a traditional book. The table of contents should be compatible with screen readers. It is necessary to check each table of contents with a screen reader to ensure that students requiring use of a screen reader have complete access to the table of contents. It is also important that the table of contents is created as an *ordered list* so that students using a screen reader or keyboard-only navigation can easily navigate through the table of content list and into the text.

    C. Working page numbers: Ebook page numbers should correspond to the print version of the book. It is important for the digital version to have working page numbers so students opting to use it are able to follow along with those in the course using the print version. HTML versions often omit page numbers and show each chapter's content on a single web page. This numbering style is more accessible for students reading the text online as they do not have to refresh each page and can scroll through the chapter. PDF and epub version of ebooks, however, should have traditional page numbers.

D. Reading layout and order: All chapters and chapter subsections of the ebook should be logically ordered and easily followed by users and screen readers. All content should be displayed left to right as well as up and down the page. It is vital for ebooks to follow the same structure and organization as traditional texts. When checking reading layout, use various screen readers to read through portions of the text to verify that content can be accurately read to students. Also, check to ensure that non-textual elements of the ebooks, such as images and graphs, are read in the correct order and in line with the text.

2. **Images**: Many textbooks include images that are informative and provide vital information that supplements the text on the page. Images are a common accessibility problem area and are often inaccessible to students using screen readers or screen modifications. Students with low vision or auditory preference use screen readers to "read" texts. Without proper markup, images are not detected by screen readers. Students with dyslexia, colorblindness, and other learning disabilities may use a colored display or other screen modification when using ebooks. As with screen readers, many images are rendered inaccessible when used with these types of AT. To assess images in an ebook, choose a minimum of 20 non-decorative and decorative images from random chapters and analyze each one individually before passing or failing the standard.

A. Non-decorative image alternative text: Images of examples, charts, and graphs or images that contain other vital information should have written alternative text in the form of an alt tag or image description. These images are essential elements of the text and should be created to be accessible for all students. A text tag accompanying the image allows students with low vision using screen readers to access images by providing a written description of the image that can be read by screen readers. Alternative tags also allow students using color overlays or monochrome displays to view the image.

B. Decorative images are marked with null text: Images that do not contribute any new educational information, or decorative images, should be marked with "null" alternative text. These images are not vital elements of the text and do not have to be accompanied by a text tag.

C. Complex images have descriptions: Images such as graphs, tables, or equations that require interpretation should have a caption that includes a description of the image and the data it presents. This helps students using screen readers to fully understand graphs, equations, etc., but also ensures that all data are presented in two ways. Students who do not perceive color or choose to listen to their ebook also benefit from image descriptions.

D. Compatibility with magnification and color contrast AT: All images should be compatible with magnification software. Test selected images with browser plug-ins, such as Zoom for Chrome, to determine whether images are compatible with this type of software. Images should be able to reflow when magnified. Additionally, all images should be viewable when magnified up to 200 percent. It is also important to test images with various screen modifications to determine whether content is viewable in alternate color schemes and display options. Images should be viewable in grayscale, with monochrome displays, and on high- and low-contrast screens.

3. **Tables:** Similar to images, tables require captions and textual descriptions, and they should be created to be compatible with assistive and non-assistive technologies. To test tables in ebooks, select a minimum of 20 tables throughout the text and check them for simplicity and viewability. Although tables are generally accessible to all, there are two main accessibility standards to consider when evaluating this element.

A. Simple tables that are compatible with AT: Tables should be simple in the sense that they are clean, single-celled, and clearly labeled. Tables should be created with a specific markup, and all information should be entered as ordered lists. All tables need to have titles and labeled rows and columns. Split cells are discouraged. When tables are not created in a simple, ordered way they are indecipherable to screen readers. Use screen readers, such as NVDA and Kurzweil, to test tables in PDF versions of open textbooks and browser plug-ins, such as Reader for Chrome, to test those in HTML versions.

B. Tables compatible with magnification AT: all tables should be compatible with magnification software and should maintain structure during text reflow. Students with low vision and certain learning disabilities need to manipulate the text size and font. Ensure tables maintain their structure and viewability when the surrounding text is reflowed. Magnify tables with plug-ins, such as Zoom for Chrome, and other magnification AT to ensure all information in the tables can be magnified to 200 percent.

4. **Hyperlinks:** Though specific only to the digital version of a text, hyperlinks are a vital part of the textbook and need to be accessible to all students. Students using screen readers or altered displays are often unable to distinguish hyperlinks from the rest of the body text. To evaluate accessibility, check up to 40 different hyperlinks throughout each text with screen readers and high- and low-contrast screens to test their universal usability.

A. In-book links function: In-book links are hyperlinks that connect to another location in the text, such as links in a table of contents that connect to specific images or locations in a chapter. These links should be a distinct color from the body text and should connect to their correct location when clicked. Test at least 20 in-book links from different locations in the chapter by clicking to check functionality and by reading them with a screen reader. Links should be created with specific markup so the link title, rather than the URL, is read by the screen reader. Often, hyperlinks are inconsistently marked, so it is important to test links from throughout the text.

B. Live hyperlinks function: Live hyperlinks are links that connect to outside webpages, usually for additional information, examples, or videos. Any content linked in an ebook should be assessed for accessibility standards. When testing links that connect to external videos and webpages, check videos for captions and webpages for compatibility with different AT. As with in-book links, live hyperlinks should be a distinct color from the text, even when underlined or italicized. All links should have a descriptive title that is not the URL. Links should be created with specific markup that allows screen readers to recognize them as links.

C. All links are descriptive: Links should be obvious and distinct from the rest of the text. Links should be descriptively titled, as noted above (e.g., "Examples of UD" vs. www.universaldesign.com/ 7principles/example/110). They should be underlined and in a different color than that of the body text. Evaluate the contrast of links with a color contrast analyzer to ensure they are visible for students using screen modifications or high/low-contrast screens.

5. **Multimedia:** Some ebooks include videos, interactive diagrams, or links to websites with interactive elements, videos, and other multimedia content. This content must be accessible by all students.

A. Open or closed captions: Any video included or linked in the text should be fully captioned, complete with action captions when necessary. Check all videos in the text for proper captioning to ensure all content is accessible to students with low vision and low hearing or to English as a Second Language (ESL) students requiring translation.

B. Transcript: Transcripts should be easily accessible for all videos linked in the text. Additionally, transcripts should be compatible with screen readers and provide a complete transcription of all multimedia content. This is helpful both for students with disabilities and those wishing to access the video without using headphones or watching a screen.

C. Audio/video media player is compatible with AT: The platform and player presenting videos and other multimedia content should be compatible with all screen readers, magnification software, and color contrast modifications.

D. Flickering: There should be no flickering content in the text. Any content that flashes more than three times per second is dangerous and inaccessible to some users. Check all parts of the text including videos, animations, and all interactive content for flickering.

6. **Formulas:** Math and engineering textbooks use formulas throughout the text. It is important that these formulas are created with a specific equation editor to ensure they are compatible with screen readers and "select and speak" functions. Test formulas from various chapter locations in the text to check for consistent markup and viewability for all students.

A. STEM (science, technology, engineering, and math) formulas and equations are created with a compatible equation editor such as LaTeX or MathML: Formulas should be created and inserted in the text with an equation editor. Formulas typed directly into text along with other body text are not distinguishable by screen readers. To test for accessibility, choose a number of formulas from different chapters and read them with a screen reader. Each should be recognizable by the reader as a formula and read in a way that makes sense to student only able to hear the formula.

B. Images of equations with alternative tags: Alternatively, equations can be inserted into the text as images with accompanying text descriptions.

7. **Font:** All body and header fonts should be compatible with assistive and non- assistive technology. It is important to check the reflowability of fonts to ensure students may adjust fonts and visibility settings to their own preferences when using open textbooks.

A. Font is adjustable and compatible with screen readers: In all ebook formats, font size and style should be adjustable. If font, color, or page background color are not adjustable with non-assistive technology, check that they are compatible with other AT. All textual information should be visible in grayscale and on high/low-contrast screens and should be compatible with screen readers and "select and speak" functions.

B. Zoom capabilities (up to 200%): Fonts should be compatible with magnification AT and capable of zoom to 200 percent. Text should be compatible with reflow. Test several locations of text to ensure when text, images, or pages are resized the text restructures and holds its original shape.

C. Standard font (12 pt. body, 9pt. footnote): Check that all body and footnote text adheres to WCAG AA size guidelines. Traditional body text should be no larger than 12 pt., and footnotes should be no larger than 9pt.

8. **Color contrast:** Color is an important element of ebooks that is often overlooked. All information presented in color should also have a text or shape alternative. For example, a graph with information represented in color should also mark data points with circles, diamonds, or

squares. Use a color contrast analyzer to test contrast ratios in the text and confirm all components of the text (e.g., images, chapter headers, section titles, interactive elements, links) are accessible to students viewing the textbook with various screen modifications. All color elements should adhere to WCAG standards.

A. All information presented with color is also conveyed in a way understood by those who do not perceive color: Any information in images or graphs presented in color must also have a textual description in order to be accessible to students with low vision or students with learning disabilities, such as dyslexia.

B. Contrast for headers passes WCAG AA standards: Headers should meet WCAG AA contrast ratio requirement of 4:4:1. Use a color contrast analyzer to check this requirement.

C. Contrast for body and footnote text passes WCAG AA standards: Contrast for text must also meet required standards.

Results

We completed 20 open textbook evaluations using the eight criteria and gained valuable insight to the usability of open textbooks and their biggest accessibility problem areas. With few exceptions, most of the open textbooks we evaluated were not universally accessible to all students. Some of the open textbooks were generally accessible, with only a few problem areas, while others managed to pass only one or two of the eight accessibility standards. The evaluations were telling, and the project team was able to identify accessibility problem areas common to most of the open textbooks in our sample.

Standard 1: Content organization. Eighteen out of the 20 open textbooks evaluated passed this standard. Many of the books were missing specific elements of this standard, such as clear headings and titles or a table of contents with navigation, but on the whole, many open textbooks were accessible in terms of organization and navigation. This standard is important as it gauges how easily a student will be able to navigate a textbook. Well-designed organizational elements benefit all students wishing to navigate through the text via keyboard-only or through an assistive technology such as VoiceOver or NVDA. Open textbooks that do not pass this standard are likely unusable for such students. Proper header and title markup are essential for easy navigation through the text.

Standard 2: Images. Eight out of 20 open textbooks evaluated passed this standard. Our project revealed images to be a huge accessibility problem area for OER. In many texts, images are central to the information and should be viewable by all students, regardless of ability. Most open textbooks that failed this standard had non-decorative images throughout the text with no alternative text. When images are not accompanied by alternative text, students with low vision are not able to access them. Additionally, students with learning disabilities that require them to listen to the text are also unable to easily "view" the image. Many of the images throughout the text were inconsistently marked with alternative tags. Such a practice suggests that the creators had some knowledge of accessibility and the need for accommodation but approached the task of integrating alternative text with carelessness.

Standard 3: Tables. Ten out of 20 open textbooks evaluated passed this standard. Tables are another accessibility problem area in the texts we analyzed. Like images, tables are often a central element of textbooks. Especially with STEM books, it is critical that tables are compatible with assistive technology and readable by all students. Many of the open textbooks we tested had complex tables, with multiple sets of information per cell. This makes it impossible for a screen reader or browser extension to decipher the table and read it to the student. Tables were also disorganized, lacked titles, and did not have clearly labeled rows and columns. Some disorganized tables are difficult to follow by able-bodied students and are impossible to navigate when reading with assistive technology. Many tables are also not adaptive to reflow, so they lose structure and viewability when the page or font is resized. Students with low vision and students requiring screen modifications are unable to properly view tables when they are not formatted correctly and inserted into the text without proper markup.

Standard 4: Hyperlinks. Seventeen of 20 open textbooks evaluated passed this standard. In general, most of the open textbooks we looked at had accessible hyperlinks that were usable by students with a wide range of abilities. Most of the texts had both in-book and live hyperlinks that functioned, connected to the correct location, and were distinct from the rest of the text. The open textbooks that did not meet this standard failed to distinguish hyperlinks from the informational body text through color or italicizing. This makes it impossible for students of all abilities to distinguish links from text. Others that failed this standard used colors that did not meet contrast requirements to distinguish links. Students who do not perceive color or who use screen modifications for other learning disabilities are not able to access the links that do not meet contrast requirements as they are not visible on their screens.

Standard 5: Multimedia. Nineteen of 20 open textbooks evaluated passed this standard. Almost all of the open textbooks we evaluated had little to no multimedia content and none had any flickering content. Like hyperlinks, as most multimedia is web-based, videos and other online content are generally compatible with different assistive technologies and usable by many students.

Standard 6: Formulas. Fourteen of 20 open textbooks evaluated passed this standard. Most of the STEM books analyzed that failed these standards are completely unusable by low vision students, despite passing other accessibility standards. In STEM books, elements like equations and formulas are central to the book and must be usable by all students if incorporated in the classroom. Many of the books tested inserted equations and formulas as text lines that are only accessible to an able-bodied student reading the ebook as a traditional book. Any student wishing to use any accommodation, or students with specific learning and physical disabilities, would be unable to access equations. Screen readers are unable to read equations correctly unless created with MathML or LaTeX. Many equations are also images without alternative text and cannot be magnified or adapted in any way to fit high- and low-contrast screens.

Standard 7: Font. Nineteen of 20 open textbooks tested passed this standard. Most versions of the open textbooks passed this standard. Font in most of the open textbooks was compatible with screen readers, high- and low-contrast screens, and magnification AT. Many books allowed for adjusting font size and style, background color, lighting, and page size with no issues. Open textbooks that do not pass this standard are difficult to use for students with specific reading preferences when using open textbooks.

Standard 8: Color contrast. Nineteen of 20 open textbooks analyzed passed this standard. Most of the open textbooks easily passed this standard, as most creators seemed to abide by WCAG AA contrast standards. Although some books failed certain requirements of this standard, color use as a whole was found to be accessible by a wide range of students and compatible with various AT.

Discussion

The results of our evaluations not only revealed common accessibility problems but also highlighted harmful assumptions about disability and higher education. As we completed the reviews, it became clear that many of the open textbooks were created with a specific student in mind: a fully able-bodied student with no physical or learning disabilities. Though often overlooked, the design of products, such as public spaces and textbooks, perpetuate common social biases against people with disabilities. In many of the open textbooks, images were inserted without captions, assuming the reader would be able to view the image with no issue. Equations were inserted as text, assuming a traditional reading of the textbook rather than one requiring a screen reader. Headers and links were created in colors and fonts that do not adhere to accessibility standards, assuming all readers fully perceive color and do not use modifications. These problem areas show the widespread and deep-reaching exclusion of people with disabilities from higher education.

These accessibility problem areas in open textbooks represent a larger problem in colleges and universities across the nation. When OER are created with faulty assumptions of students' mental and physical abilities, OER become part of a larger social problem that systematically excludes students with disabilities from equal education. Though licensed openly, many of the OER we reviewed were completely closed to students with disabilities and students wishing to access texts through nontraditional accommodations.

In order to gain a better understanding of the issues these students face when using ebooks for university courses, the disability studies intern met with students to discuss the problem areas identified in our evaluations. The practice of treating accessibility and accommodation as an ongoing conversation revealed additional aspects of ebook accessibility that should be considered. By the end of the semester we reworked the evaluation rubric to include two additional standards, Interactive Elements and Accessibility Documentation. Interactive elements in ebooks (e.g., animations, quizzes and knowledge checks, calculators) should also be checked for accessibility. Like photos and tables, interactive functions should be compatible with adaptive and nonadaptive technologies. The revised rubric is included in the Appendix. It is now used at UTA to guide, evaluate, and revise (if necessary) OER creation projects that are currently underway. Future projects could refine rubrics further to evaluate OER for accessibility for a specific set of students or for compatibility with a specific AT.

Finally, the intern expressed gratitude for the experiential learning opportunity and noted the value of speaking with students on campus about their struggles in confirming the importance of this project. Her summative reflection also demonstrated an increased understanding of issues surrounding access to information and of student behaviors in response to access barriers. Additionally, our work revealed that students use accommodations and AT for a multitude of reasons and that universal accessibility benefits all students and not just those with physical and learning disabilities. The experience shed light on student frustrations and invisible barriers that hinder students' education and provided a useful perspective to the intern as a prospective teacher. It also provided her the opportunity to share her expertise and scholarship publicly through co-authorship of this chapter.

Conclusion

The partnership between the two UTA units was a win for all stakeholders. The Libraries benefited by being able to contribute to experiential learning at UTA and by growing expertise on accessibility and universal design; the student benefited from the opportunity to apply coursework in a real-world setting and reference the experience in résumés, portfolios, and future applications; and the program administrators benefited from having a reliable site to recommend to students with an interest in publishing, education, or other relevant fields.

The results of the evaluation project, however, demonstrated that there is significant room for growth in OER and in how we as a community discuss and prioritize accessibility. Future interns matched with the UTA Libraries will be asked to contribute to this growth by conducting similar evaluations of both existing resources and OER currently under development by UTA faculty and staff, by providing remediation assistance as necessary to improve the accessibility of OER, and by investigating strategies for sharing findings and best practices in order to benefit the greater OER community and the students we serve. Open education coordinators and project managers at other institutions are encouraged to explore similar partnership opportunities with students and staff with expertise in disability studies in order to expand their own knowledge of the subject, provide meaningful learning experiences for students, and ensure that the open resources we create are truly open to all.

References

Burgstahler, S. (2012). Universal design in education: Principles and applications. *Do-It: Disabilities, opportunities, internetworking, and technology.* Retrieved from http://www.washington.edu/doit/universal-design-education-principles-and-applications

Coolidge, A., Doner, S., & Robertson, T. (2015). *BCcampus open education accessibility toolkit.* Retrieved from https://opentextbc.ca/accessibilitytoolkit/

EDUCAUSE Learning Initiative. (2010). 7 things you should know about open educational resources. Retrieved from https://library.educause.edu/resources/2010/5/7-things-you-should-know-about-open-educational-resources

Henry, S. L. (Ed.). (2017, March 10). Web content accessibility guidelines (WCAG) overview. *Web Accessibility Initiative.* Retrieved from https://www.w3.org/WAI/intro/wcag

Kuh, G. D. (2008). *High-impact educational practices: What they are, who has access to them, and why they matter.* Washington, D.C.: Association of American Colleges and Universities.

Margulies, A., Sinou, V., & Thille, C. (2005). Models of open educational resources: OpenCourseWare, Sofia, and the Open Learning Initiative. *EDUCAUSE Center for Analysis and Research: Research Bulletin, 2005*(22). Retrieved from https://library.educause.edu/resources/2005/10/models-of-open-educational-resources-opencourseware-sofia-and-the-open-learning-initiative

Treviranus, J., Mitchell, J., & Clark, C. (n.d.). *Flexible learning for open education.* Retrieved from https://floeproject.org/

Web Accessibility In Mind. (n.d.). *WAVE web accessibility evaluation tool.* Retrieved from http://wave.webaim.org/

Appendix: Accessibility Evaluation Rubric

Open Textbook:

    Format:

    Accessibility Standards Passed:

    Accessibility documentation:

1. The organization providing materials has a formal accessibility policy.
2. The organization providing materials has an accessibility statement.

Pass/Fail:
Additional Information:

Content organization:

1. Chapter titles and section headers should be marked as headers and distinct from body text.
2. Table of contents should be present and allow navigation.
3. Page numbers should be present and correspond with print numbers.
4. Content should remain organized after user 'reflows' page.

Pass/Fail:
Additional Information:

Images:

1. Non-decorative images should be marked with alternative text.
2. Images should be compatible with screen reader and magnification software.
3. Decorative images should be marked with null alternative text.

Pass/Fail:
Additional Information:

Tables:

1. Tables should be simple and compatible with screen readers and magnification software.
2. Tables should be single celled and contain ordered lists.
3. Tables should include markup that identify their rows and columns.

> **Pass/Fail:**
> **Additional Information:**

Hyperlinks:

1. In-book links should function and connect to their correct location in the text.
2. Hyperlinks should connect to a working webpage. Hyperlinks should open pages in the same window or alert the reader that a new tab is open.
3. All links should be distinct from body text. They should be descriptively titled and a different color or italicized.

> **Pass/Fail:**
> **Additional Information:**

Multimedia:

1. Closed captions should be provided for any video content.
2. Descriptive transcripts should be provided for any video content.
3. Audio or video player used for multimedia content should be compatible with assistive technology.
4. No content should flash more than 3 times per second.

> **Pass/Fail:**
> **Additional Information:**

STEM Content

1. STEM formulas and equation should be created with an editor compatible with screen readers such as LaTex or MathML.
2. If equations are inserted as images they should be described in an alt tag.

> **Pass/Fail:**
> **Additional Information:**

Font

1. Font should be adjustable and compatible with screen readers, magnification software, and colored displays. Text must remain accessible when any font size is selected.
2. All font should have zoom capabilities to 200%.
3. Font should meet standard size requirements (12 pt. body, 9 pt. footnote).
4. Alternative color and line spacing adjustments should be available.

Pass/Fail:
Additional Information:

Color Contrast:

1. All information presented in color should also be conveyed in text or other images.
2. Headers should meet WCAG AA contrast standards.
3. Body text should meet WCAG AA contrast standards.
4. Simple images should meet WCAG AA contrast standards.

Pass/Fail:
Additional Information:

Interactive Elements:

1. Interactive elements (such as menus, examples, practice questions) allow keyboard only operation with and without assistive technology.
2. All instructions, error messages, and prompts are in text and compatible with assistive technology.
3. Text should allow for keyboard only operation.
4. Text should be accessible on mobile devices.

Pass/Fail:
Additional Information:

Notes:
Recommendations:

Course Material Decisions and Factors: Unpacking the Opaque Box

Anita Walz

Introduction

Course material adoption within higher education is a complex, pedagogically driven, but relatively opaque process. To students, librarians, and those not teaching semester-length courses or involved in curriculum design, course material evaluation and selection in higher education can feel like a black box: opaque, proprietary, and mysterious, minimally transparent with only a few clues available through institutional policy requirements or instructor disclosures. Few instructors seem to openly discuss course materials among themselves or others. For open education advocates this opacity poses a problem. How can one provide relevant, customized information regarding open options when scant information is available regarding instructor motivations, criteria, processes, and ultimately curriculum or pedagogy decisions?

Several reasons exist for this opacity: a lack of training during instructors' college and graduate programs, and cultural factors which perpetuate limited discussion of course material selection processes. Authors in both K–12 and higher education indicated that there are few training opportunities (Stein, Steuen, Carnine, & Long, 2001, p. 8; Allen & Seaman, 2014, p. 5) or that they have "little formal knowledge" (Smith & DeRidder, 1997, p. 367) of criteria used to evaluate textbooks or of protocols used by other institutions for textbook selection. A humanities faculty member reflects the limited, but changing culture of sharing within higher education:

> There is a strangely idiosyncratic culture around course resources that is perhaps the consequence of academic freedom traditions in the US. There is little centralized sharing of best

practices [regarding learning resource evaluation], although social media has changed this somewhat—I have witnessed substantial Facebook threads on textbook selection and approaches to teaching specific topics. Resource awareness and selection should be part of teacher training, which graduate students at Research I institutions do not receive. (Full-time humanities faculty in Allen & Seaman, 2014, p. 5)

There are likely other reasons including limited time, few perceived rewards for sharing, political factors, or a perception that course material selection falls outside of one's area of research and expertise.

To education advocates, this lack of transparency may be viewed a missed learning opportunity for instructors and graduate students bound for teaching, as well as students themselves who might miss out on the benefits of their instructors' knowledge and skill. For open education advocates, especially those based within libraries, the lack of transparency also poses some practical problems. The least of these problems is the barrier to joining and contributing to existing conversations and processes. At worst, lack of transparency regarding course material selection negatively affects the abilities of open advocates and librarians to carefully design appropriate, insightful, scalable, and effective programs and services for a range of open education applications. Open education advocates and librarians have a great deal to gain in better understanding course material evaluation processes and selection decisions. Better understanding these processes means a greater ability to join existing conversations, better understanding of the particulars of how their specific institution works, opportunities to expand one's area of expertise, and the opportunity to add value regardless of the processes found.

Why it Matters

In 2007, the Advisory Committee on Student Financial Assistance issued a report stating "faculty have been faulted for largely ignoring price, routinely assigning textbooks only partially relevant to the course, switching from textbook to textbook on a whim, selecting lower-priced alternatives very rarely and failing to use all the material in the bundles students are required to buy" (p. 1). Students groan under the cost of course materials, many choosing to download illegal in-copyright copies, share, borrow, or go without. Students may express frustration when very little of the course material they purchased is actually used, or when they are required to spend extra money to rent homework software in order to submit homework (Walz, 2015). Students are increasingly deciding to not to acquire access to required textbooks, believing that lecture material is a substitute for textbooks. Many feel overwhelmed by the expanding amount and variety of resources (Berry, Cook, Hill, & Stevens, 2011).

Applying the dialectic concept of "open" as sharing, give-and-take, contributing, and giving credit, open practices are quite possibly the antithesis of the current idiosyncratic culture around course resources. However, as applied to many other aspects of higher education, the ethic or concept of "openness" is highly valued and directly relevant to the purpose and practices valued in higher education teaching and learning, research, and service activities, not to mention professional ethics and responsible use of resources. A lack of transparency and exchange of learning and expertise regarding course material selection appears to be a missed opportunity that affects instructors as well as students.

Conceptions of open education vary. Open education does not just include OER (open educational resources) or just open pedagogy or open source infrastructure. Open practices described in *Librarians as Open Education Advocates* describe a foundation which I believe has potential applications for teaching, research and scholarship, publishing, system design, outreach, service, and nearly any other function championed in higher education (McKernan, Skirko, & West, 2015). The authors describe these open practices as: sharing, giving (and receiving) [constructive] feedback, sharing and integrating new ideas about teaching and learning, understanding and using open licenses whenever possible, giving credit to others for their work, and "considering students and their needs as central to the activity of teaching and learning" (McKernan, Skirko, & West, 2015).

As practitioner-scholars, many academic librarians and instructional designers are already involved in open educational practices and engaged in modeling, championing, critiquing, improving, inventing, and/or supporting various open educational practices. Many instructors also within higher education adhere to and implement these values by sharing, valuing student learning, and providing service to their community, institution, and disciplinary associations. Sharing potentially messy processes regarding teaching and learning is perhaps not easy. My intent is to identify what we *can* know about this seemingly hidden process.

This chapter is intended to provide an introduction to the myriad ways that course materials are or could be evaluated, selected, and incorporated into curricular design with an emphasis on the contributions that could be made regarding course material selection by open education librarians. It reviews the literature in which instructors in higher education describe their learning material selection processes, the very few large studies covering course material selection evaluations in multiple disciplines, and the prescriptive literature describing how course material can—or should—be selected. This chapter touches on traditional course materials and those that have emerged as educational theory, technology, and instructor readiness have changed over time, making this one snapshot in a quickly changing environment.[1] And it asks the question: Where can an open education advocate, or simply someone that cares about teaching and learning, start to make a contribution if they are not the course material decision-maker?

My hope in writing this chapter is that librarians and others involved in the open education movement who are also interested in applying open principles as a way to add value to teaching and learning processes will benefit from additional information regarding course material production, evaluation, and selection practices. I also hope that readers will be motivated to become increasingly savvy and valuable consultants and experts regarding course material selection in general and openly licensed course material use, production, or publishing, in particular, and that they will leverage open practices to solve problems in higher education.

What is in that Box? Course Material Evaluation and Selection

Several groups of literature predominate this area of study: Descriptive articles document rigorous processes of course material selection for particu-

---

[1] While written for the US higher education sphere, some characteristics will be applicable to countries beyond the United States and/or to the K–12 environment, though both these groups differ enough in regulatory context, procedures (especially regarding state or local control or alignment to standards), and pedagogical practices that the reader will need to carefully consider their particular context.

lar college-level disciplines (accounting, foreign language, psychology, and history). Prescriptive documents, such as the dated but otherwise excellent *Handbook for Evaluating and Selecting Curriculum Materials* (Gall, 1981), and various shorter guides and rubrics provide recommended approaches. Thoughtful analyses of how course materials, philosophies of education, pedagogical approaches, and differing levels of teaching expertise interact with one another are relevant in this area. Last are the very few recent large quantitative studies, which explore instructors' values in course materials and activities undertaken by instructors in selecting materials for courses.

Aspects of Course Materials Instructors Value Most

Recent large-scale studies on this topic in the U.S. or Canada reported that teachers in higher education most highly value comprehensiveness, effectiveness, cost, and writing quality in their evaluation of textbooks or course materials. A number of large-scale studies identify the top reported values. Individual articles supplement these with additional values not listed in the large-scale studies. And finally, the rubric used in the Open Textbook Library adds several.

Table 1. Top values of faculty in course content selection (multi-site research and individual reflections)

Scope of study	Top values reported	Source
Large-scale study	Efficacy, proven quality, cover a wide range of subjects	"Babson report" Allen and Seaman, 2014, pp. 8, 34
Large-scale study	Cost to the student, comprehensive content and activities, easy to find	"Babson report" Allen and Seaman, 2016, p. 7
Large-scale study	How well they address course objectives, accuracy, currency, consistency	Florida Virtual Campus, 2012, p. 5

Scope of study	Top values reported	Source
Large-scale study	Clear and accessible writing, comprehensive coverage, ease of fit	Jhangiani, 2017
Individual (regarding digital course materials)	"My own assessment of [digital course materials]," cost to my students, and colleague comments	Green, 2016
Economics	Faculty time saving	McMahan, 2013, p. 45
Hospitality-tourism	Currency, subject-specific examples; interesting writing style	Hsu and Lin, 1999, p. 25
Accounting	"Relevance of the text material and its exposition quality, and compatibility between the text material and homework problems"	Smith and DeRidder, 1997
Psychology	Accuracy, readability/writing quality, and examples	Landrum and Hormel, 2002
Any	Comprehensiveness, content accuracy, relevant longevity [currency], and clarity of text	Open Textbook Library, n.d.

Given the ongoing public dialog regarding the cost of course materials (*Are College Textbooks Priced Fairly?*, 2004; U.S. Government Accountability Office, 2005; Popken, 2015) and the orientation of many institutions and some open education advocates toward cost, readers may have a particular interest in how instructors value cost. While cost appeared periodically in the top three most important factors, suggesting that cost is a factor, it was rarely reported as the most important factor. Hsu and Lin (1999) affirmed cost "as a relatively important conversation in textbook adoption … but [not] important enough to dictate the textbook selection decision" (p. 25). In reviewing Allen and Seaman's 2014 survey,[2] cost ranked as the lowest factor of all of the factors listed, but jumped to the top of the list in 2016 (Allen & Seaman, 2014, 2016). The 2016 report clarified this: it appears that faculty consider cost *ceteris paribus*: all other things being equal. "Faculty reinforce the idea that cost to the student is important, but only after content, relevance, quality, and presentation have been considered. Cost alone is not sufficient to drive the resource selection" (Allen & Seaman, 2016, p. 10). Factors which could be described as reflecting accuracy, effectiveness, and appropriateness of "fit" to subject and the given context seem to summarize the values well.

Course Material Selection Activities

We turn now to the literature on course material selection activities. The research literature on systematic course material selection processes abounds in K–12 literature. The literature, however within higher education is limited in quantity and tends to be highly discipline-specific. Further, higher education literature on systematic course material evaluation and selection leans toward novel high-effort approaches rather than repeatable, manageable, sustainable, and likely less flashy practices.

A few examples of these novel and wide-ranging approaches however may be helpful: One article examined five leading American Government texts, comparing their structure, guiding perspectives, in-text and electronic features for students and faculty, and notable strengths and weaknesses "with the goal of identifying appealing textbooks for instructors who value different approaches" (Knutson, 2017, p. 536). In the field of foreign languages, a study summarized an admittedly "time consuming" two-year collaborative textbook selection process for Spanish language instruction, which included the development of a 19-item evaluation rubric suitable for application to foreign language texts, collaborative and reflective review of results, and satisfaction rankings one year later (Czerwionka & Gorokhovsky, 2015, p. 4). A student, medical resident, and faculty textbook review process for pharmacy students aims to understand a learner-centric approach to textbook evaluation and selection, and to describe differences in textbook selection preferences between students and faculty (Peeters, Churchwell, Maura, Cappelletty, & Stone, 2010, p. 31). To complete an apparent gap in the literature, a dissertation by Tate

---

[2] Reports from this series are informally referenced as "the Babson report."

reported on the determinants for selecting a successful principles of economics textbook based on an analysis of six adoptive criteria: textbook-integrated learning aids, organization format or layout, content, readability and rigor, and ancillaries for students and ancillaries for instructors (Tate, 1991, p. 66).

These are likely some of the exemplars illustrating new and novel practices. But how do all of the other time-strapped instructors in higher education select course materials? What are their roles? And what do they actually do?

The policies, strategies, and cultures of an institution and department determine how decisions regarding how to teach and what course materials to use are resolved. In general, and consistent with academic freedom in universities, decisions are made by an individual instructor or staff member, by teams of instructors, or by departmental curriculum committees. While often championed as an individual right, a department may choose not to extend the freedom to select course materials to individuals, seating this authority in committees. Given the importance of academic freedom in higher education, course material decisions are rarely made at the administrative level, but it does happen (Jhangiani, 2017).

Every educational institution is different from the next. At the large Research 1 Polytechnic University where I am employed, I have not found a consistent pattern of course material decision processes based on discipline type or level of course. For example: learning materials for some introductory courses in the sciences are decided by a committee which identifies core knowledge and skills students must master as a foundation for more advanced courses. Other large introductory courses on the more analytic side of social sciences are taught in sections by three or four different instructors, each using different textbooks and/or homework software, presumably equally able to prepare students to build on the subject material, but taking a different approach. Some departments choose a common text for fall and spring semesters but allow for experiments and other types of course material during summer or online sessions. Other departments in which large introductory courses are team-taught appoint a course coordinator who either builds consensus or decides about course materials. These committees and individuals may have formal or informal processes for course material selection.

Two patterns that seem to be prevalent pertain to textbook authors and tenure-track faculty. These observations vary widely from one institution or institutional type to the next, where different structures, traditions, and culture prevail. This implies value in knowing one's own institution and interpretation of academic freedom. For textbook authors, the decision at my institution is simple: current policy allows authors to require the book they authored in their course.[3] For tenure-track faculty teaching upper division and graduate levels, decisions about course design, teaching methods, and course content are solely their prerogative. This practice opens the door to a growing number of faculty that increasingly teach from their notes and/or select course readings from a variety of sources, an approach suggested by several authors (Novotny, 2011; Landrum, 2012) and anecdotally more common. When a tenure-track instructor suddenly inherits a course and the instructor's predecessor is accessible, the inheriting instructor is likely to seriously consider the previous instructor's recommendation regarding course material and teaching methods. In contrast, and common to most institutions grappling with an increase in temporary, adjunct, graduate teaching assistant, or non-tenure line instructors, is the assignment of course materials by someone other than the course instructor. External choice often leaves few happy with the selection of text or the proscribed role of the text in the course. The divide between teaching-focused and tenure faculty continues and is an important characteristic to know about.

Prescriptive Perspectives and Processes for Review of Course Materials

Process matters and many scholars have opinions and suggestions regarding how learning materials *should be* selected. Again, this literature is weighted toward analysis of traditional print textbooks, though some concepts may be transferable to interactive electronic resources. By far, the most insightful one-volume handbook I located is Meredith Gall's 1981 *Handbook for Evaluating and Selecting Curriculum Materials*. While out of

---

[3] See *Virginia Tech Faculty Handbook*, Section 9.4: Textbooks and other Instructional Materials http://provost.vt.edu/faculty_affairs/faculty_handbook/chapter09/chapter09.html

print and far out of date for electronic, internet-hosted, or interactive content, the handbook, I believe, accurately and succinctly describes issues related to any era of course material selection. Especially helpful for those wanting an introduction to curriculum studies, Gall mentions the timeless issues of: curriculum quality and commercialization, roles for various actors in higher education, the wide range of types of curriculum objects, the propensity of instructors to limit their searches to what's easily available, the lack of instructor time and expertise in selecting course materials, relationships between instruction and course materials, and differences in learning resources even when options appear to be equivalent. Several helpful tools are included in the book, including an inventory and description of dimensions for analyzing curriculum materials (Chapters 4–6), a high-level course material process relevant for any topic and level of education, even higher education, and an appendix of featured curriculum materials that may facilitate learning. While updates would be needed, this source is very helpful and takes seriously the importance of selection of instructional materials in light of the fact that students spend far more time using instructional material than anyone else (Gall, 1981). (See the note below for guidance on accessing this out-of-print resource.)[4]

Several other authors report on prescriptive course materials selection processes or report on processes they have created or use. Prosser offers a summary of text readability analysis processes, prominent in the literature in the 1970s and 80s, namely using SMOG (Simple Measure of Gobbledygook) readability and the cloze test (Prosser, 1978). Heye offers a tool and process for evaluation of textbooks for nursing that enabled her school to include input from faculty members not initially involved in course material selection. Implementation of this process eliminated the need for supplementation of a main outdated text, reduced costs to students, and resulted in the use of materials that included updated health care developments (Heye, Jordan, Taylor Harden, & Edwards, 1987). Novotny provided a checklist for selection

---

[4] The *Handbook for Evaluating and Selecting Curriculum Materials* book is out of print. A digitized version is available electronically with permission of the copyright holder at: https://vtechworks.lib.vt.edu/handle/10919/79783

of nursing textbooks and provided guidance in assigning textbooks and journal reading assignments (Novotny, 2011).

Several scholars suggest value in having different levels of review. Lawrence summarized suggestions that the best of textbook evaluation schemes adopt a "leveled" approach: an initial overview of the strengths and weaknesses of the book with regard to design and structure, sequence, visual attractiveness, and availability of ancillary materials, and a further evaluation which is more detailed and determines whether text, skills and activities meet syllabus and learner needs (Lawrence, 2011). Kato affirms multipart approaches, indicating that textbook evaluation conversations should consist of pre-use evaluation, in-use evaluation, and post-use evaluation (Kato, 2014). Arnold's research adds the insight that faculty valued being part of (textbook) pre-publication review (Arnold, 1989). Multiple authors cited a need for more instructor training and knowledge regarding course material selection (Gall, 1981; Stein, Steuen, Carnine & Long, 2001).

Course Materials, Pedagogy, and Levels of Instructor Expertise

Open education advocates and librarians can benefit from understanding the intended role or purpose of a text within a course. Texts may be adopted as a course reference, because textbook adoption is expected even though the textbook is not well integrated into the course, to aid students in building a resource collection, for ease in scaffolding the course or countering an instructor's self-perceived deficiencies (Lawrence, 2011, p. 7, Confrey & Stohl, 2004, p. 43-46), or a combination of these reasons. In theory, course material selection should support course objectives, instructor pedagogies, and efficacious student learning habits. New instructors or instructors with new courses are more likely to adopt "book in a box" course materials but as they become comfortable with the course or less risk averse to changing the course away from parts that are not working, they may become more open to alternate pedagogies and curricular materials. It is into this dynamic environment that the open education advocate steps. The open education advocate or librarian may encounter a wide range of instructor comfort or discomfort with teaching and learning processes. Some instructors may be experimenting with incremental or major course design changes. Others may be content with limited investment in teaching or feel obligated to focus most of their energies on research endeavors. The librarian may also observe the impact of the institution or department's politics and practices, governance and budgeting constraints, relative importance of career advancement via tenure and promotion, and individual instructors' tolerance of risk, comfort, and perceived available support; each of these factors can and do influence student learning outcomes, selection of pedagogical processes, course materials, an instructor's decision to go without traditional or emerging course materials, or an instructor's openness to experiment with open pedagogical approaches. Beyond pressures related to an instructor's career advancement, the relationship between instructor risk tolerance, comfort, and support, pedagogical understanding and openness to pedagogical and assessment methods, and beliefs regarding the purpose of course materials should not be understated.

Usage and types of course materials have changed over time due to educational philosophies, legal environments, cultural expectations, availability of trained educators, and commercial and technological changes. The earliest and most traditional course materials were printed textbooks and readers for children, designed to lead to literacy using catechism (question and answer) as their instructional mode. In the late 19th century, changing educational philosophies, the increased availability of trained teachers, and orientation toward deductive approaches and generalized morals in response to high immigration resulted in changes in curriculum resources (Wakefield, 1998).[5] One hundred years later, and in the scope of higher education we see continued evolution of educational philosophies, development of cultures of tenure-track and adjunct faculty, an increased proportion of the population expected to engage in higher education, and impacts of technological change on course materials and instructional practices. Print resources are supplemented or replaced by digital course materials and systems. Not dismissing persistent digital divide issues, course materials and learning processes are now embedded in closed learning manage-

---

[5] A helpful summary of the history of curriculum can be found in McCulloch, G. (2016). History of the Curriculum. In Wyse, D., Hayward, L., and Pandya, J. (Eds.), *The Sage Handbook of Curriculum, Pedagogy and Assessment* (vol. 1, pp. 47–62). Thousand Oaks: Sage Publications, 2016.

ment systems, blogs and wikis, ebooks, online discussion boards, online homework systems, adaptive learning and intelligent tutors, student-driven platforms for authoring, game-based learning, and all manner of tools, clickers, and software systems. All bring pedagogical assumptions, some evidence-based. Regardless, many are adopted for classroom use.

Technology-enhanced learning resources represent some of the most creative, interesting, useful, and potentially responsive but constantly changing options within learning spaces. Many provide student metrics, allowing instructors a view of student time on task, theoretical opportunities for early interventions, and a research platform in which to start to learn what works and what does not work. Some offer freemium services, with more advanced premium services available at a fee. Open source projects are also present in the mix, some with an open business model (where content costs nothing) and in which services are rented on a subscription basis. The options are constantly changing. Current and new instructors with limited prior exposure to digital instructional methods or constantly changing digital learning environments are likely to be overwhelmed and feel disrupted when changes are foisted on them—such as the change of an enterprise-wide learning management system or techno-pedagogical changes such as flipping a classroom or converting a course to a blended or online format, which are willingly undertaken to improve a course which is otherwise not working, or for department, institutional, or financial reasons. Instructors at research institutions may lack adequate incentives—or support—to envision or achieve these types of changes in their classrooms (Gregory & Lodge, 2015). While there are many reasons to experiment with emerging technologies, some choose not to but regularly update their course notes and are perhaps less engaged by new technologies. For those who embrace new technologies, there are several potential downsides: needing time to teach a new tool, neglect of student privacy,[6] and setting students up to game a system rather than engage in deep learning and authentic reflection.

---

[6] See also: Meineke, B. (2018, March 27) Signing Students Up for Surveillance: Textbook publisher terms of use for data [blog post]. Retrieved from https://medium.com/@billymeinke/signing-students-up-for-surveillance-textbook-publisher-terms-of-use-for-data-24514fb7dbe4

While this chapter does not cover in depth selection methods for educational technologies including software programs, audience response clickers, homework software access codes, or other electronic ancillary tools, sometimes thought of as instructor conveniences and sometimes thought of as student aids,[7] I do want to note that implementation of educational technology tools seems to be growing. I have observed two main responses: instructors who select materials based on research evidence are often slow to adopt such tools when their effectiveness is insufficiently documented, and instructors attempting to manage very large courses tend to adopt them quickly out of convenience if not survival; sometimes they are abandoned just as quickly.

Incentives Influencing Design and Selection of Course Materials

To the innocent bystander, the presumed aim of course materials in mediated instruction within higher education is student learning. As discussed above, this goal can be muddled by various incentives. Several influential factors still remain:

- Perceived quality (sometimes signaled by a trusted brand name)
- Author authority/accuracy and currency of content
- Reliable scope, sequence, or structure for instructors and students to follow
- Perceived fit for the student's level of expertise
- Perceived fit with instructor's methods of teaching
- Use of emerging technology (this factor can encourage or discourage, depending on instructor comfort)
- Time savings for faculty (including pre-made lecture slides and assessments)
- The selector's valuation of meaningful promised student analytics[8]

---

[7] For a more detailed treatment of homework software access codes, see Seneck, E., Donoghue, R., O'Connor Grant, K., Steen, K. (2016). *Access denied: The new face of the textbook monopoly.* Washington, D.C.: Student Public Interest Research Groups. Retrieved from: http://www.studentpirgs.org/reports/sp/access-denied

[8] Learning resources that collect usage metrics or interaction data also

- Authoritative resource for student reference now and in the future (Arnold, 1989)
- Departmental/institutional expectations or requirements regarding always assigning a text even if the text is not heavily used

For novice instructors, part-time adjuncts without preparation time, graduate teaching assistants, and faculty teaching a course for the first time, course resources fit best as a support structure for the instructor. Experienced instructors and those with a more comfortable grasp of teaching the content area are likely to not need to rely as heavily on course resources, may be more likely to teach with learning resources they developed themselves, might not require student acquisition of learning resources, but may still assign course materials for student benefit, because students expect it, or because assigning a text is just what you do.[9] Sometimes, an instructor's long-time habits dictate assigning a required textbook as a "resource" even when it will not be used very much in the course.

Of course, disciplinary differences in pedagogy and student needs come into play. Course materials in different disciplines may have quite different functions. For example: student learning activities in literature, foreign language, and biology differ quite a bit and affect the types of course materials selected. Students studying literature may focus primarily on reading and writing activities; students in foreign language experience a much greater emphasis on listening, speaking, and, at the lower levels, grammar and basic sentence construction. Students studying biology are involved in learning the scientific method, maintaining a lab notebook, experiments, and hands-on activities in a laboratory.

---

have a new type of audience: statisticians, researchers, administrators, and sometimes commercial actors who analyze data to better gauge student engagement (often without institutional permission) and to understand how systems are or aren't being used. Vendors of this sort often aim to sell this data back to institutions if ownership and access to this data by the individuals or institution was not contractually negotiated.

[9] Due to course changes and faculty not always complying with requirements to submit information about course material adoptions, it is difficult to quantify what percentage of faculty assign don't assign course materials which students must acquire themselves.

Since purposeful learning materials were developed, they have helped instructors solve complex teaching problems (Wakefield, 1998). A generous example is the instructor who selects course materials that fit the course learning outcomes and offer students helpful problem sets, real-life applications, case studies, or other examples that help students transfer knowledge to other domains. A more cynical example is the likely overworked or unsupported instructor, perhaps with too many students, who assigns course materials primarily for the instructor's own benefit. Course materials, especially commercial ones "have been written, edited and marketed as teaching and learning aids" (Wakefield, 1998, p. 23) and are often interpreted by instructors as such. Required homework software access codes and classroom response tools or clickers primarily for instructor time savings in grading or as an expensive experiment in innovative teaching are a prime example. In my experience, I've seen these decisions justified by having to teach a very heavy course load, large classes, or the promise that the tools will make students who don't complete their reading assignments engage with the materials. These tools unfortunately pass on the burdens of an instructor struggling with getting students to engage in course material and/or trying to manage interaction and assessment of a very large class directly to students, often in the form of multiple required learning resources such as clickers, quizzing or classroom interaction tools, print or electronic texts, and/or homework software access codes.

This conflict between instructor and student needs is not condemnation of instructors who make these decisions, but a reflection a common problem cited in economics and political science literature, called a principal–agent problem. A principal–agent problem features a decision-maker (the agent), in this case the instructor, who to varying degrees reflects (or doesn't reflect) the values and interests of the person or people she represents (the principal), in this case the students. When the agent or instructor is motivated to act in his or her own interest to the detriment of the interests of the principal or students, economists identify "moral hazard" as an outcome (Eisenhardt, 1989). One may argue that the instructor is indeed in a difficult situation, often teaching as a non–tenure-track professor, without leverage, and in a somewhat impossible situation where implementing all sorts of tools is the only solution. Whether intended or not by the department which created such large courses or by the instructor, moral hazard, or "harm," is likely to occur when an agent puts their own needs above those of their principal—or when instructors assign course materials too expensive for students to access. Students may be harmed by losing the freedom to take a class or a major because it is too expensive, by taking on additional debt, additional work hours, or at minimum by additional financial stress. Further, students may lose consistent and reliable access by sharing course materials, or by participating in peer-to-peer copyright infringement in the forms of digitizing, sharing, and/or downloading illegal copies of learning materials. Again, this is not a condemnation that instructors or departments in these types of situations are malicious actors, but an observation that care needs to be taken to proactively identify and remediate situations in which incentives encourage an agent to act in a way that may be harmful to the principal.

Introducing a Paradigm Shift

What can an open education advocate do? For starters, engaging faculty in conversation regarding their particular contexts, what they like or do not like about their course materials. What kind of content do they wish existed? What kind of content (including questions and other artifacts for assessment) could they or students create? What freedoms do they have to pilot or repeatedly create small quantities of content or assessments over long periods of time? What do they wish was happening in their class that isn't? These can be tender topics, so trust and diplomacy is called for. Six open educational practices or values may scaffold instructors in their early and late attempts in openness: sharing, early drafting, supportive feedback, studying licenses, giving credit, and putting students at the center (West, 2017). Understanding open practices and values as a paradigm shift, and introducing, discussing the relative merits, supporting, and implementing each of these values can provide a clear focus for one's activities and assist in navigating where to spend scarce time and resources.

Ideally, instructors will develop courses around course learning outcomes, mapping content, activities, and assessments to course learning outcomes. Instructors exhibiting this type of teaching tend to have a sufficient if not high level of mastery over their subject and a high level of comfort with regard to teaching. A deep interest in one's discipline and care for one's students, relevant and reflective professional development opportunities, practicing teaching improvements, and valuing instructional practices are paths to developing efficacious instruction. Instruction which increasingly prioritizes these types of practices strikes a different balance between instructor expertise, teaching methods, and critical selection and use of course materials.

Learning and working to understand the realities of one's campus or campuses, campus cultures, policies, practices, values, pressures, motivators and incentives are the probably the hardest part of this work and take the most time, but are well worth the investment. Understanding course material evaluation and selection process will likely require a brief review of institutional policy regarding textbook or learning resource selection. Conversations with each of the departments on your campuses can be helpful. A call to each departmental administrative assistant or advisor with the following questions is a good place to start:

- Do the majority of your instructors assign required books?
- Are course materials selected by committee or individual instructors?
- Who are the point people regarding committee-selected course materials?
- What is the course material adoption schedule look like in your department?
- How does reporting of textbook adoptions (to the bookstore or other) work?
- I'm interested in learning more about how course materials are selected. Who else do you suggest I contact?

The registrar of your institution will be able to direct you to someone who can explain how your institution handles approvals for new or updated courses and whether there are requirements to list learning resources used in the course.

Liaison librarians may be aware of department-wide curriculum initiatives and needs. If your campus has a Center for Excellence in Teaching and Learning or instructional design support embedded in another unit, you may also be able to glean useful information about course design/redesign assistance and helpful insight regarding learning resource selection processes and motivations.

Your bookstore, if cooperative, may also be a useful source of information regarding textbook and other learning resource adoptions. Some helpful ideas for building a relationship with your bookstore can be found in Bell's 2018 article.

As you gather information and build trust, think about what open resources and open practices might contribute to resolving stated problems in current departmental resource selection processes. Some academic librarians have gone as far as to contribute to and coordinate year-long textbook evaluation processes for selected high-enrollment courses within willing campus departments. For those instructors overwhelmed with large-scale changes toward open educational resources, piloting an open resource as an alternative text is an option, as are incremental changes to incorporate open pedagogical practices which replace one reading or assignment over a period of time. The *Open Pedagogy Notebook* is one place to look for or share examples of open pedagogical practices (DeRosa & Jhangiani, 2018). The text *A Guide to Making Open Textbooks with Students* (Mays, 2017) may also be a helpful resource.

Novel and Purpose-made Course Materials

Course materials include any discrete media, format, or system deployed in support of the learning process. Cost and copyright concerns notwithstanding, course materials can now be almost anything. Some materials and processes used in courses today were not designed to be used in courses: news and academic journal articles, movie clips, equipment designed for industry, household items, 3D printers, beach balls, Twitter, Wikipedia authoring, and so on. These items and processes are used outside of classrooms and have made their way into courses. This is a refreshing trend, as the application of these materials on teaching and learning may enrich students' lives and help them to see the world around them as having potential for learning and exploration.

Purpose-built course materials are different than materials not specifically designed for learning. Textbooks, educational videos, workbooks, digital flashcards, lab environments, problem sets, online modules, interactive quizzes, clickers, educational apps, learning management systems, and various assessment and engagement tools are created specifically for learning and are most often purpose-built for educational contexts. They are intended to be consumed or acted upon by students in specific ways with specific outcomes in mind. Purpose-built learning resources always have embedded assumptions about what constitutes learning, how people learn, what learning is for, and how the system supports or facilitates that learning. Because educational technology is built by a wide variety of people, some systems may reflect sophisticated and well-conceived pedagogical philosophies; others might not. Rather than engaging with learning as a process, some may envision students primarily as containers for content provided by instructors as seen in this public domain illustration.

At School

[Public Domain] France in the 21st Century

Interactive systems designed by those with expertise in various pedagogical philosophies may rely heavily on pedagogical philosophies of behaviorism, constructivism, cognitivism, and any number of other pedagogical approaches.[10] Learning resources and approaches are not pedagogically neutral.

---

[10] For an excellent introduction to instructional design and principles therein, see Chapter 1: Introduction to Instructional Design by Gagne, R., Wager, W., Golas, K., and Keller, J. (2005). *Principles of Instructional Design*, 5th edition. Belmont, CA : Cengage.

Even as learning resources have changed with the times, they continue to be marketed as "teaching and learning aids" to solve problems (Wakefield, 1998). For the most part in the United States, development of course materials and educational technologies is a for-profit endeavor. This raises some ethical issues. For-profit ed tech companies serve two or more masters: student learning, generating a profit for shareholders, developing their research base, capturing market share and so on. Competition between these factors may challenge the most ethically minded ed tech company to deviate from valuing student learning above other factors. It is certainly possible to imagine the existence of a company that sells learning resources of value without being overly swayed by a profit motive. However, this is very difficult to do without powerful and built-in accountability structures. Like any business, commercial publishers are responsible to their shareholders for financial gains, so the conflict between product quality for ultimate end users (e.g., instructors and students) vs. shareholders is often difficult to navigate. (Potential authors courted by publishers also face these conflicts in deciding whether or not to sign a publication agreement. They are encouraged by potential royalties and legitimately enjoy attention, respect, and relationships with publishers. They often transfer copyrights to the degree possible, limiting access to their work, and give up control to write the book they want to write.)

Commercial approaches also have an impact on the development of learning resources. Publishing industry veteran Beverlee Jobrack's book about the K–12 textbook industry describes how commercial incentives shape the K–12 textbook publication process. Jobrack explores how market research, competitor analysis, and focus groups lead to the development of educational materials rather than educational research, rigorous study, and effectiveness of past use of course materials. Publishers rarely fund studies to understand the development of a subject and how it has been taught in the past, strengths and weaknesses of previously used materials, nor the educational research literature. In focus group sessions "publishers confirm that teachers rarely care about program effectiveness when weighted against a perceived useful design ... and when curriculum specialists are in the room, they nearly always prefer research-based materials, but realize that it would be an upward battle for their teachers to accept them" (Jobrack, 2012, p. 62). As a result, textbook development focuses mainly on features that are appealing rather than effective. While disheartening, Jobrack's observation that the development process for commercial textbooks focuses on aspects that appeal rather than being chosen for their effectiveness is an observation for open education advocates and instructors who develop or adapt open educational resources. At the end of the day, if effectiveness is more important than appeal, openly licensed resources focused on effectiveness should be different in important ways than those developed with appeal in mind.

Some faculty feel compelled out of habit to require a textbook even if it is not used very much in the course. Other faculty explore pedagogies as far away as possible from passive, consumable resources, some using Wikipedia assignments or creating a textbook as part of their course (DeRosa & Robinson, 2017). Others are implementing practices to encourage student agency, such as giving students flex or pink time (Baird, Kniola, Lewis & Fowler, 2015). Increasingly, instructors are seeing student engagement with the course and course content as the key to improve learning (Hunt et al., 2016)

A Way Forward?

Let's return to the question posed early in this chapter: Where can an open education advocate, or simply someone that cares about teaching and learning, start to make a contribution if they are not the course material decision-maker? For open education advocates, the keys to addressing the course material adoption issues on campus rest in working to understand the distinct realities of campus and departmental contexts and cultures, gathering information, building trust among instructors, decision-makers, and others working to address course material and teaching-related issues on campus, introducing a new paradigm of values and open educational practices (West, 2017).

Academic librarians and instructional designers already do many things to model, champion, critique, invent, improve upon, and/or support open educational practices. These may include but are not limited to: open access authoring and publication, creating and building sustainable, Creative Commons-licensed editable curriculum materials, modeling pedagogies and web development strategies dependent upon openly licensed content and open source software, contributing to open source infrastructure, developing open and sustainable models of operation through collaborative networks, and implementing student-centric pedagogies which grant increased student agency or emphasize creation of artifacts which have value beyond the classroom.

Others contribute to and aid faculty, staff and students to interact with authored content in ethical and sustainable ways by creating, remixing, and sharing research outputs with open licenses. OER are just one of many possible ways to implement the ethic or concept of openness. Librarians may be engaged or desiring to be engaged in course material or learning resource initiatives at their academic institution, including organizing evaluation or selection of openly licensed or other course materials and course material formats.

Building new expertise helpful to processes where there is no or minimal expertise may have even more potential. A few examples from this brief overview of course material production and selection where open advocates could add value include: provide more support for faculty training in course material evaluation and selection, curate tools and methods for all effort levels of course material review, and when developing openly licensed course materials, focus on effectiveness more than appeal.

And finally, build trust. Everything runs on trust and, in an ideal world, accurate information, sharing, and trustworthy processes and systems. Course material selection decisions are based on trust in people, information, and/or processes. Accurate information, reliable services that provide needed information, support, logistics or somehow add value, and a willingness to listen, learn, and respond with integrity should greatly add to creating a way forward that keeps learners at the center, values transparency, requests and accepts constructive feedback, gives credit, and promotes sharing.

References

Advisory Committee on Student Financial Assistance. (2007). *Turn the page: Making college textbooks more affordable.* Washington, D.C. Retrieved from http://files.eric.ed.gov/fulltext/ED497026.pdf

Allen, I. E., Seaman, J. (2014) *Opening the curriculum: Open educational resources in U.S. higher education.* Babson Survey Research Group. Retrieved from https://www.onlinelearningsurvey.com/reports/openingthecurriculum2014.pdf

Allen, I. E., Seaman, J. (2016) *Opening the textbook: Open educational resources in U.S. higher education, 2015–16.* Babson Survey Research Group: Retrieved from http://www.onlinelearningsurvey.com/reports/openingthetextbook2016.pdf

Are College Textbooks Priced Fairly? Hearing before the Subcommittee on 21st Century Competitiveness of the Committee on Education and the Workforce, House, 108th Cong. 2.

(2004). Retrieved from purl.access.gpo.gov/GPO/LPS56745

Arnold, D. (1989, November 2–5,). *A discipline sensitive model of textbook selection criteria in the higher education faculty.* Paper presented at the Annual Meeting of the Association for the Study of Higher Education, Atlanta, GA. Abstract retrieved from https://eric.ed.gov/?q=ED313985&id=ED313985

Baird, T. D., Kniola, D. J., Lewis, A. L., & Fowler, S. B. (2015). Pink time: Evidence of self-regulated learning and academic motivation among undergraduate students. *Journal of geography, 114*(4), 146–157. http://dx.doi.org/10.1080/00221341.2014.977334

Bell, S., (March 15, 2018). Ideas for building a better relationship with your campus bookstore. *Library Journal.* Retrieved from: https://lj.libraryjournal.com/2018/03/opinion/steven-bell/ideas-building-better-relationship-campus-bookstore-bell-tower

Berry, T., Cook, L., Hill, N., & Stevens, K. (2011). An exploratory analysis of textbook usage and study habits: Misperceptions and barriers to success. *College Teaching 59,* 31–39. http://dx.doi.org/10.1080/87567555.2010.509376

Confrey, J., & Stohl, V. (2004). Framework for evaluating curricular effectiveness. In J. Confrey, & V. Stohl (Eds.), *On evaluating curricular effectiveness: Judging the quality of K-12 mathematics evaluations* (pp. 36–64). Washington, D.C.: National Academies Press. Retrieved from https://www.nap.edu/read/11025/chapter/5

Czerwionka, L., & Gorokhovsky, B. (2015). Collaborative textbook selection: A case study leading to practical and theoretical considerations. *L2 Journal, 7*(2), 1–12. Retrieved from http://escholarship.org/uc/item/1sd802w7

DeRosa, R., & Jhangiani, R. (2018). *Open pedagogy notebook.* Retrieved from http://openpedagogy.org

DeRosa, R., & Robinson, S. (2017). From OER to open pedagogy: Harnessing the power of open. In R. S. Jhangiani, & R. Biswas-Diener (Eds.), *Open: The philosophy and practices that are revolutionizing education and science* (pp. 115–124). London: Ubiquity Press. Retrieved from https://doi.org/10.5334/bbc.i

Eisenhardt, K. M. (1989). Agency theory: An assessment and review. *The Academy of Management Review, 14*(1), 57–74. Retrieved from https://www.jstor.org/stable/258191

Florida Virtual Campus. (2012). *2012 faculty and administrator open educational resources survey.* Retrieved from https://florida.theorangegrove.org/og/items/7976fe31-6282-9f81-6dcb-5ea0b6ca037b/1/

Gall, M. (1981). *Handbook for evaluating and selecting curriculum materials.* Boston: Allyn and Bacon.

Green, K. (2016). *Going digital: Faculty perspectives on digital and OER course materials.* The Campus Computing Survey, Independent College Bookstore Association. Retrieved from https://kenneth-green-pln7.squarespace.com/s/GOING-DIGITAL-2016-ICBA-Faculty-Survey_3.pdf

Gregory, M., & Lodge, J. (2015). Academic workload: The silent barrier to the implementation of technology-enhanced learning strategies in higher education, *Distance Education, 36*(2), 201–230. doi: 10.1080/01587919.2015.1055056

Heye, M. L., Jordan, L. E., Taylor Harden, J., & Edwards, M. J. (1987). A textbook selection process. *Nurse Educator, 12*(1), 14–18.

Hsu, C. H. C., & Lin, L. (1999). Hospitality marketing: Textbook selection and course content. *Journal of Hospitality & Tourism Education, 11*(1), 22–29. http://dx.doi.org/10.1080/10963758.1999.10685218

Hunt, K. A., Trent, M. N., Jackson, J. R., Marquis, J. M., Barrett-Williams, S., Gurvitch, R., & Metzler, M., (2016). The effect of content delivery media on student engagement and learning outcomes. *The Journal of Effective Teaching, 16*(1), 5–18. Retrieved from http://files.eric.ed.gov/fulltext/EJ1092702.pdf

Jhangiani, R. (2017, May 24). *Factors the influence the selection of open (and commercial) educational resources.* Presentation at the 2017 Open Textbook Summit, Vancouver, BC.

Jobrack, B. (2012). *Tyranny of the textbook: An insider exposes how educational materials undermine reforms.* Lanham: Roman & Littlefield.

Kato, S. (2014). Using analytic hierarchy process in textbook evaluation. *TESOL Journal, 5*(4), 678–697.

Knutson, K. (2017). US government textbook review. *PS: Political Science & Politics, 50*(2), 536–541. doi:10.1017/S1049096516003152

Landrum, E., & Hormel, L. (2002). Textbook selection: Balance between the pedagogy, the publisher, and the student. *Teaching of Psychology, 29*(3), 245–248.

Landrum, R. E. (2012). Selection of textbooks or readings for your course. In B. N. Schwartz & R. A. R. Gurung (Eds.), *Evidence-based teaching for higher education* (pp. 117–129). Washington, D.C.: American Psychological Association. http://dx.doi.org/10.1037/13745-000

Lawrence, W. P. W. (2011). *Textbook evaluation: A framework for evaluating the fitness of the Hong Kong New Secondary School (NSS) curriculum* (Master's thesis). Retrieved from http://www.asian-efl-journal.com/Thesis/Thesis-Wong.pdf

Mays, E. (Ed.). (2017). *A guide to making open textbooks with students.* Retrieved from https://press.rebus.community/makingopentextbookswithstudents

McKernan, R., Skirko, T., & West, Q. (2015). Definition of open education. In R. McKernan, T. Skirko, & Q. West (Eds.), *Librarians as open education advocates.* Retrieved from https://openedadvocates.pressbooks.com/chapter/definition-of-open-education

McMahan, C. (2013). *Theory and evidence of switching costs in the market for college textbooks* (Doctoral dissertation). Retrieved from http://scholar.colorado.edu/cgi/ viewcontent.cgi?article=1039&context=econ_gradetds

Novotny, J. M. (2011). Textbook and reading assignment selection. In M. S. Quinn Griffin, & J. M. Novotny (Eds.), *A nuts and bolts approach to teaching nursing* (fourth edition). Springer. Retrieved from http://www.ovid.com/site/catalog/books/ 7878.jsp

Open Textbook Library. (n.d.). Open textbooks review criteria. Retrieved from https://open.umn.edu/opentextbooks/ReviewRubric.aspx

Peeters, M., Churchwell, M., Maura, L., Cappelletty, D., & Stone, G. (2010). A student-inclusive pharmacotherapeutics textbook selection process. *Currents in Pharmacy Teaching and Learning, 2,* 31–38. doi:10.1016/j.cptl.2009.12.004

Popken, B. (2015, August 2). College textbook prices have risen 1,041 percent since 1977. *NBC News.* Retrieved from https://www.nbcnews.com/feature/freshman-year/ college-textbook-prices-have-risen-812-percent-1978-n399926

Prosser, D., & Bondavalli, B. (1978, March 14–16). *A textbook selection process.* Paper presented at the Annual Meeting of the Remedial/Developmental Studies in Post-Secondary Institutions, Chicago, IL, March 14-16, 1978. Abstract retrieved from https://eric.ed.gov/?id=ED174941

Smith, K., & DeRidder, J. (1997). The selection process for accounting textbooks: General criteria and publisher incentives—A survey. *Issues in Accounting Education, 12*(2), 367–384.

Stein, M., Steuen, C., Carnine, D., & Long, R. (2001). Textbook evaluation and adoption. *Reading & Writing Quarterly 17,* 5–23. Retrieved from http://dx.doi.org/10.1080/ 105735601455710

Tate, J. (1991). *A study of the determinants in selecting a successful principles of economics textbook* (Doctoral dissertation). Retrieved from http://jewlscholar.mtsu.edu/ handle/mtsu/4116

U.S. Government Accountability Office. (2005). *College textbooks: Enhanced offerings appear to drive recent price increases.* Retrieved from purl.access.gpo.gov/GPO/LPS64226

Wakefield, J. F. (1998, June). *A brief history of textbooks: Where have we been all these years?* Paper presented at the meeting of Text and Academic Authors, St. Petersburg, FL. Abstract retrieved from https://eric.ed.gov/?id=ED419246

Walz, A. R. (2015, March 23). University libraries host open education week [Blog post]. *Open@VT: Access to information at Virginia Tech.* Retrieved from https://blogs.lt.vt.edu/openvt/2015/03/23/ university-libraries-host-open-education-week-2015

West, Q. (2017). Librarians in the pursuit of open practices. In R. S. Jhangiani, & R. Biswas-Diener (Eds.), *Open: The philosophy and practices that are revolutionizing education and science* (pp. 139–146). London: Ubiquity Press. https://doi.org/ 10.5334/bbc.k

An Open Athenaeum: Creating an Institutional Home for Open Pedagogy

Rajiv S. Jhangiani & Arthur G. Green

Introduction

At its core, open pedagogy describes an intervention aimed at improving teaching and learning. Open pedagogues recognize that education is never value-free or politically neutral. For us, education at its finest is liberatory, democratizing, critical, antiracist, and decolonized (hooks, 1994). As such, open pedagogy is a vehement rejection of the incumbent and predominant "banking model" of education, in which knowledge is something to be deposited, stored, and withdrawn at a later date (Freire, 1970). Open pedagogy instead represents a vision for education that replaces classrooms of control with communities of possibility. This is precisely why open pedagogues seek to empower students and educators to interrogate and subvert power structures that systematically limit their agency and restrict their access to high-impact education practices. Open pedagogy—an integral part of the contemporary open education movement (OEM)—is firmly and explicitly grounded in concerns about social justice.

In this chapter, we examine how to build an institutional home for open pedagogy, with particular attention to recommendations for libraries and librarians. While librarians have always been central to disseminating public knowledge, more recently they have engaged diverse ways of becoming community-led agents of social change (Morales, Knowles, & Bourg, 2014) and leading social justice activists (Library Freedom Project, n.d.). We believe that it is no coincidence that librarians are found at every frontier of open education. Indeed, academic librarians' expertise and their interstitial, consultative relationships make libraries a natural home for open pedagogy.

As we write this chapter (2017), it is an exciting time to be part of a growing and vibrant international community of open education practitioners, one that hails from all segments of academia. Librarians are of course already an essential part of this community. They are enhancing the formal, informal, and professional learning support that they already perform by training their communities in open licensing, providing physical places for workshops on open pedagogy and other open educational practices (OEP), cataloging open educational resources (OER), and engaging in numerous other activities that support open education. The support of librarians is essential as the community debates and experiments with ways to implement more socially just, open approaches to supporting the universal human right to education (United Nations, n.d.). This support is essential given the experimental nature of open pedagogy, as it allows us to leverage collaborations across faculties and institutions as well as learn lessons from previous open pedagogical experiments.

In this chapter we examine the experimental terrain of open pedagogy as an approach and clarify how we are using the term. We then illuminate ways in which open pedagogy in higher education not only involves but often relies on academic librarians and libraries by exploring diverse, real-world examples of open pedagogy projects. Finally, we draw some common themes from the examples and offer an outline of ways in which academic librarians can support OEP in their various institutional contexts.

Open Pedagogy: Past and Present

The ways in which we define open pedagogy undoubtedly impact the ways in which we can support open pedagogy. While open pedagogues tend to engage deeply in constructivist and critical approaches to learning, the lack of a common understanding of the role of OER in open pedagogy has recently become a point of debate. While use of the term open pedagogy can be traced back to learner-centered approaches dating to at least the 1970s (see for example Cronin, 2017; DeRosa & Jhangiani, 2017; Jordan, 2017; Morgan, 2016), contemporary use of the term has most often been linked to the development of OER and OEP. The spectrum of narrow to broad definitions of open pedagogy that have formed the basis for recent debates tend to emphasize either OER or OEP (Green, 2017). Narrower definitions are closely related to the development and use of OER as defined by the 5 Rs (Wiley, n.d.; described fully in Section 1 of this volume) whereas broader definitions tend to link open pedagogy to a spirit of openness that underpins a wide array of educational practices that do not necessarily involve openly licensing (Grush, 2014), such as syllabus co-creation, public scholarship, and service learning.

These terminology debates reflect the experimental nature of open pedagogy and are the result of three factors. First, open pedagogy is a relatively new approach, so understandings of what activities it entails are under healthy and vigorous debate. Second, open pedagogy is a syncretic blend of several critical and constructivist pedagogies, so the ways in which relationships are framed among the subject matter, learners, teachers, learning objects, and their human environment can be profoundly divergent. Third, open pedagogues grapple on a daily basis with emerging practices devised for the unique challenges and possibilities entailed in using OER and integrating the radical transparency of open education practices into courses.

In the case of the open pedagogy debate, the community has to a large extent agreed to disagree. In fact, by early 2017 David Wiley (an influential writer, organizer, and advocate for open education) relabeled his earlier, oft-cited but narrower version of open pedagogy as "OER-enabled pedagogy" in order to move beyond terminology debates and establish a term that could be operationalized to research the use of OER within a constructivist teaching approach. He writes,

> OER-enabled pedagogy is the set of teaching and learning practices only possible or practical when you have permission to engage in the 5R activities…. We learn by the things we do. Copyright restricts what we are permitted to do. Consequently, copyright restricts the ways we are permitted to learn. Open removes these restrictions, permitting us to do new things. Consequently, open permits us to learn in new ways. (Wiley, 2017b, para. 5, 9)

In this chapter, we engage primarily with this latter definition of open pedagogy (or OER-enabled pedagogy), to which the creation, adaptation, and adoption of OER are central.

To the extent that engagement with open pedagogy increases the use and prevalence of OER, this pedagogical approach supports students and institutions. Indeed, a rapidly growing body of research attests to the positive impacts of OER use on student and institutional cost savings (Hilton, Robinson, Wiley, & Ackerman, 2014; Hilton, Gaudet, Clark, Robinson, & Wiley, 2013) as well as on student performance, persistence, and completion (Hilton, Fischer, Wiley, & Williams, 2016). While a focus on OER-enabled pedagogy may seem to overly weigh the importance of OER artifacts in relation to other open practices, we argue that it actually recognizes that open education is fundamentally a community of practice.

The open education community of practice involves diverse stakeholders interested in lowering barriers to education. The community is maintained and built through formal conferences (e.g. the annual Open Education Conference and OE Global), workshops (e.g. Digital Pedagogy), and informal networks that focus on sharing and learning practices such as ways to create OER, implement OEP, support open education policy, and build strategic initiatives. The activities and organizing that define OER-enabled pedagogy reflect lively and sustainable ways of invigorating the relationships in the community of practice and maintaining momentum towards the above goals.

The title of this chapter invokes an open athenaeum. An athenaeum can be an institution, library, or reading room that contains artifacts; it can also be a group of people that engages in the promotion of literary and scientific learning. The idea of the open athenaeum metaphorically represents the contemporary transitions that librarians successfully navigate and that we face in the OEM. It represents the challenges of transitioning from archiving and supplying materials to consulting and serving communities, from focusing on artifacts to focusing on teaching and learning ecosystems, from conveying to co-creating knowledge, and from focusing on OER to facilitating OEP. The open athenaeum thus enables open pedagogy as both a community of practice and as shared physical and digital resources.

Open Pedagogy in Practice

A broad range of approaches to understanding and defining open pedagogy offers a diverse slate of potential examples of what these projects may look like in practice. Although the six project examples that follow represent different aspects of the open pedagogy spectrum, they should each be recognizable for the manner in which they trust and empower students, encourage faculty to relinquish tight control and to depart from the familiar, provide authentic and meaningful learning experiences, serve the wider community, and make use of the permissions that accompany OER. In each case, the description of the open pedagogy project is followed by a reflection on the role and significance of librarians in supporting similar projects.

Project Management for Instructional Designers

Successive cohorts of graduate students enrolled in a course on project management at Brigham Young University revised and remixed an open textbook on project management to suit their needs and the needs of future formal and informal learners. The students aligned the book chapters with professional certification standards, filmed and integrated video case studies into the chapters, replaced generic examples with those written from an instructional design perspective, completed a word-for-word re-editing to improve readability, created text-to-speech audio recordings of each section, replaced copyrighted images throughout the book with openly licensed ones, and added a glossary of key terms. The revised and remixed book was republished as an open textbook, *Project Management for Instructional Designers*.[1] David Wiley, the faculty lead for the project, wrote:

> Each time I give this kind of assignment, I find that my students invest in their work at a completely different level and go far above and beyond what I ever imagined they could do. Now these students are co-authors on a book that is being used in programs across the US (and world? let me know if you're using PM4ID in your class!) and have an incredible portfolio piece to showcase to future potential employers and their moms. (Wiley, 2012, para. 5)

It is worth noting that PM4ID was adapted using technology from Pressbooks.com.[2] While the choice to use the Pressbooks website or the

---

[1] Available from: https://pm4id.org/

Pressbook plugin on a personal WordPress installation is perfectly suitable for publishing open textbooks, there may be advantages to having student work integrated into local, institutional installations of Pressbooks. Academic libraries can play a central role in making such local, institutional installations open to successive cohorts in one or several courses, making sure the book is cataloged and discoverable, and using Pressbooks to encourage awareness of OER and possibilities for open pedagogy projects.

Environmental Science Bites

Undergraduate students enrolled in a lower-division Introduction to Environmental Science course at the Ohio State University were tasked with describing some of Earth's major environmental challenges and discussing ways that humans are using cutting-edge science and engineering to provide sustainable solutions to these problems. Their work would eventually form the different chapters in the open textbook *Environmental Science Bites*.[3] In the words of Brian Lower, the faculty lead of the project,

> In writing these chapters, our students learned a great deal about the publication process. They learned: (1) How to find information from primary and secondary sources and critically evaluate topics, issues, results and conclusion. (2) How scientific research is conducted and how results and conclusions are reported to the public so that people can make more informed decisions in their own lives. (3) That the peer-review evaluation system is an integral part of the scientific process, which enables scientists to maintain high quality standards and provides credibility to research and scholarly works. And (4) that peer reviews are a necessary part of the writing process because it focuses attention on particular details and considers the input of an actual audience. (Lower, 2015, para. 2)

The role of librarians in facilitating the above lessons in the creation process is central. Modules addressing open licensing, peer review, and

---

[2] See: https://pressbooks.com/

[3] Available from: https://osu.pb.unizin.org/sciencebites/

information sourcing and evaluation can be made ready for use by students across the institution in different disciplines. Another interesting aspect of this project is that it is published on a Pressbooks installation on Unizin.org. Unizin is a consortium formed by several major research institutions in the US and currently supports digital learning technologies for 22 institutions. While it hosts an open textbook, it does not necessarily provide an openly available catalog of the OER students at partner institutions have contributed to their platform. Integrating these digital learning objects into the search functions of the partner institution libraries might increase their discoverability, increase their use, and allow professors across institutions teaching environmental science or other subjects to contribute to the collection.

Wiki Education Foundation

With the assistance of the Wiki Education Foundation, more than 22,000 students enrolled in >1,000 courses at institutions across the world have participated in the Wikipedia assignments, collectively revising and refining more than 37,000 articles. This includes medical students working with Dr. Amin Azzam at the University of California, who receive course credit in exchange for improving this public resource while improving their own ability to describe complex processes in layperson's terms.[4] Dr. Azzam feels that "it should be part of a physician's social contract to provide high quality health-information on open repositories like Wikipedia" and that "as a result of all this training, my medical students are well-qualified to be improving the medical and health-related content on Wikipedia pages" (Salvaggio, 2016, para. 11, 14).

This open pedagogy project encourages students to interpret scientific knowledge and create accurate, up-to-date resources for public knowledge dissemination. Libraries and librarians can help navigate Wikipedia's unique framework for contributions, create formal or informal working groups that allow faculty members across campus to smoothly integrate Wikipedia assignments into their courses by drawing from institutional knowledge of best practices and existing human con-

---

[4] For more information, see: https://en.wikipedia.org/wiki/Wikipedia:UCSF_School_of_Medicine

nections (such as a campus Wikipedia ambassador[5]) to the Wiki Education Foundation and the Wikipedia community itself.

The Noba Project

The Noba Project's efforts to address a wide array of psychology topics led to the creation of an annual competition in which students create short topical videos. The competition offers $10,000 in prizes for three-minute videos that best help viewers understand and remember the concepts around the topic. The students' Noba Student Video Award projects are openly licensed for review and reuse under a Creative Commons license. The process empowers the students who create the content and results in learning tools for other psychology students (DeRosa & Robinson, 2017, p. 119).

In the words of Michael Harris, co-author of one of the award-winning videos about Personality Traits during the 2016–17 competition,

> They say that teaching a subject is the best way to truly learn it, and I now see why they say that. After writing the script, filming many takes of talking to the camera and our (hopefully funny) examples of the big 5, then editing it with my very talented friend Matt all into a final product, I feel that I know this content in a way I never did before. I am incredibly grateful for the opportunity and had a great time making the film. I hope we see more media-meets-psychology projects like this in the future. (Harris, 2017, para. 1)

While many large institutions have special units focused on producing professional audiovisual content, the ability of libraries to provide facilities for learning and audiovisual production for students across the campus can be a key to success in projects such as the one above. Provision of physical infrastructure, a repository for the produced digital materials, and expertise in the Learning Commons of the library helps open pedagogy projects flourish and can create synergies across courses.

---

[5] For an in-depth explanation of Wikipedia ambassadors, see: https://en.wikipedia.org/wiki/Wikipedia:Education_program/Ambassadors

Geographic Information Science, Open Science, and Land Policy

In 2016, nearly one hundred students in the Department of Geography at the University of British Columbia (UBC) undertook an open pedagogy project to contribute scientific knowledge regarding British Columbia's Agricultural Land Reserve (ALR).[6] Using open science principles and open data, over 20 teams of students conducted independent analyses of subsections of the ALR in order to measure how much agricultural land was actually in the protected farmland zone. The key question here was whether official estimates of agricultural land used by the province and media refer to actual agricultural land or just to everything within the administrative boundaries of the ALR.

Student feedback on the project was positive. Many students noted their increased ability to critically analyze open data sources and open data accessing, processing, handling, analyzing, and interpretation. Many students expressed shock at the types of data that the British Columbia provincial authorities did not provide to the public under open licenses. They were also surprised to find instances where crowdsourced, open data (like Open Street Map) appeared to be more detailed than proprietary data sets. The students learned many core ideas about data quality in GIScience (geographic information science), yet the project also presented many pedagogical questions and quandaries for the instructors. For example, many students pointed out possible outcome differences between using open data and proprietary data for analyses. As an open science project, we needed to share our data yet proprietary data could not be shared. Given different methodological decisions taken by student groups, should the results be framed as part of the learning process or should the results, even if problematic, enter into the public debate to stimulate more research? How is it possible to design and use an open science project for successive cohorts? How do we assess learning in the context of open science? The students' final reports, maps, and spatial data were published on a public-facing website providing open resources for people interested in BC's agricultural lands. The project website provides a brief overview

---

[6] For background information on the Agricultural Land Reserve, see: http://blogs.ubc.ca/alrmap/alr-background/

of the project process and groups of outcomes from the project, including lessons learned by the instructors for implementing GIScience, open science, and open pedagogy projects.

Once again, librarians were fundamental to the success of this project. The UBC Data & GIS Librarian came into the course to provide an overview of open and proprietary data sources, how to access them and attribute them, how to understand metadata, and how to use some basic software for visualizing data. Students and faculty were able to rely on the librarian's technical expertise in data and vast knowledge of data sources while building their methodological approaches for the actual GIScience analyses.

Open Pedagogy in Broader Terms

While all of the above examples convey open pedagogy work with an array of openly licensed resources (from open textbooks to open data to open science documentation), broader understandings of open pedagogy practices can also be supported by libraries. For example, open pedagogy can be understood as openness in co-creating course outlines with students. As Kevin Gannon argues, current course outlines are not learner-centered:

> The role of a syllabus has become contested for a variety of reasons, resulting in maladroit attempts to balance institutional needs and effective pedagogy. Because syllabi are now interpreted as contracts in addition to curricular documents, they have become the default landing site for university policies, accreditation box-checking, and myriad other items attracted to the platform like cat hair to a black shirt. (Gannon, 2016, para. 6)

What could be more learner-centered than the openness of having the students themselves agree upon the learning outcomes, course conduct, behaviors, and even the assessment strategies (Monsen, Cook, & Hannant, 2017)? This openness to engaging the learners in framing their relationships to each other, to the subject matter, and to the instructor provides an honest model of learning together. However, it is scary for many faculty to relinquish control over the course. While arguments about course outlines being an unbending contract or the intellectual property of the instructor need to be addressed, much of this fear might simply be because it is hard to imagine what a student-created course outline might look like and we have very few among us with experience in co-creating course outlines. So, we need more examples and best practices.

Librarians can make a major contribution to this type of openness. There is a valid argument for course outlines being cataloged and referenced in institutional repositories in the same way that other scholarly materials are treated. These repositories can be tagged with many keywords, and not just disciplines and departments. Some of these keywords might focus on the pedagogy employed and if students were involved in the creation of the course outline. This would provide faculty with invaluable insights into openness. How is it being done, who is doing it, and what are the expected outcomes and best practices?

Several other projects that do not focus necessarily on OER but rather on opening the teaching and learning process might also be supported by librarians. For example, Robin DeRosa's work on an open anthology not only involved students creating OER, but making curatorial decisions in the selection of types of texts to include (DeRosa, 2016). Her students' open pedagogy project resulted in *The Open Anthology of Earlier American Literature*.[7] Other examples include Rajiv Jhangiani's (one of the authors of this chapter) work with students to create a question bank to accompany an open textbook for social psychology (Jhangiani, 2017c). As well, projects emphasizing public scholarship as a type of openness might be important. For example, UBC Geography students in an environmental geography course developed dozens of case studies analyzing wicked environmental problems (see https://environment.geog.ubc.ca/); these case studies are not openly licensed but emphasize creating and disseminating scientific knowledge through public scholarship. While we believe that openly licensing public scholarship provides greater potential utility for learners, these efforts nonetheless reflect a push towards openness and getting away from disposable assignments.

Whether or not these projects openly license their products and can be considered OER-enabled pedagogy, the above examples reflect open and collaborative approaches to effective pedagogy. Librarians can support the above examples of openness in pedagogy by working on dis-

---

[7] Available at: https://openamlit.pressbooks.com

coverability, creating institutional repositories for types of resources, and hosting workshops that feature open educational practices. Below we distill many of the lessons learned from these cases into six recommendations. While these recommendations are easiest to implement in cases where institutional resources support full- or part-time support positions to support open education, the recommendations can be pursued through collaborative, sustainable partnerships with other units on campus.

Building an Open Athenaeum

So, just how does an institution facilitate open pedagogy? Let's get down to brass tacks to look at some concrete actions that librarians can take to champion open pedagogy from the library. Our list draws from the above cases and our professional experience as faculty working closely with librarians and students, but it is certainly not meant to be exhaustive. Anita Walz points out, "Depending on our main roles and the needs of our institution we may implement and connect open educational practices very differently. There is no single model for librarian involvement in open education; I think this is a good thing" (Walz, 2017, p. 153). Towards locating a suitable model, Quill West proposes a useful framework of habits that librarians can focus on. She writes: "We achieve openness by exploring and encouraging the six habits of open practice: sharing, early drafting, supportive feedback, studying licenses, giving credit, and putting students at the center" (West, 2017, p. 140). The embodiment of these different habits within your particular institutional culture needs to be creative and contextualized. Likewise, you can adapt our suggested actions as they are relevant to your situation and how you approach open pedagogy.

Collaborate and Grow a Community of Open Practitioners: A Campus Working Group

If your campus does not already have a formal, cross-functional Open Education Working Group (OEWG), librarians can be the driving force to create one. The group might include faculty, administrators, union representatives, students, and staff from the bookstore, accessibility services, and the teaching and learning center. Although the composition of an OEWG may vary across institutions, the critical guiding principle is to not omit interested internal stakeholders, as the recommendations of the group may otherwise be perceived as confrontational. Moreover, the natural temporal turnover of students as well as the particular politics of administration and faculty units might unnecessarily undermine or politicize open education.

Having the OEWG run by librarians brings several benefits. First, it gives the work of the group the veneer of institutional approval and a stability that individual stakeholders cannot easily manage. Second, the formal group can serve as the go-to point for people interested in learning more (the provision of this information is a natural function of the library—the official commons—in the campus ecosystem). Third, the working group can plan and offer professional development opportunities for faculty (e.g., how to adapt an open textbook, how to design a Wikipedia assignment), run an open textbook review program that provides honoraria to faculty willing to write a peer review of an open textbook within their area of expertise (an especially handy way of countering the low-quality myth), run an OER grant program (to support faculty to make necessary changes prior to adopting OER), manage an institutional listserv for OEP, and apply for internal and external funding to support all of the above.

The technical expertise of librarians and the physical and digital spaces that the library supports are key assets for all of the above working group actions. This is the group that can ensure that OER are widely understood in terms of their permissions, so that even if people "come for the cost savings, they stay for the pedagogy" (Wiley, 2017a, para. 6). This approach—one that highlights both social justice and pedagogical innovation—carries the additional benefit of widening the appeal of OER adoption as only the first stop on a journey of exploration into open pedagogy.

Collaborate and Grow a Community of Open Practitioners: Informal Networks

One of the reasons why working groups are such a useful mechanism is that collaboration and partnerships are key to the success of this grassroots movement. So even if not formally connected within working groups or written partnerships, librarians may collaborate with the campus store to help them explore revenue models based on OER (e.g., selling print copies of open textbooks, including on demand) and the campus student association to help raise awareness about the impact of high textbook costs and the availability of OER. Librarians may also work directly with faculty interested in revising and remixing OER to build course-specific LibGuides (see, for example, http://nmc.libguides.com/psy250mccord/welcome) that allow faculty to share their work with institutional support but outside of the closed institutional learning management system (LMS).

In order to provide support for open pedagogy librarians should especially explore collaborations with the teaching and learning center (TLC). The TLC administrators and staff are the ones who will most likely be aware of the innovative pedagogues across different faculties, the teachers who are eager to explore new technologies and who might be excited at the prospect of empowering their students via open pedagogy.

Strongly supporting these innovators (especially within high-enrollment departments or flagship programs) as they engage with OEP is a strategy that can pay dividends, for when their efforts are recorded, recognized, and celebrated these innovative pedagogues become carriers for the message of OEP for the many early adopters waiting in the wings across campus. In addition to the organic spread of ideas through pedagogical mavens, librarian- advocates are then able to point to respected peer innovators on campus, a powerful strategy that aligns both injunctive norms (what people ought to be doing) and descriptive norms (what people are actually doing).

Assuming the goal is to normalize the adoption of OEP on campus, collaborating with the TLC once again provides several mechanisms to build and grow a community of practitioners, whether by creating faculty learning communities or other communities of practice (ideally led by the faculty innovators) that collaboratively explore the full potential of working in the open. Once again, fostering interinstitutional collaborations can help by reducing individual workloads, enhancing quality via peer review, and widening impact.

Raise Awareness

As you might have intuited from reading the above, a critical action is to raise awareness of both OER and open pedagogy, and here librarians can really flex their technical expertise and leverage their interstitial position. Awareness of OER remains relatively low among the academic community. Speaking from our experience, many students have never heard of open education and therefore cannot be effective advocates. Likewise, many administrators confuse open education with online education and therefore do not see how or why additional institutional support might be necessary or beneficial to the institutional goals. Faculty are not immune either as studies show that most faculty continue to confuse what is "open" with what is merely free or what happens to be in digital format.

This all points to the critical need for more education. We describe this as critical because, after all, it is not the "free" that enables open pedagogy but rather the "freedom" or the 5R permissions. Fortunately, this is precisely the sort of education that librarians are perfectly positioned to provide, both online through licensing guides and modules and face-to-face during consultations or professional development workshops. Organizing campus events that bring in external speakers is an effective strategy, partly because doing so provides inspiration with concrete examples of practice, but also partly because all too often the identical message conveyed by an internal expert is readily discounted.

Address Discoverability

Once the awareness barrier has been tackled, basic strategies to address the discoverability of OER can help ensure that open resources get into the hands of teachers and learners, who may then decide to take advantage of the 5R permissions. Addressing discoverability can take many forms—such as importing MARC records for open textbooks into the library catalog, integrating open repository searches into the discovery layer, or developing LibGuides for OER.

One interesting strategy that has been found to work at institutions across British Columbia is integrating open educational materials into seasonal displays that are often found near the entrance of the physical library. While a wide array of OER can be displayed and discovered, printing open textbooks and including examples of open pedagogy (student-created) projects can lead faculty, staff, and students to discoveries that stimulate curiosity, raises awareness, and encourages adoption.

Similar efforts to support OEP include gathering and publishing course outlines (if they are not made public elsewhere), publishing rubrics to assess renewable assignments, writing case studies to profile diverse examples of open pedagogy, or facilitating the deposit of students' creative and academic work in the institutional open repository. Whether for OER or OEP, the goal is the same: ensure that practical tools and resources are made available and discoverable to faculty who learn about open practices and wish to adopt them. Happily, addressing discoverability is something that can be more easily achieved by proactively reaching out to and collaborating with peers at other, like-minded institutions or via consortia.

Enable Adaptation

Enabling adaptation across the institution can contribute to and in many cases may rely upon the technical expertise of librarians and the physical and digital infrastructure of libraries. While the physical infrastructure enables workshops on creating openly licensed materials for both students and faculty, the digital infrastructure and technical expertise in project management can be just as valuable. For example, drawing from ongoing work at the Rebus Foundation, Billy Meinke at University of Hawai i emphasizes teaching OER production workflows (Meinke, 2017). Teaching these soft skills of navigating and managing the OER creation process allows faculty to see entry points for learner activities and for learners to better able to conceptualize how their contributions are part of a larger picture that perhaps involves learners at other institutions.

Libraries have the potential to lead the needed implementation of digital architecture for enabling adaptation. OER are not always in an ideal format for remixing or adapting (Levine, 2017). This poses limitations not just to adoption but also for the use of OER in open pedagogy projects. For example, in British Columbia, BCcampus led the successful implementation of Pressbooks as an open textbook repository. The repository allows people to freely access online and download digital copies of textbooks in several different file formats. In Alberta, Manitoba, and Ontario, the BCcampus Pressbooks model and content is mirrored by agencies advancing open education in their respective provinces. While widely dispersed, these repositories often contain static editions of learning objects. So faculty and students are unable to easily edit and contribute in the same way they might through a more dynamic shared wiki or website. This limits adaptation and the use of OER in open pedagogy. UBC librarians Leonora Crema and Erin Fields recognized this hurdle and decided to experiment with implementing a locally hosted Pressbooks installation that allows faculty and learners to import and edit openly licensed materials from other repositories. This enables long-term OER adaptation projects across courses and departments. It is likely that enabling local adaptation of OER will translate into better rates of adoption and to learning objects more relevant and engaging for students in their local contexts.

Inspire and Emphasize Practices

Librarians can provide multiple entry points to meet people at their understanding level of open education and broaden the open education discourse beyond OER cost savings to OEP and open pedagogy. After all, "if cost savings were the only goal, then OERs are not the only answer. Materials could be made free, or subsidized, which are not openly licensed" (Weller, de los Arcos, Farrow, Pitt, & McAndrew, 2016, pp. 84–85). Open pedagogy offers other benefits such as peer-to-peer efficiency in the adaptation and dynamic updating of materials. When faculty move from being consumers of texts to realizing the potential power of adapting and creating OER for enabling OEP then "we've come within striking distance of realizing the full power of open" (Wiley, 2016, para. 16).

Aside from making fuller use of the available permissions, the broader takeaway for those of us seeking to advance the open education movement is that when we advocate for OER we can engage in aspirational visions of education and avoid the appearance of judgment or guilt. Aspiration better supports innovation and engages in "approach motivation" (Elliot & Covington, 2001). In a broad aspirational vision of what we may be able to accomplish in open pedagogy and OEP, material cost savings may be the *least* significant benefit of OER (Jhangiani, 2017a).

Indeed, "for faculty who enjoy experimenting and innovating, open textbook adoption does feel like a meagre position to advocate. These are instructors who care deeply about authentic and open pedagogy, who may take full advantage of the permissions to revise and remix, and who understand that adopting OEP is really just about good pedagogy ..." (Jhangiani, 2017b, p. 275). On the other hand, as principled agents in a principal-agent dilemma, faculty who adopt high-priced textbooks may feel guilty about their decision and bend a course to better conform to and utilize an expensive textbook. These empathetic teachers are cases where the social justice reasoning for open textbooks may resonate particularly well (Jhangiani, 2017b, p. 275).

The above recommendations indicate the need for librarian-advocates to know their audience and meet them where they are, something that is made easier by the multiple entry points to OEP. These entry points are described by Weller and colleagues (2016) as three categories of OER users:

Of course these categories are neither static nor mutually exclusive, as individual faculty will evolve, whether in terms of the specific Creative Commons license they are comfortable applying to their newly created work or their motivation for adopting OEP. Nonetheless, they offer some insight into the different starting points for different faculty in their journey towards greater openness. Librarians can chart the typical paths of these different types of users, link these users to one another, and provide the ligaments of the community of practice so necessary for open pedagogy.

1. The OER active are engaged with issues around open education, are aware of open licenses, and are often advocates for OERs ... An example of this type of user might be the community college teacher who adopts an openly licensed textbook, adapts it and contributes to open textbooks. (pp. 80–81)

2. OER as facilitator may have some awareness of OER, or open licenses, but they have a pragmatic approach toward them. OERs are of secondary interest to their primary task, which is usually teaching ... Their interest is in innovation in their own area, and therefore OERs are only of interest to the extent that they facilitate innovation or efficiency in this. An example would be a teacher who uses Khan Academy, TED talks and some OER in their teaching. (p. 82)

3. Finally, OER consumers will use OER amongst a mix of other media and often not differentiate between them. Awareness of licenses is low and not a priority. OERs are a "nice to have" option but not essential, and users are often largely consuming rather than creating and sharing. An example might be students studying at university who use iTunes U materials to supplement their taught material. For this type of user, the main features of OERs are their free use, reliability and quality. (p. 85)

Conclusion

We reiterate that it is no coincidence that librarians are to be found at every frontier of the open education movement. Librarians are the ones whom students approach when they need to borrow a textbook that has been placed on course reserve. Librarians witness pairs of students daisy-chaining interlibrary loans to last the length of a semester. Librarians conceive of and manage alternative textbook programs. Librarians try to persuade their faculty to make greater use of the institutional repository. Librarians build guides to help faculty and students locate the subscription-based resources for which the institution has dedicated precious resources. Librarians deal with increasingly exorbitant and opaque database subscription fees. Librarians are the perennial champions of improved access and student support because they have benefited from hard-won lessons learned along their profession's journey from print to digital and from resources to services. From conversations about open textbook publishing to the push for embedding inclusive design principles within OER creation, librarians are offering expertise, infrastructure, insights, and communal cornerstones for OER and OEP.

These experiences, combined with their expertise and the consultative nature of their relationship with faculty perfectly position the library to be the open athenaeum—the institutional home for open pedagogy.

References

Cronin, C. (2017, April 24). Opening up open pedagogy [Blog post]. Retrieved from http://catherinecronin.net/research/opening-up-open-pedagogy/

DeRosa, R. (2016, May 18). My open textbook: Pedagogy and practice [Blog post]. Retrieved from http://robinderosa.net/uncategorized/my-open-textbook-pedagogy-and-practice/

DeRosa, R., & Jhangiani, R. S. (2017). Open pedagogy. In E. Mays (Ed.), *A guide to making open textbooks with students* (pp. 6–21). Montreal: Rebus Community. Retrieved from https://press.rebus.community/makingopentextbookswithstudents/chapter/open-pedagogy/

DeRosa, R., & Robinson, S. (2017). From OER to open pedagogy: Harnessing the power of open. In R. S. Jhangiani & R. Biswas-Diener (Eds.), *Open: The philosophy and practices that are revolutionizing education and science* (pp. 115–124). London: Ubiquity Press. doi: doi.org/10.5334/bbc.i

Elliot, A. J., & Covington, M. V. (2001). Approach and avoidance motivation. *Educational Psychology Review, 13*(2), 73–92. https://doi.org/10.1023/A:1009009018235

Freire, P. (1970). *Pedagogy of the oppressed.* New York: Continuum.

Gannon, K. (2016, September). DIY syllabus: What is a syllabus really for, anyway? *ChronicleVitae.com*. Retrieved from https://chroniclevitae.com/news/1545-diy-syllabus-what-is-a-syllabus-really-for-anyway

Green, A. G. (2017, April 11). What is open pedagogy? [Blog post] Retrieved from: http://greengeographer.com/what-is-open-pedagogy/

Grush, M. (2014). *Open pedagogy: Connection, community, and transparency—A Q&A with Tom Woodward*. Retrieved from https://campustechnology.com/Articles/2014/11/12/Open-Pedagogy-Connection-Community-and-Transparency.aspx?Page=1

Harris, M. (2017). Personality traits—the Big 5 and more. *Noba Project*. Retrieved from http://nobaproject.com/student-video-award/winners

Hilton J., III, Fischer, L., Wiley, D., and Williams, L. (2016). Maintaining momentum toward graduation: OER and the course throughput rate. *The International Review of Research in Open and Distributed Learning, 17*(6). http://dx.doi.org/10.19173/irrodl.v17i6.2686

Hilton J., III, Gaudet, D., Clark, P., Robinson, J., and Wiley, D. (2013). The adoption of open educational resources by one community college math department. *The International Review of Research in Open and Distributed Learning, 14*(4). http://dx.doi.org/10.19173/irrodl.v14i4.1523.

Hilton J., III, Robinson, T. J., Wiley, D., & Ackerman, J. D. (2014). Cost-savings achieved in two semesters through the adoption of open educational resources. *The International Review of Research in Open and Distributed Learning, 15*(2). http://www.irrodl.org/index.php/irrodl/article/view/1700/2833

hooks, b. (1994). *Teaching to transgress: Education as the practice of freedom* (Vol. 1). New York: Routledge.

Jhangiani, R. S. (2017a). Open as default: The future of education and scholarship. In R. S. Jhangiani & R. Biswas-Diener (Eds.), *Open: The philosophy and practices that are revolutionizing education and science* (pp. 267–279). London: Ubiquity Press. https://doi.org/10.5334/bbc.v

Jhangiani, R. S. (2017b). Pragmatism vs. idealism and the identity crisis of OER advocacy. *Open Praxis, 9*(2), 141–150. https://doi.org/10.5944/OPENPRAXIS.9.2.569

Jhangiani, R. S. (2017c, January 12). Why have students answer questions when they can write them? [Blog post] Retrieved from http://thatpsychprof.com/why-have-students-answer-questions-when-they-can-write-them/

Jordan, K. (2017). The history of open education—a timeline and bibliography. Retrieved from http://www.katyjordan.com/opened_draft.html

Levine, A. (2017, June 21). Open as in not PDF [Blog post]. Retrieved from http://cogdogblog.com/2017/06/open-as-in-not-pdf/

Library Freedom Project. (n.d.). *What does the Library Freedom Project do?* Retrieved from https://libraryfreedomproject.org/

Lower, B. H. (2015). Letter to the readers. In K. A. Clark, T. R. Shaul, & B. H. Lower (Eds.), *Environmental ScienceBites*. Retrieved from https://osu.pb.unizin.org/sciencebites/front-matter/letter-to-the-readers/

Meinke, B. (2017). Discovering OER production workflows [Blog post]. Retrieved from https://oer.hawaii.edu/discovering-oer-production-workflows/

Monsen, S., Cook, S., & Hannant, L. (2017). Students as partners in negotiated assessment in a teacher education course. *Teaching and Learning Together in Higher Education, 21*. Retrieved from: https://repository.brynmawr.edu/tlthe/vol1/iss21/2

Morales, M., Knowles, E. C., & Bourg, C. (2014). Diversity, social justice, and the future of libraries. *Portal: Libraries and the Academy, 14*(3), 439–451. https://doi.org/10.1353/pla.2014.0017

Morgan, T. (2016, December 21). Open pedagogy and a very brief history of the concept—explorations in the ed tech world [Blog post]. Retrieved from https://homonym.ca/uncategorized/open-pedagogy-and-a-very-brief-history-of-the-concept/

Salvaggio, E. (2016, April 5). For Wikipedia, the Doctor is in … class [Blog post]. Retrieved from https://wikiedu.org/blog/2016/04/05/medical-students-wikipedia/

United Nations. (n.d.). *Universal declaration of human rights.* Retrieved from http://www.un.org/en/universal-declaration-human-rights/

Walz, A. (2017). A library viewpoint: Exploring open educational practices. In R. S. Jhangiani & R. Biswas-Diener (Eds.), *Open: The philosophy and practices that are revolutionizing education and science* (pp. 147–162). London: Ubiquity Press. https://doi.org/10.5334/bbc.l

Weller, M., de los Arcos, B., Farrow, R., Pitt, R., & McAndrew, P. (2016). Identifying categories of open educational resource users. In P. Blessinger & T. Bliss (Eds.), *Open education: International perspectives in higher education* (pp. 73–92). Open Book Publishers. https://doi.org/10.11647/OBP.0103.04

West, Q. (2017). Librarians in the pursuit of open practices. In In R. S. Jhangiani & R. Biswas-Diener (Eds.), *Open: The philosophy and practices that are revolutionizing education and science* (pp. 139–146). London: Ubiquity Press. https://doi.org/10.5334/bbc.k

Wiley, D. A. (n.d.). Defining the "open" in open content and open educational resources. Retrieved from http://opencontent.org/definition/

Wiley, D. A. (2012, December 11). The best OER revise/remix ever? [Blog post] Retrieved from https://opencontent.org/blog/archives/2629

Wiley, D. A. (2016, October 27). Underselling open: The problem with cost framing [Blog post]. Retrieved from https://opencontent.org/blog/archives/4774

Wiley, D. A. (2017a, February 16). Evolution vs revolution [Blog post]. Retrieved from https://opencontent.org/blog/archives/4910

Wiley, D. A. (2017b, May 2). OER-enabled pedagogy [Blog post]. Retrieved from https://opencontent.org/blog/archives/5009

Section 3:
OER Advocacy, Partnerships, Sustainability, and Student Engagement

Throughout this book, particularly in this third section, we see themes of the librarian as both catalyst and central collaborative leader for awareness building, adoption oversight, and project management. Librarians are central in supporting OER adoption. Here, we investigate the roles librarians play in identifying and cultivating partnerships with student organizations, government entities, multiple institutions, and the profession.

As described previously, advocating for a broad adoption of OER can be a challenge to organizational culture, and changing culture takes time and true collaboration. Our hope is that practitioners will learn about how to cultivate productive partnerships with a variety of stakeholders to support broad cultural change and uncover concrete strategies for finding and evaluating existing OER in preparation for adoption, modification, and creation of OER.

In the first chapter, Cummings-Sauls et al. highlight the role of the librarian in catalyzing partnerships across a broad array of stakeholders. The authors offer clear advice on how to engage with a variety of partners within one's institution and with broader external communities.

Rigling and Cross outline the creation and implementation of an OER program at North Carolina State University (NCSU). The authors describe how they built partnerships with their student population to support wider advocacy for the program. Readers will find valuable insights on strategies for partnering with students and assessing outcomes.

Further emphasis on the importance of student engagement comes in Ivie and Eillis' chapter on advancing access for first-generation college students. Here, the authors discuss the role of the library in advancing OER through integration with various campus entities, and in particular advocacy work focused on multiple student organizations. The authors offer practical suggestions in working with students to market and assess programs.

Continuing with this focus on student engagement, Baker and Ippoliti describe how they engaged students at Oklahoma State University to become advocates for OER adoption and how they worked with student organizations, supported by a development grant, to design OER and advocate for their adoption.

Kirstin Dean describes the multi-pronged approach to library-led OER adoption at Clemson University. Dean frames the issue as a communication challenge, and describes the methods she has used in effectively communicating the importance of OER to student organizations and other campus stakeholders.

To complete the section, we shift focus to extra-institutional and professional partnerships. First, LaMagna describes an approach at Delaware County Community Colleges, in which faculty librarians advocate for OER and train colleagues in implementation strategies though professional development programming. Readers will learn about the creation of the program, the funding sources, and the design of the curriculum.

Frank and Gallaway outline the train the trainer approach, outreach efforts, and how library leadership manifests in OER initiatives carried out by Louisiana's state library consortium. Their description of coordinating OER efforts at a statewide level, in concert with a legislative body, includes discussion of a variety of challenges and opportunities.

Finally, Hare, et al. explore inter institutional collaborations to implement OER programming across the Duke Endowment Libraries. This case study explores the different settings and campus cultures across the endowment libraries and how working with endowment support to train the trainer, engage faculty, and assess their collaboration.

Open Partnerships: Identifying and Recruiting Allies for Open Educational Resources Initiatives

Rebel Cummings-Sauls, Matt Ruen, Sarah Beaubien, & Jeremy Smith

Introduction: The Value of Having Partners—Why You Don't Want to Go It Alone

Leading or partnering with others on an open educational resources (OER) initiative is one of many ways libraries provide value to students, as well as visibility on campus. As Joseph A. Salem Jr. suggests, "… partnering early in the process will allow the library to lead in areas where expertise is needed and missing. If no programmatic approach is underway, these partnerships offer the library an opportunity to lead overall on an initiative focused on student success" (Salem, 2017). Combining library services with others across the institution may result in a robust, enriching initiative, leveraging various types of expertise or infrastructure throughout an institution.

The successful OER initiatives that we discuss here have been built upon partnerships. Partnerships may include any number of individuals or groups ranging from libraries, the Student Government Association (SGA), faculty support offices, bookstores, administration, and more (including outside your institution). A possible starting point for a partnership is to first consider your available resources, the needs at your institution, and what would help bridge the gaps. Promoting what you have to offer, while seeking others to complement those resources or services, can naturally lead to opportunities to partner. Libraries, for example, may have key services in place that contribute to OER initiatives, such as assistance finding high-quality OER, copyright consultation, central infrastructure, expertise in publishing, and existing relationships with campus departments. While partnerships are not necessary for implementing an OER initiative, for our universities' partners they have been invaluable in increasing awareness, building and sustaining momentum, and bringing a variety of perspectives, skills, and resources that contribute to long-term success.

Throughout departments, colleges, and universities there are shared goals involving education affordability and student success, which dovetail with OER goals. "Combining the strengths of key campus units to build OER into the campus culture" is a powerful way to move these goals forward (Woodward, 2017). Partnerships can bring many benefits, but require effort, ongoing development, and flexibility. Partnerships may be a time-consuming, labor-intensive way to move an initiative forward, yet the authors have found the rewards can be exponential in return. Goodset, Loomis, and Miles found that the "greatest challenge in collaborating with a faculty member, perhaps unsurprisingly, was navigating schedules and deadlines," and that agreed-upon methods of communication were "essential" (Goodset, Loomis, & Miles, 2016). This holds true of all partnerships, and becomes more challenging and critical as additional partners join the initiative. Goals and expectations should be clearly stated, agreed upon, and periodically revisited throughout collaborations. That being said, it is also important to be flexible in your goals and expectations.

In this chapter, we describe OER partnerships at three institutions: University of Massachusetts Amherst (UMass Amherst), Kansas State University (K-State), and Grand Valley State University (GVSU). In each institution, the libraries are a leading partner in OER initiatives, joined and supported by a variety of partners from the university community. Throughout the chapter, our discussion of these partnerships will illustrate a variety of different goals and outcomes. In some instances, the nature of the partnership is focused largely on advocacy. In others, new services were developed to meet faculty pedagogy and student learning needs. And in other examples, existing services and infrastructure were combined to provide more cohesive support for supporting OER. With each stakeholder, we highlight potential hooks and motivations for the partner's involvement, roadblocks you may encounter recruiting them, and benefits of their participation. Our goal is to share our experiences through this framework so that you may be able to identify similar partners within your institution, customize and implement strategies we describe, and overcome the challenges inherent in OER collaboration.

Library

Following the path blazed by educational technologists, distance educators, and instructional designers at Massachusetts Institute of Technology (MIT) with the creation of their OpenCourseWare program in the early 2000s (Abelson, 2008) libraries have begun to fully embrace and support the development of OER in the last decade. Initially thought of as content locators, contributors, and organizers (Atkins, Brown, & Hammond, 2007), libraries are now leading OER funding initiatives, educating faculty, and providing infrastructure for the storage, creation, and dissemination of OER (Kleymeer, Kleinman, & Hanss, 2010; Santos-Hermosa, 2012; Gallant, 2015). The authors' libraries have recognized the connections between OER efforts, which work to remove the barrier of high-cost resources for students and encourage new teaching methods for faculty, and existing open access (OA) and open data work. To address the faculty concern that they do not have time to find or create alternatives to their existing teaching materials, libraries have begun to initiate and coordinate incentive and grant programs, develop or support the work of other campus OER efforts, and dedicate staff time to supporting and advocating on behalf of OER.

OER efforts may be led by or centralized in one of many different library units. Many germinate in scholarly communication departments due to their expertise in OA publishing, institutional repositories (IR), fair use, and guidance on the use of Creative Commons and other copyright/intellectual property rights issues (Wesolek et al., 2017). Library teaching and learning, collections, or administration units are similarly well suited to support OER programs (Yano, 2017). For academic department liaisons, reference and reserves staff, library administrators, and student support teams, collaboration on OER may be an opportunity to build new relationships with departments, demonstrate the library's value to campus, or meet student information needs. No matter what library unit they belong to, find someone who is passionate about these issues and willing to advocate on behalf of your efforts. If you are not a librarian and planning to launch an OER program, the library should be one of your first partners.

In addition to material support, libraries may offer funding opportunities for OER. With the growing trend of library budgets moving away from "big deal" journal packages (Anderson, 2017), there is an opportunity to reallocate these funds towards OA projects. Many libraries have Friends of the Library or other community groups willing to support initiatives that directly impact students. Library development offices can be great at finding alumni or large donors who want to support the library in a meaningful way. Libraries may also have access to federal grant funds from the National Endowment for the Humanities (NEH) and the Institute for Museum and Library Services (IMLS), which both support the development of open materials. However, it's no secret that library budgets are tight; since OER is a relatively new area for libraries it has not, with some exceptions, established a foothold in traditional library budgets. OER funding often falls into the "special projects" category and is thus not necessarily sustainable over the long term. Greater efforts to institutionalize funding for OER within libraries will need to happen in the future to guarantee their viability as a core library service.

Currently, full-time OER positions in libraries are rare. Many OER efforts on U.S. campuses are managed by someone with other responsibilities, such as IR management, reference, or undergraduate support (Okamoto, 2013; Kleymeer et al., 2010). One way to gradually introduce more OER work into the library is by including it in revised job descriptions following retirements and vacancies. But even without new positions there is a plethora of existing staff who can help spread the word about OER. Library subject specialists or reference staff, who interact with faculty regularly and are great promoters of library services, can introduce faculty to the concept of OER and recruit them to participate in a program. They can also create or assist with creating OER subject guides. Reserves departments can plug OER when faculty are looking for course materials or placing textbooks in the reserves collection. Archives and special collections departments can present faculty with untapped, unique archival material that can be used as teaching materials. Metadata staff can assist with resource description that helps surface OER in local catalogs and worldwide indexes. Acquisitions staff can identify and ingest quality OA journals, monographs, and textbooks. Library development and communications departments can promote OER efforts as well as develop possible funding streams for an OER initiative. Libraries can also provide infrastructure support for OER projects. Many academic libraries have stable fiscal processing ingest for processing grants/awards. Libraries also often support an institutional repository or OA press that provides hosting and publishing of locally created OER. The fabric of support for OER runs throughout almost every unit in the library.

Libraries, however, are not always equipped to provide expert advice on all OER matters. Support for the mechanics of publishing (copy editing, proofreading, editorial decisions, layout, graphic design, etc.) is something that OER authors frequently need that libraries can't always provide—as with GVSU's library publishing program, which has relied on authors to prepare and format OER before they are made available online. Libraries have increasingly started to collaborate with university presses and others to address this need (Sutton & Chadwell, 2014). The accessibility of the variety of formats generated with OER content, especially video and audio material, is oftentimes outside the area of libraries' expertise as well. Partnerships, vendors, and training are some of the ways to address this important aspect of OER creation, but there are others. K-State, for instance, addresses accessibility issues in one way by inviting someone from the Student Access Center to sit on each application review board. UMass Amherst Libraries recently partnered with the Assistive Technology Center to provide training for staff and students on closed captioning and audio description of video material.

Even when a library has the potential to support all aspects of an OER program, collaborating with allies on campus enables the resources and time of the library and librarians to have faster, greater, and better impact. Let's look at some other campus stakeholders you may want to include in an OER initiative.

Faculty

Faculty members are an absolutely vital partner in OER initiatives on your campus. Plain and simple, because faculty teach the courses, if faculty do not become involved in the process you cannot have a successful OER initiative. The good news is that it takes just one to start. Most likely you already have at least one faculty member in mind or as a friend on campus where you may be able to begin. Reaching out to connections that you already know, or know exist, is a great first step in building faculty partners. If you are new to campus or don't feel that your connections are right, reach out to the individuals within the library, who we discussed above, that may have or may want to have a vested interest in OER. Ask these individuals to introduce you to their faculty connections, which can be as simple as a forwarded email with a short message or meeting for coffee.

You may also have faculty on campus who are already using an open or alternative resource. These faculty may be able to convert another course to OER and they may let you know which faculty have shown interest in their efforts on campus. Plus, they can be the obvious, great examples of how OER can work on your campus. Once you have worked with faculty on campus, you may be able to call upon them to participate in future OER events, share their experiences in promotional material, and to convert other courses that they have in their course load. It is important to remain in contact with faculty who have participated in the initiative, to ensure that they are continuing use of the resource and have been satisfied with the process. Use their feedback to make improvements when possible and be sure to communicate your efforts with them, as faculty word of mouth can be a powerful tool in making future faculty partners.

Beyond being trailblazers for selecting and implementing OER, faculty also serve as advocates among their colleagues. Faculty may be sources of expertise, bringing direct hands-on experience of using OER. These faculty can be great allies in creating and supporting the initiative on campus and in some cases may become an initiative partner or member of your OER committee. In fact, the K-State Open/Alternative Textbook Initiative Team consists of faculty members from three different departments on campus and several others are asked to join the review committee each year.

In addition to individual connections, there are several other ways to connect to faculty on campus. Calls for applicants or interested faculty should be placed in your campus communications channels (i.e. email, newsletters, magazines, flyers) that you have available. Holding events and activities on OER during nationally recognized open access or open education weeks can draw in faculty and highlight OER efforts on your local campus. Attend other faculty-focused events and make small talk with other attendees. Where appropriate, mention that you may be able to provide grant funding and/or support for their transition to OER. Even when you can't talk about your initiative, you are expanding your connections.

When possible, reach out to those you met to reintroduce yourself, and don't forget a link to your OER website in your email signature.

Some universities have, on their own or working with an external partner like Open Textbook Network, held workshops to inform faculty about the impact of open textbooks. During these workshops, faculty are asked to complete a review on an existing open textbook to gain familiarity with a resource that they may want to use in their course. Faculty may receive a small stipend or award for their participation, depending on your local policy and resources. At K-State, some faculty have reported uncertainty in completing the OER grant application itself. If you have an application for participation, providing information sessions where the application process is explained and discussed can provide faculty an added comfort level in completing the process. At the very least, this provides you an opportunity to interact with faculty who show some level of interest in participation.

Soured or unsatisfied faculty relationships with commercial publishers can also lead faculty towards OER. At GSVU, the general chemistry course has adopted an OpenStax textbook in reaction to publisher price hikes. Faculty at K-State frequently report dissatisfaction with commercial options as a prime reason they are looking at OER. OER has given faculty the ability to produce a textbook for a discipline that commercial publishers have not yet shown interest in or that is too niche to recoup investments. Faculty with a passion for these areas may be looking for an outlet and OER is the perfect option. The most important thing to keep in mind with faculty partners is to not dictate what you want them to incorporate into their course. You may even hold off on suggesting content until they have asked you for possible options.

Faculty members, at our universities and more generally, have some degree of freedom to select their desired course materials. The AAUP Statement of Principles on Academic Freedom and Tenure states academic freedom "is fundamental for the protection of the rights of the teacher in teaching and of the student to freedom in learning" (American Association of University Professors, 1940). Whether committees or individual instructors select the resource, faculty usually decide on the text. If doing so by committee, you just have more people to enlist. Ultimately, faculty are the ones who can make the decision to move a course to OER.

Research by Tyton Partners support "Faculty time/effort" as a reported obstacle for all faculty by administrators in digital learning (Lammers & Tyton Partners, 2017). As OER coordinators, we see that this is especially true as it pertains to reviewing OER content for use in courses. Faculty may have more opportunity to conduct these tasks during the summer months, when they have fewer demands on their daily routines. Some faculty are off-contract with their college or university over the summer and can use grants/awards for stipends to cover their efforts during this time. Faculty without publishing experience may have concerns over their lack of expertise. These faculty should factor the costs of publishing, such as copy editing, into their applications when applying for their grant award.

To alleviate quality concerns, faculty should be encouraged to gather and reflect on reviews of their OER. For newly created content, authors are asked to receive traditional textbook reviews from internal/campus and external reviewers in their discipline. Along with gathering and incorporating feedback from traditional reviews, each semester students in the course will provide or should be asked about their perceptions on the quality and relevance of the content to their needs. Hearing that students valued and appreciated the OER has led faculty at K-State to convert additional courses to using OER.

Multiple faculty members at each of the authors' institutions have explored, adopted, adapted, or created OER. By the end of spring 2017 K-State had granted OER awards to approximately 80 faculty from 26 different departments. The faculty of the math departments at both GSVU and K-State have been actively involved in converting their courses to OER to provide innovative teaching to their students. Faculty members from our initiatives have reported that they are interested in OER as a way to provide flexibility in their teaching and more learning options for their students. Faculty instructors report concern for student costs as a major factor in the selection of course materials, as well as the quality of the resource, providing a fair and equitable resource, and student engagement (Green, 2016). Faculty have discipline-specific and pedagogical expertise that make them excellent OER partners for evaluating and creating resources to use in their courses.

Academic Department Heads

Department heads make a strong partner in OER as they may stall or accelerate your OER program. Unlike many other partners whose primary focus is on student success, department heads are more focused on their faculty and departmental success, even if they still teach one or two courses. You may be able to identify the department's current priorities by reviewing their goals, mission, and other documents (if any are available to you). Often, a department head's first consideration will be the faculty tenure and promotion process and how a faculty member's commitment of time on a textbook fits in with their other duties and requirements. Also, for some faculty, the creation of OER is not an added value to their portfolio. Working on an open textbook project could lead to a department head discouraging participation. Unknown challenges for new faculty can mean added stress, mainly due to limited faculty and/or department time. Showing how an open textbook could impact positively on a particular discipline, improve teaching evaluations, bring the faculty teaching awards, or provide opportunities to produce research on the integration of OER in the classroom, can help persuade a resistant department head. It is also beneficial to know, in advance, where to find and create OER before approaching the department head. This will show the department head that you are ready to assist their faculty if they are ready to encourage the change.

Some departments on our campuses have struggled in the past with unifying courses taught by several graduate/teaching assistants. Suggesting the adoption of a single OA textbook can elevate this issue and ensures that, even if the teaching styles still vary, all the students are learning from the same content. This strategy has brought whole teams of faculty on board at once for some K-State courses. Using a $100 average cost savings for a course with 1,800 yearly student enrollments provides department heads evidence that moving large courses to open educational resources means the department is able to show the students large savings and the dean a large return on investment. However, moving smaller courses to OER allows the department and faculty to experiment with the process, ensure they will receive a reward or see a benefit, and encourages faculty or the department to do what they want to do first. With either approach, departments have had success, so encourage the department head to use the approach that feels most comfortable. You should work with the department head to prepare for rotation of faculty and staff and discuss the possibilities of the course being cancelled. These can be signs of courses that may not be ready for conversion, or the opposite—those that are primed for OER.

In our experience, certain departments have internal peer pressure to not go open. The best counterweight to this is education. On the other hand, some subject areas are embracing OER wholeheartedly and at the authors' institutions, department head allies are providing support to faculty for additional resources that go beyond grant funding. We have even seen department heads providing funds to cover commercial textbook conversions when OER initiatives cannot. Money is far from the only support a department head can offer: asking a department head at GSVU to help promote an OER event resulted in that department's faculty contributing over half of the event's participants.

Department heads at K-State have also begun to show interest in being able to identify courses, (through an icon next to that department's courses in the course catalog), that are using OER as a draw for students. Since this has only been implemented for a couple of semesters we are not able to determine the rate of positive draw or negative push of this icon, but we have had faculty requesting the icon be added to their course and report of a faculty member worried that the icon would have students enrolling in the other section instead of their own. In addition, with easy identification and searching the OER icon can be used in future marketing of their department to draw in new students.

K-State has the benefit of having department heads as lead developers and participants on the Open/Alternative Textbook Initiative team. Most direct outreach to other campus department heads has been directly from our mathematics department head partner, which, as colleagues in this role at the university, has made for an easier, and often more candid conversation about the possibilities of converting department courses. These open discussions have aided in identifying barriers that may be an obstacle for specific areas. A recently implemented student fee for approved courses using an open or alternative textbook has caught the attention of several department heads on campus. With this, 89 percent of the $10.00 fee (per student) goes directly to the department. Having department heads on the team who understand budget constraints it was very important to not limit the funds, apart from following already approved university guidelines for spending. For the K-State mathematics department last year, that was over $30,000 for the first year of participation.

Department heads are the captains of the department "ship" whose job it is to set the direction and look out for the "shipmates." For these partners you will need to let them choose the path, demonstrate that you are prepared, and find a way to show there are big rewards for the efforts. With these strategies, we hope to see more department heads encouraging strong support and adoption over next few years.

Students

In discussions surrounding the cost of textbooks and OER, the student voice is central. Students are the stakeholders who are most directly impacted by textbook costs and should be involved in working toward alternatives. The high cost of textbooks is often the cause of students not buying required textbooks, taking fewer courses, or receiving poor grades because they didn't have the books (Florida Virtual Campus, 2016). With the increased availability and awareness of OER, there is now an alternative that can help mitigate the cost issue. Because of the tangible impact on their day-to-day finances, it is very easy for students to see the benefits of OER. The challenge is finding ways to channel that awareness into action. But it is worth it. Students can be the most passionate, articulate, and authoritative voices on behalf of OER efforts. On our campuses, collaboration with students range from activism to advocacy. Students, if well organized, can have significant influence over their peers, professors, and administrators.

One place to begin to collaborate with students is your local SGA. The common goal of the SGA is to advocate on behalf of students, and as a result, SGAs have a built-in infrastructure where they can encourage faculty and administrators to support OER. SGAs also often have access to funds that can be used for OER incentive programs. At K-State, the SGA supplied funds for the local initiative, edited, paid for, and wrote promotional materials, and successfully advocated for an "OER icon" that is included in the course catalog next to classes that use open or alternative materials.[1]

---

[1] K-State open or alternative resources can include: the use or adaptation

They also supported and helped advocate for a student fee to help pay for open/alternative courses.

SGAs frequently have close connections with other student representatives in the region, so you may encourage them to reach out and discuss how OER programs are working on other campuses. GVSU's SGA has focused on awareness, helping to raise the profile of OER by distributing promotional materials, holding events, and passing resolutions to encourage OER adoption. At UMass Amherst, the SGA, with the assistance of the library, began recognizing faculty "OER Champions". The SGA publicly recognizes the faculty member for their efforts to ease the financial burden on students. Non-monetary student recognition of faculty OER use can be a valuable incentive: a similar initiative at Texas A&M University was designed so that the SGA's award could be used by the faculty as evidence of teaching quality for tenure and promotion (Herbert, 2016).

The SGA can reach campus leaders through representation in faculty governance, meetings with administrators, and Boards of Trustees meetings. Libraries or other campus OER partners can support student leaders as they meet one-on-one with provosts to advocate for increased support of OER programs. OER leaders may "coach" students before these meetings with general facts about OER as well as local qualitative and quantitative data illustrating the need for, and benefits of, OER. During faculty governance meetings, the SGA has an opportunity to speak on a topic of their choice. They can use this opportunity to educate faculty about OER and encourage them to seek local support for the use and development of OER in the classroom. SGA candidates running for office may also use OER as part of their election platform. Students at K-State did this and were successfully elected (K-State Today, 2015). Partnering with the SGA can prove to be very effective at advancing an OER campaign at the grassroots level.

In addition to the SGA, any student groups working on issues of affordability, student debt, or access to higher education are great candidates for collaboration. At UMass Amherst, the state PIRG (Public Interest Research Group) has followed the lead of U.S.PIRG and begun working

---

of an existing open access textbook, library resources, high quality OER, media, and/or faculty-authored materials.

on a textbook affordability campaign. The UMass Amherst Libraries has worked with MassPIRG to support their #TextbookBroke campaign (Student Government Resource Center, 2014). They have set up information tables in high student traffic areas, collected data about textbook costs, and handed out postcards for students to give professors that encourage them to consider OER. Although cost is not the sole consideration for faculty when choosing textbooks, it is a factor, along with quality and effectiveness (Allen & Seaman, 2016). If faculty hear from students that they cannot, or will not, buy a book because of the cost, it can help motivate faculty to look more closely at OER.

Of course, not all work with students may be fruitful. Because of their transient nature, it is hard to nurture long-term partnerships and maintain relationships with administrators and faculty. Students may rotate out of SGA, graduate, become consumed with classwork, or lose interest. This means that you will have to frequently re-engage with new students to keep partnerships going. One way to do this it to invite SGA or student representatives to serve on grant application review committees. If you make a major announcement, release news, or produce a report on the initiative, forward it to the student groups with a note about why it is important to them. Include students in the planning of OER events and be sure to send them a special, personalized invite where appropriate. Connect with new officers following every election. Set up meetings with the new SGA officers to review their successful OER election platform and see how it aligns with your goals. There is no guarantee that students will share the goals of your initiative, but informing them of your efforts will at least allow them to make educated decisions about their future strategies.

Students may be OER advocates in other ways as well. Students who have used OER in the classroom can be featured in promotional content about OER, encourage other students to enroll in OER courses, and encourage faculty to use OER in other classes. Students are able to provide classroom feedback about OER resources used in a course in student teacher evaluations. Some faculty are enlisting students to become co-authors on collaborative OER as alternatives to traditional "throwaway assignments" (Wiley, 2013). When coordinating student contributions to OER projects consider copyright and the Family Educational Rights and Privacy Act of 1974.

Students are often integrated with OER initiatives at many levels, from SGA to taking an OER course. Making them a partner instead of just a participant can have lasting impacts. Students can provide advocacy, funding, feedback, and much more; just ask.

Faculty Support Offices

If faculty partners are an essential key to the success of an OER initiative, then faculty support offices can be the key to faculty participation. This broad category of stakeholders may include instructional designers, educational technology specialists, teaching and learning centers, accessibility experts, or other administrative and professional specialists. Faculty support can also encompass institution-wide committees, centers, or projects focused on particular issues, like digital humanities/digital scholarship, big data, or community engagement. The exact constellation of resources, people, and organizations often varies by institution—GVSU's instructional designers, for example, are part of the information technology (IT) department, while at UMass Amherst instructional designers are employed by both IT and the teaching and learning center. In any context, however, these stakeholders are united by a shared focus on supporting the scholarly and pedagogical practices of faculty members, through professional development programming, grant funds, consultations, and other services. As a result, faculty support offices—whatever form they take—have broadly similar motivations, face some of the same obstacles, and bring similar benefits as an OER partner.

Faculty support offices, more than many campus stakeholders, reflect and help to realize their institution's strategic priorities: a research-driven institution may have more services and support to help researchers compete for grant funding, while GVSU's instructional design and technology specialists, for example, enable progress towards the university's goal of increased online course offerings. By linking OER with the priorities and values of your institution, you can frame OER engagement as an opportunity for faculty support offices to be more effective and successful. Strategic documents, vision statements, and institutional culture can reveal key values and concepts—innovation, sustainability, equity, student success, recognition, research impact, competitive rankings, and more—which offer an entry point to recruit these partners. With some critical and creative thought, you could pitch OER to faculty support offices as an engaging pedagogical practice, a more sustainable approach to textbooks, an opportunity to make higher education more equitable and affordable, or an innovative form of scholarship with global reach. By doing so, you position OER engagement as something that advances the partner's own goals, instead of diverting resources from core services.

Other OER narratives have more universal appeal, like the growing body of research surveyed by John Hilton (2016) which suggests that, beyond affordability, OER adoption leads to similar or better student learning outcomes compared to traditional textbooks. Perhaps the simplest reason for faculty support offices to join an OER initiative is if faculty begin asking them for OER-related support. For example, grant management offices may see more OER needs due to the U.S. Department of Education's recent policy requiring open licenses of educational resources produced through Department of Education grants (U.S. Department of Education, 2017). Participation in an OER initiative can thus enable faculty support offices to address emerging needs and connect the faculty they serve with other campus resources.

Recruiting faculty support offices for an OER initiative can be challenging, of course. These stakeholders probably have far more opportunities for collaboration on campus than resources to meet every request, especially if they award grant funding. OER-related grants or new services may come at the cost of other grants and services, and may be preempted by higher-profile or higher-priority needs (hence the value of positioning OER as a path towards a support office's core mission). If your institution's faculty support offices are not well informed about OER, it may take sustained relationship building and information sharing before they are ready to be enthusiastic OER allies: GVSU's OER collaboration with faculty support offices only occurred after several years of communication and groundwork. Even faculty support offices that are informed and engaged OER partners face a continual learning curve as the theory, praxis, and communities around OER emerge and evolve. As always, ongoing outreach and information sharing are essential to breaking down silos, continuing existing partnerships, and welcoming new parties to the OER conversation.

Once on board with an OER initiative, faculty support offices can be tremendously valuable allies: their relationships with and services for faculty provide additional conduits to the stakeholders ultimately responsible for adopting and creating OER. The connections that faculty support offices build in the course of their normal activities offer a ready audience for OER promotion and education, while also raising the profile of OER projects among faculty. The GVSU grants office has systems in place to support scholarly and creative activities, whether through funding, a lighter teaching load, or sabbaticals, and faculty across campus are keenly aware of these advantageous resources; by explicitly including OER as a supportable activity, the office raises the profile of OER-as-scholarship at the same time as directly empowering faculty OER creation.

With practical expertise and dedicated programming on instructional design, educational technology, or grant management, faculty support offices allow an OER initiative to provide more, better, and faster support than a library could offer on its own. At both K-State and GVSU, faculty support specialists regularly help faculty develop online courses, create digital learning materials, or work with learning management systems. This assistance generates excellent opportunities to highlight the benefits of OER, encourage open licenses on faculty-created materials, and inspire faculty exploration of OER-enabled practices.

Faculty support offices can both amplify OER awareness efforts and directly assist faculty OER engagement through existing resources or services, especially if you have successfully framed OER as an aspect of effective teaching, innovative scholarship, or other priorities. With high demand on these offices, it is important to locate their strategic priorities and tie OER into those areas.

Administration and Foundation

Senior administration and foundation offices can be challenging and sometimes intimidating to approach, but are exceptionally valuable partners in an OER initiative. Presidents' and provosts' offices represent both prestige and direct financial resources, while a foundation, alumni center, development office, or other fundraising arm could be a conduit to external funding and influential community members. Compared to other stakeholders in this chapter, administration and foundation offices are less likely to be aware of OER and will have substantially more high-profile demands on their time and resources. Persistent engagement and ongoing education are essential early steps: take the time to invite these leaders to OER events or activities and share great things happening in OER both locally and nationally. Universities have also employed the competitive spirit of showing off regional rivals' figures and highlights to entice their leaders to act. The height of the football season, or whichever sport is popular on campus, may be a great time to send this communication.

K-State received minimal support from these areas for the first year or two, but once we were able to engage the leaders in OER, show the local return on investment, and provide evidence of the strong student and faculty support, they were easily brought on board. In fact, the previous president of K-State, Kirk Schultz, participated in marketing, fully supported the open/alternative student fee, and brought our initiative to his new university. Which brings us to the point that, like students and faculty partners, administrative partners will also have turnover and it is important to actively engage with each new member. The major hook for getting these players on board is the ability to market the vast student savings with communications and marketing promotions. K-State's Foundation Office interest was piqued after seeing donor reactions to the initiative. Administration at K-State has provided substantial funding to the OER initiative since the first year, and now actively seeks new donors to K-State's Open/Alternative Textbook Initiative.

Although difficult to engage at first, administration at your institution can bring a high-level spotlight on your initiative. This light will make your efforts visible to a wider audience. Use this wisely and you can increase your impact even further.

Campus Bookstores

"But what about the bookstore?" It's a common question in OER conversations, and an understandable one. Free online textbooks can seem like a direct threat to the business of bookstores, but bookstores—whether independent, university-owned, or vendor-managed—can be beneficial stakeholders for an OER initiative. Depending on your context and the bookstore's willingness to engage, you may seek to enlist the bookstore as an active partner, soothe concerns from the bookstore or their stakeholders, or simply keep the bookstore's staff informed and in the loop.

Strategies that work for enlisting other campus partners are effective at engaging the bookstore, too. For GVSU's university-run bookstore, involvement with OER is a way to advance the university's student-centric mission and values. For externally-run bookstores, meanwhile, OER engagement can be an opportunity to generate goodwill with students or with the vendor's contractual partners at the institution. At UMass Amherst, the transition to Amazon as the campus bookstore in 2016 gave the library an opportunity to push for the surfacing of OER content and to receive valuable data on assigned class materials. This was mostly due to the library having representation on the team that selected Amazon as the new campus vendor.

OER can also generate new sales opportunities: a GVSU bookstore manager noted that if they sold fewer textbooks, they'd have more space for technology and for university-branded merchandise (both of these sales opportunities offer higher profit margins than the competitive textbook market that is currently taking up this space). A bookstore may remain able to sell physical OER materials, from the traditionally published OpenStax print textbooks to print shop or print-on-demand copies of OER (depending on the licensing). In 2016–17, GVSU's bookstore sold physical books to more than 10 percent of students enrolled in a course that adopted an OpenStax book, even though the book was freely available online.

In many cases, recruiting a bookstore as an OER ally may be more challenging than other stakeholders. It is important to note that some bookstores' contracts with the college or university may have strict policies (in which case, you may want to target the institutional contract-holder as a potential OER ally). If a bookstore is expected to be a revenue source for the university or for student government, the store's financial concerns about OER could inspire concern from university or student leaders. This presents an opportunity to emphasize the financial benefits of OER to those leaders and explore alternative revenue sources to reduce dependence on textbook sales. A bookstore that is already facing difficulties with the evolving textbook market might see an OER initiative as the most immediate, visible cause of their financial trouble: a formerly independent bookstore for K-State knew online competition had hurt sales, but also blamed the university's OER projects for financial difficulties. Early and ongoing outreach to the bookstore and its own stakeholders can be helpful in identifying obstacles like these and deciding how—or whether—to address them. In some cases, the best approach may simply be sharing information in good faith and keeping a door open for bookstore engagement while you focus on other partners. Ideally, however, the bookstore will benefit from engaging at some level with an OER program, even if that engagement is preparing for a future with decreased textbook sales.

Bookstores' relationships with students and faculty are valuable assets for their business that can similarly benefit an OER program. Whether independent, institution-run, or vendor-managed, bookstores communicate regularly with faculty to explore options for course materials and liaise with publishers or vendors. These relationships are an opportunity to present OER as one of many options for course materials and to connect faculty with other OER support at their point of need. By facilitating the adoption of an OpenStax textbook for the chemistry department, GVSU's bookstore strengthened their relationship with the department while simultaneously enabling an OER adoption that affected more than 1,700 students in the 2016–17 academic year. Some bookstores are becoming active partners in OER: bookstore management company Follet recently launched a collaboration with OER service vendor Lumen Learning (Follet, 2017), and while Follet and Lumen benefit from new revenue streams, institutions with Follet bookstores will benefit from new resources to support faculty OER adoptions. Bookstores have similarly high-value connections to students, which can help raise the profile of OER and the faculty who have adopted OER.

A bookstore's network of relationships and role as a hub of textbook activity also makes them an unparalleled source of data on course material use and practices. The data they collect in the course of normal operations—faculty selecting materials to assign or deciding not to require any texts, student purchasing behaviors, specific cost data—could be a treasure trove for an OER initiative. GVSU's OER program is beginning to explore the potential of bookstore data for both outreach opportunities and for more accurately estimating the monetary impact of OER adoptions. UMass Amherst is using data from Amazon to begin an experimental textbook affordability program in the Acquisitions and Reserves departments.

After reading this, you are probably still wondering "But what about the bookstore?" Ultimately, that's a question only you can answer for your own institutional context, but in many cases advocating for OER may not prevent a rewarding collaboration with the campus stakeholder who sells textbooks. There are advantages that can be gained on both sides when this partnership is successful. Begin with information sharing and see where this partner is willing to go from there.

External Partners

For the purposes of this chapter, we define external partners as anyone outside of the college or university governance structure and alumni community. Many of these we briefly describe below are library-centric and some may require a fee for different levels of participation. However, we encourage you to look for OER partners in any institutional connection, whether or not they currently have an OER focus or library relationship. Your community and institutional context undoubtedly contains other distinctive organizations that could be valuable allies.

OER Communities

The professional and practice communities that have emerged around OER communities are usually pretty "open" and welcoming, so becoming a part of the community is rather easy. That being said, several of the communities do require a fee to participate in depth. Some of these communities still provide resources to the general public, but the "good stuff" is members-only or behind a sign-in. An OER community can be a valuable source of information, provide opportunities for partnership on OER or research, and offer colleagues to lean on with your challenges and celebrate your successes.

The Open Textbook Network (n.d.-a) is a nonprofit organization of libraries and universities supporting the use and creation of OER. This support includes the Open Textbook Library, a portal for finding high-quality OER with publicly posted reviews by faculty members, which is open to any and all users. Membership in the Open Textbook Network itself brings further benefits, including professional development events as well as resources for creating and remixing OER (n.d.-b). Membership in the Open Textbook Network offers outside legitimacy for OER efforts, valuable training to empower OER allies, and access to an engaged community of OER users and creators—benefits that have made the Open Textbook Network a worthwhile partner for OER programs at K-State and UMass Amherst.

OpenStax (n.d.-a), a nonprofit textbook publisher affiliated with Rice University, is an easy entry point into OER for many instructors, but also a potential partner for an OER initiative. Beyond their high-quality open textbooks and supporting resources, OpenStax (n.d.-b) offers a grant-supported institutional partnership program for institutions interested in rapidly expanding the use of OER on their campus. This program, open to new applicants annually, includes professional development, strategy guidance, and community support for OER adoption programs. Although the extensive OpenStax library often plays a central role in partners' efforts, the program supports adoption of any OER.

Scholarly, professional, and advocacy organizations, in addition to state and regional associations, have thriving networks of librarians and instructors engaged in OER practices. OER-focused sessions are increasingly common in conferences focused on academic libraries, educational technology, and instruction, not to mention the annual Open Education Conference. The events and communities facilitated by organizations like SPARC (the Scholarly Publishing and Academic Resources Coalition, https://sparcopen.org/), the Library Publishing Coalition (https://www.librarypublishing.org/), and the Association of College & Research Libraries (http://ala.org/acrl/) make these groups valuable as informal partners, allowing your OER initiative to connect to other communities of practice, share ideas and information, collaborate, and innovate.

Of particular note are community college organizations and associations, no matter your institution type. Community colleges are among the leading OER innovators, from the "Z-Degree" pioneered by Tidewater Community College (Wiley, Williams, DeMarte, & Hilton, 2016) to Washington State Board for Community and Technical Colleges' Open Washington initiative (2017), and can be an inspirational partner as you grow your OER program. On a regional level, GVSU's OER initiative benefits from connections with enthusiastic OER champions at Michigan community colleges who have organized public events and shared information resources focused on OER. The Community College Consortium for Open Educational Resources (CCCOER) is a national organization with a lively community of practice around OER (https://groups.google.com/forum/#!forum/cccoer-advisory) where participants can share their successes and failures and benefit from cross-institutional support.

Commercial OER Service Providers

A myriad of commercial services have emerged in response to increasing attention to OER at colleges and universities. Companies like Lumen Learning, PanOpen, bepress, and Pressbooks typically provide tools, expertise, or platforms that make it easier for instructors to adopt, use, and create OER. For example, Lumen Learning's suite of services includes assessment instruments, student learning aids, and course design support, while Pressbooks' open source publishing platform supports user-friendly book creation. These commercial partners can provide an OER initiative with immediate, scalable support for faculty instructors, thereby making OER adoption easier and more appealing.

The Digital Commons platform from bepress enabled GVSU's library to begin publishing faculty-created OER in 2012 with minimal additional staff time and money. However, this example highlights a potential problem with commercial partners, beyond the obvious cost consideration: bepress' acquisition by mega-publisher Elsevier in 2017 refreshed concerns among many institutions and organizations over the implications and consequences of scholarly infrastructures controlled by profit-driven organizations (Joseph & Shearer, 2017; Schonfeld, 2017).

Government Offices

Local and regional governments—and the members of the public whom they serve—are practical stakeholders and potentially transformative allies in an OER initiative. Arguments in favor of OER can appeal across the political spectrum, from innovative pedagogy and equitable access to knowledge, to college affordability and efficient use of taxpayer dollars (given Senack and Donoghue's 2016 estimate that every year, U.S. students spend $3 billion of government-subsidized financial aid on textbooks). In return, government partners might be a source of additional funding, can raise the profile and legitimacy of OER, and can influence the priorities of publicly funded colleges and universities.

The #GoOpen program developed by the U.S. Department of Education, and adopted by a growing number of state Departments of Education, focuses on OER in K–12 education (Leu, 2017). Even so, post-secondary OER programs can benefit from making connections with their state's #GoOpen project, building relationships with a broader educational community and sharing OER expertise. Institutions with teacher education programs can also use #GoOpen engagement as an entry point into conversations with the institution's education faculty. In the long run, K–12 OER adoptions may change students' and parents' expectations for post-secondary institutions, providing additional pressure in favor of OER.

Conclusion

Throughout this chapter, we have highlighted stakeholders with significant potential as allies in an OER program, based on experiences at GVSU, UMass Amherst, and K-State. Although in many cases our individual relationships with these partners formed organically or opportunistically, exploring these partnerships through the framework of motivations, challenges, and benefits is a useful model for any form of advocacy, as well as a template for building partnerships from scratch. Any goal is easier to achieve when the people and organizations involved are united by common ground, yet motivated to participate by their own reasons, values and priorities.

If you are involved in an OER program, your work with partners and potential allies will undoubtedly be different, dependent as each stakeholder is on your individual institution's context. Your institution's mission and goals, demographics, internal and external pressures, and the individual people who make up any organization create an environment that you can and should approach on its own terms.

As a result, it is natural that different OER initiatives will have different definitions of what makes a successful collaboration. Even in the three institutions represented in this article, the authors' OER programs have developed along unique paths with different goals. GVSU's OER partnerships mostly involve building awareness of OER across campus and keeping OER in the forefront of partners' existing services and conversations. Success in this collaboration has led to more workshops and professional development opportunities around OER, growing faculty interest in OER creation, and a network of supportive stakeholders potentially positioned to support new activities or resources for OER. At K-State, partners have made their program grow from a pilot OER grant project enabled by students and the libraries to collaborations with administrative offices to both expand the program and develop long-term funding from external donors. Those partnerships are continuing to generate high-impact collaborations with faculty OER creators and sustainable funding for new projects. And at UMass Amherst, successful collaboration has meant more funding, sharing the burden of promoting and supporting our OER program, and increased awareness across campus.

Regardless of what success means for your context and your program right now, a wide network of partners can help you achieve and advance beyond that success. OER initiatives can require a significant investment of time and resources, but they are a rare and exciting opportunity for stakeholders across an institution to collaborate on an issue because the collaboration benefits every stakeholder's own mission.

Hewlett Foundation President Larry Kramer (2015) wrote that, "'No brainers' are incredibly rare in education, where strongly held, widely disparate values all too often stymie potential reforms. Well, OER is a no brainer." We would argue that building partnerships for OER programs is an equal no brainer. An OER initiative may begin as a small collaboration with an individual faculty member or department. Undoubtedly, a well-resourced and focused library could develop and implement an entire program of OER advocacy and support on its own, if it wanted to devote the necessary resources. So too could many of the stakeholders we describe, and of course individual faculty have been creating and using OER since before OER was a common term. Maybe you can go it alone on an OER initiative, but since working with partners can help your initiative advance faster, reach farther, and be more efficient, why would you want to?

This chapter outlines several partners the authors have worked with and can be a starting point for potential collaborators for your OER initiative. Remember that each campus is unique; some partnerships work better on certain campuses, and even if you engaged a partner once and it was not successful, there may yet be an opportunity for successful collaboration in the future. Finding the partner's hook, incorporating their needs, and recognizing the value that they bring to the table will carry your OER partnership into the future and hopefully on to new programs too.

List of Partners

Internal (University/College/Campus)

Library Partners: Scholarly Communications Department, Academic Department Liaisons

Reference Staff: Library Administrators, Student Support, Library Development Office—Friends of the Library

Reserves Department

University Archives

Special Collections

Metadata and Acquisitions

Library Fiscal Staff

Faculty: Classroom Faculty, Research Faculty

Department Heads

Students: Student Government Association

Faculty Support Offices: Teaching and Learning Centers, Instructional Designer, IT

Educational Technology

Accessibility Services

Professional Development Programming

Internal and External Grant Fund Management

Administration & Foundation: President, Provost, Foundation

Alumni

Campus Bookstore

External

OER Communities

OER Commercial Services

References

Abelson, H. (2008). The creation of OpenCourseWare at MIT. *Journal of Science Education and Technology, 17*(2), 164–174. http://dx.doi.org/10.1007/s10956-007-9060-8

Allen, I. E. & Seaman, J. (2016). *Opening the textbook: Open educational resources in U.S. higher education, 2015–16.* Babson Survey Research Group. Retrieved from https://www.onlinelearningsurvey.com/reports/openingthetextbook2016.pdf

American Association of University Professors. (1940). *1940 statement of principles on academic freedom and tenure.* Retrieved from https://www.aaup.org/report/1940-statement-principles-academic-freedom-and-tenure

Anderson, R. (2017, May 1). When the wolf finally arrives: Big deal cancellations in North American libraries [Blog post]. Retrieved from https://scholarlykitchen.sspnet.org/2017/05/01/ wolf-finally-arrives-big-deal-cancelations-north-american-libraries/

Atkins, D. E., Brown, J. S., & Hammond, A. L. (2007). *A review of the open educational resources (OER) movement: Achievements, challenges, and new opportunities* (pp. 1–84). Retreived from William and Flora Hewlett Foundation website: https://hewlett.org/wp-content/uploads/2016/08/ReviewoftheOERMovement.pdf

Florida Virtual Campus. (2016). *2016 student textbook and course materials survey.* Retrieved from https://florida.theorangegrove.org/og/items/ 3a65c507-2510-42d7-814c-ffdefd394b6c/1/

Follett. (2017). Follett and Lumen Learning to expand adoption of OER courseware. Retrieved from https://follett.com/lumen/

Gallant, J. (2015). Librarians transforming textbooks: The past, present, and future of the Affordable Learning Georgia Initiative. *Georgia Library Quarterly, 52*(2), 8.

Goodsett, M., Loomis, B., & Miles, M. (2016). Leading campus OER initiatives through library–faculty collaboration. *College & Undergraduate Libraries, 23*(3), 335–342. http://dx.doi.org/10.1080/10691316.2016.1206328

Green, K. (2016). Going digital: Faculty perspectives on digital and OER course materials. Retrieved from https://campuscomputing.net/goingdigital2016

Herbert, B. (2016). Texas A&M Student Government OER Teaching Awards. Retrieved from http://hdl.handle.net/1969.1/156092

Hilton, J., III. (2016). Open educational resources and college textbook choices: A review of research on efficacy and perceptions. *Educational Technology Research Development, 64*(4), 573–590. http://dx.doi.org/10.1007/s11423-016-9434-9

Joseph, H. & Shearer, K. (2017, September 6). Elsevier acquisition highlights the need for community-based scholarly communication infrastructure [Blog post]. Retrieved from https://sparcopen.org/news/2017/ elsevier-acquisition-highlights-the-need-for-community-based-scholarly-communication-infras

Kleymeer, P., Kleinman, M., & Hanss, T. (2010, November). *Reaching the heart of the university: Libraries and the future of OER.* Paper presented at the Open Education 2010 Conference, Barcelona, Spain. Retrieved from http://hdl.handle.net/2027.42/ 78006

Kramer, L. (2015, December 9). Sharing the benefits of open educational resources with everyone [Blog post]. Retrieved from https://hewlett.org/ sharing-the-benefits-of-open-educational-resources-with-everyone/

K-State Today. (2015). *Hurtig, Tinker new Kansas State University Student Governing Association leaders.* Retrieved from http://www.k-state.edu/media/newsreleases/ mar15/sgaelections3615.html

Lammers, E. & Tyton Partners. (2017). *Time for class 2017.* Retrieved from http://tytonpartners.com/library/time-class-2017-2/

Leu, S. (2017, May 10) #GoOpen: More than a hashtag [Blog post]. Retrieved from https://medium.com/@OfficeofEdTech/ goopen-more-than-a-hashtag-293357a550f1

Okamoto, K. (2013). Making higher education more affordable, one course reading at a time: Academic libraries as key advocates for open access textbooks and educational resources. *Public Services Quarterly, 9*(4), 267–283.

Open Textbook Network. (n.d. -a). About us. Retrieved from https://research.cehd.umn.edu/otn/about-us

Open Textbook Network. (n.d. -b). Impact and benefits. Retrieved from https://research.cehd.umn.edu/otn/impact-and-benefits/

OpenStax. (n.d. -a). FAQ. Retrieved from https://openstax.org/faq

OpenStax. (n.d. -b). OpenStax institutional partnership program. Retrieved from https://openstax.org/blog/openstax-institutional-partnership-program

Salem, J. A. (2017). Open pathways to student success: Academic library partnerships for open educational resource and affordable course content creation and adoption. *Journal of Academic Librarianship, 43*(1), 34–38. https://doi.org/10.1016/j.acalib.2016.10.003

Santos-Hermosa, G. (2012). *Faculty-librarians collaboration in an e-learning experience: resources management and training in Open University of Catalonia (UOC).* Retrieved from http://hdl.handle.net/10609/18482

Schonfeld, R. (2017, August 7). Reflections on "Elsevier Acquires bepress" [Blog post]. Retrieved from http://www.sr.ithaka.org/blog/reflections-on-elsevier-acquires-bepress/

Senack, E., & Donoghue, R. (2016). *Covering the cost: why we can no longer afford to ignore high textbook prices.* Retrieved from https://studentpirgs.org/reports/sp/covering-cost

Student Government Resource Center. (2014, February 18). #TextbookBroke: Campaign for affordable textbooks [Blog post]. Retrieved from http://studentgovresources.org/textbookbroke-campaign-for-affordable-textbooks/

Sutton, S., & Chadwell, F. (2014). Open textbooks at Oregon State University: A case study of new opportunities for academic libraries and university presses. *Journal of Librarianship and Scholarly Communication, 2*(4). http://doi.org/10.7710/2162-3309.1174

U.S. Department of Education. (2017). Open licensing requirement for competitive grant programs; Rule. Federal Register (82), 7376-7397. https://www.federalregister.gov/d/2017-00910

Washington State Board for Community and Technical Colleges. (2017). Open Washington open educational resources network. Retrieved from http://www.openwa.org/

Wesolek, A., Thomas, W., Dresselhaus, A., Fielding, J., Simser, C., Sutton, S., ... & Appleton, B. (2017). NASIG Core Competencies for Scholarly Communication Librarians. Retrieved from http://www.nasig.org/site_page.cfm?pk_association_webpage_menu=310&pk_association_webpage=9435

Wiley, D. (2013, October 21). What is open pedagogy? [Blog post]. Retrieved from https://opencontent.org/blog/archives/2975

Wiley, D., Williams, L., DeMarte, D., & Hilton, J., III. (2016). The Tidewater Z-Degree and the INTRO model for sustaining OER adoption. *Education Policy Analysis Archives, 24*(41). http://dx.doi.org/10.14507/epaa.24.1828

Woodward, K. M. (2017). Building a path to college success: Advocacy, discovery and OER adoption in emerging educational models. *Journal of Library & Information Services in Distance Learning, 11*(1/2), 206–212. http://dx.doi.org/10.1080/1533290X.2016.1232053

Yano, B. (2017). *Connect OER Annual Report, 2016–2017.* Washington, DC: SPARC. Retrieved from https://sparcopen.org/our-work/connect-oer/reports

Getting to Know You: How We Turned Community Knowledge into Open Advocacy

Lillian Rigling & William Cross

Introduction

Textbook affordability has been a priority for the North Carolina State University (NCSU) Libraries for the better part of the past decade. As a large public land-grant institution, NCSU has a deep commitment to welcoming all students, particularly first-generation students and those from underrepresented populations. As a science, technology, engineering, and math (STEM)-focused institution, NCSU must balance this commitment against the high cost of STEM textbooks, which are often significantly more expensive than textbooks for humanities courses. As the space on campus where students, faculty, the campus bookstore, and others can meet to work collaboratively, the Libraries have a unique opportunity to meet our own stated mission to be the "competitive advantage" for students working to navigate this challenging textbook marketplace. This chapter details our efforts to not only encourage the use of open educational resources on our campus, but also to understand how our students were navigating the information marketplace, and to educate and empower our students to leverage the rise of open culture into meaningful and sustainable support for open education.

Library Support for Textbook Affordability

Our initial efforts date back to a 2009 student-led proposal submitted to our University Library Committee, which led the NCSU Libraries to pilot a textbook lending program. In partnership with the NCSU Bookstores, the Libraries committed to purchasing at least one copy of every required textbook for fall and spring semester classes and made them available to students for a short-term loan. This program ensures that any student who does not have the funds to purchase a textbook can have access to the textbook through the Libraries. In the first year of the program, the Libraries purchased approximately 1,200 textbooks to seed the collection, and after the success of the pilot, we have continued to purchase around 700 textbooks each year. Textbooks are added to a "Textbook Collection" in our integrated library system (ILS) and interfiled with our traditional course reserves, available for a two-hour checkout in each library (Thompson, Cross, Rigling, & Vickery, 2017).

Our textbook lending program is designed to address an immediate burden of the cost of textbooks and learning materials on our students, but we also have taken steps to address the culture of faculty and departments assigning expensive textbooks to students by initiating library collaborations with faculty, students, and external partners to provide free or lower cost alternatives to traditional textbooks. In 2010, the Libraries partnered with the NCSU Physics Department to license a physics textbook used for all introductory physics courses. The Libraries paid a one-time licensing fee of approximately $1,500 to the publisher to allow all NCSU students to have free access to an electronic version of this textbook and any future editions through the library catalog (Laster, 2010; Rashke & Shanks, 2012). The impact of this program on our students did not go unnoticed by our students, faculty, and the media. Nearly 1,300 students take a physics course which requires this textbook each year, saving students nearly $90,000 in textbook costs annually.

The success of this open physics textbook laid the groundwork for the Libraries to continue to address the financial burden of buying textbooks through collaborating with faculty to seed innovation. In 2013, NCSU Libraries received a grant from The NC State University Foundation to develop our Alt-Textbook project. This program was inspired by similar programs hosted in the Temple University Libraries and University of Massachusetts at Amherst Libraries. Like these programs, NCSU's Alt-Textbook project provides small grants of between $500 and $2,000 to individual instructors who are willing to replace an existing commercial textbook with an openly licensed or freely available resource. This program solicited proposals from instructors who were interested in developing a new resource, remixing existing resources, or following the open physics textbook model to license a copyrighted resource. A review team comprised of librarians and other campus stakeholders, including a student, a faculty member, representatives from the university Distance Education and Learning Technology Applications office, and a representative from the university Office of Faculty Development, voted on applications and awarded nine grants. This project received press nationally in publications such as *Library Journal*, and locally, including articles in NC State's student-run newspaper, *The Technician*. After the first round of Alt-Textbook grants, our student senate passed a bill stating their support of this program and expressing gratitude to the Libraries.

After the first year, the Alt-Textbook project received internal funding from the NCSU Libraries. Over the course of three years, the Alt-Textbook project has successfully converted 20 courses to using open or free educational resources in place of costly textbooks. NCSU Libraries estimates, based on course enrollment and the cost of the replaced commercial textbooks, that the Alt-Textbook project has saved students nearly $300,000 in textbook costs. This program encouraged the adoption of pre-existing open resources, and sought to engage students in the creation of open resources. These resources have explored innovative instruction such as student made-videos, 3D scan files and renderings, remixed popular articles, interactive tutorials, and iterative courses developed through versioning tools like GitHub. These learning materials are not just free to use, but have added value that is not provided by a print resource.[1]

As the footprint of Alt-Textbook grew, the Alt-Textbook team of librarians' contact with students did not always follow suit. This faculty-facing grant program didn't have obvious opportunities for students to engage. Librarians involved in the Alt-Textbook project focused their advocacy efforts for open textbooks on individual faculty members, departments, and faculty-facing offices or groups on campus. Yet students were an important driving force behind our commitment to textbook affordability. The cost of textbooks affects our students above all, and students have the potential to be the loudest and most persuasive voice

---

[1] See https://www.lib.ncsu.edu/alttextbook/projects for existing Alt-Textbook projects.

in a move towards open education on campus. This chapter discusses the strategies and tactics we took to re-engage our students and empower them to become advocates for open education on campus and beyond.

Getting to Know our Student Community

In order to build connections with our students around open education and open culture, we focused on two approaches: researching the needs of our students through analysis of textbook usage and communication on social media, and interacting with them directly, through existing student groups and with one-on-one conversations. By combining direct engagement with a deeper understanding of student needs, the Libraries have been able to develop partnerships that improved educational outcomes for students.

One of the first steps for our engagement was for us to develop a deeper understanding of student needs and practices related to the assigned learning materials in their courses. Because we could rely on existing research done at the national level related to the financial burden of textbooks, we began our research with a focus on textbook affordability at NCSU. To do this, we analyzed student use of two campus resources: the Libraries textbook lending program and online communities devoted to informal textbook exchange and information sharing. Significant work has been done by groups such as the Student Public Interest Research Group (PIRG) on the needs and practices of students at the national level, but information about the needs of NCSU's students was limited, and we needed to design engagement activities that would be meaningful and effective at the campus level.

Our textbook lending program has been a significant boon for our students. Because it has been so heavily used, data gathered from the program provided important insights into the needs it was meeting. By tracking student use of the program and cross-referencing it with data from the university bookstore about course size and textbook cost, we were able to use it to identify a large set of granular data that informed our broader understanding of student needs and behaviors (Thompson et al., 2017). This research revealed clear areas where students were relying heavily on textbook lending, either to replace an expensive textbook or to provide access to a book that was physically unavailable or inconvenient to use on campus. Although these areas crossed disciplines and instructors, a clear set of especially high-enrollment courses with expensive assigned textbooks emerged that delineated pain points for students. These specific courses—often, but not always introductory level—clustered around a few discrete areas of study are clearly putting significant financial pressure on our students. By identifying these courses, this research helped us map courses, majors, and communities that were struggling with textbooks and gave us the information to speak credibly about student needs.

This information dovetailed with our second area of research: analysis of informal textbook exchange and information sharing that we have called "student survivalism." In order to better understand students' use of informal channels such as social media to share information about courses and develop gray markets for buying and selling used materials, we harvested data representing student activity on an institution-specific Facebook group. We posted a question to an institutional-specific subreddit, and a local online forum, requesting guidance for a new student navigating these issues (Thompson et al., 2017).

This research revealed an impressive community of students engaged in social commerce at NCSU. Students have developed robust markets for buying and selling not only textbooks, but also supplemental materials, from classroom "clickers" and lab kits to forestry vests and handball equipment. Students also use these markets for exchanging materials such as parking passes, loft beds for a dorm room, and, in one case, a bald cap.

In particular, students are using these exchanges to mitigate not only the costs of textbooks, but also to mitigate the challenges created by digital materials that require access codes, which allow access to course materials but which often expire after a single use or remain tied to a single user. In some cases, access code materials were shared in this gray market. Students also used these spaces for information sharing about assigned materials, asking whether they "really need to buy" an expensive textbook or set of materials. This exchange often went further, with discussions about whether a particular instructor was an engaging speaker, whether an elective course was worth enrolling in, and how to navigate their academic career.

Taken together, this research on student survivalism revealed important trends about student needs around the cost of textbooks, but also provided insight into students' lives on campus. We discovered new things about the way informal channels developed communities of students that offered support and guidance for one another.

The result of all of this research confirmed our sense that students' engagement with issues of access to resources goes far beyond concerns about open education and the costs of textbooks. Our research reaffirmed that physical, commercial textbooks pose logistical and pedagogical challenges for students. At the same time, student consideration of the value of educational materials goes far beyond the financial costs, leading to questions about how a text fits into a course and whether instructors are thoughtful about their assigned texts. These communities for unmoderated discussion are valuable for students in a variety of ways and point to the potential value of open culture for other aspects of student life. We know students are also creators of scholarly and popular content that benefits from openness. They value communities that connect them to new collaborators and allow them to share their work.

To understand the different ways that open culture resonates with students, we reached out to students directly to understand their perspective and to begin to share the work we had been doing. As the environment of students' lives and academic work came into view, these conversations illuminated our shared aims: making student work openly available, creating open spaces, and promoting open culture to facilitate collaboration, discovery, and community. These conversations also began to suggest opportunities to work together to meet these aims.

Our first formal work in this space was a series of pop-up interviews done as part of our Open Access Week programming. Held in October 2016, our Open Access Week events included exhibits of open source art, training on use of open scholarly tools, and our "Power of Open" events that connected work in the makerspace with open licensing. Along with these events, we set up a small kiosk in our main library and asked students about their experience with open culture.

Open Access Week Pop-ups

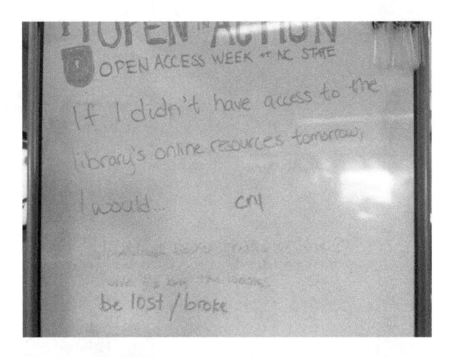

Open Access Week Pop-ups

Using a set of simple prompts such as "what percentage of the materials in the library will be available after you graduate?" or "what would you do if you didn't have access to the library's databases tomorrow?" we asked students about their information privilege and their experiences with open materials and open culture. As an incentive, we provided candy.

Over the course of the week we spoke to roughly 300 students from across multiple departments and classes. These conversations revealed student interest in open culture on a variety of fronts. Unsurprisingly, many students had little or no awareness of open culture. Since they were unlikely to be familiar with traditional points of references such as open access, students often had, at most, a colloquial understanding of open as "free." The idea that databases may not be available after graduation took some by surprise. One student, when asked to estimate how much the Libraries paid for a journal subscription guessed "$50." Responding to questions about how they would cope if licensed resources were suddenly unavailable, students suggested they would "be totally lost" or "cry." Some students did suggest student survivalism strategies similar to those we examined in our research, such as the student who wrote that they could always "download books illegally online."

Some students did have familiarity with certain aspects of open culture. For example, students engaged with computer science identified a strong commitment to open source licensing for software. Many students were also familiar with openly licensed resources such as Creative Commons or with gray market sites such as torrents. In many cases, however, this awareness was connected to the idea of free resources, rather than the more robust "5R" understanding of open that librarians and open culture advocates are dedicated to.

The other major takeaway from these pop-up sessions was that there was a desire to learn more and to develop a community. Although students may have been surprised to discover that licensed databases would not be available once they graduated, they wanted to do something about the issue. Naturally, reducing the cost of textbooks resonated particularly deeply, but larger discussions about issues such as public access to scholarship and global access inequity also animated lively discussion. More often than not, students left the pop-up sessions energized about the issues and more aware of the Libraries' role in addressing them.

We had a similar experience when we reached out to individual students through other contexts. We had productive and exciting discussions with several of our student workers, who often had a better understanding of library resources but still had much to learn about open culture. Conversations with student workers confirmed many of the ideas we identified in pop-up sessions: open was often conflated with "free." Student workers also confirmed that many students did not understand how open practice was a meaningful advantage for students, especially those who were not planning to become scholars.

As in the pop-ups, however, students were enthusiastic about issues of access and quickly connected them with the value of open as a way to develop communities of practice. Conversations about open access publishing often seemed abstract to these students, but sharing work to develop a portfolio for potential collaborators or employers made sense in a very concrete way. Students were clear that library engagement with open would need to spell out how open culture could make their lives better by finding a job, completing coursework, or identifying new collaborators with shared or complementary interests.

The final group we reached out to was student leaders. The responses from student government representatives and students on campus committees shared many similarities with their fellow students. Knowledge of open culture beyond free resources was scattered across campus and generally tied to the majors or organizations they were engaged with on campus. Even more than their counterparts however, these leaders were enthusiastic about tackling these issues once they understood them. In a few cases, student groups had partnered with the Libraries on small efforts in the past. We were pleasantly surprised to discover that the student senate had passed a resolution commending our Alt-Textbook project several years earlier, although we were a bit puzzled that we had never been made aware of the commendation.

Without exception, committee members were happy to spread the word about Libraries programs. Members of student government immediately pledged to use their offices to help their fellow students and their next question was often "how can we help?" Our job was to find an answer to that question.

Turning Knowledge into Outreach

Armed with a new understanding of how our students understand and approach both textbook affordability and information access, we were ready to find meaningful places to intervene with information about open culture. Our approach centered largely on the idea that, if students could understand the value of openness in the work that they create or are interested in, they could apply this concept to their course materials and become great advocates for open education. This process, which we call "stealth advocacy," involved identifying pre-existing Libraries or on-campus services that could be enhanced by a conversation about ownership and openness and approaching this service to build a partnership. As a library with an active makerspace community that regularly engages with open source software, open hardware, and openly licensed materials, we chose to integrate this content into pre-existing makerspace instruction.

This partnership began as an effort to create local programming for *International Open Access Week 2016: Open for Collaboration*. We redesigned the curriculum for the existing Arduino and 3D printing workshops for a mini workshop series we called *Power of Open*. We chose these workshops because existing curriculum required students to engage with open hardware, open source software, and openly licensed materials. The content was designed in a partnership between librarians with tool expertise from the NCSU Libraries' makerspace and librarians from the NCSU Libraries' Copyright and Digital Scholarship Center with deep knowledge of copyright, licensing, and the scholarly life cycle. These workshops began with a primer on ownership and licensing, and then delved deeply into hands-on tool training. We taught students how their individual making activity is shaped by a larger community of makers who use open tools and open licensing to enable sharing and community-building and mitigate or eliminate barriers to access.

Power of Open

The *Power of Open* miniseries drew an engaged audience of faculty, staff, graduate students, and undergraduate students. The feedback was overwhelmingly positive; participants filled out anonymous feedback forms after the session where they were asked to rate the session on a scale of 1 (poor) to 5 (excellent) and all reported the session as a 4 or a 5. Additionally, Harris Kenny, the Vice President of Marketing at Aleph Objects, Inc.

maker of the LulzBot desktop 3D printers we used in our workshop, attended the *Power of Open: Introduction to 3D Printing and Design* workshop. In a letter he wrote about his experience he said, "It is impressive that Lauren and Lillian's workshop taught foundational lessons about free licensing, copyright, and operating a 3D printer, while providing hands-on experience. The workshop also showed what makes makerspaces so special: bringing the community together."

After the success of the *Power of Open* miniseries and the feedback from Harris Kenny, it was clear that this content had the potential to be core to our students' learning experience. We redesigned the workshops to include content about copyright, licensing, and sharing throughout, and offered them as introductory Arduino and 3D Printing and Design workshops. The new curriculum integrated hands-on activities with the Arduino kits or LulzBot Mini 3D Printers into instruction on open licensing in the making community. For example, in the 3D Printing and Design workshops, after a basic primer on Creative Commons licensing, students were asked to download a CC-licensed remixable file from Thingiverse—a digital repository of files for laser cutting or 3D printing. They then worked with this openly licensed file to remix and print the file. Finally, we discussed what their rights to the remixed file were, and how they might upload or share their altered file or their original design to Thingiverse or a similar repository of openly licensed files. We continued to receive positive feedback on these workshops through our anonymous feedback forms, and many students responded to the question "What was the most useful thing you learned in today's session?" with a reference to the licensing section of the curriculum. One student even responded, "Copyright - refreshing topic!"

We have continued to take this stealth advocacy approach for the value of open with other workshops offered through the library. In spring 2017, we piloted a workshop for our digital media lab titled "Making Music: Uncovering Copyright." This workshop was a collaborative effort between NCSU Libraries' Copyright and Digital Scholarship Center, and the Digital Media Librarian from NCSU Libraries' Learning Spaces and Services Department. This workshop not only taught students about ownership and licensing in music through hands-on beatmaking and sampling activities, but also pointed students to sources for openly licensed music files, like ccMixter, and platforms which allowed students to upload and openly license their own creations, like SoundCloud. In both of these workshop series, students reported feeling more informed about ownership, and, in multiple cases, feedback forms specifically indicated that students felt the most valuable topic covered was Creative Commons and open licensing. We continue to identify partners with existing information literacy programming where we can find a way to talk about openness to continue to build a community of engaged students that care about open.

We also took a straightforward approach to educating our students about open. In an attempt to connect with motivated students across multiple disciplines and departments, we hosted a full-day student-oriented conference on open culture and open creation. With the support of the Scholarly Publishing and Academic Resources Coalition (SPARC) and the Right to Research Coalition (R2RC) we applied to host an Open-Con Satellite Event—a local meeting that leverages the momentum of the international OpenCon meeting, designed with the mission of "Empowering the Next Generation to Advance Open Access, Open Education and Open Data." We hosted this event as part of Open Education Week 2017.

We used the information we had learned through our informational interviews and other information-gathering to design programming that we felt would attract a wide array of students. In addition to bringing in speakers from various library departments, including Collections and Research Strategy, Digital Library Initiatives, and the Copyright and Digital Scholarship Center, we brought in a local open advocate, Tom Callaway. In Tom's work as the University Outreach Lead for Red Hat, he works to help students and educators understand, use, and contribute to open source efforts. We consulted with the NCSU Center for Student Leadership, Ethics, and Public Service on the design and promotion of the event.

The event was marketed as an opportunity to gain valuable skills for careers in and outside of academia that hinged on openness and leadership. We incentivized students to attend by providing the opportunity for students to create personal web pages and have headshots taken throughout the day. *OpenCon 2017: North Carolina Student Leaders* saw deep engagement with a group of undergraduate and graduate students from the sciences, social sciences, and humanities to explain the power of openness and open licensing in retaining control of their early work while simultaneously engaging with a broader community of scholars and practitioners. Throughout the day, students engaged with various facets of openness through hands-on tool-based sessions, workshops, and talks with established open advocates. Students received a brief introduction to the concept of openness and how it applies to concepts like education, data, and scholarship. Next, students attended a brief how-to session on openly licensing their own work or identifying and using openly licensed works. Students then had the opportunity to make their own online portfolio using GitHub Pages where they can host a résumé or student work.

Students also had the opportunity to meet Tom Callaway, who has made a career working with open tools and openly licensing his own work. In his keynote address, he told his own story of working on open source and openly licensed projects in his early career and the doors that it opened for him. He also discussed how he values visibility and openness of a candidate's work when hiring new professionals. Finally, students participated in advocacy training, where they learned how to demonstrate the value of open to key stakeholders, including employers, professors, or administrators. They had the opportunity to practice not only advocating for open, but also explaining why open was important to each student as an individual and as a community member, in small groups. This experience gave students the confidence to speak to those in positions of authority about the importance of openness.

Finally, we reached out to our student senate, the same group that had previously issued a statement in support of Alt-Textbook, about helping us inform students about the services the Copyright & Digital Scholarship Center at the NCSU Libraries could offer. We were able to engage with their President-elect. After a frank conversation with him about the success of Alt-Textbook, the textbook lending program, and the other open programming the libraries supported, we offered our support in any way possible. We invited him to attend *OpenCon 2017: North Carolina Student Leaders,* and followed up with him specifically about his experience. Our student government has the potential to be the most persuasive body on campus to advocate for open education, and we were willing and eager work with and support students in any way possible. We were invited to the inaugural meeting of the student senate for the 2017–18 academic year and allotted 15 minutes for a presentation.

We led our student senators in a discussion about textbook affordability, prompting them with questions about the cost of their textbooks such as "What is the most expensive textbook you have ever purchased?" and "How many of you have not purchased an assigned textbook? Can you tell us why?" We devoted most of our presentation time to fielding questions, positioning the Libraries as a partner and support on campus, rather than presenting Alt-Textbook as a service offered by the Libraries. It was important that we opened the floor to feedback on our existing services in order to provide room to create a partnership. We spoke candidly to the students about our previous information-gathering conversations as well as the data we had collected about the cost of textbooks on campus. Personalizing and contextualizing the conversation about open education to NCSU's campus allowed the student senate to connect with the issue.

Shall We Dance? Funneling from "Open" to "OER"

By the summer of 2017, we had developed a two-way relationship between the Libraries and students at NCSU. The Alt-Textbook project is well known, with stories in our student newspaper and student engagement at the individual and student government level. Open is also understood as an integral part of student work in and beyond the classroom. Where there had been so little communication that library resources were unrecognized and a student senate resolution of support went unreported, there was now fertile ground for collaboration.

One of the major results of this new relationship is a fundamental change to our OER program. In its initial form, the Alt-Textbook project was focused primarily on transformative pedagogy, inviting faculty instructors to "do something a textbook can't!" In collaboration with students, we are reconfiguring the project to reflect the two aims of our work. Instead of asking every project to both save students money and create innovative instruction, we have split our grants into two complementary programs.

Grounded in our discussion with students about immediate, concrete impacts, we offer Student Success grants that save students money. These can be simple adoption of an OER, use of licensed library resources, or any other approach that reduces the burden on students in the current semester.

In order to connect students with the power of open in the larger "5R" sense, we also offer open pedagogy grants that transform teaching and learning. These courses, which replace static, one-size-fits-all materials with shared learning, sustain our efforts to make open a tool to change the environment in the long term. An early partnership with the Wiki Education Foundation provides a promising prototype for these projects. Replacing disposable research assignments that end up in the trash can with research products that contribute to Wikipedia has energized both students and faculty (Jhangiani, 2016; Wiley, 2013). By raising the level of understanding about open culture as a transformative force, we know our students are better prepared to engage with these courses.

In addition to changing the program itself, we have begun to develop strategies that empower students to drive change in open education more broadly. One of our priorities will be to help students tell their stories. We are proud of the advocacy work we have done with faculty and administration, but we recognize that students have a unique perspective that can be a powerful force for change. By raising their awareness of the potential of open culture, we have already seen students make more sophisticated and impactful arguments about open education. Now our role is to amplify those voices and connect them to decision-makers on campus and beyond.

Connecting student voices to faculty is a clear first step. Many faculty are unaware of the burden placed on students by commercial textbooks, and too many more choose to prioritize convenience or even personal financial gain over student success. In the Libraries we have heard and been moved by students' stories and we aim to give faculty the same chance to hear and react. This is especially true at the departmental level, where engagement with a single faculty member may not be able to change textbook assignments in adjunct-led introductory classes. No amount of faculty outreach can solve this problem, but connecting students in a department with that department's administration can make a difference.

Student voices can have significant impact on other campus stakeholders such as our campus bookstore. We are fortunate to have a store that is genuinely dedicated to student success and has been a willing partner in our efforts around open education. Nevertheless, decisions made without student input can seem appealing but miss crucial effects that students are best positioned to notice. For example, the recent trend of adopting "inclusive access" models where all students pay a course fee that provides access to course materials may be appealing to a bookstore dazzled by potential savings and the promise of 100 percent sell-through. Our students, however, are often suspicious of the inclusive access model, which they fear will lock them out of long-term access and the ability to avail themselves of the student survivalism skills discussed above. By connecting our students with the bookstore, these concerns can be raised directly so the bookstore is better able to meet its mission and students can be assured their concerns are heard.

We are also committed to giving our students the ability to share their stories beyond campus. Our own advocacy has been strengthened immeasurably by stories from students at other campuses and we need to add our students' voices to the national conversation. This is particularly true since students benefit so much from hearing from their peers on issues of openness. Trumpeting their success can be an inspiration for students at other campuses. Just as significantly, the quiet communities engaged in student survivalism on individual campuses will be strengthened when connected to a national and global community.

In addition to broadcasting the voices of our students, the Libraries are committed to giving students' voices greater impact on campus. As frustrating as it was to engage and energize students in our initial pop-ups, only to leave them with nothing to do with that energy, we must provide actionable steps for individual students and the student groups such as student government that want to make a difference. Early efforts in this area have included discussion with student government about naming a student-voted Faculty Champion. We are working to meet stated student demands for early access to course syllabi, as required by the Federal Higher Education Opportunity Act 2008, so they know more about individual courses before they register. If this is successful, we would like to have our course listings indicate which courses have adopted free and open materials so students can vote with their feet. This approach, which empowers students to use their market power to address the imbalance in the textbook market, is especially appealing because it is student- rather than library-driven.

Finally, we are excited about building on our shared commitment to open culture to empower students in other areas. Partnerships with student journals that are published open access and student groups that use open source code for projects have built openness into student lives in ways that are meaningful for them, not just assigned by an instructor or administrator. Engagement with unmediated communication on social media to tell students' stories and measure the impact of creative works have prepared them for public science and lifelong learning. Use of open platforms like GitHub and Creative Commons have made their works openly available so they can find new collaborators and showcase their work for employers as they move beyond our campus and into the next phase of their lives. As an institution committed to openness, these student benefits also benefit everyone, since a new generation of citizens, artists, and entrepreneurs are conversant with and enthusiastic about open culture.

Conclusion

In one year of open advocacy we have transformed the conversation about openness on campus, and invited our students to not only participate in, but to direct this conversation. However, with the rapid turnover in an undergraduate population at a college or university we must continue to be active in encouraging advocacy. This presents an additional challenge at a large university where you rarely see the same face twice. Working "on student time" means working at a much quicker pace than comes naturally, and it means we need to continually make ourselves, our services, and our accomplishments visible on campus. Though we want to encourage students to be the voice of open education on campus, the Libraries must be diligent in providing support for students to do so.

In the coming academic year, librarians from the Copyright & Digital Scholarship Center, as well as any other librarians invested in open education on campus, must continue to engage face-to-face with students. We must continue to get to know our students as they grow and change, and we must continue to educate our students on the value of openness in education and beyond. The process laid out in this chapter is not linear and finite. Rather, the steps need to be performed continually and in concert.

But now that we have the ear of student leaders, we need to keep them engaged, active, and listening, finding the delicate balance of encouraging students to prioritize open education advocacy while giving students space to advocate in their own voice with their own methods. Our student leaders expressed the need for guidance, support, and leadership with respect to advocacy, which will allow us to be more hands-on. But they have also asserted that NCSU's campus is unique, and the ways that other student governments on other campuses have promoted open education may not cut and paste easily onto our campus. We must step back and allow students who are in place to represent the student body to decide what will work best for our campus. We plan to stay involved and active in this dialog, as NCSU students push our community to care not only about affordability, but also about openness in scholarship, code, art, and more.

References

Jhangiani, R. (2016, December 7). Ditching the "Disposable assignment" in favor of open pedagogy. Retrieved from osf.io/rc82h

Laster, J. (2010, February 12). North Carolina State U. gives students free access to physics textbook online [Blog post]. Retrieved from https://www.chronicle.com/blogs/wiredcampus/north-carolina-state-u-gives-students-free-access-to-physics-textbook-online/21238

Rashke, G., & Shanks, S. (2012). Water on a hot skillet: Textbooks, open educational resources, and the role of the library. In S. Polanka (Ed.), *The no shelf required guide to e-book purchasing from library technology reports* (pp. 52–57). Chicago, IL: American Library Association.

Thompson, S., Cross, W., Rigling, L., & Vickery, J. (2017). Data-informed open education advocacy: A new approach to saving students money and backaches. *Journal of Access Services,14*(3), 118–125. doi:10.1080/15367967.2017.1333911

Wiley, D. (2013, October 21). What is Open Pedagogy? [Blog post]. Retrieved from https://opencontent.org/blog/archives/2975

Advancing Access for First-Generation College Students: OER Advocacy at UT San Antonio

DeeAnn Ivie & Carolyn Ellis

UTSA Background

The University of Texas at San Antonio (UTSA) was founded in 1969 by the Texas Legislature in order to provide access to quality higher education for South Texans. Over the last 10 years, UTSA has expanded its vision to become a Top Tier research institution, while still preserving its founding mission to provide access.

UTSA is designated as a Hispanic-Serving Institution (HSI), where almost 60 percent are students of color. Over 40 percent of UTSA's undergraduate students who have graduated within the last five years are first-generation college students, with 40 percent qualifying for Pell federal grants (UTSA, 2017b).

Typically, Latino students face economic barriers more acutely than other groups starting college. In a Pew Research Study on Latinos and Education, 74 percent of Latinos surveyed who had a high school diploma or less stated that the reason they could not pursue higher education was because they needed to support their families (Lopez, 2009). College costs can range from equal to many times greater than the average median net worth of Latino households (Dowd & For, 2012). From 2005 to 2009, Latino households' net worth shrank from $18,359 to $6,325 (Kochhar, Fry, & Taylor, 2011). During the same period, tuition and fees for a four-year public university rose to $6,695—approximately the same amount as the average Latino family's net worth (National Center for Education Statistics, 2010).

Over the next 20 years, the vast majority of growth in the student population in South Texas will be driven by Latinos (Greater Texas Foundation et al., 2011). The success of the region is increasingly becoming inextricably tied to their success. As an HSI, UTSA has a significant role to play in the continued growth and development of the South Texas region.

Providing Access to Quality Education in South Texas

In December 2011, UTSA kicked off an initiative to address two of the biggest indicators of student success: student retention and graduation rates. Out of the freshman cohort admitted to UTSA in fall 2011, only 15.2 percent graduated within four years (UTSA, 2017a). Research has shown that HSIs have lower retention and completion rates when compared with their non-HSI peers (Contreras & Contreras, 2015; New America, 2015).

UTSA set a goal to improve the four-year graduation rate to 25 percent for the 2021 freshman cohort (UTSA, 2011). The Graduation Rate Improvement Plan (GRIP) identified numerous ways to address the issues of lower graduation and retention rates, including streamlining the curriculum, financial incentives to finish on time, expansion of faculty and student support, as well as raising admission standards (UTSA, 2011).

More recently, UTSA has refined its approach to addressing graduation and retention rates, with a new initiative called CLASS: Coordinated and Linked Approach to Student Success. The new approach includes strategies focused on integrated approaches to student support services, including advising, onboarding, leadership development, financial aid, and enhancing the first-year experience (UTSA Office of the Provost, 2016). One of the innovative efforts to support the financial aid needs of students is the offering of micro-retention grants, where small amounts of funds can be the difference between staying in school or dropping out (UTSA Office of the Provost, 2016).

OER as a Strategy for Student Success

Across the nation, there have been efforts made by numerous community colleges, specifically through the Achieving the Dream Network, to construct entire degree programs using only OER materials. These efforts build on the success of institutions like Tidewater Community College's Z-Degree program, which has created an Associate of Science degree program with no textbook costs (Tidewater Community College, 2015).

UTSA's leadership selected Georgia State as an exemplar institution due to its incredible success raising graduation rates and its diverse student population. There have been many discussions about how we can adopt Georgia State's best practices and create new strategies to fuel student success. OER is one of many identified supporting strategies that can help us reach our student success goals.

In 2003, Georgia State had an institutional graduation rate of 32 percent, with underserved minority student populations having an even lower rate (Georgia State University, 2016). Through multiple strategic efforts, they have since increased their graduation rate to 58 percent in 2016 for their students of color. Although not one of the major strategies for student success, Georgia State and the University System of Georgia (USG) have funded efforts to promote OER as a means to reduce the financial burden on students. Affordable Learning Georgia is a statewide program offering financial incentives (grants), coordination between institutions, and online resources that support OER growth and sustainability. Numerous studies and data support a positive correlation between students' overall financial situation and their likelihood of persisting and graduating (Alon, 2007; Hossler, Ziskin, Gross, Kim, & Cekic, 2009; Tinto, 2004).

USG piloted a new open textbook for US History I in the fall of 2013, and found a 6 percent increase in retention when compared with the same semester the previous year (Affordable Learning Georgia, 2014). Interestingly, an even greater improvement was seen in grades. Successful completion of the course (grades A, B, or C) increased from 56 percent to 84 percent when using the open textbook.

The Potential for OER at UTSA

The cost of textbooks has increased at a rate of over 80 percent in the last 10 years (Senack, 2014). Students have felt that increase acutely, resulting in many students forgoing purchasing the textbook or buying a used, older edition. In a survey we conducted of 568 students who used OER in our grant pilot program, many alternatives to purchasing their textbooks were identified: not purchasing textbooks at all, renting, borrowing from friends, or using library copies. Given UTSA's status as an HSI as well as the economic challenges faced by our students, the adoption of OER seemed like a strong strategy in support of increased retention and graduation rates. It has been established that there is a clear link between family income level, college retention, and graduation. The National Center for Education Studies report, *Placing College Graduation Rates in Context*, concluded that across universities with similar attributes, those that enroll larger numbers of low-income students tend to have lower graduation rates (2006). OER is one way that we can alleviate the financial strain that students bear when faced with rising textbook costs; we hope it will contribute positively to student retention at UTSA.

In response to the cost of textbooks and students' financial limitations, over the past six years the UTSA Libraries has purchased textbooks actively being used in classes for circulation in reserves. Our reserves circulation is primarily driven by textbooks, with circulation increasing 28 percent from 2013 to 2016, while circulation of other reserve materials overall falling by 30 percent during the same period (UTSA Libraries, 2015). Although providing print textbooks is a helpful service for students, check out periods are limited to two hours, and there is often a wait list during peak times of the semester. OER present us with a better alternative—textbooks that are completely accessible at any given time, from anywhere.

UTSA Faculty

As of fall 2016, UTSA employed 1,396 faculty with 41 percent tenured, 15 percent tenure-track, and 44 percent non–tenure-track (UTSA Office of Institutional Research, 2016, p. 2). Though total enrolment is hovering at just under 30,000, the campus has a student to professor ratio of 22:1 (UTSA, n.d.).

UTSA Libraries' 11 research and instruction librarians provide support for faculty and students in the 165 degree programs across the university: University College; College of Architecture, Construction and Planning; College of Business; College of Education and Human Development; College of Engineering; College of Liberal and Fine Arts; Honors College; College of Public Policy; College of Sciences, and the Graduate School (UTSA, 2018).

The UTSA Libraries' subject librarians partner regularly with faculty in their academic departments to support teaching by: tailoring library sessions to courses and assignments; creating online tutorials and research guides; providing copyright support and guidance on fair use; and providing innovative teaching spaces for class sessions throughout the semester. In addition to teaching support, librarians are heavily involved in events sponsored by their academic departments, including beginning of semester departmental orientations, student welcome events, and graduate student orientation. Librarians also maintain a steady stream of communication with faculty in their areas to build the collection in support of faculty research and new academic programs through new acquisitions in all formats.

UTSA librarians realized in the earliest stages of OER exploration just how crucial faculty engagement would be to the successful adoption and growth of OER at UTSA. Faculty are the key decision-makers when it comes to textbook selection, which can greatly influence a student's success or failure in a course. UTSA subject librarians have cultivated lasting relationships with faculty in their areas and have a great foundation on which to build current and future conversations with faculty interested in growing OER at UTSA. Strong relationships with the Faculty Center and Center for Teaching and Learning Services, and a constant presence at faculty events, have supported new faculty–librarian partnerships and reinvigorated existing ones.

Grant Program

At the writing of this chapter, the UTSA Libraries had completed the first grant cycle (2015–16), collected student and faculty feedback on the OER trials, and had awarded the second round of grants (2016–17). Even though our program is still in the beginning stages, we've continued to refine it and are constantly evaluating and incorporating new strategies for growing OER adoption.

During the first funding cycle, the Libraries offered $1,500 minigrants for faculty interested in adopting OER for their courses. The minigrants were funded solely from the library's budget, and we were able to award a total of $7,500 to five faculty for using OER in their courses; these five faculty are currently featured on our website (UTSA Libraries, 2017).

Though we recognize there are many other incentives at play in order for faculty to adopt and integrate OER into their courses, librarians offered mini-grants to fast-track OER adoption in order to make an immediate impact on our students. Although textbooks are only a fraction of total college costs, every dollar saved can be used by our students to meet other needs. Our thinking was that once the program took off, the push for integrating OER into more courses would come from other faculty that had adopted OER with success, students that have successfully completed OER courses, and, finally, campus administrative and student leaders advocating for OER adoption.

Because many of the courses we were targeting are taught by adjuncts and sometimes graduate and PhD students, the only requirement the library imposed, as far as faculty status, is that the applicants be the instructor of record for the course. To encourage collaboration and provide additional support, applicants were also required to partner with their subject librarian in order to identify and locate potential OER for their course. Adoption of low- or no-cost materials for the class, completion of an adoption impact report, including student and faculty feedback on the OER used, and participation in a Faculty Center/UTSA Libraries workshop rounded out the requirements (UTSA Libraries, 2017).

Grants were announced on February 1st (with an application deadline of March 13th) and were promoted on websites, social media, emails, and newsletters owned and managed by UTSA Libraries and the Faculty Center. Librarians scheduled a workshop with Nicole Finkbeiner and Kedrienne Day of OpenStax for February 29th in the Faculty Center: *Leaping into Open Educational Resources: The Virtues of Free Textbooks* (UTSA Libraries, 2016c). In addition to the OpenStax reps, faculty that had successfully integrated OER into courses were invited to speak on a panel and were also encouraged to apply for the grants. One faculty panelist invited a student from a past class where an open textbook was used so that attendees could hear his perspective. Approximately 20 faculty attended.

For the 2016 funding cycle, we received 11 applications and ranked them on application quality, number of students impacted, textbook cost, and drop/fail/withdraw rate for the course. During the 2017 application round, we received three times the number of applications received in 2016, so the ranking and selection process became more complex. We developed a scoring system based on textbook cost, enrollment, drop/fail/ withdraw rate for the course, and whether the applicant's course would increase OER adoption; this became a significant factor because a good number of the 2017 applications were OER continuations. Our campus bookstore textbook adoption date for the fall is mid-April, so we notified all applicants by April 1st.

For the 2016–17 funding cycle, we retained the same grant structure but made some adjustments. In order to make the highest impact, we offered, in addition to individual grants, departmental grants, defined as collaboration by two or more instructors to adopt OER in all sections of a course. We asked applicants to provide the new price for their current textbook and to explain how they would advocate for OER adoption to their peers. In order to coordinate an earlier meeting between the grant recipient and their librarian and to also establish firmer spending guidelines, librarians and UTSA Libraries' Dean's Office staff drafted a document that recipients were to sign and return within 30 days of award notification; see Appendix 5. In addition to defining expectations, librarians also provided boilerplate language for integration into the course syllabus. The purpose of the language was to promote awareness among enrolled students of the use of OER for the coming semester and to spur a conversation between the professor and the students about OER. The language provides clarification on what might be an otherwise unfamiliar concept for students and also helps provide context for the end-of-semester OER survey.

Program Launch and Barriers to Adoption

UTSA librarians began exploring OER at the end of fall 2015. With increased change in our university and library environment in recent years, we created a process to streamline any projects that have a university-wide impact or that would involve multiple stakeholders, internal or external. The initial stage of any new project, including OER, starts with drafting of a project plan that outlines the project scope, goals, stakeholders, and identifies an implementation timeline.

We also had initial conversations with OpenStax, with whom we started an official partnership. As an OpenStax partner, we participated in monthly calls with other schools in the same cohort, sharing tactics for growing OER adoption at our respective institutions. Monthly partner discussions centered on the crafting of institutional strategic plans, adoption tracking, and sharing strategies for overcoming adoption roadblocks. OpenStax membership has also helped us stay abreast of new developments in the OER landscape through a partner distribution list, and direct connection with one of the leading OER developers in the United States. As we now enter the intermediary stages of adoption and begin formulating a blueprint for a statewide OER initiative, OpenStax continues to provide structure, support, and grounding, helping to ease the inevitable uncertainty that arises when exploring uncharted territory.

After just a few meetings with OpenStax and project stakeholders, we were excited about the potential for OER at UTSA. We realized we had a lot of work to do in order to achieve the goals laid out in our project plan. During these initial explorations, we uncovered roadblocks and barriers, some expected and some unexpected, to faculty OER adoption. These discoveries shed light on issues faculty face when selecting and adapting teaching resources, and have given us increased insight into our teaching faculty and the struggles they face. Some barriers were unearthed through our own explorations of OER repositories while others surfaced in one-on-one and group conversations with faculty.

The first and most obvious barrier to OER adoption is awareness and discovery by faculty. A 2016 Babson Research Group Survey found that while faculty awareness of OER has increased 20 percent from 2015, adoption and use among faculty is still low with only 6.6 percent of faculty reporting they are "Very aware" and 19 percent of faculty report being "Aware" of OER (Allen & Seaman, 2016). Additionally, 49 percent of faculty report "there are not enough resources for my subject"; 48 percent report it is "too hard to find what I need"; 45 percent report "there is no comprehensive catalog of resources" (Allen & Seaman, 2016). While we have yet to roll out a university-wide faculty survey on OER awareness, discussions with faculty reveal that their knowledge of OpenStax has increased since the initial stages of our program, while awareness of other OER providers remains low.

While numerous OER repositories exist, there is not a comprehensive single search for OER, so UTSA librarians mine repositories separately in order to successfully match OER to courses. Merlot II (Multimedia Educational Resource for Learning and Online Teaching), a California State University initiative, is UTSA Librarians first go-to for OER discovery since it compiles OER from many repositories and features an ISBN search that retrieves more accurate matches. UTSA librarians will often point faculty to this, but the tool is not perfect, and it can still take time to sort through results to find viable options. To help overcome this barrier, UTSA librarians created two OER guides for the disciplines and programs at UTSA, organized by format: textbooks, courses/ancillary materials, videos, and a search for ebooks at the UTSA Libraries (UTSA Libraries, 2016a, 2016b). When we receive a request for materials from a faculty member, we check our guides first to see if that course has already been matched. If not, we do a deep dive into repositories and develop a custom list of potential OER, including ebooks in our collection when no viable OER exist.

Lack of ancillary materials has been identified by UTSA faculty and librarians as another barrier to OER adoption and growth. While thousands of OER are available and searchable through the various repositories, there is a much lower number of open textbooks neatly outfitted with ancillary materials that integrate seamlessly with learning management systems. Meanwhile, traditional textbook publishers have this market cornered and offer an appealing package for our overburdened faculty. To overcome this, UTSA Libraries has initiated conversations with UTSA's bookstore managers. UTSA's bookstore is Follett-owned and features Lumen Courses in its IncludeEd faculty textbook discoverability tool, many of which pair well with OpenStax textbooks. We are also heartened by the recent release of OpenStax Tutor Beta and the gaps it will fill in the OER ancillary landscape and are sharing these tools with faculty that have adopted OpenStax texts.

In spring 2016, UTSA librarians began meeting with faculty, both in departmental meetings and one-on-one, to advocate for OER adoption. During these meetings, we learned that faculty perceptions of OER vary, and these perceptions influence other faculty's willingness to adopt. Some of the hesitancy may be attributed to the availability of quality OER for the discipline. In some cases, faculty that have authored or edited textbooks and have received royalties can be opposed to OER for personal reasons. To overcome these barriers, UTSA librarians have continued one-on-one conversations with interested faculty and have hosted annual workshops that highlight the virtues of free textbooks. Though initial conversations with academic departments revealed hesitations about OER adoption, attitudes have shifted since our program's inception. We even had one department chair that was initially resistant submit an application to our grant program; he now plans to continue using OER in his course indefinitely. These conversations with faculty have also reminded librarians that the decision to choose a certain textbook over another is not always made by the individual faculty member teaching the course, but instead by textbook committees. While some departments allow instructors greater academic freedom in select learning materials, others employ a committee structure. We quickly realized that a hybrid communication strategy for our grant program would be essential in order to reach all levels of faculty at UTSA.

Ultimately, the largest factor influencing OER adoption is part of a much bigger conversation: how do faculty use their textbooks; how much of the test material comes from the textbook; and how do faculty communicate with their students about their expectations and recommendations for using course learning materials? Faculty that have been using a textbook for a number of years that rely heavily on textbook publisher ancillary materials will require more persuasion in order to transition to OER. Likewise, faculty that test primarily from lecture notes may be more easily convinced to transition due to decreased or no reliance on textbook publishers' out-of-the-box tools.

Strategies for overcoming these barriers and more are all tackled in a Scholarly Publishing and Academic Resources Coalition (SPARC, a division of the Association of College and Research Libraries dedicated to advancing the open agenda) adaptation of an OER Mythbusting document currently in the works. UTSA Librarians are using this document in conversations with OER-resistant faculty and plan to incorporate it into the faculty adoption toolkit on our website.

Communication Strategies and Advocacy

OER advocacy requires consistent and comprehensive effort. Our work has been impactful and far-reaching due to multiple factors: the development of an OER communication strategy and timeline, leveraging our campus partnerships to get the word out, and our research and education librarians' direct outreach to faculty. At UTSA, both tenure and non-tenure faculty teach high-enrollment courses that we are targeting for OER course transformation. Considering this, we worked with our communications director to develop tailored messages for targeted venues in order to achieve the widest reach.

After the beginning of semester rush in fall 2016, we contacted the Office of the Registrar to get a list of the 100 courses with the highest enrollment in order to begin the OER matching process. These matches would be incorporated into custom emails to all course instructors and paired with the spring grant application deadline and OER workshop registration. Librarians worked intensely to match open textbooks, ancillary materials, and media to high-enrollment courses in November and December 2016, one of our quietest times of the year. The goal of the matching served many purposes: to alleviate OER discovery work for faculty, to demonstrate that matches exist for courses, and to pique adoption interest. Since lack of awareness is a major hurdle to adoption, providing matches seemed like an easy way to get faculty over the initial hump, and it worked. We received applications from several faculty that were direct emailed, and even if they weren't completely happy with the provided matches, they wanted to know about other options.

UTSA Libraries set the application deadline for the 2017 funding cycle to March 20th, so all communication centered on this. Having produced a great deal of administrative and promotional materials during the 2016 cycle that didn't cleanly fit into either of our OER LibGuides, coupled with the realization that a space for recognizing our diligent OER adopters would be needed, we began developing an OER website. Librarians met with our communications director and our web designer, presented a draft of text for the OER website, and finalized the page design. On the cusp of a major website redesign, we opted for a practical and basic layout that we could refine over time. UTSA Libraries launched its OER website early spring 2017; the website highlights our faculty OER adopters, provides background on student success initiatives at UTSA with a segue into OER adoption, and serves a starting point for faculty interested in transitioning courses to OER (UTSA Libraries, 2017).

Once the website launched, we used it as the basis for our communications with faculty. Though we did not survey faculty applicants in order to determine which strategy was the most effective, this is something we may do in the future. See Appendix 1 for our Adopt a Free

Textbook communication timeline in its entirety and succeeding appendices for sample communication pieces.

Campus Partners

Developing lasting partner relationships is critical to the success of any OER program. Partner collaborations make OER an institutional effort, increasing support for all aspects of OER discovery, adoption, and adaptation for the classroom.

One of the most obvious and important partners in an OER initiative is the campus bookstore. The bookstore provides faculty with the discovery source for textbooks, as well as serving as the de facto place students go for their class materials.

In order to ensure OER textbooks are presented alongside traditional textbooks for course selection, we worked with our Follett campus bookstore to include all major OER providers in their online textbook selection tool. The library has been granted access to this tool, so that we can see what our faculty see, which allows us to better promote OER through familiar channels. To facilitate communication between faculty, the bookstore, and students, we are sharing OER courses with the bookstore; enrolled students may also opt for a print copy of these OER texts.

In addition to facilitating discoverability for faculty when selecting textbooks, it is also important to increase visibility of OER courses for students who are registering. Because of this, the registrar's office is another campus partner that can help promote OER on campus. UTSA uses Banner as the student information system, and students use the ASAP web interface for registration. We have been working with the registrar to include a new filter by which students can search for classes using OER (free) textbooks. This effort is still in process, but we hope to have it fully functional by fall of 2018.

Partnerships with the Faculty Center and Teaching and Learning Services are critical because they provide additional outlets for the UTSA Libraries to communicate with faculty and cultivate lasting relationships. The Faculty Center is a collaboration between UTSA's Office of Research, Office of the Vice Provost for Academic and Faculty Support, and the UTSA Libraries that exists as both a physical and virtual space to support faculty needs (The Faculty Center, n.d.). Librarians and faculty often meet in this physical space to collaborate on projects, including OER. Teaching and Learning Services, which reports directly to the Vice Provost for Faculty Academic Support, is a division charged with supporting faculty teaching. Teaching and Learning Services has been an active partner in our OER effort by inviting librarians to speak at the end-of-semester Provost's Academy for Teaching Excellence, which is marketed to those same non-tenured faculty that teach high-enrollment courses that the library is also targeting. Partnerships between the library and both the Faculty Center and Teaching and Learning Services are critical foundations upon which we are basing current and future OER strategies and communication.

Outside Partnerships and Opportunities

While most partnerships associated with our initiative have been formed within the campus community, some significant external partnerships have also emerged. Most important is the partnership we began with OpenStax in 2016, a nonprofit organization dedicated to the development and promotion of OER textbooks. The OpenStax partnership has connected us with other institutions pursuing OER adoption and growth and provided not only a sounding board for barriers but also given us venues for sharing creative ideas, strategies, and models for implementation and expansion. Starting in 2015, we began participating in monthly calls with OpenStax partners, creating adoption goals for our individual institutions, and we were also added to the OpenStax email distribution list.

While OpenStax and OpenStax partner schools have been our primary external supports, we have also sought out and joined other OER communities. While not formal partnerships like our partnership with OpenStax, they have been critical in keeping us abreast of OER updates, including new open textbooks, legislative updates, information about new ancillary initiatives, and matching OER to specific courses here at UTSA. We are currently in conversations with the Open Textbook Network regarding membership and hope to take advantage of their many textbook development communities, OER tracking, staff training, and faculty workshops. Other external opportunities we have pursued are open education conferences including the SPARC Meeting on Openness in Research and Education, the National Association of College Stores' Textbook Affordability Conference, and an array of other regional and Texas conferences. The Association of College and Research Libraries' SPARC and Scholarly Communication discussion lists (ScholCOMM) have also been helpful for growing and sharing our expertise in this area.

Students

During our fall 2016 pilot, we were able to impact over 568 students with our OER program. From our survey of these students, certain themes emerged after the initial analysis that helped us better understand student perspectives and have also revealed their perceptions of OER. Of the 568 respondents to our end-of-semester survey, over 40 percent relied on Pell grants and student loans for tuition and textbook costs. Data from the College Board reveals that "83% of Pell grant recipients had family incomes of $40,000 or less, including 42% with incomes of $15,000 or less" (2016, p. 28). For UTSA students, many of whom receive Pell grants, every dollar is critical. Over 40 percent of the students we surveyed are spending $400–600 per semester on textbooks, and 25 percent said they don't purchase textbooks simply because they cannot afford them. Perhaps the strongest argument for increased OER adoption at UTSA is that over 88 percent of those surveyed rated the open textbooks used in their courses as good or better than a traditional text in helping them prepare for tests, content quality, ease of use and accessibility, and practice opportunities.

In addition to data gathered through our survey for the fall 2016 pilot, we had individual conversations with students about the use of OER in their courses and invited them to speak as part of faculty panels during "Adopt a Free Textbook" workshops. The most compelling was a student veteran's account of his experience receiving funding for tuition and books through the G.I. Bill. He contrasted his use of an open textbook that same semester in one class with his experience in another class using a traditional textbook; since the release of funds came too late, he was forced to drop the course with a traditional textbook, but was able to successfully complete the course that used an open textbook. His account of accessibility through mobile devices and helpfulness in preparing for tests is compelling (UTSA Libraries, 2016c).

In addition to the student survey data and the individual student testimonies in our faculty workshops, we started the process of meeting with our Student Government Association (SGA) this past spring. The Academic Affairs Committee is a subgroup of UTSA's SGA, and we learned that many of the candidates running for SGA president had free textbooks on their platforms. Our primary focus until this point was reaching out to faculty, who could be resistant, so our conversations with students were enlightening and reinvigorating. We also shared data from Student PIRGs to provide a step-by-step guide for advocacy (Student Public Interest Research Groups, 2016). Since we are at an early stage of OER growth at UTSA, we hope to partner with our UTSA Libraries Student Engagement Committee and UTSA Student Government to plan and host a Textbook Broke event for fall 2017 or spring 2018 (Student Government Resource Center, 2014).

Measuring OER Success

Much of the research on OER has focused on how to best assess the impact of using OER in the classroom. One of the frameworks that we have found useful is the Cost, Outcomes, Usage, Perceptions (COUP) approach, developed by the Open Education Group, which evaluates OER impact using four factors (Open Ed Group, n.d.).

Given the economic challenges our students face, the most immediate benefit of using OER is the cost savings. As an institutional partner with Rice's OpenStax College, we have been tracking metrics related to cost savings to students. In our pilot grant program, we were able to save students $94,000. As we continue to mature our grant program, and increase the number and type of grants given, we expect that number to increase significantly. One of the most compelling metrics related to cost is determining ROI (return on investment) for the grant program, comparing investment (grants awarded) to the cost savings for students. In our pilot program, we determined an ROI of 1,153 percent.

Assessing outcomes is a much more complex process. Many researchers have evaluated outcomes by looking at grades and retention in the course using OER versus the same course taught with a traditional textbook. The OER Research Hub, in their 2013–14 report found that only 27 percent of instructors surveyed found that OER improved performance in classes using OER textbooks (OER Research Hub, 2014). Hilton, Fischer, Wiley, and Williams (2016) looked at outcomes using a new measure they called course throughput rates—an aggregation of drop rates, withdrawal rates, and C or better rates. They found when looking at multiple variables together such as drop, withdrawal, and pass rates, OER has been found to significantly affect outcomes (Hilton, Fischer, Wiley, & Williams, 2016).

Another way to evaluate the success of OER materials is faculty usage. Usage is defined as the level to which faculty engage with the open content, by embellishing, deleting, inserting, and rearranging content within the open resource (Open Ed Group, n.d.). By itself, this engagement is not necessarily significant, however it was found to be a leading indicator of a few positive outcomes for students. Faculty who are more engaged with the course material are more like to be engaged in their teaching practice. The OER Research Hub reported in a survey that 92.2 percent of instructors strongly agreed or agreed that using OER "broadened their range of teaching and learning methods" (OER Research Hub, 2014). Instructors who used OER materials reported an increased level of collaboration with their colleagues.

Faculty and student perception of OER materials is an additional way to look at OER success. Numerous studies have been conducted to assess faculty and student perception of OER. A few studies with students have focused on asking them to compare OER textbooks to traditional textbooks. Feldstein et al., in their survey of 991 students at Virginia State University School of Business, found a positive response to OER used in nine core courses (Feldstein et al., 2012). Almost 95 percent of students surveyed agreed that their open textbook was "easy to use" and 78 percent of students liked "how the textbook linked to other resources." We also conducted a survey of 568 students who participated in four courses in our pilot OER grant program. We found 75 percent of our student respondents felt that "accessibility" was better than traditional textbooks, as well as 63 percent of students who thought that "ease of use" was better. In a survey which included eight community colleges, Bliss, Robinson, Hilton, and Wiley found that instructor perceptions of OER were mostly positive, with any negative feedback focusing on issues of quality (Bliss, Robinson, Hilton, & Wiley, 2013). In our work with faculty at UTSA, perceived poor quality was one of the major deterrents to considering adopting an OER. It is important to assess student and faculty perception of OER (both before and after using an open text) in order to understand impediments to adoption and use.

Currently, we are only using the cost factor to evaluate the success of OER, as it is the easiest attribute to assess. We do have future plans analyze the relationship between outcomes, such as grades and/or persistence, to the kind of textbook used (open, no-cost, low-cost, traditional). The factor of faculty usage is more difficult to gauge. Many of our faculty may not necessarily rearrange/change/embellish within an open textbook, but they may use the open textbook as part of a greater body of materials used for a class. These other materials may be open or low-cost. This mix and match approach still shows engagement with the materials, but not in the way defined by the COUP model. We are currently tracking faculty and staff perception of OER materials used in courses, but we have not yet begun analyzing the data. This is part of our future plan to assess our OER program.

Future Directions

We see a very positive future for OER at UTSA. The 2017 academic year wraps up our second round of grants incentivizing OER adoption, with 24 grants given—five times the number of grants awarded during our pilot year. Once fully implemented, we will see $1,063,594 in student money saved in one semester alone, with a total of $4,348,376 in student savings over four semesters. We estimated this savings using OpenStax's methodology—the retail cost of the textbook, multiplied by the average number of students in each course, multiplied by the number of semesters.

We plan to increase our assessment activities for the grants this academic year, applying the full COUP model to more broadly determine the impact on our students and faculty. Given the larger grant program this last year, we will have a greater sample of students and faculty to study, likely to yield more meaningful results (Open Ed Group, n.d.).

Finally, over the last few months, OER has advanced at the state level. On June 6, 2017 the Governor of Texas signed a law that will establish a statewide OER grant program to be overseen by the Coordinating Board, in addition to the creation of a Texas repository for open materials. We hope this is just the beginning for coordinated, statewide progress for OER in Texas.

References

Affordable Learning Georgia. (2014). *Retention and completion with OER implementation* [PowerPoint slides]. Retrieved from http://www.affordablelearninggeorgia.org/documents/Retention_and_Completion_with_OER.pptx

Allen, I. E., & Seaman, J. (2016). *Opening the textbook: Educational resources in U.S. higher education, 2015–16.* Babson Survey Research Group. Retrieved from http://www.onlinelearningsurvey.com/reports/openingthetextbook2016.pdf

Alon, S. (2007). The influence of financial aid in leveling group differences in graduating from elite institutions. *Economics of Education Review, 26*(3), 296–311.

Bliss, T. J., Robinson, T. J., Hilton, J., III, & Wiley, D. A. (2013). An OER COUP: College teacher and student perceptions of open educational resources. *Journal of Interactive Media in Education, 2013*(1), 4.

College Board. (2016). *Trends in student aid 2016* (Trends in higher education series). Retrieved from https://trends.collegeboard.org/sites/default/files/2016-trends-student-aid_0.pdf

Contreras, F., & Contreras, G. J. (2015). Raising the bar for Hispanic serving institutions: An analysis of college completion and success rates. *Journal of Hispanic Higher Education, 14*(2), 151–170.

Dowd, A. C., & For, A. N. (2012). *Priced out: A closer look at postsecondary affordability for Latinos.* Pell Institute. Retrieved from http://education.utsa.edu/images/uploads/Priced_Out_8_5_12_(Rendon_Nora_Dowd).pdf

Feldstein, A., Martin, M., Hudson, A., Warren, K., Hilton, J., III, & Wiley, D. (2012). Open textbooks and increased student access and outcomes. *European Journal of Open, Distance and E-Learning, 15*(2). Retrieved from http://www.eurodl.org/?p=archives&year=2012&halfyear=2&article&article=533

Georgia State University. (2016). Georgia State University campus plan update 2016. Retrieved from http://www.completegeorgia.org/georgia-state-university-campus-plan-update-2016

Greater Texas Foundation, et al. (2011). *South Texas Regional Overview.* Greater Texas Foundation.

Hilton, J., III, Fischer, L., Wiley, D., & William, L. (2016). Maintaining momentum toward graduation: OER and the course throughput rate. *The International Review of Research in Open and Distributed Learning, 17*(6). Retrieved from http://www.irrodl.org/index.php/irrodl/article/view/2686

Hossler, D., Ziskin, M., Gross, J. P. K., Kim, S., & Cekic, O. (2009). Student aid and its role in encouraging persistence. In J. C. Smart (Ed.), *Higher education: Handbook of theory and research* (pp. 389–425). Springer Netherlands.

Kochhar, R., Fry, R., & Taylor, P. (2011). Wealth gaps rise to record highs between whites, blacks, Hispanics. Retrieved from http://www.pewsocialtrends.org/2011/07/26/wealth-gaps-rise-to-record-highs-between-whites-blacks-hispanics/

Lopez, M. H. (2009). Latinos and education: Explaining the attainment gap. Retrieved from http://www.pewhispanic.org/2009/10/07/latinos-and-education-explaining-the-attainment-gap/

National Center for Education Statistics. (2006). *Placing college graduation rates in context: How 4-year college graduation rates vary with selectivity and the size of low-income enrollment* (NCES 2006-161). Retrieved from https://nces.ed.gov/pubs2007/2007161.pdf

National Center for Education Statistics. (2010). Digest of education statistics, 2010. Retrieved from https://nces.ed.gov/programs/digest/d10/tables/dt10_346.asp

New America. (2015, January 1). Hispanic-serving institutions (HISs): A background primer [Blog post]. Retrieved from https://www.newamerica.org/post-secondary-national-policy-institute/our-blog/hispanic-serving-institutions-hsis/

OER Research Hub. (2014). *OER evidence report 2013–2014.* Retrieved from https://oerresearchhub.files.wordpress.com/2014/11/oerrh-evidence-report-2014.pdf

Open Ed Group. (n.d.). The COUP framework. Retrieved from http://openedgroup.org/coup

Senack, E. (2014). *Fixing the broken textbook market: How students respond to high textbook costs and demand alternatives.* US Public Interest Research Group & Student PIRGS. Retrieved from http://www.uspirg.org/sites/pirg/files/reports/NATIONAL%20Fixing%20Broken%20Textbooks%20Report1.pdf

Student Government Resource Center. (2014, February 18). #TextbookBroke: Campaign for affordable textbooks [Blog post]. Retrieved from http://studentgovresources.org/textbookbroke-campaign-for-affordable-textbooks/

Student Public Interest Research Groups. (2016). Make textbooks affordable. Retrieved from http://www.studentpirgs.org/campaigns/sp/make-textbooks-affordable

The Faculty Center. (n.d.). About the Faculty Center. Retrieved from http://faculty.utsa.edu/about/

Tidewater Community College. (2015). *The "Z-degree": Removing textbook costs as a barrier to student success through an OER-based curriculum.* Tidewater Community College.

Tinto, V. (2004). *Student retention and graduation: Facing the truth, living with the consequences* (Pell Institute Occasional Paper 1). Retrieved from http://files.eric.ed.gov/fulltext/ED519709.pdf

UTSA. (n.d.). Welcome to The University of Texas at San Antonio: UTSA—Financial affairs.

UTSA. (2011). *Four-year graduation rate improvement plan.* Retrieved from http://provost.utsa.edu/home/docs/UTSA_Graduation_Rate_Plan_2011-FINAL.PDF

UTSA. (2017a). Graduation rates. Retrieved from http://www.utsa.edu/ir/content/student-graduation-rates.html

UTSA. (2017b). Student achievements at UTSA. Retrieved from http://www.utsa.edu/ir/content/achievement.html

UTSA. (2018). *Fast facts: UTSA at a glance.* Retrieved from http://www.utsa.edu/about/doc/fastfacts.pdf

UTSA Libraries. (2015). *UTSA Libraries access services semester report.* UTSA Libraries.

UTSA Libraries. (2016a). OER course matches UTSA: OER at UTSA. Retrieved from http://libguides.utsa.edu/oercoursematches

UTSA Libraries. (2016b). Open educational resources at UTSA: About OER. Retrieved from http://libguides.utsa.edu/oer/about

UTSA Libraries. (2016c). *OpenStax workshop* [Video]. Retrieved from https://www.youtube.com/watch?v=Ji-dl3RAjfA

UTSA Libraries. (2017). Open educational resources. Retrieved from https://lib.utsa.edu/services/faculty/open-educational-resources

UTSA Office of Institutional Research. (2016). *Faculty information: The UTSA fact book.* Retrieved from http://www.utsa.edu/ir/pub/factbook/2016/faculty.pdf

UTSA Office of the Provost. (2016). CLASS: Coordinated and linked approaches to student success. Retrieved from http://provost.utsa.edu/class/financial-aid.asp

Appendix 1: Communication Timeline for Adopt a Free Textbook Grants (2017)

- OER Website Launched 1/9
- Email to Dept Chairs 1/11
- Faculty Infobites 1/13
- Social Media Posts 1/18
- Website story 1/25
- Flyer emailed to Academic Affairs Admins 1/30
- Department Chair Presentation 2/8
- Faculty Infobites: Workshop 2/15
- Email Broadcast to Faculty: Workshop 2/21
- Social Media Posts 2/24
- Librarian Emails to Faculty 2/25
- Email Broadcast to Faculty: Workshop 2/27
- OER Workshop 2/27
- Faculty InfoBites 3/1: Grant Application
- Social Media Posts 3/6: Grant Application
- Email Broadcast to Faculty 3/6

Appendix 2: Library Dean Email to Department Chairs

Subject: Faculty Grants Available Fall 2017

As part of UTSA's efforts to increase student success, retention and completion, the UTSA Libraries has partnered with the Teaching and Learning Center to offer **individual and departmental grants** to faculty who pilot a free textbook in a course this fall.

The grant application deadline is **March 20, 2017**. There are two types available:

- **Individual**: $1,000 for a faculty member to use a free textbook in one of their courses.
- **Departmental**: $1,500–$7,000 (calculated based on number of students impacted) for faculty to adopt a free textbook in a course across the entire department.

Why are we offering these grants? All too often, the high cost of textbooks is a reason students delay or discontinue their educational path. By using free, high quality textbooks, UTSA can make great strides in higher education affordability for our students.

I hope you will visit our **Open Educational Resources website** to learn more. You'll find **a video** showing what UTSA students have to say about textbooks, and a **plethora of research** on the benefits of using free textbooks on our guide to free textbooks that most closely align with high enrollment courses in your discipline.

We hope you'll encourage faculty in your department to apply for the grant! Please don't hesitate to contact me or your departmental librarian with any questions you may have.

Appendix 3: Adopt a Free Textbook Flyer

Adopt a free textbook
FACULTY GRANTS

If you're looking for an opportunity to try out a free textbook in one of your courses, this grant is for you!

$1,000 individual faculty grants   **$1,500-7,000** departmental grants

The high cost of textbooks is a reason students delay or discontinue their educational path. By using free, high quality learning materials, UTSA can make great strides in higher education affordability for our students.

APPLICATION DEADLINE: MARCH 20, 2017

lib.utsa.edu/freetextbooks
for more information

UTSA Libraries   **UTSA**
Teaching and Learning Services

Appendix 4: Adopt a Free Textbook Social Media Posts

 **Faculty Center at UTSA** ⊘   •••
January 19 · ⊛

Be a hero to your students! The UTSA Libraries is offering grants to faculty
who try out a free textbook in one of their courses next year. The availability
of high-quality free textbooks has exploded in recent years, and a librarian
will help you find the right one for your class. #WinWin #TextbookHeroes
#MakingCollegeAffordable

Faculty Grants - UTSA Libraries
Application deadline: March 20, 2017

LIB.UTSA.EDU   Learn More

Appendix 5: Adopt a Free Textbook Grant Spending Requirements & Reimbursement Guidelines

Please read, complete, sign, and return to DeeAnn Ivie by 05/01/2017.

Grantee Expectations

For your course, you will be expected to:

- Collaborate with a librarian to identify a free textbook (or other open materials).
- Adopt a free textbook, replacing the primary, traditional textbook and incorporate the following text and OER logo into your course syllabus:

Open educational resources (OER) are textbooks and learning materials that are available at no cost to students, accessible from mobile devices, and available from class day one. Research has shown that OER can improve student engagement and course outcomes. This course is part of UTSA Libraries' OER initiative, a collaboration between your professor and UTSA Libraries to encourage faculty adoption of free and low-cost instructional materials into courses.

- Complete a course impact report that includes a final syllabus, assessment, student evaluations of the textbook, analysis and future plans based on findings, and anonymous data on grades, including D/F/W rates.
- Share experience using a free textbook with colleagues by participating in a free textbook workshop as a panelist.
- Commit to adopting a free textbook for a minimum of four semesters, including the pilot semester.

Recipients of an **Individual Grant** will adopt a free textbook in one section (or more) of a course.

Recipients of a **Departmental Grant** will adopt a free textbook across at least three instructors teaching the same course OR all instructors teaching the same course.

Grant Spending Guidelines

As a recipient of the OER Free Textbook Grant, I agree that I will abide by the following spending requirements:

Appendix 5: Adopt a Free Textbook Grant Spending Requirements & Reimbursement Guidelines (cont.)

1. Professional travel expenses (airfare, conference registration, per diem)

2. Equipment/technology that directly supports teaching. Equipment and/or materials purchased become property of your academic department.

3. Funding for teaching assistants to develop ancillary and support materials for OER course (for each student assistant, a maximum number of hours needs to be stipulated so that the student wages do not exceed grant funds).

Funds received by grant recipients may **not** be used for personal purchases or as a salary supplement.

Funds must be fully expended by May 1, 2018.

1. What do you plan on using grant funds for? Please select and describe all that apply.

___ Conference travel/professional development

Estimated Cost	
Describe	

___Equipment/materials (Note: all equipment purchased with grant funds are property of your UTSA department)

Estimated Cost	
Describe	

___Development of ancillary and support materials by students

Estimated Cost	
Describe	

2. Who is your departmental admin?

Name	
Phone Number	
Email	

1. Print, sign, and date.

Printed Name (primary faculty applicant)	
Signature	
Date	

Student-Driven OER: Championing the Student Voice in Campus-Wide Efforts

Alesha Baker & Cinthya Ippoliti

Introduction

This chapter will discuss how students can actively collaborate with libraries and other campus entities to provide their much-needed perspective, as well as present a case study of how Oklahoma State University (OSU), a public land-grant university, is using student participation to increase campus awareness and provide additional support for the development and implementation of open educational resources (OER). OSU is a research university with high research activity. The total student population at OSU's primary campus in Stillwater, Oklahoma is approximately 24,000, with an undergraduate population of approximately 20,000. Edmon Low Library is the primary library on campus and is used by undergraduates, graduates, and faculty. Our initial efforts began due to informal interest on the part of a few librarians and has since started to take additional shape and direction as we continue to explore more formalized approaches to integrating OER and discussions about open access in general into campus culture and infrastructure.

Finding the Student Voice

There is a surprising lack of information about how university campuses are including students in the OER conversation, at least on a formal level. A scan of the journal literature indicates that student input is either not included or is not a major factor in decisions surrounding the adoption and use of OER. In order to understand why and how students might be involved in OER efforts, it is important to consider the broader social and pedagogical context in which these efforts might occur. Joyce (2006) states "The prevailing culture in higher education places the responsibility for innovation in the hands of academics, rather than students who may have stronger incentives to experiment with and advance teaching and learning methods" (p. 9).

When an institution decides to adopt an innovation, the institution as a whole and individuals within the institution progress through a complex process. This innovation-decision process includes five stages, (1) knowledge, (2) persuasion, (3) decision, (4) implementation, and (5) confirmation. Those involved in this process make up a social system. Rogers (2003) defines a social system as "a set of interrelated units engaged in joint problem-solving to accomplish a common goal" (p. 23). Students in higher education institutions are included in the social system and should be a considered as part of this process as faculty begins to adopt and use open textbooks. Faculty, students, and all involved in the implementation process collaborate to identify needs and work together to solve problems that arise from the initial identification of the challenges that need to be addressed. According to Rogers, when individuals within a social system can work together, the rate of adoption of an innovation should increase. Ed Hegarty asserts that OER provide a unique opportunity for students to take an active role in their own learning processes in a way that traditional textbooks and pedagogical approaches do not, as he defines an arc-of-life model as "a seamless process that occurs throughout life when participants engage in open and collaborative networks, communities, and openly shared repositories of information in a structured way to create their own culture of learning" (2015, p. 3). He goes on to discuss eight attributes necessary to achieve this type of learning: participatory technologies, people/openness/trust, innovation and creativity, sharing ideas and resources, connected community, learner generated, reflective practice, and peer review (2015, p. 5). By their very nature, OER allow for the type of activities that Hegarty outlines and provide an opportunity for collaboration by helping to shape learner motivation so that the word "open" takes on a much broader meaning than simply available to all: one that invites engagement, reworking, and experimentation from both a learner as well as an instructor perspective. By being able to change the course materials themselves, students are responsible for both the learning experience as well as its application not only throughout the course itself but also in other academic and even professional contexts as students become used to this repurposing of information as a way to help them define and achieve their goals. For example, through open pedagogy, students can modify or create information for wikis, remix audiovisual content, write or revise open textbooks, create and openly license supplemental content to share with their peers, assist in developing test banks, or even create their own course assignments (Hilton & Mason, 2016).

Flavin (2012) offers an interesting perspective on the use of technology and control over the learning process, which can be extrapolated to include the use of OER within the classroom setting. He asserts that "when digital technologies are brought into the classroom setting, the lecturer may have to relinquish some of their authority" (p. 104). While this may seem to disrupt the balance of knowledge, arguably this furthers the notion that students can take control of their learning process by interacting with this open content in a way that makes sense for them, as opposed to being forced to utilize a printed source that may or may not support their educational habits and goals simply because it was simple for the faculty member to adopt. This point is also supported by Shaffer (2014) who mentions that open platforms where students and instructors can pedagogically interact "facilitate student access to existing knowledge, and empower them to critique it, dismantle it, and create new knowledge," which highlights a two-way experience where both students and instructors can learn from one another.

Finally, in a recent posting on the Open Oregon Educational Resources blog, Lin Hanick and Amy Hofer (2017) discuss how open pedagogy can also influence how librarians teach information literacy. While the discussion of the Association of College and Research Libraries (ACRL) *Framework for Information Literacy* is beyond the scope of this chapter, it does mention concepts and ideas that are related to OER. Specifically, it states that "open education is simultaneously content and practice" (p. 1) and that by integrating these practices into the classroom, students are learning about issues such as intellectual property, the value of information, and the other costs associated with these "free" resources that they may not be aware of, by acting "like practitioners" (p. 5) where they take on "a disciplinary perspective and engage with a community of practice" (p. 5). These methods have deeply influenced our efforts at OSU, where the Library has taken an active role in soliciting student input as part of all of its services and programs, and OER is no exception. We view the student perspective as central to our efforts and hope to integrate the feedback we receive so that it will inform our outreach efforts as we continue to work with faculty in raising awareness of OER on campus and build on or existing initiatives.

Institutional Context

Our initial efforts began when we received a donation to begin an Open Educational Textbook pilot (http://info.library.okstate.edu/wiseinitiative). The Wise OSU Libraries' Open Textbook Initiative was made possible through generous initial funding from Dr. James Wise, an OSU alumnus who is a member of the Friends of the Library Board. Dr. Wise has supported a wide variety of library projects over the years, most of them focusing on innovation and technology. The goal of the Wise OSU Libraries' Open Textbook Initiative is to encourage faculty by providing a stipend for OER adoption or creation to consider open textbooks as less costly alternatives for their students. The types of materials that could qualify for the open textbook project can include material from different media—articles, audio, video, websites—or the use of an existing open access textbook. While some entities that are developing or funding the development of OER focus on high- enrollment courses, OSU encourages faculty in all areas and at all levels to consider using an open textbook. The project is open to either individual faculty members or a group of faculty members teaching multiple sections of the same course (in the case of partnered projects, the monetary award goes to a single representative of the group). A major goal of the open textbook project is to demonstrate how savings may be achieved for students while maintaining or improving the quality of their learning process.

To assist with some of this work, we have developed our own publication platform, dubbed the OSU Libraries ePress (site is in progress), which has allowed us to begin developing workflows for how these manuscripts are copy edited and transformed into their respective epub and PDF formats. In addition, we are offering a more interactive WordPress option for those faculty who are interested in being able to make ongoing changes to their materials and take advantage of the platform's features. To date, seven faculty members have applied, and each project is in various stages of development.

1. LSB 3010/5010: Patent Law and Managing Investments in Technology
2. ENGL 1123: International Composition
3. EDTC 5030: Learning in a Digital World
4. EDTC 5203: Foundations of Educational Technology
5. SOIL 4683: Soil, Water, and Weather
6. POLS 3103: Introduction to Political Inquiry
7. PHIL 1313: Logic and Critical Thinking

Open Pedagogy Project

One of the first courses to develop an OER was EDTC 5030: Learning in a Digital World. In order to accomplish this task, the faculty member reached out to graduate students asking if they would be willing to contribute to its creation; 15 students agreed to help. The student writers began this collaborative effort by selecting a project manager and brainstorming ideas for topics which turned into chapters. The faculty member took the topics to the department faculty to ensure the open textbook would align with the objectives of the program. The focus of the open textbook is learning in a digital world and includes sections such as History and Theory, Digital Literacy, Digital Divide, Pre-K to 12, Adult Learning, Digital Learning Groups, Learning in Emerging Spaces, and Tools and Strategies. Once the topics were agreed upon, the student writers determined which chapters they each would write. After the chapters are written, the student writers and the faculty member will participate in a peer review and editing process. The faculty member's role is the same as the students', in that he will be writing and be part of the peer review process. The practice of open pedagogy will continue after the open textbook is used each semester. The students in future sections of EDTC 5053 will have an opportunity to modify or add to the resources through an iterative process with continual input from the students. Students who participate in this Wise initiative by helping write the text for the new open textbooks do not receive monetary compensation, but they do participate in the creation process to gain experience and lend their authors' voices to the creation of the very tool that will enhance their learning.

Collaborating with students is an important component to the OER initiative. In addition to including students in the creation of OER through open pedagogy, the Library collaborated with an OSU graduate student who was an OER Fellow in the Department of Educational Technology within the College of Education. We were able to hire this student as a graduate research assistant for a semester to assist us with key projects as part of our OER program. The research fellowship was sponsored by the William and Flora Hewlett Foundation and administered by the Open Education Group. The fellowships are meant to encourage research on the cost, outcomes, use, and perceptions of OER. The partnership between OSU and the student led to several exciting initiatives. One activity the student assisted with is co-teaching of workshops. The workshops included educating interested faculty on OER, information on the Wise initiative, and how to get started with finding or writing an open textbook. Through research and the trial of potential platforms and templates, the student provided input on how to progress to the development stage when faculty needed to go beyond the writing or curation of content.

Partnering with other departments and organizations on campus has proven invaluable for developing stronger collaborations and extending the reach of our programs. The Library is in the process of working with the Student Government Association (SGA) to develop joint programming for Open Access Week in fall of 2017. As part of this project, we hope to build on our previous efforts which, though impactful, were one-sided and did not engage students beyond a quick interaction. We hope to co-develop an interactive exhibit during Open Access Week that will serve a dual purpose of informing other students about these resources, as well as give us additional data that we can utilize with campus administration and faculty. This will help drive a more strategic and programmatic approach via our Textbook Affordability Committee and possibly add OER to the campus textbook adoption guidelines that are sent out each year from the Provost's Office. Although we have not yet discussed the details of what the initiative might encompass, we are confident that with the inroads we have made with the SGA thus far, we will be able to continue collaborating and establishing some concrete action items for fall of this year.

Another partnership which developed and which continues to grow is between the Library and the bookstore as a result of the creation of a textbook affordability program. This partnership is taking a holistic look at options for students, and we are seeing OER being included as part of that suite of materials. Moreover, the Library was recently invited to serve on the Textbook Affordability Committee, and we are optimistic that our inclusion will allow us to take a broad look at how these efforts can be scaled and adapted at a university-wide level. As a small start, the Library collaborated with an economics course in fall of 2016 to survey students about their textbook needs and discovered that over 75 percent would use an OER, and 46 percent would purchase a print copy of an OER textbook and would be willing to pay about $20 for it. This percent is similar to a previous study cited in Hilton and Wiley (2011) that shows 40 percent of students continued to purchase print versions of their required textbooks even when free online copies were available to them. The option of purchasing a print copy is helpful for the students who prefer this format over the digital version alone.

This preliminary research has allowed the Library to work with the bookstore to offer an on-demand printing model via our FedEx office on campus, which gives students the opportunity to print only the sections of an open textbook that they need for a nominal fee of approximately $8 and also allows them to pay for added customization, such as color images and different binding options, depending on their preferences. Anecdotal evidence from the bookstore indicates that students are unwilling to pay $35 for an OpenStax textbook (which had been sitting on their shelves for this course with virtually no demand) simply because they did not need all of it and we hope that this model will encourage students to print what they need. We plan to continue marketing this program campus-wide as we get a better sense of how we can continue campus-wide conversations around these topics.

Finally, the Library regularly surveys students about their textbook costs as part of their Open Access Week programming. During Open Textbook Week 2014 and 2015, we set up whiteboards in the south lobby to solicit student feedback/input on the cost of their textbooks with an accompanying table display on open textbooks. Students would stop by, and if they did not ask questions, they often made a hash mark or comment on the whiteboards. There was one constant question: *How Much Did Your Textbooks Cost This Year?* The second board featured a question that changed every other day:

- *What Is Your Most Expensive Textbook?*
- *For What Class Did You Not Purchase the Textbook, and Why?*

The images below detail the presentation as well as the responses from students that we compiled during each of these sessions. This information has allowed us to gather some informal evidence for our campus which has supported national trends and which continues to lend the student perspective to these issues especially as we determine ways we can continue working with campus administration to make our efforts more visible and impactful.

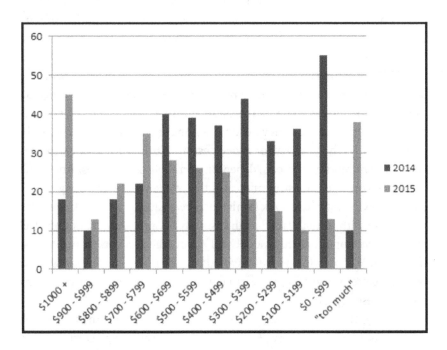

What Students Told Us: How Much Did Your Textbooks Cost This Year?

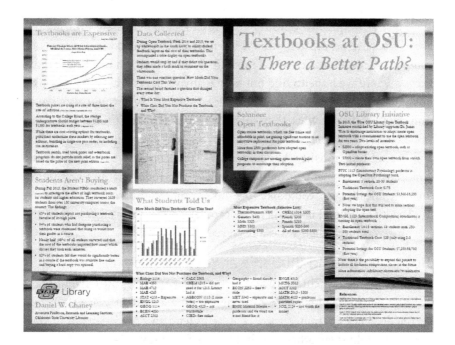

Future Plans for the Program at OSU

While we have covered some ground through these initial efforts, we recognize that there is much that still needs to be done. We would like to scale up the pilot into a full-blown program, where we receive proposals on an ongoing basis that are reviewed by a formal board comprised of campus faculty and students. This would allow us to develop a more cohesive workflow for the entire process from the initial idea all the way to the published product and its integration within the curriculum. This model will require significant effort on our part to develop an outreach and marketing program, as well as further develop the underlying infrastructure so that authors are fully supported throughout the duration of the project and the implementation of the resource. We would also like to include these OER into our institutional repository as a way to make them even more discoverable, and also to highlight these works as part of the university's scholarly output. In addition to the board, we hope to partner with our Technical Writing Program where students can act as copy editors and gain professional experience while helping us in an area where the Library might not have sufficient expertise.

Finally, we plan to develop a survey to gather baseline information about students' perception of their learning and overall course experience using these resources. This will most likely take the form of a brief online survey where we hope to find out how many students accessed the books, how many printed them versus downloaded them. We would also like to find out specifically what they thought of the format of these texts, and ask them for ways that we can improve their discoverability, accessibility, and overall functionality. We hope this will allow us to pave the way for a more robust assessment model once we have additional projects under our belt. Ideally, we would like to conduct some comparative analysis using faculty anecdotal data where we can determine how the quality of the learning was impacted by these resources.

Tips for Engaging Students at Your Institution

It is important to include student input into any OER initiative to maximize the chances of success. Although adding a student voice to library efforts does not guarantee success, it helps lend an added element of support that might sway other stakeholders, such as university administration and faculty, to listen where they might not have before. A formal needs assessment might help pave the way for some of these discussions and secure additional buy-in from students and student groups. There are many different ways to go about this, and the University of Idaho Extension program details the most commonly used methods in a concise and useful fashion. The main elements of any needs assessment consist of the following steps (McCawley, 2009):

- What is it that you want to learn from the needs assessment?
- Who is the target audience? Whose needs are you measuring, and to whom will you give the information?
- How will you collect data that will tell you what you need to know? Will you collect data directly from the target audience or indirectly?
- How will you select a sample of respondents who represent the target audience?
- What instruments and techniques will you use to collect data?
- How will you analyze the data you collect?
- What will you do with the information that you gather?

An important point to consider about this type of assessment is to include information about student needs that go beyond content. For example, based on OSU's modest survey, we were able to determine that students just wanted to pay for the content they needed and were not interested in an entire textbook, even if it was fully bound and in color. They were more likely to choose a "stripped down" bound version in black and white if it meant they would get the information they had to have and nothing extraneous. Without asking students what they preferred, we might have made some erroneous assumptions about their desire to have better looking, yet less useful, versions of their textbook, when in fact that was not the case.

Another important step is to reach out to student organizations such as governing bodies, resident life, and Greek organizations. This approach is a more effective and scalable than trying to target individuals, and it can result in a broader reach. The good news is that this issue should be a fairly simple one to address with these groups because OER benefit students directly. The question then becomes one of execution. Establishing a clear yet flexible plan will allow these organizations to determine how they would like to move forward. In the case of OSU for example, we are discussing both developing some shared programming as well as approaching faculty members directly about the use of OER in their high-enrollment courses.

Using some of the evidence you have gathered (such as the statistics above, for example) will also help lend more weight to your arguments and proposed planning, and if they are collected by students at your institution and shared through those same students, they will have a much stronger impact than simply citing statistics that may or may not provide enough compelling evidence about how these costs are affecting local populations. Also, student groups can assist with marketing and outreach efforts and can go with you when you make visits to faculty or talk with administrators. They can actively participate in any open access programming that is held on campus, and it is up to you to ensure that for every faculty panel or participant, students have an equally strong presence to keep momentum going and serve as a reminder of the purpose of championing OER. Crafting a uniform and consistent message will ensure that everyone is working towards a unified goal.

Finally, plan for success by establishing a committee or taskforce comprised of library, faculty, student, and other campus representatives, to look at these issues at a strategic level. Ensuring that students are invited to the table as part of this work will not only signal that their feedback is valued, but can also help shape how these resources are developed, implemented, and assessed as part of an overall program. Thinking about both in-class as well as out-of-class elements should provide a holistic picture of how these resources are integrated and utilized throughout the entire student experience. The former may require collaborations with the campus institute for teaching and learning and the faculty council. This will prevent pedagogical considerations that are implemented from being seen as trying to usurp existing processes for how faculty modify their curriculum, especially since open pedagogy practices can require what some may see as a radical shift in teaching habits and approaches. This work could necessitate additional training for faculty in working with students in a more collaborative capacity than they might have previously done, and might require additional practice with assessing and grading the types of artifacts that would emerge.

This might be met with significant resistance and necessitate having involvement from a higher administrative capacity in order to pave the way for pilots and other smaller-scale implementations before a broader open access program is announced, but having a group that is focused on these issues should help you anticipate and resolve these types of challenges as they arise. This more expansive approach can help shift the focus away from objections related to publisher kickbacks and long-held preconceptions about these resources, because they are furthering student learning and success which is everyone's ultimate goal.

Conclusion

There is no magic formula when it comes to championing campus-wide OER efforts, and as we have explored throughout this chapter, there are several ways in which students can become active participants both in and out of the classroom. One of the most important lessons to be taken away from these conversations is that of providing opportunities for faculty and students alike to engage in the types of pedagogical and programmatic activities that allow for deeper collaboration and re-imagining of both the learning process as well as the content itself. This is not an easy thing to accomplish, as there are decades of preconceived notions, habits, and practices in existence on both sides, but the library can provide a platform where new projects and initiatives have an opportunity to be explored and become successful as we continue on the path to redefining the way in which OER influence the world of higher education and beyond.

References

Flavin, M. (2012). *Disruptive technologies in higher education.* Presented at the Annual Conference of the Association for Learning Technology, London, UK.

Hanick, S., & Hofer, A. (2017, May 31). Opening the framework: Connecting open education practices and information literacy [Blog post]. Retrieved from http://openoregon.org/opening-the-framework/

Hegarty, B. (2015). Attributes of open pedagogy: A model for using open educational resources. *Education Technology, 4.* Retrieved from https://upload.wikimedia.org/wikipedia/commons/c/ca/Ed_Tech_Hegarty_2015_article_attributes_of_open_pedagogy.pdf

Hilton, J. L., III, & Mason, S. (2016). Open pedagogy library. Retrieved from http://openedgroup.org/openpedagogy

Hilton J. L., III, & Wiley, D. (2011). Open access textbooks and financial sustainability: A case study on Flat World Knowledge. *The International Review of Research in Open and Distributed Learning, 12*(5), 18–26.

Joyce, A. (2006). *OECD study of OER: Forum report.* Retrieved from https://www.researchgate.net/profile/Alexa_Joyce2/publication/265183257_OECD_study_of_OER_forum_report/links/564b064e08ae9cd9c827cf5a.pdf

McCawley, P. F. (2009). Methods for conducting an educational needs assessment. *University of Idaho, 23.*

Open Education Group (2017). *Open education library.* Retrieved from http://openedgroup.org/openpedagogy

Rogers, E. M. (2003). *Diffusion of innovations* (5th ed.). New York: The Free Press.

Senack, E. (2014). *Fixing the broken textbook market: How students respond to high textbook costs and demand alternatives.* US Public Interest Research Group & Student PIRGS. Retrieved from http://www.uspirg.org/sites/pirg/files/reports/NATIONAL%20Fixing%20Broken%20Textbooks%20Report1.pdf

Shaffer, K. (2014). The Critical Textbook. *Hybrid Pedagogy.* Retrieved from http://hybridpedagogy.org/critical-textbook/

Wiley, D. (2014, March 5). The access compromise and the 5th R [Blog post]. Retrieved from http://opencontent.org/blog/archives/3221

From Conversation to Cultural Change: Strategies for Connecting with Students and Faculty to Promote OER Adoption

Kirsten N. Dean

[S]hifting the mainstream public discourse is the best—and in most cases the only—way to achieve lasting change. Without this crucial ingredient, other movement successes—recruiting and empowering members in an expanding social organization; raising public awareness; and even convincing power holders to change policy in a desired direction—may prove ephemeral. By contrast, a movement that effectively alters the terms of discourse can overcome considerable opposition and structural disadvantages to achieve sustained, meaningful change (Woodly, 2015, p. 1).

Although Woodly was writing about national social movements, this argument may just as well apply to the promotion of open education (OE). Even if librarians and our allies succeed in advocating for open educational resources (OER) by recruiting participatory faculty, raising awareness across our communities, and gaining support from university administrators, our best chance at achieving sustainable and ever-deepening change requires a focus on discourse.

This chapter presents the practical details of how my colleagues and I increased OE awareness and incentivized OER adoption through a faculty stipend program at a public land-grant state university over the course of one year. Our communication strategies, timelines, and preliminary outcomes are grounded in the underlying assumptions that (1) conversations can promote lasting change and (2) grassroots-led action is preferable to top-down mandates. Although these assumptions may not apply in every context, my goal is to conceptualize our local progress in terms that may contribute to collectively developed models of successful and sustainable initiatives. Therefore, I emphasize discourse—that is, foreground "semantic tools and social processes" (Woodly, 2015, p. 22)—in this narrative of our successes and failures. This fits our story because I initially approached this work from a rhetorically influenced viewpoint. But I also contend that careful attention to discourse is vital for all library-led OE programs, since so much of our work can be classified as advocacy or persuasion. For this reason, frameworks drawn from political science and communication studies serve as useful analytic tools.

In the following sections, I will describe the situation of OE at Clemson University; offer a one-year timeline of our major activities; analyze our communicative approach; and reflect upon lessons learned and future directions.

Open Education at Clemson University

Clemson University is a public land-grant university in South Carolina with approximately 23,000 graduate and undergraduate students. While we know that, as on most campuses, there are faculty members engaging independently with OER, at the start of 2016 there was no coordinated effort to promote open education at the University. The Head of Digital Scholarship at the Clemson Libraries and colleagues at Clemson Online (the distance education department) had discussed and even budgeted for OER initiatives in previous years, but a lack of dedicated staff combined with major administrative changes in both units meant that the efforts remained speculative.

Despite these barriers, they laid the groundwork for more concerted action. In November 2014, the Clemson Libraries and Clemson Online co-sponsored an invited presentation by Dr. Cable Green, a prominent figure in the Open community. In early 2016, thanks to the Libraries' membership in SPARC (the Scholarly Publishing and Academic Resources Coalition), we sponsored a faculty member from the College of Education to participate in OpenCon. On his return, he addressed the campus community on "Making the Most of Open Educational Resources." These activities began conversations on campus as our local Open advocates sought dedicated institutional support. The effects of this preliminary work to connect interested parties, which in Clemson's case meant representatives from the Libraries, Clemson Online, and the College of Education, are still evident. These early allies remain our strongest, indicating the simple power of repeated social contact.

In July 2016, I accepted the newly created position of Undergraduate Instruction and Open Educational Resources Librarian. The Libraries had decided to try out an official and specific investment in open education by allocating 40 percent of the position to OER work. Classified as a temporary lecturer, I was tasked with working to transition classes from traditional textbooks to open materials through outreach to students and faculty. (The remainder of the position is dedicated to undergraduate information literacy instruction.) Since my position was fixed for a two-year term expiring in July 2018, we knew that we had to move quickly to capitalize on previous action and attempt to prove the lasting value of open education for the Clemson community.

The first challenge was clear and personal: at the start of 2016, I could barely define "OER." I had vague understandings of open access and copyright issues from nearly three years as a library specialist, but in order to take the lead on OER initiatives, I had a lot to learn. Throughout August and September, I attended webinars, read as much as I could, explored OER repositories and content types, and leaned heavily on the expertise of colleagues across campus and external partners such as SPARC. (Special thanks to SPARC's Assistant Director of Open Education, Brady Yano, for his invaluable support during these early days and beyond.)

These first few months were also about planning, defining, and connecting. The Head of Digital Scholarship, my supervisor and closest collaborator on the OER side of my job, introduced me to our indispensable partners at Clemson Online. As we discussed our programmatic aspirations, and as my knowledge of the OER universe slowly expanded, I began to understand my task as a communications challenge. The general charge to "establish an OER program" felt vague and daunting. So, like all good research librarians, we started by seeking models. Unsurprisingly, most institutions emphasized "awareness" as a vital first step. This, however, *still* felt vague and daunting. "Awareness" was a job for marketing or public relations or brand managers, not for introverted librarians! Failure loomed whenever I attempted to imagine myself as a salesperson with OER as my product, or even as a protestor agitating for policy changes. Doubtful of my role, I looked around for context clues—and realized that

I barely knew my own context. I had learned about open education abstractly, but still needed to break down our specific rhetorical situation at Clemson. This heuristic, a familiar one from my background in rhetoric and composition, provided guiding questions:

- Who is the audience?
- What is the purpose, message, and exigence?
- What is the medium and channel of communication?

Since each answer informs the others, I started by identifying our *audiences*. After all, we can hardly "raise awareness" without defining whose awareness we wish to raise. There are multiple stakeholders in the OE movement, but the most obvious audiences on a university campus are students, faculty, and administrators. As previously mentioned, we were already operating under the belief that top-down mandates would be slow, unsustainable, and potentially threatening to academic freedom. In their reflection on leading change at the University of Michigan-Flint, Gano-Phillips and Barnett (2008) concluded that they were only able to achieve "sweeping cultural change" (p. 41) by avoiding heavy-handed, top-down approaches. Instead, they "depended upon collective action" and "used existing faculty governance structures" (Phillips & Barnett, 2008, p. 41). This echoes much of the common wisdom about institutional reform. In accordance, we prioritized grassroots-led efforts over administrative action. Thus, two target audiences remained: students and faculty.

Our *purpose* was also twofold. Raising awareness may be an obvious first step, but its success is difficult to assess, and we had a two-year timeframe in which to produce outcomes that could inspire more permanent institutional support. We clearly needed measurable action, not just awareness. Previous conversations between the Libraries and Clemson Online had laid the groundwork for a faculty stipend program inspired by initiatives at other institutions. Establishing this stipend became a primary action item, with the goal of incentivizing faculty adoption, adaptation, or creation of OER for courses offered in fall 2017.

The *exigence* of OER initiatives, as explored in detail throughout this volume, is difficult to refute. Higher education costs are generally untenable, and textbook prices in particular have skyrocketed; most students lack required learning materials at some point due to these financial realities and/or the belief that such materials are unnecessary; open resources, practices, and pedagogy offer exciting and relatively easy solutions to these problems. However, the details and definitions embedded within this seemingly straightforward *message* mean that translating it for those with inconsistent OER knowledge requires careful tailoring—particularly when trying to keep it succinct enough to capture the limited time and attention of faculty and students. Moreover, convincing an audience of your argument's validity does not automatically lead them to act. I will further detail our messaging challenges and strategies later in this chapter.

Lastly, the communicative *mediums and channels* available on Clemson's campus have always posed difficulties. As in any large organization or community, and especially any decentralized university, multiple voices vie for the limited time and attention of their audiences. Therefore, gatekeepers often attempt to mediate this chaos by controlling access to channels such as email listservs and campus-wide news publications. Once again, the strength of an argument is inconsequential if it never reaches its intended audience. Knowing that this was a likely roadblock, opening channels quickly became a priority.

The Libraries already offered several avenues toward faculty. Liaison librarians communicated with their assigned academic departments, the Head of Digital Scholarship served on the Faculty Senate, and our administrative office provided me with contact information for each college's coordinator. More broadly, we could reach a self-selected population of faculty and students through the Libraries' blog and social media. But we still lacked a direct line to students, a larger and more diverse group than faculty and one whose communicative habits remained opaque. I needed insight and inroads.

As the fall 2016 semester began in earnest, I reached out to the Clemson Undergraduate Student Government (CUSG). I emailed the president, introduced myself and my task, and asked if we could meet to discuss student needs and possible collaborations. After our discussion, he delegated the (potential and undefined) project to CUSG's Academic Affairs Committee. The committee chair suggested that one member, a senator in her junior year, take the lead in working with me. Luckily for us, she was enthusiastic and committed, and Clemson's burgeoning OER movement gained a powerful ally armed with suggestions and networks for reaching other students. Her work led to the passage of a CUSG resolution expressing student support for OER adoption (see Appendix I).

Most of my conversations in these first three months were with colleagues and OER advocates as I developed content knowledge, learned from others' experiences, defined goals, and decided how to approach our local context. The following timeline describes what came next by charting our major events and activities up to May 2017.

Timeline of Major Activities

October 2016
In celebration of Open Access Week:

- Organized a pizza party for students with a presentation about OER basics by SPARC's Brady Yano via Google Hangouts.
- Assembled a display in the main library lobby that asked students to report their textbook expenditures on a whiteboard and to pick up a flyer about open alternatives.
- Offered students a chance to win gift cards if they recorded a brief testimonial about their experiences with textbook costs in our Adobe Studio's video recording room and signed a release allowing us to use the footage as needed for future media campaigns.
- Held two informational presentations for faculty: one by the Head of Digital Scholarship on open access publishing and one by me on defining and adopting OER.

November 2016
Attended the Annual Open Education Conference ("OpenEd") and Open-Con 2016, which both offered energizing opportunities to gather ideas, make connections (e.g., meeting with an Open Textbook Network representative), and get inspired. CUSG passed a Resolution in Support of Open Educational Resources (see Appendix I).

December 2016
Held final meetings with campus partners at Clemson Online and Human Resources to establish a faculty stipend program (see Appendix II for call for proposals). Updated web presence in the form of a LibGuide listing

OER repositories and related resources. Proposed membership in the Open Textbook Network to library leadership.

January 2017

Presented to the CUSG on the possibilities of OER and asked for volunteers to assist with Open Education Week in March. Presented to the Clemson Faculty Senate on OER benefits and campus support for adoption. Presented OER stipend details to liaison librarians in the Research Services unit. Advertised the faculty stipend program via Libraries' channels (including: blog, social media, and paper flyers in interlibrary loan books sent to faculty) and submissions to campus-wide news media.

February 2017

Continued soliciting applications for faculty stipend program, including direct emails to coordinators in each college who forwarded the message to their faculty listservs. Planned Open Education Week activities in collaboration with CUSG volunteers and advertised events via library channels, CUSG newsletter (sent to all students) and social media, and CUSG volunteers' personal networks of friends, Greek organizations, etc. Began receiving faculty stipend applications, primarily from the College of Education.

March 2017

In celebration of Open Education Week:

- Offered students a chance to win a gift card for creating a meme about OE and tagging the Libraries on Twitter.
- Set up a table on the high-traffic footbridge in front of the main library, staffed throughout the week by student volunteers, with candy, a sign advertising the meme contest, and flyers encouraging student advocacy for OER.
- Started a petition on Change.org (as per student suggestions) for students to sign in an expression of support for OER.
- Held two drop-in sessions for faculty with questions about the stipend.

Began receiving requests from faculty for consultations about stipend applications (by phone, email, and in person). Officially joined the Open Textbook Network and announced membership via press release sent to campus-wide publications. Contacted by the student newspaper, *The Tiger*, for an interview about our initiatives.

April 2017

Continued to meet with faculty as requested. Faculty stipend committee (with two representatives from the Libraries and two from Clemson Online) met to review applications and select award recipients.

May 2017

Updated CUSG partners on outcomes from Open Education Week and stipend process (e.g., number of petition signatures, estimated fall savings for students, etc.) before students left for summer break. Notified stipend recipients with award details. Emailed remaining stipend applicants with offers of assistance and suggestions of relevant OER for their courses.

Crafting Our Message

As evidenced by this timeline, most of our efforts in this first year have been various forms of outreach: media and advertising; presentations to both self-selected groups and influential campus bodies; contests; flyers; displays; networking; one-on-one discussions; etc. The hope is that these social processes will eventually transform our campus culture into one that not only accepts but expects OE practices. (Although this chapter focuses on Clemson's current work to encourage OER adoption in particular, I continually reference "OE practices" in general because I believe that our strategies can and will be applied more broadly.) At that point, the Libraries would primarily serve in a supporting role, offering expert advice to faculty. But, for now, we must continue to actively shape the discourse on campus. In this section, I will consider some of the approaches that helped us craft the messages behind our outreach activities.

I have already referenced my rhetorical approach to analyzing our local context, but the utility of rhetoric's classic emphasis on interactions between speaker/author, message/text, and audience(s) cannot be overstated. Prominent commentators in the OE community are also reflecting this. For example, in a blog post comparing pragmatic and idealistic approaches to OER advocacy, Jhangiani (2017) considered different identities that we may adopt as speakers/authors and how these stances affect our choice of messaging. That is, "whereas idealists emphasize student-centered, personalized solutions that foreground process and agency, pragmatists emphasize instructor-centered turnkey solutions that foreground content and efficiency" (Jhangiani, 2017). In his response to this post, Wiley (2017) shifted the emphasis from speaker to audience and argued that our messages should be shaped as specifically as possible, not only by distinguishing between groups such as faculty or students, but by tailoring our discursive choices to the individual. "Rather than a static framing like 'what kind of advocate should I be?,' I think a more useful framing would be dynamic, like 'as I'm advocating for open with this specific faculty member, should I advocate for an evolutionary approach to open ... or should my advocacy go straight to revolution?'" (Wiley, 2017). In short, both Jhangiani and Wiley are reminding us to be rhetorically aware.

What does this all mean in terms of message content? We know that, on most campuses, a majority of faculty still lack basic awareness and understanding of OER. In a recent qualitative study, Belikov and Bodily (2016) found that 73.9 percent of faculty still, quite simply, needed more information (p. 243). In consideration of our audience's limited knowledge, I have tried to ensure that every piece of general communication includes a brief definition of OER and summary of their benefits, regardless of the rest of the content (see Appendix III for press release example).

However, we are also attempting to incite action. When addressing students, our goal this year has been to encourage advocacy. By asking students to record testimonials, report textbook costs, and sign a petition, we have been able to collect student voices for use in future campaigns. Our direct requests for student action in the form of emails to, or office hours discussions with, professors is difficult to assess and, admittedly, can be a rather daunting task. Student participation in Open events, including contests with gift card incentives, has also been low in this first year. Clearly, garnering student involvement is an ongoing project. While messages about lowering textbook costs are highly resonant, as evidenced by enthusiastic responses from both individuals and groups of students such as CUSG, we are still seeking inroads and effective expectations for student action.

Realistically, when it comes to course material selection, faculty hold the power. When addressing faculty, we have been trying to encourage adoption of OE practices, with an emphasis on stipend applications and OER use in this first year. Many others have noted the limitations of cost savings arguments when addressing faculty, including Jhangiani (2017). To craft messages that resonate more deeply, I once again turn to advocacy strategies from political science. Woodly (2015) argued that "resonance is rooted in ... combining familiar values, common concepts, and new ideas into presumptive wholes that can come to be taken for granted" (p. 125). In other words, resonant arguments aim to shift the status quo by merging "existing understandings of the way things work or relate, with new arguments about what is significant or what is to be done" (Woodly, 2015, p. 97). This requires knowledge of underlying values and existing motivators. While, ideally, such knowledge is gained at the local level, we can make some assumptions about what drives university faculty at all institutions.

Wergin (2001) usefully summarized key themes found throughout research on faculty motivation, reporting that *autonomy, community, recognition*, and *efficacy* (p. 50) are the most important factors. This research provides another set of frames with which to analyze and organize our activities. For example, our commitment to grassroots rather than administrative action reinforces faculty *autonomy*, although we must be careful not to send the message that OER adoption is always the "best" or "only" way. So far, the only direct sign of pushback that I have received was during a conversation with an influential faculty member, in which he warned that some of his colleagues might interpret our efforts as an encroachment on their freedom to choose course materials.

We are working to develop a *community* around OE, although this is an ongoing project that requires wider awareness and participation. The faculty stipend recipients will, we hope, become the core of a growing community of practice that the Libraries and our allies can nurture through events and social networking. The stipend itself is one form of *recognition*, although our limited communication channels means that this recognition may not always spread as far as we would like. In future, the goal is for news of faculty accomplishments to trickle up, reaching the ears of influential campus figures (from department chairs to upper administration) who have the power to broadcast more widely in voices with more weight.

Lastly, we know that faculty care about their students. Proving the *efficacy* of OE is currently a research emphasis throughout the open community. Locally, part of our job is to collect, focus, and amplify the voices of Clemson students. Anecdotal feedback gathered through displays, video testimonials, petition signatures, the CUSG resolution, and personal interactions indicates that students believe OER can help them succeed. However, we have also found that they are understandably reluctant to directly advocate for OE to faculty members. Therefore, it falls on us to help faculty recognize the value of OE practices for their students.

These motivational factors serve as helpful frames when crafting messages directed toward faculty. However, it is still incredibly easy to fall into the "carrots and sticks" mentality that Wergin (2001) maligned. Even the widely popular stipend approach, which can be seen as offering a "carrot" of monetary rewards to faculty who agree to adopt or create OER, has obvious weaknesses: stipends are only sustainable if libraries or other advocates include them in their budgets, and—even more crucially when viewed from a discourse perspective—they imply that adopting OE practices is "above and beyond" a faculty member's normal responsibilities, and thus warranting additional compensation, rather than an expected part of routine course planning activities. Similarly, although I believe that OE efforts should eventually be recognized in tenure and promotion guidelines, any attempts to force such deep institutional changes, rather than allowing them to organically grow as a result of cultural shifts, could have unintended negative consequences. Once again, this leaves us to rely on conversations, rather than carrots or sticks, as the core of our work—and makes patience a necessary correlate.

Measuring Our Success

Happily, we do have some measures of success available at the end of this first year. These outcomes are not only vital on a personal level, helping advocates to avoid burnout by providing evidence of efficacy, but are also required to garner continued institutional support.

Our clearest measurable success is the faculty stipend program. We awarded six $2,000 stipends and expect to save students nearly $100,000 in textbook costs in fall 2017. These savings should continue each semester. Our monetary inputs to yield this return include: $12,000 in direct stipend funding provided by Clemson Online plus related expenditures by the Libraries to fund 40 percent of a temporary lecturer position, SPARC and Open Textbook Network membership fees, and professional development funds used for OpenEd and OpenCon attendance.

We can also measure faculty buy-in beyond that of the six stipend recipients by considering total numbers of applicants and faculty consultations. For example, at least two faculty members (one from the College of Engineering and one from the communications department) are planning to adopt OER in their classes this fall even though they did not receive a stipend. I have also had recent conversations with a group of mathematics faculty who, prompted by my visit to the Faculty Senate, are interested in adopting open homework systems. It may be difficult to track these ripple effects with precision, but they certainly indicate an increase in OE-related action across campus.

Ultimately, it is difficult to quantify the effects that I argue are even more important: steps toward a change in discourse, behavior, and culture. But there are some frameworks at our disposal to help chart this movement. Raneri and Young (2016), in their discussion of OER programs at Maricopa Community Colleges, pointed to their use of John Kotter's eight steps for leading change as one useful model (p. 583). According to Kotter, we must "establish urgency, form guiding coalition[s], create vision, communicate vision, empower others to act, plan for short-term wins, produce more change, and institutionalize new approaches" (Raneri & Young, 2016, p. 583). In our case, the urgency of OE is already globally established and locally confirmed; we have formed a guiding coalition between the Libraries and Clemson Online, though its sustainability is uncertain due to budgets and changing leadership; and we have created and communicated a vision of OER adoption on campus through our messaging. Our faculty stipend program is already enacting "short-term wins," and we hope that it will instigate further change. By this metric, our efforts to lead change are well underway.

We might also look to measurements of behavioral change such as Patrick Jackson's approach. I stumbled across this model while exploring public relations basics in the hope of finding guidance for OER outreach. Jackson listed these steps toward change: awareness, knowledge, interest, desire to change, preference for new behaviors, and adoption of new behaviors (Black, 2014, pp. 26–27). Under this framework, I would locate Clemson's progress toward the middle. We have been striving throughout this year to raise awareness, knowledge, and interest in OE among faculty. The stipend program has led some to adopt, or at least try out, the new behavior of incorporating OER into their courses. However, on a larger scale, we are still in the early stages of cultivating faculty interest in change. This is a long-term project, and Jackson's stages help us preview our intended path.

Reflection: Why Discourse Matters

Our choice of communication strategies (whether targeted toward students, faculty, administrators, or other campus publics) not only affects the quantitative success of OE programs (e.g., numbers of OER adoptions or dollar amounts of student savings) but also lays the groundwork for long-lasting cultural change within our institutions. In this context, I use "cultural change" to mean embedded shifts in routines, behaviors, values, and expectations at both individual and institutional levels. For example: expanding student and faculty expectations of what a "textbook" looks like and how it can be used; changing instructors' processes for finding and selecting teaching resources; and establishing institutionalized structures with budgets, staff, and policies to support OE. Discourse allows or impedes these changes because "the way that we talk about issues in public both reflects and determines what solutions are considered desirable or plausible" (Woodly, 2015, p. 19). In other words, discourse constitutes possibilities—and, in classical rhetorical terms, determines "the available means of persuasion" (Aristotle, 350BCE) available to us as we plan our advocacy work.

In an essay about the rise of discourse perspectives in organizational communications research, Putnam (1999) argued:

> Discourse, in this orientation, is the way that organizational understanding is produced and reproduced. Labels such as "ideal patient" and "healthcare provider" are not simply terms that classify occupational groups; rather *they define expectations, forms of knowledge, and task activities for organizational groups.* (p. 60, emphasis added)

The same is true for labels like "textbook" and "open" and "educational resource": the way that academic librarians represent them in conversations or advertisements affects institutional activities. Schoeneborn and

Blaschke (2017) confirmed the continuing influence of perspectives that examine "the formative role of communication in constituting organizational phenomena of various kinds" (p. xiii). This resonates with the concept of constitutive rhetoric, which further defines how communication strategies can form, cohere, or "constitute" definitions, identities, and realities (White, 1984; Charland, 1987). Accepting and leveraging the idea that discourse has constitutive power can help us to sustainably achieve our goals.

A focus on discourse lends itself particularly well to decentralized university contexts in which faculty governance and academic freedom should stand at the forefront of any attempts at institutional change. Rather than creating and passing down ideas about OE through administrative policies, starting with conversations among faculty and students encourages OE practices to be constituted naturally and eventually routinized. This grassroots approach to change management also allows for the fractures and contradictions (Putnam, 1999, p. 63) inherent in academia, from disciplinary or departmental differences to individual idiosyncrasies among faculty members.

Moreover, this belief in the power of conversations helps us choose strategies. At Clemson, we have decided that encouraging grassroots action by students and faculty, drawing on existing values and motivations, and working to change routinized behaviors will—slowly, but surely—change our campus culture. After all, "National political agendas do not merely develop; they are made by and through the speech and action of officials, elite opinion leaders, news media, interpersonal interactions, and the organized efforts of grass-roots" (Woodly, 2015, p. 33). Similarly, a campus focus on open education does not spontaneously arise, but instead requires initiatives led by OER advocates and carried forward by organizations such as student and faculty governments; recruitment of influential voices; campus-wide messaging strategies; and those all-important conversations, conducted at every turn.

Next Steps: Sustainability and Growth

By incentivizing initial OER adoptions and then gathering data, narratives, and advocates, we hope to translate grassroots efforts among students and faculty into part of our institutional identity, prompting wide-scale adoption and administrative support. Our success, at Clemson and beyond, will ultimately be measured not only by number of adoptions, depth of pedagogical integration, and amount of money saved for students, but also by the institutionalized structures—such as funding, policies, and staff—put in place to provide sustainable support for OE practices.

Clearly, we still have a great deal to accomplish before successfully changing the discourse around educational resources and practices at Clemson University. As I complete the first year of my position, we already have several firm goals ahead. Our membership in the Open Textbook Network means that we will host workshops in September 2017 for faculty to learn more about the process and possibilities of OER and for librarians and other personnel to learn how to support faculty adoption. We will also continue to support the faculty stipend recipients as they implement OER in their courses and highlight their progress to demonstrate new possibilities for their colleagues. Further, since CUSG's involvement has proven to be a useful representation of student interest, I will reconnect with our contacts when they return to campus in the fall. My goal is to institutionalize support for OER at the student level by encouraging the formation of a standing committee or work group in CUSG. Lastly, contingent upon the success of the stipend program's fall semester results, we should have funding available to offer a second round of stipends in 2018.

As awareness increases, so does the need for resources. One pressing project is to improve our web presence and distinguish it from Clemson Online's Open Education web site. Although the basic distinction between our departments is that the Libraries provide support with discovery and adaptation of resources while Clemson Online supports the development of pedagogical strategies, our roles naturally overlap. Luckily, we work well together and share a passion for our goals. Unfortunately, however, our websites do not currently help visitors clarify our differences or take advantage of our connections.

We must also capitalize on our first stipend program's results in order to promote an anticipated repetition of the program in 2018 and to recruit participation in other OE initiatives such as the Open Textbook Network workshop. Media campaigns and future presentations to student and faculty governments will feature the accomplishments of our stipend recipients.

Furthermore, although we have an estimate of student savings from stipend recipients, we do not know how much OE practices are helping students across campus to succeed in their programs. I plan to survey our faculty to compile a comprehensive picture of OE activities, particularly among faculty with whom I have not yet been in contact. The survey itself will raise awareness, and its results will allow us to describe the current state of open education at Clemson with far better accuracy. Ideally, this survey will also gauge faculty understanding of OER and their primary motivations for interest in OE, helping us to craft more resonant arguments. Once we have evidence in hand of OE on Clemson's campus, rather than trying to generalize from the experiences of other institutions, I will target high-enrollment classes and large programs (such as introductory math, writing, and chemistry) to expand our reach. This could, of course, be a first step for other open advocates in their local contexts. However, I consider these classes to be such important targets that I would like to test our strategies, hone our arguments, and collect more data before approaching program leaders.

I firmly believe that all of these efforts can only be made sustainable through cultural change. If faculty and students start talking about and expecting education in new ways, then administrative buy-in and institutional structures to support OE will follow out of necessity. Unfortunately, cultural change tends to be slow and difficult to measure, meaning that most of our successes and failures will be proven only by time. However, the current structure of education in the United States is tipping toward the untenable. We are due for widespread changes. If we, as open advocates, can help to change the discourse around educational materials and practices on our campuses, then we may just be able to shape these new conceptualizations in ways that broaden opportunities for all students.

References

Aristotle (350 BCE). *Rhetoric.* (W. R. Roberts, Trans.). Retrieved from
http://classics.mit.edu/Aristotle/rhetoric.1.i.html
Belikov, O.M., & Bodily, R. (2016). Incentives and barriers to OER adoption: A qualitative analysis of faculty perceptions. *Open Praxis, 8*(3), 235-246. doi: dx.doi.org/10.5944/openpraxis.8.3.308
Black, C. (2014). *The PR professional's handbook: Powerful, practical communications.* London: Kogan Page.

Charland, M. (1987). Constitutive rhetoric: The case of the peuple Québécois. *Quarterly Journal of Speech, 73*(2), 133–150.

Gano-Phillips, S., & Barnett, R.W. (2008). Against all odds: Transforming institutional culture. *Liberal Education, (94)*2, 36–41.

Jhangiani, R. (2017, February 15). Pragmatism vs. idealism and the identity crisis or OER advocacy. [Blog post]. Retrieved from http://thatpsychprof.com/pragmatism-vs-idealism-and-the-identity-crisis-of-oer-advocacy/

Putnam, L. L. (1999). Shifting metaphors of organizational communication: The rise of discourse perspectives. In P. Salem (Ed.), *Organizational communication and change* (pp. 45–65). Cresskill, NJ: Hampton.

Raneri, A., & Young, L. (2016). Leading the Maricopa millions OER project. *Community College Journal of Research and Practice,40*(7), 580–588. doi: 10.1080/10668926.2016.1143413

Schoeneborn, D., & Blaschke, S. (2017). Introduction. In S. Blaschke & D. Schoeneborn (Eds.), *Organization as communication: Perspectives in dialogue* (pp. xiii–xxii). New York: Routledge.

Wergin, J.F. (2001). Beyond carrots and sticks: What really motivates faculty. *Liberal Education, 87*(1), 50–53.

White, J. B. (1984). *When words lost their meaning: Constitutions and reconstitutions of language, character, and community.* Chicago: University of Chicago Press.

Wiley, D. (2017, February 16). Evolution vs. revolution [Blog post]. Retrieved from https://opencontent.org/blog/archives/4910

Woodly, D. (2015). *The politics of common sense: How social movements use public discourse to change politics and win acceptance.* Oxford: Oxford University Press.

Appendix I: A Resolution To Support The Use of Open Educational Resources

Resolution No. 6

Date Submitted: 11/03/2016

2016/2017 Clemson Undergraduate Student Senate

Committee: Academic Affairs

Purpose: To express Undergraduate Student Senate support for reducing textbook costs and increasing the use of open educational resources at Clemson University.

Whereas, as a result of regular increases in student tuition and fees, many Clemson University students face economic challenges while completing their degrees, and

Whereas, open educational resources are low-cost yet effective substitutes for traditional textbook materials, and

Whereas, traditional textbooks may fail to arrive on time, but open educational resources

Whereas, in an informal poll conducted by the Clemson University Libraries, 84% of the 445 respondents reported not buying a required textbook due to cost, and 29% of respondents reported dropping a class due to textbook cost, and

Whereas, in another informal poll of similar size conducted by the Clemson University Libraries, 27% of respondents reported incurring more debt due to textbook cost, and 13% of respondents reported forgoing basic necessities to purchase required textbooks.

Therefore, **Be it Resolved** by the Clemson Undergraduate Student Senate assembled in regular session the following:

That the Clemson Undergraduate Student Senate supports the use of more affordable educational materials including, but not limited to, open educational resources.

Appendix II: Faculty Stipend Call for Proposals

The Clemson University Libraries and Clemson Online seek proposals for the implementation of Open Educational Resources (OER) into existing Clemson courses. OER are instructional materials such as textbooks that are free to users and openly licensed to allow unlimited distribution and modification. To pilot the introduction of OER on campus and assist with course transitions, we are awarding $2,000 to one faculty member in each college.

Proposals Due: April 14th, 2017

Eligibility: All faculty.

Requirements: Adopt, adapt, or create Open Educational Resources (OER) to replace existing materials in a course currently offered at Clemson University. All implemented OER must be licensed under a Creative Commons Attribution (CC-BY) license or similar.

Selection Committee: Two representatives from Clemson University Libraries (Head of Digital Scholarship and OER Librarian) and two representatives from Clemson Online (Deputy Director of Curriculum and Instruction and Manager of Learning Systems and Resources).

Evaluation Criteria:

1. Potential savings and remaining costs for Clemson students
2. Applicant's preparation to successfully implement OER
3. Feasibility of implementing OER transition by Fall 2017
4. Creativity of proposed adoption/adaptation/creation

Application Instructions: Complete and submit the following form and email your C.V. to Kirsten Dean, Clemson Libraries, at kirsted@clemson.edu. Stipend recipients will be notified in May. Note that one stipend is available for each college, but each college is not guaranteed a stipend.

Appendix III: Press Release

Clemson Joins Open Textbook Network, Offers $2,000 to Faculty Members

Clemson University is a proud new member of the Open Textbook Network, an alliance of colleges and universities working to promote "access, affordability, and student success through the use of open textbooks." Open textbooks are written by experts and peer-reviewed, just like traditional textbooks — but because they're published online under open licenses, they're free to use and customize!

The average college student spends over $1,000 each year on textbooks, and many Clemson students report spending even more. As textbook costs continue to rise at over four times the rate of inflation and student debt reaches unprecedented levels, students are increasingly forced to make tough decisions about how to afford their education. For too many, that means not buying required textbooks, taking fewer classes, and suffering both academically and financially.

Joining the Open Textbook Network is just one part of a larger initiative sponsored by the Clemson University Libraries and Clemson Online to bring open educational resources (OER) to campus and reduce costs for students. Last November, the Clemson Undergraduate Student Government (CUSG) declared its endorsement by passing a Resolution to Support the Use of Open Educational Resources. CUSG senators are continuing to raise awareness and make student voices heard. You may have recently seen them on the library bridge during Open Education Week, a global celebration of educational equity.

We know that change isn't easy, so the Clemson Libraries and Clemson Online are offering professional support along with **$2,000 stipends to help faculty transition to OER**. Faculty interested in replacing their course materials with OER may apply here by April 14th.

As part of our Open Textbook Network (OTN) membership, we will also be hosting a workshop this fall with financial incentives for participating faculty. A team of OTN experts will be on hand to provide training in OER assessment and adoption, along with continuing support. Stay tuned for more details!

Questions or comments? Contact Kirsten Dean, OER Librarian, at kirsted@clemson.edu.

Making the Connections: The Role of Professional Development in Advocating for OER

Michael LaMagna

Introduction

Although faculty awareness and use of open educational resources (OER) is currently growing at many institutions of higher education given the continued conversation about course content access, course material costs, and retention and completion efforts, in 2012, the level of awareness among college and university faculty members was not as widespread. Given the gap in faculty awareness and adoption of OER, faculty librarians at Delaware County Community College (DCCC) wanted to not only bring increased awareness on campus through advocacy but also take a leadership role in the process. Using a model of advocacy through institutional professional development, faculty librarians at the college were able to build awareness and use of OER. The Professional Development Committee drives all professional development at the College. This is a committee made up of representatives from all constituencies at the college to design and implement a total of eight days of mandatory professional development opportunities for members of the college community. Although these professional development days were originally designed exclusively for faculty, these experiences have evolved to address the overall needs of the college community. These days consist of several approximately 90-minute sessions that utilize a variety of modalities including lectures, panel discussions, workshops, and meetings.

College costs continue to dominate the discussion among politicians, parents, and prospective students. Since the recession in 2008, colleges and universities have looked at ways to reduce tuition, room, board, and ancillary costs to attract prospective students. Students at all institutions of higher education face financial challenges related to housing, food cost, and rising tuition prices. At the macro level, within the greater Philadelphia area where DCCC is located, Rosemont College made national news by announcing a significant reduction in the cost of tuition to attract new students (Snyder, 2015). In addition to reducing the tuition costs of attendance, colleges and universities also understand the importance of reducing the number of obstacles students may face at the micro level to improve retention and completion rates. Specifically, for community college students, there are additional financial obstacles that are not necessarily faced by students at other institutions of higher education. In addition to tuition costs, community college students often struggle when faced with personal financial obstacles as well as other non-tuition educational costs (Camera, 2016). These non-tuition financial obstacles include housing, food, transportation and the cost of educational resources and materials (Camera, 2016). While these obstacles are not exclusive to community college students, as this impacts students at all institutions of higher education, the nontraditional population of community college students makes the use of OER in the community college environment a natural fit (Vitez, 2018).

OER "demonstrate great potential as a mechanism for instructional innovation as networks of teachers and learners share best practices" (William and Flora Hewlett Foundation, 2011). The case to migrate course content away from traditional publisher content toward OER has never been stronger. The growth in the range and quality of content now available to faculty members from across disciplines demonstrates that OER have a place in higher education. Academic libraries and professional librarians are well positioned to advocate for the use of OER based on our service to the college community at large and our professional knowledge, skills, and abilities.

Beginning in 2012, faculty librarians at DCCC offered institutional professional development programs during the college's faculty in-service days related to OER. The first professional development program, titled "Alternatives to the Textbook: Open Educational Resources and Open Access Journals" was well received by faculty members throughout the college and resulted in a second professional development program titled "Open Educational Resources: Alternatives to the Traditional Textbook" the following year. This advocacy of OER by the faculty librarian built interest among the general faculty and administration, which led to the formation of the Alternatives to the Textbook Committee—later shortened to Alt Text Committee. As interest in the use of OER continued to grow at the college, members of the Alt Text Committee created additional professional development programs for faculty related to licensing, creation, and adoption of OER. The continued advocacy of OER via institutional professional development opportunities inspired the college to invite an outside keynote speaker to a faculty in-service professional development day to discuss OER.

This continued focus on OER through institutional professional development has further contributed to the realization of several institution-wide OER initiatives, including: an awarded grant to fund the migration of business courses away from traditional textbooks toward OER, an increased interest by the general faculty in the application of OER, and a formal discussion among administration on the feasibility of developing a zero textbook cost degree program. The role of the academic library in building an OER program centered on an information campaign focused on the larger college community about the growing importance and practicality of these resources. This case study describes the importance of advocacy through the use of institutional professional development at DCCC; it will also interweave how other approaches to advocacy intersect with professional development.

Literature Review

Through the examination of the specific literature stream related to approaches utilized by academic libraries when advocating the use of OER at the institutional level, the literature provided relevant and practical approaches to ensure positive results. When academic libraries advocate for the use of OER, they need to move beyond the basic marketing efforts that have been a hallmark of library services promotions. This will require moving beyond writing columns for the library's newsletter or posting information on the library's website (Kachel, 2017). The American Association of School Librarians (AASL) offers a relevant definition of advocacy that can be applied in the higher education setting. The AASL (n.d.) defines advocacy as an "ongoing process of building partnership so that others will act for and with you, turning passive support into educated action for the library program. It begins with a vision and a plan for the library program that is then matched to the agenda and priorities of stakeholders." Using this definition to inform the process to develop an impactful OER program, Fasimpaur (2012) offers four concrete steps to advocating for the use of OER. The first step that Fasimpaur (2012) identifies is "start with your curriculum goals and involve teachers from the start" (p. 38). This is followed by "offering high quality professional development – early and often" (Fasimpaur, 2012, p. 38). The final two steps are "find the OER that are right for your students" and "use OER to customize curriculum and differentiate learning" (Fasimpaur, 2012, p. 39–40).

The academic library's role in developing OER programs is outlined within the four steps put forward by Fasimpaur (2012). Most importantly, academic libraries can build awareness and advocate for the use of OER by first educating the college community, specifically teaching faculty, about the resources that are available. As Allen and Seaman (2014) note, there is a lack of knowledge among faculty concerning OER, how to find the content, and how to use the materials in a legal and ethical manner. This lack of knowledge concerning OER offers libraries the opportunity to develop professional development programs that advocate for the proper use of these materials. These educational and professional development opportunities can be workshops, learning communities both within the library and outside, and other opportunities (Hess, Nann, & Riddle, 2016; Miller & Homol, 2016; Smith & Lee, 2017; Woodward, 2017). Grant programs are another approach and provide a similar opportunity to advocate for OER use on campus through the creation and/or adoption of content (Blick & Marcus, 2017). Ultimately, successfully advocating for the use of OER and building a successful program require collaboration between the library and the faculty members (Goodsett, Loomis, & Miles, 2016). Using these collaborative approaches to providing educational or professional development opportunities within the college or university, libraries can take a leadership role in advocating for the use of OER.

Institutional Profile

Founded in 1967, DCCC serves suburban, urban, and rural populations in two counties in Southeastern Pennsylvania. Currently, DCCC has nine campus locations in Delaware and Chester counties. As of the spring 2017 semester, the College has a total student population of 10,998 students and a full-time equivalency of 7,765 students in a range of transfer and career and professional degree programs (Institutional Effectiveness Office, 2017). Currently, 60 percent of students enrolled at the College take classes on the main Marple Campus, with the remaining 40 percent of students enrolled at branch campus locations in Delaware and Chester counties (Institutional Effectiveness Office, 2017). At DCCC, the Online Campus offering distance learning courses and programs continues to grow with a 3.1 percent increase from 2016 to 2017 and a total enrollment of 6,936 students (Institutional Effectiveness Office, 2017). Teaching these students are approximately 830 full- and part-time faculty members (Delaware County Community College, 2017).

Institutional Professional Development Priorities

As part of DCCC's shared governance structure, the College Advisory System (CAS) focuses on "support[ing] the college's mission to facilitate learning by providing quality educational programs and services that are student-focused, accessible, comprehensive and flexible to meet the educational needs of the diverse communities it serves. In doing so, the college will enable its students to develop themselves to the limit of their desires and capabilities and to be successful" (College Advisory System, 2016, p. 3). One standing committee associated with CAS is the Professional Development Committee (PDC). This committee is charged with identifying "professional development needs, interests, and priorities of full- and part-time faculty members, support staff, and administrative employees through committee members and general advertisement to the College community" (College Advisory System, 2016, p. 22) (see Appendix A for a complete list of committee functions).

Part of the work of the PDC is to develop faculty in-service opportunities twice each semester for a total of four professional development in-services each academic year. Before the start of each semester in August and January, faculty members are required to attend two days of professional development. During the fall semester in October and during the spring semester in February, faculty members are required to attend two additional days of professional development. Recently, these professional development days have grown to include administrators, staff, and adjunct faculty as participants. In addition to faculty, divisional, and administrative meetings, professional development programs are offered throughout the day. It is during this period that faculty librarians offered professional development programs related to resources and services with specific attention to new resources or important topics. With an increased focus on the rising costs of textbooks, faculty librarians began exploring the feasibility of using OER at the College.

Faculty librarians examined the textbook costs at DCCC. Using prices from 2012, the faculty librarians determined what the cost would be for students taking four typical courses during a semester at the College, based on existing academic program structures. At that time, the total cost would be $646.33. For comparison, those textbooks were found on Amazon at a less expensive price of $505.12.

Table 1. Textbook Costs Comparisons from 2012

Course Number	Course Title	Citation	Amazon Price	Bookstore Price
DPR100	Introduction to Information Technology	Evans, A. R., Martin, K., & Poatsy, M. A. S. (2011). *Technology in action, complete* (8th ed.). Upper Saddle River, NJ: Prentice Hall.	$103.51	$145.33
BIO110	Introductory Biology	Reece, J. B., Urry, L. A., Cain, M. L. Wasserman, S. A., Minorsky, P. V., & Jackson, R. B (2010). *Campbell Biology* (9th ed.). San Francisco, CA: Benjamin Cummings.	$161.49	$202.67

Course Number	Course Title	Citation	Amazon Price	Bookstore Price
ENG112	English Composition II	Roberts, E. V., & Zweig, G. (2011). *Literature: An introduction to reading and writing* (10th ed.). Upper Saddle River, NJ: Prentice Hall.	$87.41	$111.00
MAT140	College Algebra and Trigonometry	Sullivan, M. (2011). *Algebra and trigonometry* (9th ed.). Boston, MA: Addison Wesley.	$152.71	$187.33

It was this information that initially convinced the faculty librarians to advocate for the use of OER, and to do so through the existing professional development program for faculty. The mandatory professional development day was ideal to begin this conversation because of the cyclical nature of these events (occurring for two consecutive days, four times per year) as well as the captive target audience they provide (mandatory for all full-time faculty). The textbook cost comparisons illustrated in Table 1 were also utilized to initiate the conversation with teaching faculty regarding the value of exploring and possibly adopting OER at the College. At the time this information was first reviewed and evaluated by the faculty librarians, there was some concern about electronic access to course material, because the Florida Distance Learning Consortium (2011) survey indicated that only 45 percent of students would prefer that some or all of their course material be available in an electronic format. While Dahlstrom, De Boor, Grunwald, and Vockley's (2011) study indicates there was an increase in personal computing device ownership at the time, they did note that "students at associate's colleges and other two-year programs are more likely to own stationary technologies, such as desktop computers and stationary gaming and video devices, particularly in comparison to students at doctorate-granting institutions" (p. 9). With these considerations in mind, the plan to advocate for the use of OER was developed and the focus was through the institution's professional development days. This provided the faculty librarians with access to the greatest number of faculty members at one time and would allow those interested in learning more about this topic to self-select into attending these sessions.

Faculty In-Service Presentations

Beginning in January 2012, two faculty librarians offered the first professional development program related to OER to the College community. As Fasimpaur (2012) stated, it is important to "offer high quality professional development – early and often" (p. 38). As part of this advocacy through professional development approach, the first program was designed to provide a foundation of knowledge about the issues of rising textbook prices and what alternatives existed at the time. The professional development program was titled *Alternatives to the Textbook: Open Educational Resources and Open Access Journals* (see Appendix B for the professional development program description).

This program was well attended and resulted in faculty members approaching the librarians to discuss both current, informal open educational projects the individual faculty members were working on and to discuss best practices on migrating away from a traditionally published textbook and adopt OER in their classes. It was clear after this session that although many faculty members showed an interest in OER adoption, they were largely isolated events without collaboration or larger vision. Some of the singular projects and ideas that were shared as a result of this session were: the adoption of an open access textbook through Flatworld Knowledge and OpenStax, the development of OER by a faculty member in the area of studio arts, and the creation of a collaborative project between the library and an English faculty member that would load OER onto Amazon Kindles to ensure students had continuous access to course material. The interest in reducing textbook costs on campus both from faculty members and administrators allowed the library to purchase these Kindles through funding from the Provost's Office. The two faculty librarians that offered this program developed a LibGuide as a starting point for faculty members interested in moving in this direction.

The interest generated from this first institutional professional development program led the PDC to request a second program on issues around OER. The use of professional development in advocating for the use of OER proved successful. A second professional development program was offered in October 2012. While the first program was offered by two librarians, the second institutional professional development program included the faculty member who used open educational content loaded on Kindles, the Director of Online Learning, and instructional design staff member in addition to two faculty librarians. The program was titled "Open Educational Resources: Alternatives to the Traditional Textbook" (see Appendix C for a complete professional development program description).

As with the first presentation, this second one was well received. It was at this time that the campus-wide Alt Text Committee was formed to examine the use of OER on campus. This committee included faculty members from across the college including librarians and interested staff and administrators. In addition to the committee, the Provost's Office offered funding for faculty members interested in developing OER for use at the college.

To support the Provost's Office's desire to create OER at the college, the next set of institutional professional development opportunities were designed to provide faculty members with the knowledge, skills, and abilities necessary to produce content. During the February 2014 Faculty In-Service there were three sessions offered specifically to continue to advocate for the use of OER by faculty members. The three professional development program titles were: *Look Ma! No textbook!*, *Building Alternative Course Content*, and *Copyright in the Academic Environment* (see Appendix D for complete list of the series professional development program descriptions).

This final set of institutional professional development opportunities included bringing to campus a nationally known figure in the library and information science field to discuss the use of OER. The combined foci of the keynote address along with three sessions showed faculty how important this work was to the institution.

Discussion

During the two years of concerted professional development opportunities the library was able to work with a range of faculty members on OER projects. This work included conducting a second pilot program using the Amazon Kindles as delivery tools for OER. It was clear this was an approach that alleviated fears among faculty members that students without home access to technology would still be able to access the content outside of class.

As these pilot programs continued, the work for advocating for the use of OER moved in a new direction based on the work of the Alt Text Committee. Because they were working with the Provost's Office, this committee soon shifted from advocating for the use of OER and instead changed to working with faculty on developing their own content for use. The desire was that faculty members would create content specifically for DCCC courses based on the Master Course Outline, which dictates how a course is taught. This would ensure that course sections taught by full-time faculty members and those taught by adjunct faculty members would use this content so as to ensure all students would benefit from the program.

To facilitate the development of OER on campus, the Provost's Office worked with the Office of Institutional Advancement, and received funding from a large local employer to fund faculty grants. These grants would fund faculty interested in producing OER during the summer months. The Alt Text Committee did not receive many applications. At this same time there were changes in senior leadership in the Provost's Office, which resulted in new directions for the OER program. Because of this uncertainty the Library and Learning Commons once again took leadership for advocating and assisting faculty in migrating and integrating OER in their classes.

In 2016, the Library Services within the Learning Commons received a $10,000 Library Services and Technology Act (LSTA) grant from the State Library of Pennsylvania, for use in working with faculty members in the business department to transition high-enrollment classes from traditional textbooks to OER (DCCC, 2016). Collaboration between Library Services and a business faculty member resulted in moving BUS 130: Business Communications from a traditional textbook course to one using

OER. The success of this collaboration resulted in additional faculty members from other departments expressing interest in participating in this program. In addition to the business course, the college was able to transition COMM 111: Public Speaking from using a traditional textbook to using OER. The LSTA grant funded professional development, OER evaluation and review, and support for the transitioning of these courses. The faculty member who participated in this grant expressed strong support for the use of OER and plans to continue using these materials.

Because of the success of the LSTA grant program, the next step for OER is to begin another round of institutional professional development programs. Currently, we plan to work with the two faculty members who participated in the LSTA grant program and ask them to offer personal accounts of their process migrating and integrating OER into online and classroom-based courses. Having faculty as part of the professional development workshops enhances the credibility of OER and provides others with professional resources who can speak directly about what to expect. In addition, through collaborating with faculty members on the professional development workshops, we plan to revisit some of the previous professional development programs and update the content so that we reach new faculty members who joined recently.

Conclusion

While DCCC has a unique model for delivering professional development to the campus community through consistent opportunities for interaction, academic libraries can replicate this approach by applying similar strategies on their campuses. Academic libraries can develop short professional development opportunities during the course of a semester at times convenient for faculty members to attend by analyzing the semester course schedule or by targeting a specific academic division through their library liaison. These short programs should be approximately 60 minutes in length and can be delivered both in person and synchronously online, using affordable or free web conferencing software. Libraries should consider creating a professional development program in which each workshop is sequential and designed to build on the work of the previous session, but would also allow for faculty members to jump into the series when needed without consequence. This allows faculty members who attend professional development workshops to become more aware and educated about OER and begin larger conversations within their own departments, divisions, or across the College. It provides them with an opportunity to discuss how they might migrate and integrate OER into their own courses.

Advocacy through professional development also ensures that the college community understands the role the library can play in leading OER initiatives. Librarians leading this project need to highlight their subject matter expertise when promoting and advocating the use of OERs on campus and discuss the value they can bring to the adoption of this content. It is essential to connect faculty members that are interested in using OER content with appropriate sources. Facilitating the use of this content will ensure librarians are viewed as subject matter experts. Librarians should be active partners in this work with faculty, be responsive to their needs and help to identify any possible pitfalls of adopting these resources. Ideally, this ongoing partnership should further strengthen the relationship between the faculty and the library. When a faculty member expresses interest in pursuing or even adopting an OER, follow-up by the faculty librarian is essential through one-on-one meetings and email. Early adopters are often the leading advocates on campus if their experience is a positive one and can be invited to present their own professional development program within the series.

Finally, librarians, while working with the library administration, need to connect with the larger institutional administration structure to ensure the support and resources necessary for OER adoption is available. The focus of this work should be through the Provost or Vice President of Academic Affairs office. For academic libraries interested in taking a leadership position on campus in advocating for the use of OER, there are a number of approaches. The literature on advocating for OER shares that collaboration, grants, and encouragement work when connections are made by librarians to the curriculum and through specific disciplines. Based on our understanding of the OER atmosphere on our own campus, our successful approach was advocacy through professional development.

References

Allen, I. E. & Seaman, J. (2014). *Opening the curriculum: Open educational resources in the U.S. higher education, 2014.* Babson Research Survey Group. Retrieved from https://www.onlinelearningsurvey.com/reports/openingthecurriculum2014.pdf

American Association of School Librarians. (n.d.). What is advocacy? Retrieved from http://www.ala.org/aasl/advocacy/definitions

Blick, W., & Marcus, S. (2017). The brightly illuminated path: Facilitating an OER program at community college. *College Student Journal, 51*(1), 29–32.

Camera, L. (2016, April 14). Financial obstacles to education go beyond tuition: Tuition isn't the only financial culprit for community college students. *US News & World Report.* Retrieved from https://www.usnews.com/news/articles/2016-04-14/financial-obstacles-go-beyond-tuition-for-community-college-students

College Advisory System. (2016). Working document. Unpublished document.

Dahlstrom, E., De Boor, T., Grunwald, P., & Vockley, M. (2011). *The ECAR national study of undergraduate students and information technology, 2011.* Retrieved from EDUCAUSE Center for Applied Research website: https://library.educause.edu/resources/2011/10/ecar-national-study-of-undergraduate-students-and-information-technology-2011-report

Delaware County Community College. (2016). College receives grant to expand access to course materials. Retrieved from https://www.dccc.edu/news/09122016/college-receives-grant-expand-access-course-materials

Delaware County Community College. (2017). Faculty. Retrieved from https://www.dccc.edu/about/faculty-staff/meet-our-faculty

Fasimpaur, K. (2012). 4 Steps to getting started with OER. *T H E Journal, 39*(8), 37–40.

Florida Distance Learning Consortium. (2011). *Florida student textbook survey.* Retrieved from http://www.openaccesstextbooks.org/pdf/2010_FSTS_Report_01SEP2011.pdf

Goodsett, M., Loomis, B., & Miles, M. (2016). Leading campus OER initiatives through library–faculty collaboration. *College & Undergraduate Libraries, 23*(3), 335–342. doi:10.1080/10691316.2016.1206328

Hess, J. I., Nann, A. J., & Riddle, K. E. (2016). Navigating OER: The library's role in bringing OER to campus. *Serials Librarian, 70*(1–4), 128–134. doi:10.1080/0361526X.2016.1153326

Institutional Effectiveness Office. (2017). Credit enrollment spring 2017. Unpublished data.

Kachel, D. (2017). The advocacy continuum. *Teacher Librarian, 44*(3), 50–52.

Miller, R., & Homol, L. (2016). Building an online curriculum based on OERs: The library's role. *Journal of Library & Information Services in Distance Learning, 10*(3/4), 349–359. doi:10.1080/1533290X.2016.1223957

Smith, B., & Lee, L. (2017). Librarians and OER: Cultivating a community of practice to be more effective advocates. *Journal of Library & Information Services in Distance Learning, 11*(1/2), 106–122. doi:10.1080/1533290X.2016.1226592

Snyder, S. (2015, September 17). Rosemont College slashes sticker price; savings vary. *Philadelphia Inquirer*. Retrieved from http://www.philly.com/philly/education/20150917_Rosemont_College_slashes_sticker_price__savings_vary.html

Vitez, K. (2018). *Open 101: An action plan for affordable textbooks*. Student PIRGs. Retrieved from https://studentpirgs.org/sites/student/files/reports/Open%20101%20-%20An%20Action%20Plan%20for%20Affordable%20Textbooks.pdf

William and Flora Hewlett Foundation. (2011). Open educational resources. Retrieved from http://www.hewlett.org/programs/education-program/open-educational-resources

Woodward, K. M. (2017). Building a path to college success: advocacy, discovery and OER adoption in emerging educational models. *Journal of Library & Information Services in Distance Learning, 11*(1/2), 206–212. doi:10.1080/1533290X.2016.1232053

Appendix A: Professional Development Committee Charge

Functions:

1. To identify professional development needs, interests, and priorities of full- and part-time faculty members, support staff, and administrative employees through committee members and general advertisement to the College community.

2. To invite, collect, and evaluate proposals for professional development activities.

3. To be responsible for organizing needs-based and participant-driven professional development activities for the College community.

4. To collect and analyze data on the evaluation of the professional development activities.

5. To advocate for College community members to obtain professional training and resources.

6. To report the status of activities and make recommendations concerning professional development needs to the Steering Panel, as well as other stakeholders.

7. To evaluate proposals for mini-grants as awarded through the Center to Promote Excellence in Teaching and Learning (College Advisory System, 2016, p. 22).

Appendix B: Initial Professional Development Program Title and Description

Alternatives to the Textbook: Open Educational Resources and Open Access Journals

Do your students complain about the high cost of textbooks? Are you looking for an alternative? Does the idea of using the best of free online content appeal to you? This session will showcase free, high-quality, open educational resources and open access journals that you can use in your teaching, either to supplement or replace textbooks. We will define open educational resources and open access journals, investigate why they are becoming increasingly relevant in higher education, and offer tips for faculty interested in finding resources appropriate for their discipline. This session will also show how, in collaboration with librarians, your open educational resources and open access journal articles can be organized in a single place through the library's subject guides.

Appendix C: Second Professional Development Program Title and Description

Open Educational Resources: Alternatives to the Traditional Textbook

Do your students complain about the high cost of textbooks? Does this lead to students not completing the assigned reading for your class? Are you looking for an alternative? This session will discuss the open educational resources movement and build on the presentation on this topic from January 2012. The panel will discuss developments in open educational resources, offer tips on locating material, address technology issues that faculty may experience when moving towards adopting OER, and offer practical advice on how to implement use of freely available resources in your courses.

Appendix D: Series of Professional Development Program Titles and Descriptions

Look Ma! No textbook!

"This idea of ditching the commercially published textbooks for free or lower cost materials sounds wonderful BUT..." If that is your response, then this discussion is for you! There are many opportunities and challenges in the adoption or editing or creation of non-commercially published course content. There are many possible formats. The pricing models are confusing. The technology might be daunting for you or your students.

The Textbook Alternatives Committee was formed in Fall 2013 to look at all of these issues (and more!) in order to determine what the possibilities are for us at the College. Please join members of this grass roots group in a discussion of what the issues are, what's already happening on campus, and what the future could look like.

Building Alternative Course Content

Have you have you been thinking about adopting or editing course content that is not coming from a commercial publisher, or even creating your own course content? Here's your chance! In this hands-on workshop, you will discover whether you want to adopt a resource completely, adopt but edit and mix content, or create content from scratch. You will explore which format might work best for your courses, e.g. an open textbook, a printed or e-course pack with both free and licensed content, a course management system-like format, a collection of digital videos, an iBook, or even something else altogether. There are many possibilities! You'll learn where to look for existing content. You'll also spend time working hands-on with online resources created to make your concept resource become a reality. (Please note: This workshop requires a working knowledge of copyright including Creative Commons licensing and the use of the Copyright Clearance Center's Annual Academic License.)

Copyright in the Academic Environment

What is "Fair Use?" Can I put commercial video clips on my faculty website? Can I load the textbook CD into WebStudy? Can I copy and paste whole journal articles I want my class to read onto my WebStudy page? What happens if I unknowingly break the copyright law? How do I get copyright permission? What is the Annual Academic Licensing Service subscribed to by DCCC?

This workshop will address the questions faculty and administrators frequently ask when working with copyrighted materials in the academic environment. In addition, the workshop will provide practical information about Creative Commons licensing and a hands-on demonstration of the Copyright Clearance Center's Annual Academic License that allows faculty and administrators to determine if the copyrighted material is covered by the site license, as well as how to request permission if it is not.

Advocacy in OER: A Statewide Strategy for Building a Sustainable Library Effort

Emily Frank & Teri Gallaway

Introduction

Efforts to encourage the adoption and creation of open educational resources (OER) have increased nationwide in recent years, with work taking place at multiple levels within the larger ecosystem. In higher education, projects are taking root at the state level and within specific schools and departments; and are being pushed by legislators, librarians, professors, students, and even publishers. It can be a challenge to achieve an approach where the work of these stakeholders at multiple levels is integrated instead of occurring in separate silos.

Recent work in Louisiana offers an example of a more unified approach. Led by the state library consortium, LOUIS: The Louisiana Library Network, stakeholders across levels have worked in tandem toward a common goal. At the same time, these stakeholders have achieved ownership of their work in order to provide specialized approaches for their audiences and to champion their individual successes to their constituencies. By linking library activities to student success, LOUIS has demonstrated how libraries, though not revenue-generating enterprises, provide value in terms of the retention and success of students. Through this program, branded as Affordable Learning LOUISiana, libraries have received new investments in a climate where annual budget reductions have become the norm. LOUIS has been able to leverage the consortial model to build capacity among librarians and to design programs that the membership could adapt and launch in order to achieve accomplishments on their campuses.

This chapter highlights how these efforts began with LOUIS responding to support that galvanized at the state level. When the Board of

Regents, a state governmental body, sought to advance OER and textbook affordability projects, they directed funds to LOUIS. This chapter discusses how LOUIS used these funds to design a project that built the capacity and infrastructure needed to develop an OER culture in the state, and how local institutions have applied this model to the degree to which they have had the ability and interest to support it.

Literature Review

State-level initiatives and funding for OER have increased in recent years, resulting in the application of top-level support to encourage OER growth through many types of approaches. This review attempts to capture the variety of the strategies being deployed and to highlight projects at different stages of maturity. For a comprehensive summary of state legislation activity, SPARC (the Scholarly Publishing and Academic Resources Coalition) provides an OER State Policy Tracker webpage: https://sparcopen.org/our-work/state-policy-tracking/.

California has been at the forefront of support for OER, passing two bills in 2012: SB 1052, *Public Postsecondary Education: California Open Education Resources Council,* and SB 1053, *Public Postsecondary Education: California Digital Open Source Library.* Together, these enabled the California public higher education system to develop an OER library, initially focused on identifying material for 50 high-impact courses. The legislation does not mandate adoption of OER but has encouraged discovery of free and open textbooks through the site COOL4ED (California Open Online Library for Education, www.cool4ed.org). COOL4ED builds on earlier initiatives by using the infrastructure of The California State University's MERLOT (Multimedia Educational Resource for Learning and Online Teaching, www.merlot.org) project, which was launched in 1997 as a tool to collect and share OER materials. Affordable Learning Solutions (AL$, http://als.csuprojects.org/), a related initiative, supports the use of OER and other free and low-cost course materials. AL$ enables adoption of affordable content through strategies such as providing faculty grant programs, highlighting available course materials, and supporting authorship. More recently, AB 798, the College Textbook Affordability Act of 2015, has established an Open Educational Resources Adoption Incentives Program to provide campuses with funds to support faculty and staff OER activity and professional development (AB 798, 2015).

The state legislature in Connecticut has been active in presenting and passing legislation for OER. In 2015, it passed SHB 6117, *An Act Concerning the Use of Digital Open-Source Textbooks in Higher Education.* This special act promoted the use of OER by requiring the Board of Regents for Higher Education to collaborate with state university and college systems to create an open source textbook consortium (HB 06117, 2015). The consortium was charged with leading a pilot program that would focus work in two areas: "(1) assess the use of high-quality digital open-source textbooks, and (2) promote the use of and access to open-source textbooks" (HB 06117, 2015). Students were instrumental in the passage of this legislation, testifying in favor of it, outlining the quality and value of OER, and sharing the consequences of high-cost traditional textbooks (Smart, 2010). More recently, the state senate passed *An Act Concerning Digital Discounts to Reduce the Cost of Textbooks and Other Educational Resources,* which provided the Board of Regents for Higher Education and the University of Connecticut the authority to "establish guidelines that encourage public and private colleges and universities to implement programs that reduce the cost of textbooks and other educational resources for students" (SB 00948, 2017). The work highlights textbooks and OER as a recognized strategy in the state for making higher education more affordable.

In the northwest, state funding, in addition to private funds from the Bill and Melinda Gates Foundation, financed Washington's Open Course Library. The collection is composed of course materials that cost $30 or less and align to 81 high-enrollment courses in the state (Reynolds, 2011, p. 182). The collection of materials primarily supports cost reduction but secondarily promotes curriculum reform by providing engaging and interactive materials that, in turn, drive completion rates (Reynolds, 2011, p. 182). In 2015, Oregon passed HB 2871, which provided $700,000 to establish an OER grant program, create an OER Resource Specialist staff position, implement a course designation that would highlight courses that use free or low-cost materials, and identify OER for 15 high-enrollment, general education courses taught commonly across institutions ("HB2871 Update," 2016).

In Georgia, the Affordable Learning Georgia (ALG) initiative developed after multiple years of OER activities in the University System of Georgia (USG). Initially, this included a partnership with California State University's MERLOT to create a repository of digital learning objects: the USG SHARE project. Subsequently, grant funding from the Institute of Museum and Library Services supported the creation of the Georgia Knowledge Repository, a project connected to academic libraries in the state. Finally in 2013, the USG, under the infrastructure of the statewide library consortia, GALILEO, and with the support of California's AL$, launched ALG (Gallant, 2015). ALG covers 30 institutions across the USG and includes projects like a competitive faculty grant program, referred to as Textbook Transformation Grants, which are given to faculty to redesign courses to reduce or eliminate the textbook costs to students. Currently in its eighth round, the Textbook Transformation Grant program prioritizes the redesign of high-enrollment courses. Some projects utilize existing OER resources, including textbooks, while others result in the creation of new textbooks.

Minnesota's OER initiatives were advanced through inclusion in the state's omnibus higher education appropriations bill, SF 1236, which was passed in the 2013–14 legislative session. This bill incentivized the development of an OER strategy to reduce student textbook expense by 1 percent. Higher education was motivated to develop this plan as one of five performance goals that, when completed, would result in an additional 5 percent appropriation for higher education (SF 1236, 2013). One programmatic example of this is the continued institutional support of the Center for Open Education at the University of Minnesota. This center is the home of the Open Textbook Network (OTN) and the Open Textbook Library. The OTN has grown to include many national member institutions, creating a community of practitioners and providing professional development in open education.

In North Dakota, an OER program was developed as a result of a legislative study committee introduced in 2013 (North Dakota Legislative Council, 2013). House Concurrent Resolution (HCR) 3009 involved the study of the potential uses of open textbooks in the state. The findings of that study committee were developed into a white paper and presented during the following legislative session to the Higher Education Funding

Committee. Subsequently, an appropriation of $110,000 was granted to the North Dakota University System for the launch of an OER program (Spilovoy, 2016). Funded initiatives included membership and training with the OTN and the launch of a grant program for redesigning courses to integrate OER.

Louisiana Higher Education Climate

Interest in OER increased in Louisiana amid a challenging budgetary environment. The national recession began in 2007 and, coupled with a shift in state budget priorities away from higher education in 2008 and steep declines in oil and gas prices, a main state revenue source, resulted in significant budget cuts for higher education. These cuts persisted in Louisiana even after funding for higher education began to rebound in many states (Mitchell, Palacios, & Leachman, 2014). From the 2007–08 to the 2015–16 academic years, the state cut higher education funding by 44 percent (Harlan, 2016). The far-reaching consequences have included reductions in the state's higher education appropriations by 43.4 percent from the start of the recession to 2017 and, as a consequence, more than doubling of in-state tuition at Louisiana State University, the state's flagship, over that period (Gluckman, 2017).

In response to an increasingly constrained budgetary environment, the legislature began to explore ways to positively impact costs in higher education. The Board of Regents, a 15-member board representing the state's seven Congressional districts, is charged with planning, coordinating, and budgeting public higher education in Louisiana. Based on recognition in the legislature of the consequences of the high cost of textbooks, the Regents provided $145,000 in funding for LOUIS to design and execute a two-year pilot project that would positively impact this issue in the state.

LOUIS and the Board of Regents

LOUIS was identified for a leadership role because of the organization's demonstrated capacity for project design and management of statewide initiatives. Formed in 1992, LOUIS serves as the statewide library consortium for 47 member institutions, composed of all public and private college and university libraries in the state. In this role, LOUIS provides cost-effective coordination of resource procurement and technology implementation and oversight. Additionally, the consortium coordinates professional development programming and information sharing. This is done through LUC, an annual LOUIS Users Conference, and Learning with LOUIS, a monthly webinar series for sharing training and best practices. LOUIS provides the communications infrastructure for service desk management; listserv hosting and coordination for systems administrators, interlibrary loan, electronic resources, and information literacy personnel; and maintains social media and a newsletter, *LOUIS Lagniappe*, for outreach to member libraries.

Although state funding is a small portion of LOUIS' overall operating budget, the vast majority being received in library membership fees, it remains critical to the success of the consortium and it also ensures a continuing connection between statewide higher education priorities and those of the library community. The state portion of funding for LOUIS originates at the Board of Regents and LOUIS cannot independently advocate for or request funding through the legislature. As a result, a reciprocal relationship has been established with the Regents, and LOUIS staff work to tell the story of their efforts to them, providing compelling data to underscore the work. As a consequence, LOUIS has been recognized as a solutions provider by the Regents, with a reputation for being able to provide cost-effective services.

The budgetary climate and LOUIS' standing converged when a member of the Louisiana legislature discussed the cost of textbooks and encouraged the Board of Regents to explore approaches to mitigate this expense. In response, the Regents provided funding to LOUIS for a proof-of-concept project. Funds were intended to provide an introduction to what the state could be doing on this issue. Thus, LOUIS set out to design a program with student-focused impacts in the area of textbook affordability. The development and branding of the Affordable Learning LOUISiana (ALL) program came soon after the initial Regents funds in order to present a cohesive and overarching project strategy.

Affordable Learning LOUISiana: Grant Program

LOUIS' initial design for ALL was informed by small-scale projects occurring locally in the state, and influenced by larger programs beyond Louisiana. Locally, two academic libraries had begun work in this area.

Louisiana State University had launched a program that aligned library-licensed ebooks with classes, specifically promoting books with user-friendly licenses ("About the E-Textbooks Initiative," n.d.). Loyola University had begun promoting open access books and OER and advocating for their use in classes in an initiative led at the library (Gallaway & Hobbs, 2015).

Considering the success of these two programs, the inaugural work of ALL focused on a statewide grant project for member libraries looking to implement or extend these strategies through multiple rounds of funding. More specifically, the first round focused on two types of projects. One asked librarians to identify a campus faculty partner and collaborate on the selection of ebooks for course use that could be licensed by the library and provided to students on that campus at no cost. LOUIS encouraged ebooks with user-friendly licenses: DRM-free, enabling students to print and save content; unlimited user simultaneous access to allow an entire class to use the title at once; and with perpetual access, maintaining the resource in the collection beyond the initial semester of use. Nonetheless, LOUIS allowed libraries to purchase or subscribe to titles that worked for their context, including single and 3-user licenses (often with multiple copies of a title to enable course use) and ebook rentals. The second option was for librarians to identify a faculty partner to collaborate with on selecting and implementing OER to replace a textbook.

In the first round, about $10,000 of grant funding was requested—less than envisioned. After reviewing the program, it was determined that the lack of training on OER support models and the limited infrastructure to support ebook procurement or licensing had resulted in modest participation and success. Additionally, there was no strategy to promote student savings or return on investment, making it difficult to communicate the impact and value of the program to the Regents, a faculty audience, or librarian stakeholders. The initial round did, however, demonstrate LOUIS' ability to engage multiple member libraries around textbook affordability. The participating libraries supported campuses from a variety of types of colleges and universities: from technical and community colleges to seminaries to large doctoral-granting institutions. Finally, regardless of the environment, all projects were student- and savings-focused, providing an opportunity to put the library at the center of a student success initiative.

Next Steps: Strategy

Reflecting on the initial work, additional LOUIS staff were assigned to the project and tasked with addressing the limitations of the first round and developing an evaluation plan for moving forward. This resulted in a program strategy revision, implemented during the fall of 2015. The strategy continued to center around OER and licensed ebook initiatives for course material affordability, but added emphasis on building and supporting a community of interested and knowledgeable librarian practitioners through professional development, communications, and assessment. For this strategy, LOUIS created an action plan (see Appendix). The primary activities of the strategy included: to provide an updated and consolidated listing of resources to enable member libraries to quickly identify existing OER, to create opportunities for state experts to share best practices, to develop a communications plan to ensure OER remained a topic of interest, and to develop an outcomes-based ebook purchasing program focused on course use titles available in DRM-free formats.

LOUIS began directing staff time toward promoting the ALL brand with a focus on reaching internal consortium member stakeholders and external audiences. The message firmly positioned libraries as expert organizations in the campus discussion relating to affordability and underscored the role of libraries in student success. Specifically, content prepared for internal and external audience emphasized that libraries are positioned to lead efforts to reduce the costs of education for students by:

- Leveraging expertise in the cooperative procurement of licensed content from textbook publishers
- Collaborating with faculty on the selection or purchase of materials within library collections that are appropriate for course adoptions
- Cooperating with campus bookstores on identifying faculty-selected materials that are owned or can be purchased
- Curating collections of OER and open access scholarly content
- Designing and supporting discovery systems and institutional repositories that enable access to and delivery of educational content
- Delivering educational programming to faculty and educational technology professionals on tenets of scholarly licensing, including Creative Commons principles

- Developing professional competencies for new roles as advocates for affordability and leaders on their campuses
- Advocating for institutional policies that support open access, open education, and open data

As librarians became exposed to the content highlighting these roles, and as they received professional development training provided by LOUIS to sharpen skills in some of these areas, they were able to internalize messages and competencies and demonstrate these roles in their local environments.

Finally, once the second round of grant funding was announced, criteria were revised to place a new emphasis on tracking student savings and to exclude projects involving textbook rentals due to sustainability concerns. Through summer 2017, five rounds of the grant program have taken place.

Institution-Level Deployment of Strategy

The grant program allowed local institutions to direct funds to reflect the local priorities and culture of the institution. In doing so, ALL enabled individual academic libraries to become campus champions for textbook affordability. This work represented a new focus in the state, and the infusion of funds enabled librarians to find and capture low-hanging fruit within their institutions. With success stories to promote, librarians could build momentum and begin developing an OER culture locally. The grant program was structured in a way that local institutions were able to apply this model to the degree to which they had the interest and capacity to support it. $50,000 was allocated to this program, with each site having an initial allocation of $1,000 for a self-selected project. Unexpended funds were reallocated in subsequent rounds of funding. This allowed as many member sites to participate as able, so long as they submitted an eligible project. After the first round, the ALL approach responded to member needs and revised the structure to support the development of state-level infrastructure. LOUIS scaled up offers of administrative assistance, such as in purchasing and licensing of ebooks.

These efforts were coupled with increased focus on professional development in the open area that launched a collaborative community of Louisiana librarians through which further learning and sharing could occur. LOUIS coordinated activities that were led by local librarians for open access and open education weeks, and encouraged institutions to share emerging best practices and accomplishments through newsletter posts and "Learning with LOUIS" webinar sessions. Encouraging librarians to tell their stories to one another contributed to the development of a culture where librarians were prepared and eager to talk about OER and textbook affordability to diverse audiences.

Next Steps: Open Textbook Network

A significant program expansion came as a result of connections to the national open education community. LOUIS began collaborating with peer groups, bringing in outside expertise for programs including a webinar with ALG on textbook transformations. In the spring of 2016, LOUIS began discussions with the OTN on joining the network as a system or consortial member. The OTN initially supported adoption of OER by working with individual campuses to deliver workshops to instructional faculty, but it was also beginning to expand its scope to support states' or systems' ability to enable librarians to host faculty workshops at campuses by using a train-the-trainer model. At the 2016 conference of the International Coalition of Library Consortia, the Boston Library Consortium (BLC) presented an overview of their system membership with OTN. LOUIS, which was already in negotiations to join the OTN, was able to design a train-the-trainer cohort model based on the experiences of the BLC.

LOUIS adopted the OTN's train-the-trainer model because of the demonstrated benefits it offered. One appeal was its outcomes-based approach that focused on how the organizing entity could demonstrate student savings through OER. Because of the focus on OER adoptions, the program aligned with LOUIS' assessment goals of tracking student savings from course textbook replacements. The model had relatively low overhead and did not require the costly support structure of other OER projects, such as extensive course redesigns using a variety of OER types and technologies. It positioned librarians as campus leaders in this affordability work. Finally, this strategy was scalable and replicable. LOUIS could invest in training and in building and maintaining a local network and then member libraries could grow their programs.

To begin work, LOUIS used a nomination process to select three participants from member libraries to attend OTN's Summer Institute, an intensive training workshop. Participants had to agree to continued involvement in terms of delivering local workshops to campus faculty following the training and supporting other librarians to do the same in the future. LOUIS' ALL project leader also attended the summer training in order to ensure that there was a coordinated statewide plan upon completion of the program to outline train-the-trainer rollout. After returning, the three librarians, with the support of the project leader, each planned a workshop at their respective campuses. Additionally, they held bi-weekly conference calls to address planning and administrative issues preceding and following these events.

The following December and January, OTN came to Louisiana to give two train-the-trainer workshops for other interested librarians. Attendees were offered the opportunity to bring a campus partner, such as a teaching and learning staff member, instructional designer, or faculty member. Through these one-day workshops, 60 individuals were trained and then placed into small groups—cohorts led by a Louisiana librarian with experience in OER and/or OTN's model. This mentoring program supported the development of a community of practice centered around open textbooks. Additionally, ALL provided small grants and administrative support for local libraries hosting faculty workshops. In total, in the fall preceding the train-the-trainer sessions and in the subsequent spring, approximately 120 faculty received an introduction to open education, open textbooks, and Creative Commons, and an invitation to complete a review of a textbook in their discipline. The number of participating faculty reflected the number of requests from librarians for funds to host workshops, therefore demonstrating alignment between librarian intentions and faculty interest. LOUIS shared these successes and the result provided positive exposure for the ALL initiative at the Board of Regents, state legislature, and on the individual campuses.

Finally, to make OER more relevant and findable in a Louisiana context, LOUIS recruited six librarians who worked alongside four LOUIS staff on the creation of a crosswalk between available content in OTN's Open Textbook Library and Louisiana's higher education curriculum. This leveraged the state's common course articulation and was modeled on the ALG's *Top 100 Undergraduate Courses*, which lists the 100 USG courses with the highest enrollment and corresponding OER. LOUIS' project provided a high-level view of potential open textbook adoptions for the state and helped to identify courses and subject areas of high priority in terms of creation of new OER content. As with other products and strategy, existing communication channels between LOUIS and member sites were harnessed to promote these tools, including the listserv and social media. In response, librarians who have used the tool while working with faculty on OER adoptions have shared that it was a helpful launching point for beginning discussions and finding materials.

Institution-Level Response

The train-the-trainer model allowed librarians to develop and demonstrate expertise. The initial three librarians to receive training served as peer librarians who could share their experiences through a Louisiana lens and highlight how approaches could be tailored in light of local opportunities (a budgetary climate that made affordability initiatives especially appealing) and restrictions (increases in teaching loads that resulted in professors valuing textbooks with integrated homework and test management systems). The train-the-trainer model created a scalable program focused on building capacity relatively quickly and fairly inexpensively. It wasn't possible to send all interested librarians to the Summer Institute, but LOUIS was able to disseminate a similar, compressed training by bringing it to Louisiana. In the process, this approach built a community of librarians and developed collaborations that extended beyond a single campus or library.

Collaborations to Advance Affordable Learning LOUISiana

The ALL initiative has prioritized the development of infrastructure and capacity. The overarching method for achieving this has been by focusing on communication of program outcomes and building an OER professional development program for librarians. To facilitate and deepen this process, LOUIS has sought out collaborations within Louisiana and beyond.

LOUIS developed ALL with other state initiatives in mind and one early program mentor was GALILEO's ALG group. ALG was natural peer group because of its administrative structure within a state library consortium. ALG offered opportunities for shared programming with a joint webinar offered to constituencies on textbook transformation strategies and a model for tracking the program's financial impacts.

LOUIS also partnered with the Louisiana Library Association (LLA), an organization that works to promote the interest of libraries in Louisiana through work including professional development and legislative advocacy. LLA's Legislative Committee has supported legislation to promote or extend OER. During the 2016 legislative session, HCR 80 was put forward and passed. This resolution was informed by the work of ALL and proposed a partnership with LLA, the state library, public libraries, and K–12 librarians to develop a study committee to investigate and recommend a virtual library and a continued textbook affordability initiative for higher education. Following the work of the study committee, a virtual library proposal, an appropriations bill, was considered but ultimately not put forward at the request of the state library due to a difficult state budget climate. Nonetheless, LOUIS has continued to pursue sustainable funding for ALL. LOUIS completed the HCR 80 study committee with a testimony to House and Senate education committees. The testimony presented ALL outcomes and acknowledged a need for legislative support for further investments in higher education for OER. While not tied to an appropriations request because of the administrative structure of LOUIS, the testimony was positively received and underscored ongoing support for Regents investment.

Future Directions

In the 2016 legislative session, Act 619 was signed into law. This mandated a "a comprehensive review of the educational demands of the state and its regions; to provide for an evaluation of the state's post-secondary education assets, needs, gaps and barriers; to provide for a report of the findings and recommendations; and to provide for related matters" (SB 446, 2016). As a consequence, the Regents supplied a formal report, *Response to Act 619 of the 2016 Regular Session of the Louisiana Legislature*, with recommendations to the Senate and House committees prior to the commencement of the 2017 legislative session. It was through this that the Regents identified ALL as a legislative priority—an acknowledgment of LOUIS' prior advocacy with the Regents and ability to provide an example of positive impacts to students of higher education in the state. The Regents' response included a commitment to develop the Affordable Learning LOUISiana Plan, a statewide plan for the "utilization of Open Educational Resources" and to "build on current efforts related to eTextbooks, eLearning and related technologies designed to significantly lower costs of course materials for students while enriching the educational experience"(Louisiana Board of Regents, 2017, p. 35). This plan is due in the fall of 2017 and is being completed by LOUIS in conjunction with the Regents and the state's eLearning Task Force—a subgroup of the Regents. Components identified for inclusion include LOUIS' successful implementation of the OTN train-the-trainer and faculty workshop model and an outline for its continuation, and the continuation of the course alignment project.

To ensure that LOUIS' ongoing participation in this and other Regents-led statewide efforts aligns with the needs and abilities of LOUIS library constituents, an Affordable Learning Taskforce is under development. This will promote greater member participation and oversight in the development of the Regents' statewide plan and provide a mechanism to connect the ALL goals with the development of LOUIS' overarching strategic plan, which may include exploration of future staffing needs and funding models.

The expanding statewide interest in textbook affordability has also resulted in institutional-level investments in OER, and LOUIS continues to support these efforts when requested. When the Louisiana Community and Technical College System (LCTCS) announced that an annual eLearning grant fund would be dedicated to OER initiatives, LOUIS was contacted by system representatives outside of the library with a request for support and coordination. LOUIS integrated the library and coordinated a successful grant-writing project for LCTCS using library-centered affordability initiatives. LOUIS staff continue to offer consultation services to other member schools designing OER projects, including for other recent grants offered by the state's eLearning Task Force. In this manner, LOUIS has been able continue to propel success stories for the state through infrastructure and administrative support.

Conclusion

The legislature-to-library consortium-to-university model has allowed multiple stakeholders to take ownership of an element of this project and apply leadership at their level while working toward shared success in the state. The financial support, administrative infrastructure, and professional development offered through ALL showed local institutions that OER are a statewide priority, backed by the Board of Regents, and a possible venue for funding and advancement in terms of skills and services. Though ALL started with one-time money, LOUIS has worked to develop a program worthy of reinvestment by continually telling the story of how students are impacted and by backing this story with numbers to show return on investment. In doing so, LOUIS has worked to rewrite a narrative in Louisiana that frames libraries as campus cost centers and that regularly results in funding cuts. Instead, LOUIS has highlighted libraries as the core of the ALL story, demonstrating libraries' ability to successfully lead initiatives on local campus and underscoring libraries' impacts on student success. This, in turn, provides the foundation for future requests for funding as a way to continue the program goals.

References

About the E-textbook Initiative (n.d.). Retrieved from http://www.lib.lsu.edu/ebooks/about

Cal. A.B. 798. *An act to amend section 69999.6 of, and to add and repeal part 40.1 (commencing with section 67420) of division 5 of title 3 of, the education code, relating to postsecondary education, 2015.* Retrieved from http://leginfo.legislature.ca.gov/faces/billNavClient.xhtml?bill_id=201520160AB798

Conn. H.R. H.B. 06117. *An act concerning the use of digital open-source textbooks in higher education, 2015.* Retrieved from https://www.cga.ct.gov/2015/fc/2015HB-06117-R000823-FC.htm

Conn. S.B. 00948. *An act concerning digital discounts to reduce the cost of textbooks and other educational resources, 2017.* Retrieved from https://www.cga.ct.gov/2017/FC/2017SB-00948-R000375-FC.htm

Gallant, J. (2015). Librarians transforming textbooks: The past, present, and future of the Affordable Learning Georgia initiative. *Georgia Library Quarterly, 52*(2), n.p. Retrieved from http://digitalcommons.kennesaw.edu/glq/vol52/iss2/8

Gallaway, T. & Hobbs, J. (2015). Open access for student success. In B. L Eden (Ed.), *Enhancing teaching and learning in the 21st-century academic library: Successful innovations that make a difference.* Lanham: Rowman & Littlefield.

Gluckman, N. (2017, July 26). How one state's budget crisis has hamstrung its public universities. *The Chronicle of Higher Education.* Retrieved from https://www.chronicle.com/article/How-One-State-s-Budget/240760

Harlan, C. (2016, March 4). Battered by drop in oil prices and Jindal's fiscal policies, Louisiana falls into budget crisis. *The Washington Post.* Retrieved from https://www.washingtonpost.com/news/wonk/wp/2016/03/04/ the-debilitating-economic-disaster-louisianas-governor-left-behind/

HB2871 update. (2016, April 22). Retrieved from http://openoregon.org/hb2871-update

Johnson, L., Adams Becker, S., Estrada, V., & Freeman, A. (2015). *NMC horizon report: 2015 higher education edition.* Austin, Texas: The New Media Consortium. Retrieved from http://cdn.nmc.org/media/2015-nmc-horizon-report-HE-EN.pdf

La. S.B. 446. *Act no. 619, 2016.* Retrieved from https://www.legis.la.gov/legis/ ViewDocument.aspx?d=1013080

Louisiana Board of Regents (2017). *Response to act 619 of the 2016 regular session of the Louisiana legislature.* Retrieved from http://www.regents.la.gov/assets/ ACT_619_BOARD_APPROVED_Final_Draft.pdf

Minn. S. F 1236. A bill for an act relating to education, 2013. Retrieved from https://www.revisor.mn.gov/bills/ text.php?number=SF1236&session_year=2013&session_number=0&version=latest

Mitchell, M., Palacios, V., & Leachman, M. (2014). States are still funding higher education below pre-recession levels. Washington DC: Center on Budget and Policy Priorities. Retrieved from http://www.cbpp.org/sites/default/files/atoms/files/ 5-1-14sfp.pdf

North Dakota Legislative Council. (2013). Higher education study—background memorandum. Retrieved from: http://www.legis.nd.gov/files/resource/ committee-memorandum/15.9039.01000.pdf

Reynolds, R. (2011). Trends influencing the growth of digital textbooks in US higher education. *Publishing Research Quarterly, 27*(2), 178–187. http://dx.doi.org/10.1007/ s12109-011-9216-5

Smart, C. (2015, February 26). UConn students testify for affordable textbooks at state capitol. *WHUS.* Retrieved from http://whus.org/2015/02/ uconn-students-testify-for-affordable-textbooks-at-state-capitol/

Spilovoy, T. (2016, August 23). North Dakota open educational resources initiative: A system-wide success story. *WCET.* Retrieved from https://wcetfrontiers.org/2016/ 08/23/ north-dakota-open-educational-resources-initiative-a-system-wide-success-story

Appendix: LOUIS Affordable Learning Action Plan, 2015

Ongoing Actions: Leverage the established criteria in negotiating pricing and policies with vendors; update availability of content for changing vendor and course offerings

Initial Actions: Complete expenditures for funds already allocated in the first round; gather and compile statistical report on the program impact; prepare and disseminate publicity materials/website feature on the outcomes

Ongoing Actions: Benchmarking and/or documenting consortia spending per student/ cost saving per student

Develop webpage/LibGuide of resources to adopt

Goal: Awareness of possible OER resources is one of the most frequently cited barriers to adoption (Johnson, Adams Becker, Estrada, & Freeman, 2015). To address this, LOUIS will provide an updated/consolidated listing of resources to enable member libraries to quickly identify existing OER to share with faculty.

Initial Actions: Identify OER; create LibGuide for LOUIS site; share link via listservs, social media, and LOUIS Lagniappe newsletter

Ongoing Actions: Update content semi-annually; notify members of new content; track page visits

Coordinate LUC roundtable/Interest Group/Best practices

Goal: Several LOUIS members are already engaged in the successful promotion of OER and DRM-free e-books. LOUIS will create a roundtable forum where these experts can share best practices within the state to enhance the effectiveness of other OER/e-book adoption efforts.

Initial Actions: Identify interested LOUIS members; schedule a roundtable discussion for the 2015 LUC; capture poignant discussion points at LUC; engage participants in editing the best practices; share via LOUIS Lagniappe Newsletter and other promotional outlets

Ongoing Actions: Annual review and republication of best practices document by an interest group

OER in the news

Goal: Ensuring OER remain a topic of interest at Louisiana academic institutions.

Initial Actions: Create a design template for recurring news items for the listserv and LOUIS Lagniappe; identify and monitor news sources that would have relevant content (The Chronicle of Higher Education, ALA publications, AAC&U, SoTL journals, NMC Horizon Report, etc.); develop a target number of annual news items to feature

Ongoing Actions: Write or solicit brief editorials on content to post in relevant publications; monitor related International Coalition of Library Consortia activities (i.e. how are other consortia engaging in the conversation)

Direct purchase of DRM-free e-book content for classroom use

Goal: In order to demonstrate the continued value proposition of LOUIS, current and future state-allocated funds for e-textbooks/e-books will be expended on resources that have direct impact on reducing student expenses. The impact of those purchases should be collected and disseminated to demonstrate cost savings (and/or cost avoidance) to students.

Mini-consortia negotiation for institutional purchases of DRM-free content for the class use/exposing DRM-free content

Goal: The information regarding availability of content and licensing terms of e-book/e-textbooks can be confusing. To assist member libraries in negotiating best possible pricing and license terms for DRM-free content, LOUIS will extend its existing mini-consortia services to these resources as well as provide technology to expose the relevant e-book/e-textbook resources that are available for purchase and meet a set of DRM-free criteria.

Initial Actions: Establish a working group to document criteria for the selection of DRM-free e-books; develop/purchase a product, mechanism or infrastructure to identify content that meet the criteria and match isbn/e-isbns of content already in use in classes

Interinstitutional Collaborations to Forge Intracampus Connections: A Case Study from the Duke Endowment Libraries

Sarah Hare, Andrea Wright, Christy Allen, Geneen E. Clinkscales, &
Julie Reed

Introduction

Academic libraries are increasingly providing education and support for faculty interested in open educational resources (OER). Some academic libraries offer comprehensive training programs and dedicated staff to support the creation and adoption of OER. Other libraries focus on smaller initiatives seeking to explore the interests of OER stakeholders on their campuses. However, there are still a significant number of academic libraries with little or no experience supporting faculty OER needs. This was the situation at Duke University, Davidson College, Furman University, and Johnson C. Smith University in early 2016.

Most of the librarians at these institutions had minimal to no experience working with OER, and had no clear concept of which of their faculty had adopted or contributed to OER. Fortunately, these institutions have access to a shared endowment that facilitates collaborative programming across their institutions. Beginning in the summer of 2016, librarians from these four schools joined together to develop a unique OER pilot program that pooled resources and created a support structure across institutions with notably different student populations, faculty interests, and library structures.

TDEL OER Pilot Program

The OER pilot program implemented by Duke, Davidson, Furman, and Johnson C. Smith benefited from external funding and interinstitutional collaboration made possible by the Duke Endowment. Established in 1924 by the tobacco and hydroelectric power magnate, James B. Duke, the Duke Endowment is a permanent trust fund with designated beneficiaries.

Among these beneficiaries are four institutions of higher learning: David-son College, Duke University, Furman University, and Johnson C. Smith University. In 2001, the libraries from these four institutions established an informal group called the Duke Endowment Libraries (TDEL) to foster collaboration and share knowledge and training across the institutions' libraries. In 2015, TDEL established a project fund to provide financial sup-port for joint projects among two or more of the Duke-endowed libraries. During preliminary discussions about possible uses of this fund, the topic of OER presented itself. With the exception of Davidson College, the OER experience among the libraries was fairly limited. Working collaboratively, the Duke-endowed libraries could realize the following benefits:

- Connect librarians at different institutions with a shared interest in supporting open access and OER.
- Collect and analyze OER information from several institutions to identify larger trends and interests in higher education.
- Maximize resource utility by pooling training and funding across in-stitutions, while still facilitating a program that best suits the needs of each individual campus.

Even with all the benefits of collaboration, it is important to note that the four beneficiary institutions of the Duke Endowment are very different from one another. They have varying missions, student bodies, and levels of involvement in scholarly communication initiatives. The TDEL library directors felt this institutional variety was an asset to the project.

Davidson College is a highly selective liberal arts college of almost 2,000 students located just outside of Charlotte, North Carolina. For its size, Davidson has been fairly progressive in the field of open education. In 2015, their Library and Center for Teaching & Learning began offering Open Educational Resources and Open Pedagogy Stipends. This program awarded $500 to five faculty interested in integrating OER into their fall 2016 classes (Center for Teaching & Learning, 2016).

Duke University is a private research university of over 14,800 un-dergraduate and graduate students located in Durham, North Carolina. While the Duke University Libraries have been active in scholarly com-munication including the management of the University's institutional repository and offering funding to support faculty open access publications, they had done very little in the realm of strategic OER programming prior to this project.

Furman University is an undergraduate liberal arts university located in Greenville, South Carolina serving 2,700 students. While Furman Libraries have been actively involved in other scholarly communication initiatives including the management of the University's institutional repository and the administration of the University's Open Access Fund, they had done virtually nothing related to OER prior to this project.

Johnson C. Smith University is a historically black college and university (HBCU) serving approximately 1,350 students in Charlotte, North Carolina. The library has a strong reputation of collaboration with faculty; however, they had very little hands-on experience with OER prior to this project.

In the spring of 2016, the TDEL library directors approved the creation of a collaborative OER pilot program for academic year 2016–17. The OER pilot program was developed to have two major elements: a Train the Trainer Workshop and a Faculty OER Review Program. The budget for the program was $12,800 with $10,000 earmarked for faculty stipends. The program had the following goals:

- Increase knowledge of OER among librarians;
- Increase awareness of OER among faculty on campus;
- Assess campus knowledge and climate regarding open access and OER;
- Inform the development and/or expansion of OER initiatives supported by the libraries.

Train the Trainer Workshop

As noted above, an important goal of this program was to increase knowledge and experience of OER among the Duke-endowed librarians. To that end, they organized a Train the Trainer Workshop where an OER expert educated the librarians on the benefits and limitations of open resources, offered hands-on experience with locating and evaluating OER, provided tips for engaging faculty, and facilitated a brainstorming session on implementing a successful faculty OER review program.

Selecting an expert for the Train the Trainer Workshop was the result of interinstitutional collaboration. Each librarian conducted research to identify possible candidates to lead the workshop. This list of candidates was then discussed and decided over the phone. William Cross, Director of the Copyright and Digital Scholarship Center at North Carolina State University (NCSU), was chosen. His knowledge and expertise in implementing the Alt-Textbook Project at NCSU was a contributing factor in his selection (North Carolina State University, 2017). Because he was located in the Carolinas, like the other institutions, it was an added benefit that he had familiarity and a strong frame of reference for the Duke-endowed libraries.

Two librarians from each institution attended the workshop, which was held in the James B. Duke Memorial Library of Johnson C. Smith University. Having two librarians in attendance was extremely beneficial. First, it increased the amount of cross-collaboration and knowledge sharing within and between the institutions. Second, it allowed for a more distributed workload in implementing and running the OER faculty review programs at each local institution. Each of the librarian participants had other duties and responsibilities within their libraries. At the same time, none of the libraries had dedicated staffing to support open education initiatives, making it even more imperative to build expertise and support across neighboring institutions. There were a myriad of tasks involved in setting up the OER pilot program, such as training, logistics, outreach and promotion, budgeting, reporting, and maintaining a commitment to the proposed timeline. Because of the amount of work required and the limitations in staffing, having two librarians from each institution allowed for a more even distribution of the workload.

In the workshop, Cross introduced the concepts of open education and OER. He also incorporated an interactive exercise in finding, evaluating, and using these materials by providing hands-on experience with the OER websites OpenStax, Open Textbook Network, OER Commons, and MERLOT (Multimedia Educational Resource for Learning and Online Teaching). He then illustrated various models for establishing a successful and engaging OER faculty review program, including the Alt-Textbook Project at NCSU. He worked with the TDEL librarians to create an action plan that defined the priorities and timelines for organizing the logistics of an OER faculty review program centrally and implementing it locally. Cross concluded with a brainstorming session on how to conduct an OER training workshop for faculty with tips for promoting the program on each of the campuses.

The materials Cross used to facilitate the TDEL training session can be accessed at https://goo.gl/S3Ac7o.

OER Faculty Review Program Overview

The second component of the OER pilot program was a faculty review program in which faculty were paid a $250 stipend to conduct a written review of one or more OER. The faculty were not required or even encouraged to adopt OER for use in the classroom. The goal of the program was simply to introduce them to the concept of OER and allow them to spend some targeted time assessing an OER to see how it might work in their classroom.

Supporting the creation of faculty OER reviews through stipends had several benefits: it created an opportunity to start conversations about OER on campus; it allowed librarians to build expertise in locating and evaluating OER; and it provided faculty with hands-on experience using OER. Finally, this program was a low-resource, high-impact way for the libraries to slowly transition into campus OER support.

The concept of implementing a review program as a first step in OER support is not a new one. The TDEL libraries were inspired by initiatives like the University of Minnesota's Open Textbook Network review program (Senack, 2015) and the University of South Carolina's SCoer! Awards (University of South Carolina, 2017) which demonstrated great success in engaging faculty by paying them stipends to conduct reviews of OER. The University of Minnesota determined that awarding stipends to faculty willing to review OER eventually led to more holistic faculty adoption. OER expert Ethan Senack (2015), writing about the Minnesota program, stated that "[w]hile the original intent of the project was to build open textbook credibility through reviews, it soon became clear that when faculty engaged with open content to provide a review, they were likely to adopt the open textbook in their class" (p. 13). This model has been highly successful for the Open Textbook Network (OTN), a consortium of over 600 campus members working to increase open textbook adoption and access to course material. While the TDEL libraries considered a consortial OTN membership, both funding and time constraints were barriers to membership. The group ultimately decided that creating a similar internal program and implementing it successfully would be a good first step to potentially asking the TDEL libraries directors for additional funding for OTN membership.

In summary, even though other libraries had conducted similar faculty review programs, the TDEL program was unique, because it was conducted collaboratively across four institutions with varying student populations, faculty interests, and library structures. For the program to be a success, it was necessary to establish cross-institutional program features for standardized results and also accommodate individual institutional customizations.

Cross-Institutional Program Features

Common Documentation

To incorporate both the standardization necessary for cross-institution analysis and the flexibility of campus-specific marketing and data, the group decided to develop base forms for program participation. These base forms included the standardized elements in a format agreed upon by the TDEL librarians. Each institution would then create a copy of the forms to customize. Colors, logos, and identifying information were customized to the individual institutions. If schools wished to gather additional information, they added unique questions to the forms. Since the core of each form was the same across institutions, results could then be easily aggregated and analyzed.

The base forms are publicly available in Google Drive for other institutions to copy, adapt, and reuse under the license CC-BY 4.0.

- Consent Form (Adobe PDF): https://bit.ly/2q5yNji

Faculty participants completed a consent form prior to official participation in the program. Because of privacy concerns, this form was not created in Google Docs. Instead, it is a fillable PDF form that was printed out and physically signed by faculty.

- OER Review Form (Google Forms): https://bit.ly/2ItHGtM

The review form was created in Google Docs, easily allowing the institutions to make copies of the base form and customize as needed.

- Stipend Form (Microsoft Word): https://bit.ly/2q8wFao

Stipends were paid by the Duke University Libraries Business Services which preferred stipend forms formatted in Microsoft Word.

- Feedback Survey (Google Forms): https://bit.ly/2Iw0dWb

The feedback form was created in Google Docs, easily allowing the institutions to make copies of the base form and customize as needed.

Institutional Review Board (IRB)

In keeping with research best practices, prior to launching the OER faculty review program, the librarians applied for Institutional Review Board (IRB) approval through Furman University. Originally, the application was submitted as Exempt Status, because the review form was similar in nature to a survey, and because the information being collected was not deemed by the librarians to pose any potential risks. However, after reviewing the application, the IRB requested it be resubmitted as Expedited Review. It is important to note that an IRB at a different institution may have come to a different conclusion and determined that Exempt Status was sufficient.

As part of the Expedited Review proposal, the librarians were required to address the following: a thorough rationale for the program, complete copies of all four forms, detailed procedures and methodologies, privacy and security of the research, and potential risks to participants. One of the major concerns expressed by the IRB related to the level of personally identifiable information that could be publicly included with the faculty reviews. Three out of the four institutions were small in size and the Board was concerned that individual faculty members could be easily identified due to limited demographic information. Given the concerns, the librarians updated the consent form to allow faculty to choose the level of personally identifiable information they were willing to share. The Board also required that the consent forms be paper-based (rather than a Google Form) and stored off-line to protect participant privacy.

The IRB process was a new one for the Furman librarians who took the lead in conducting this portion of the project. As such, they were required to go through extensive training on IRB procedures, and also had a much greater learning curve in understanding and completing the application. This process added several weeks onto the faculty review program. Because IRB approval was not built into the initial timeline, it did delay the launch of the program by a week. However, approval was well worth the delay because it enabled the librarians to publish and present on the results of the faculty review program.

Faculty Participant Requirements

Faculty participants from all the TDEL institutions went through essentially the same process, although its implementation differed slightly from institution to institution.

The format of the consultation was the most varied part of this process. In some cases, workshops were used to allow multiple faculty to be introduced to OER and the program process simultaneously. In other cases, the specific interest of a faculty member coupled with the difficulty of scheduling group meetings led to one-on-one consultations. In all formats, the consultation included: an overview of OER, particularly licensing; a discussion of the review criteria; and an introduction to platforms and sites designed for OER discovery.

As required by the IRB, all participants completed a hard copy consent form to participate. This detailed the program and allowed participants to indicate what level of identifying information they would allow to be included in any written or publicly available materials resulting from the study. The form also indicated the title and URL for all OER to be reviewed. Faculty were allowed to choose one large curricular component, such as an online course or textbook, or several small components such as videos or content modules.

A standardized review form was utilized across all four institutions. The first section covered basic demographics and contact information. The second section asked for basic metadata about the OER, including license and content level. The main body included a professional review that was based on the BCcampus OER review criteria (BCcampus, 2013). Faculty ranked and commented on the following areas:

A fourth section completed the survey with a personal review where faculty reflected on strengths and weaknesses of the OER as well as how the resource might be used in their own teaching.

Once the completed review was received by librarians at the faculty member's home institution, they were directed to the Business Services Office at Duke University which collected the sensitive information required for issuing payment from the Duke Endowment funds. External payment processes are complex, particularly when compensating faculty at different institutions. It's important to plan ahead, document how the compensation process will work, and think through the collection of sensitive information beforehand to ensure that expectations of faculty participants are clear.

1. *Attend a workshop or one-on-one consultation with a librarian, which included identifying possible OER.*
2. *Sign a consent form to participate.*
3. *Complete a written review for each OER using a standardized form.*

   - Comprehensiveness
   - Content Accuracy
   - Relevance/Longevity
   - Clarity
   - Consistency
   - Modularity
   - Organization/Structure/Flow
   - Interface
   - Grammatical Errors
   - Cultural Relevance

4. *Submit personal information required for $250 stipend to be issued.*
5. *Complete a follow-up survey.*

Participants who completed a review were sent a follow-up survey in early summer after the program. This survey aimed at determining the success of the program as both a specific OER review and a larger OER awareness campaign.

The first section asked participants to rank their experience and knowledge of OER before and after the program, as well as reflecting on benefits and challenges to OER adoption in their teaching. A second section asked about perceived OER knowledge and challenges at the department and institutional level, including whether faculty would consider adopting OER in their classroom. The final section rated the various elements of the OER review program individually as well as a whole.

Questions about concrete textbook savings were not asked as this project was an introductory effort intended to build knowledge and understanding of the concept of OER.

Individual Institution Customization

Even though the faculty review program was largely standardized, each institution also had the flexibility to make its own customizations. Librarians utilized their knowledge of successful communication strategies, effective outreach tactics, and existing culture around openness on their campus to maximize success. As previously mentioned, while faculty across institutions were required to meet with a librarian to learn more about OER, each institution could decide what that meeting looked like.

At Davidson College, the program was promoted through the faculty listserv, internal web pages, and an OER tab on the Davidson Open Access guide (https://davidson.libguides.com/open/oer). Librarians met with interested faculty in one-on-one consultations where they could tailor their searches to each faculty member's interest, as this aligned with the small, liberal arts college culture at Davidson.

At Duke University, the program was promoted through the Center for Instructional Technology (CIT) newsletter, a blog post on the Duke University Libraries website, and a presentation at the CIT Showcase. The program was also promoted to library staff through presentations at a staff digital scholarship discussion group, departmental meetings, and a discussion series about scholarly communication topics entitled "ScholComm in the Edge." A website was also created: https://scholarworks.duke.edu/open-access/open-educational-resources/.

At Furman University, the OER faculty review program was promoted at the New Faculty Orientation and an Undergraduate Evening Studies Faculty Orientation. An OER Guide (http://libguides.furman.edu/oer) and information about the review program in specific was created and posted to the library website. Because of significant interest from these two orientations, the program was not actively marketed elsewhere. Group workshops to introduce OER and the program requirements were held to reach multiple faculty at once. A few faculty members who could not attend the workshop or joined the program later had one-on-one consultations with a librarian.

At Johnson C. Smith University (JCSU), there was no familiarity in general with OER. Some faculty were using OER without realizing it, however, when teaching with public domain materials and Creative Commons-licensed journal articles. To publicize the pilot program, liaison librarians for different subject areas attended meetings for their respective departments as well as meetings of the library committee and with departmental chairs. A LibGuide was also created to assist in promoting the iniative (http://jcsu.libguides.com/OER). Word of mouth about the $250 stipend also assisted in recruitment and outreach efforts. Like Davidson, Johnson C. Smith found that meeting with professors for one-on-one OER consultations was a better model than a group workshop, because faculty could more easily receive individualized and modified assistance for their particular courses.

It was important to balance standardization across the TDEL group with institutional customization. Others hoping to create a similar program should aim to balance data collection across institutions with customization to each institution's goals, mission, and culture in order to be effective.

Results

OER Review Results

As of June 12, 2017, 28 faculty members had completed 37 professional reviews of OER for the program. Johnson C. Smith and Furman had robust faculty response, with 11 and 10 faculty participants, respectively. Duke and Davidson had a smaller response, with 3 and 4 faculty participants, respectively, on each campus. Every possible rank of faculty was represented across all four campuses (see Table 1), with Assistant Professor and Instructor being the most common. The participants also represented a wide variety of disciplines and departments, (see Table 2), though the social sciences dominated the group. Also of note, 10 of the participants taught in nontraditional undergraduate programs. Introductory level material and textbooks where the most popular content levels and format, but there was a good bit of variety in both of these areas (see Table 3).

Table 1. Participant Ranks

Rank	Count
Assistant Professor	11
Associate Professor	3
Instructional Designer	1
Instructor	9
Professor	4
Grand Total	**28**

Table 2. Participant Disciplines & Departments

Disciplines & Departments	Count
Arts & Humanities	**6**
Classical Studies	1
English	1
Interdisciplinary Studies	1
Religion	1
Theatre Arts	1
Visual & Performing Arts	1
Sciences	**6**
Chemistry	1
Computer Science	1
Environmental Sciences	1

Disciplines & Departments	Count
Mathematics	1
Nursing	2
Social Sciences	**16**
Anthropology	1
Business & Accounting	6
Communication Studies	2
Education	1
Ethnic Studies	1
Health Sciences	1
Interdisciplinary Studies	1
Psychology	1
Social Work	1
Sports Management	1
Grand Total	**28**

Table 3. OER Formats & Content Levels

Format & Content Level	Count
Article	**2**
Graduate Student/Professional	1
Introductory/Survey	1
Class Assignment/Exercise	**1**
Graduate Student/Professional	1
Online Course	**4**

Format & Content Level	Count
Advanced Undergraduate	1
Graduate Student/Professional	1
Introductory/Survey	2
Other	**1**
Introductory/Survey	1
Textbook	**23**
Advanced Undergraduate	8
Graduate Student/Professional	2
Introductory/Survey	13
Video	**6**
Advanced Undergraduate	1
Graduate Student/Professional	1
Introductory/Survey	4
Grand Total	**37**

As noted previously, the professional review categories were developed from an OER evaluation rubric developed by BCcampus. This same rubric is utilized by Open Textbook Library and other organizations, making it a common and accepted tool for evaluation of OER.

Considering the variety of faculty and resources being reviewed, the professional reviews consistently gave high marks across all categories (see Table 4). On a five-point Likert scale, each area received above average scores.

Table 4. OER Review Rankings

Category	Average	Median	Mode	Stand Dev
Comprehensiveness Rating	3.65	4	4	1.23
Content Accuracy Rating	4.22	4	5	0.98
Relevance/Longevity Rating	4.00	4	5	1.11
Clarity Rating	3.89	4	4	1.10
Consistency Rating	4.22	5	5	1.11
Modularity Rating	4.19	5	5	1.17
Organization/Flow/Structure Rating	4.16	5	5	1.14
Interface Rating	3.95	4	5	1.25
Grammar Rating	4.41	5	5	0.93

Faculty participants were also asked about how they might use the resource, with the ability to choose more than one option. Participants indicated that they would not use the resource at all in its current form with only four OER, with the majority indicating that they would use it as supplementary material and several indicating that they would replace their textbook with the resource (see Table 5). When asked about changes to the resources, suggestions ranged from updating and expanding content coverage to supplemental resources such as bibliographies, timelines, and glossaries. With these changes, only two resources were still listed as not having a potential use for the faculty member (see Table 6).

Table 5. How might you use this resource in its current state?

Option	Count
As a textbook replacement	13
As a unit replacement	7

Option	Count
As an assignment or exercise	10
As supplemental material	29
I would not use this resource	4
Grand Total	**63**

Table 6. How might you use this resource with your recommended changes?

Option	Count
As a textbook replacement	20
As a unit replacement	10
As an assignment or exercise	8
As supplemental material	26
I would not use this resource	2
Grand Total	**66**

Feedback Survey Results

As of June 12, 2017, 23 faculty participants representing all four institutions had completed a program feedback survey (see Table 7). Paired-samples t-tests were conducted to compare self-reported OER knowledge and OER experience before and after participation in the review program. There was a significant difference in the pre-program knowledge ranking (M=2.22, SD=1.04) and the post-program knowledge ranking (M=4.04, SD=0.77); t(22)=-7.59, p=0.01). There was also a significant difference in the pre-program experience ranking (M=2.09, SD=1.04) and the post-program experience ranking (M=3.91, SD=0.79); t(22)=-6.72, p=0.01). This supports a finding that the program met its stated goals of increasing OER knowledge and experience on the campuses.

Interestingly, while faculty ranked their own OER knowledge before the program fairly low (Average rank=2.2; 1=None, 5=Expert), they perceived the knowledge amongst their colleagues as moderate (Average rank=3.2; 1=None, 5=Expert). Faculty participants also indicated that they were more likely than not to adopt the OER they reviewed for the program (Average rank=3.6; 1=Not at all, 5=Guaranteed) and to consider OER in future course development/revision (Average rank=4.4; 1=Not at all, 5=Guaranteed). The most consistent challenge to adopting OER was time and discovering appropriate resources. The program itself was well received, with faculty ranking indicating general satisfaction with the review form and the entire faculty review program. The most common suggestion for improving the program was to increase recruitment of participants.

Table 7. Program Feedback Survey Rankings

	Average	Median	Mode	Stand. Dev.
Rate your knowledge of OERs prior to your participation in this program	2.22	2	2	1.04
Rate your knowledge of OERs since your participation in this program	4.04	4	4	0.77
Rate your experience with OERs prior to your participation in this program	2.09	2	1	1.04
Rate your experience with OERs since your participation in this program	3.91	4	4	0.79
How likely are you to adopt the OER(s) you reviewed for the program?	3.61	4	4	1.16
How likely are you to consider OERs in future course development/revision?	4.39	5	5	0.72
How would you rate OER knowl-	3.22	3	4	1.04

	Average	Median	Mode	Stand. Dev.
edge amongst your colleagues?				
Please rate your satisfaction with the OER Review Form	4.30	5	5	0.82
Please rate your satisfaction with the entire OER Review Program	4.43	5	5	0.66

Engagement Results

In addition to the quantitative outcomes, the review program had some unexpected and exciting outcomes related to library and faculty engagement. The new connections made between faculty members and librarians were valuable, even at institutions that did not see high participation in their review programs.

While all of the library/faculty interactions were positive, some faculty became incredibly engaged with OER as a result of their participation. At Furman University, one program participant was so interested in OER, he began conducting research about OER in his discipline. He developed a survey to determine the impact of OER in his discipline at other liberal arts colleges. He also conducted informal research by teaching one of his classes with OER and another with traditional textbooks. He then surveyed the students throughout the semester to compare their experiences with the course materials. Finally, he is actively partnering with the librarians at Furman to create presentations and publications on his research. At Johnson C. Smith University, a faculty member is planning a new course on LGBTQ and gender studies using OER exclusively. She is working with the librarians to choose materials for the class. Another professor plans to use the resource she reviewed as the main textbook in her class beginning fall 2017.

Faculty members from two different institutions were inspired to author their own OER. At Davidson, librarians were embedded in two spring 2017 courses (History 338: Berlin in Translation and Religion 278: Islamic City) where students learned more about copyright, intellectual property, and openness. One librarian at Davidson traveled to Berlin with the class to teach students about open access and privacy as a result of a Faculty OER Review Program consultation. At Furman University, a faculty participant in the program conducted a review of a LibreText. She liked the general content of the LibreText but felt that it needed significant revisions and additions before she could use it in her class. Since her review, she has been working with the LibreText website to create her own LibreText for an upcoming class in the fall.

Perhaps the most exciting outcome for the program was that it sparked broader discussions of OER adoption within the library and at the campus level. For example, at Duke University, the program triggered interest in rolling out a larger strategy for the use of OER in their MOOCs (massive open online courses). Through its MOOCs, Duke University has taught over 2.8 million students (Manturuk & Ruiz-Esparza, 2015). Adopting OER for MOOCs would have significant positive results for these enrollees. In addition, the Furman University Undergraduate Evening Studies (UES) program offers a small selection of bachelor's degrees to nontraditional students. Five of the faculty from Furman's OER review program taught in the UES program. Their participation has led UES directors to begin investigating the feasibility of converting the UES classes to OER-only.

All four institutions enjoy strong relationships between librarians and faculty. The faculty review program served to strengthen these relationships in several significant ways. The one-on-one consultations afforded faculty and librarians an opportunity to learn about one another's expertise more deeply. Librarians gained a deeper understanding of the faculty members, their teaching focus, their classes, and their research. Similarly, faculty members gained a greater appreciation for the services, programs, resources, and research available to them from the library. For example, faculty who initially expressed interest in OER began to have discussions related to the use of the library's print and electronic subscriptions and databases to support their classes. Moreover, the rapport built among librarians and faculty enabled some faculty members to begin collaborating with the library on unrelated, but equally valuable projects. These conversations would likely not have occurred if not triggered by the Faculty OER Review Program.

Lessons Learned

The TDEL OER pilot program was an experiment in interinstitutional collaboration with the goals of increasing knowledge of OER among librarians and faculty; assessing campus knowledge and climate regarding open access and OER; and informing the development and/or expansion of OER initiatives supported by the libraries. The pilot program achieved these goals all while fostering knowledge sharing, cooperative program management, and distribution of resources among the TDEL libraries. The success of this program can be attributed to four major factors:

1. Building an OER support network;
2. Providing opportunities for frequent virtual and in-person collaboration;
3. Establishing a flexible timeline;
4. Managing expectations and goals.

Building an OER support network was a critical component to the OER pilot program. The Train the Trainer Workshop served as a catalyst for forming this network, building trust, and giving all of the librarians a baseline understanding of OER. Through the workshop, Will Cross not only provided participating librarians with a wealth of information about OER, but also provided an interactive session allowing them to brainstorm, share ideas, and build a sense of trust and community. The workshop also included an informal lunch, allowing the TDEL librarians to chat personally, thereby increasing their camaraderie. These in-person interactions were a critical component to the success of their future virtual interactions.

To foster the rapport and collaborative spirit that was developed during the workshop, it was important for the TDEL librarians to meet on a frequent basis. These one-hour meetings were held every four to six weeks virtually using the online conference software Zoom. While a conference call would have sufficed, Zoom offered the added benefit of virtual face-to-face discussions and screen-sharing capabilities. During these meetings, the TDEL partners shared their progress in implementing the OER faculty review program. They also brainstormed about next steps, shared ideas about outreach efforts, discussed challenges, and celebrated successes. In between the scheduled meetings, the librarians used email and Google Drive to communicate. As a group, the TDEL librarians found that having a support structure of eight librarians (two librarians from each institution) was invaluable. Being able to share tactics for success and brainstorm solutions to challenges collaboratively has enabled the librarians to be more effective on their campuses.

Another important component to the success of the program was flexibility. As with any program, unexpected difficulties arose, so building in flexibility during the planning process was critical. This was especially true with the timeline. When establishing the timeline, the TDEL librarians failed to take into account the need for IRB approval. Adding this step to the timeline caused delays in rolling out the program, which was originally scheduled to launch at the beginning of the fall semester. Luckily, the general flexibility of the schedule allowed them to easily adjust the deadlines to compensate for the delay.

In addition to flexibility, it was also important for the librarians to manage their goals and expectations. This was especially important when it became clear that all four institutions would not be able to contribute the anticipated 10 faculty reviews. This happened for a variety of reasons, including faculty time constraints, lack of interest, and a lack of OER in niche topic areas. While this was a disappointing outcome, the number of completed reviews was not and never had been the only goal of the program. The reviews were simply a means to broaden faculty awareness of OER and start fruitful conversations about how the library could support teaching and research in nontraditional ways. Keeping this in mind throughout the duration of the program allowed the TDEL librarians to manage their expectations, and to celebrate their successes, even if those successes were different at each institution.

Due to privacy restrictions of the IRB process, faculty reviews were not shared. Developing a joint repository of reviews could be a goal of a prospective partnership; however, due to staffing and managerial changes at our institutions, next steps for future collaborative efforts have not yet been determined. One of the goals of this particular program was to spark OER interest on our respective campuses and that objective was definitively met.

Libraries wishing to pursue a cross-institutional collaboration to further their OER outreach should focus on not only creating efficiencies but also community. Starting OER outreach with a faculty review program can be a useful way to gauge campus climate while demonstrating librarian expertise and building connections on campus. Pooling financial resources and creating a shared OER faculty review program were an effective means for building a support structure, creating shared resources and workflows, and collaboratively working toward a better understanding of OER.

References

BCcampus. (2013). BC open textbooks review criteria. Retrieved from
https://www.bccampus.ca/files/2013/10/
BC-Open-Textbooks-Review-Criteria_Oct2013.pdf

Center for Teaching & Learning. (2016). Open educational resources and open pedagogy stipends—submission request. Retrieved from https://www.davidson.edu/news/ctl-news/151215-open-educational-resources-and-open-pedagogy-stipends

Manturuk, K, & Ruiz-Esparza, Q.M. (2015). On-campus impacts of MOOCs at Duke University. *EDUCAUSEreview*. Retrieved from http://er.educause.edu/articles/2015/8/on-campus-impacts-of-moocs-at-duke-university

North Carolina State University. (2017). Alt-textbook project. Retrieved from https://www.lib.ncsu.edu/alttextbook

Senack, E. (2015). *Open textbooks: The billion-dollar solution*. The Student PIRGs. Retrieved from http://studentpirgs.org/sites/student/files/reports/The%20Billion%20Dollar%20Solution.pdf

University of South Carolina. (2017). SCoer! 2017 faculty awards. Retrieved from: https://guides.library.sc.edu/OER/affordableclass

Section 4:
Library-Supported Adoption and Creation Programs

In this final section, we explore the shifting emphases in more mature OER initiatives. The maturation of OER initiatives brings with it a shift in focus from advocacy and education efforts to adopting or adapting existing OER for use in the classroom, and in some cases, facilitating the creation and dissemination of new OER. In addition to their roles as educators and occasional advocates, librarians have a long and rich history of connecting researchers with relevant information, preserving material, and facilitating access to that material. In the OER space, these skill sets are being augmented to include the integration of existing OER into curricula, and in some cases catalyzing the creation or adaptation of new OER through innovative award programming and external partnerships. This section explores the role of the library in adopting and creating OER through a series of case studies. Readers are offered a variety of strategies to support OER discovery, adoption, and creation within a range of institutional environments. Whatever the realities of one's home institution, the pages ahead will offer transferable practices.

The section begins with two chapters outlining the maturation of OER programs at the University of Massachusetts Amherst and the University of Oklahoma. First, Smith explores the mature OER program at U. Mass Amherst, with a focus on developing partnerships to cultivate true open education. He offers an introduction to creating a library support program and strategies for sustainably supporting it. Second, Waller, Taylor, and Zemke map out the maturation of OER initiatives at the University of Oklahoma. While the program at their institution is aided by substantial top-down support, the authors detail the creation of an OER position and planning committee, along with strategies for assessing OER technology and course design.

Pivoting to a bottom-up approach to OER adoption, Ross and Francis describe the approach taken at the University of Saskatchewan. Here, the authors focus on cultivating individual champions to serve as instruments of change. The authors describe their use of the university's institutional repository in support of OER adoption efforts.

Miller takes a similar approach, viewed through the institutional context at Rollins College, a small liberal arts college in Florida. In his chapter, Miller describes the OER initiatives in this environment, including the unique challenges facing professors of art and art history, political science, and physics.

We end this section with a concrete example of the potential success inherent in combining OER initiatives with library-based publishing programs. Batchelor details a case study in publishing OER through the University of Washington and Reebus foundation. In this new space of OER publishing, as is illuminated by the author, partnerships, both within the institution and broadly, are critical, but librarians can and do serve as important connectors and catalysts in these important partnerships.

Seeking Alternatives to High-Cost Textbooks: Six Years of The Open Education Initiative at the University of Massachusetts Amherst

Jeremy Smith

Introduction

This article explores the development of the Open Education Initiative at the University of Massachusetts Amherst, one of the earliest library-led OER initiatives. The Open Education Initiative is an incentive program that offers UMass Amherst instructors small stipends or grants to explore alternatives to high-cost textbooks. The origins of the program in 2009–11 through its use today are discussed. Strategies around funding, campus partnerships, implementation, and assessment are considered.

Origins

In the winter of 2009, Scholarly Communication and Special Initiatives librarian Marilyn Billings traveled to the ALA Midwinter meeting in Denver. Along with former W.E.B. Du Bois Library Director Jay Schafer, she attended a panel sponsored by the Association of College and Research Libraries (ACRL) and the Scholarly Publishing and Academic Resources Coalition (SPARC) entitled "The Transformative Potential of Open Educational Resources (OER)" (Malenfant, 2008). The panel featured OER pioneers Richard Barniuk, the founder of Connexions, now OpenStax; David Wiley, a leading openness advocate and thinker; Nicole Allen, then an organizer with PIRG (Public Interest Research Group), now Director of Open Education for SPARC; and Mark Nelson, of the National Association of College Stores, NACS. Billings and Schafer came back to Amherst inspired by the panel and began to contemplate how they might introduce some of the ideas at UMass Amherst.

The idea of incorporating open educational resources (OER) into the work of the library was a natural one. In 2006, Billings had launched

ScholarWorks, a Digital Commons–hosted institutional repository, to house the scholarly output of the University. While building Scholar-Works between 2006 and 2009, Billings reached out to college deans, the Graduate School, Faculty Senate, and administrators about the value of open access publishing of scholarly material. This became even more topical as federal funding agencies, such as the National Institutes of Health, began to issue open access mandates for all grants, which opened an opportunity to work with the Office of Research on guiding the campus policy around open access.

As Billings and the library thought about new ways to encourage faculty to consider using OER, SPARC hosted a member phone call with Stephen Bell, the Associate University Librarian for Research & Instructional Services at Temple University, and Eric Frank, a UMass Amherst grad and co-founder of Flat World Knowledge. At the time, Flat World Knowledge was a publisher of free openly licensed textbooks.[1] On the February 2011 call, Bell discussed Temple's then brand new Alternate Textbook Project, (subsequently renamed the Textbook Affordability Program), which seeks to "encourage faculty experimentation and innovation in finding new, better and less costly ways to deliver learning materials to their students" (Bell, 2007). Temple's program offers "incentive grants" of $500 for faculty to: "create an alternate to the traditional textbook using a combination of Open Educational Resources (OER) and licensed library content" or "adopt an existing open textbook and use it to replace the existing commercially published textbook". Bell's program inspired Billings to create a similar program at UMass Amherst and in April of 2011, the first round of grants for the effort, billed as the Open Education Initiative (OEI), was announced and disbursed.

It should be noted here that one of the driving forces for launching the OEI in 2011 was the seemingly unending rise in the cost of textbooks and the increased attention being paid to student debt. In addition to the cost of textbooks, UMass Amherst also had a serious budget cut in

---

[1] Flat World has since rebranded and focuses on low-cost customizable textbooks and homework systems instead of free openly licensed ones. Their new content is no longer published with an open license, but the original line of open textbooks is still available in places like the Open Textbook Library.

2008 that led to a larger than usual increase in the cost of attendance. The institution was still feeling the effects of that in 2009–10. As Sara Goldrick-Rab has so eloquently explored in her devastating study of the cost of college for today's students, *Paying the Price,* students sometimes drop classes, work an extraordinary amount of hours outside of school, purchase course materials with student loan money, lack food and housing, or leave school with no degree and a generation of debt (Goldrick-Rab, 2016).

The 2002 UNESCO Forum on the Impact of Open Courseware for Higher Education in Developing Countries, which ostensibly launched the current wave of the OER movement, recognized the potential that OER had to overcome educational barriers in the developing world. The report issued at the end of that conference pledged to "develop together a universal educational resource available for the whole of humanity" (UNESCO, 2002). It has become increasingly clear in the ensuing decade and a half that this need is as great in the United States as it is throughout the world.

Implementation

Building a grant program in a large academic library with no permanent support staff was not easy. Fortunately, support for the program came easily from Schafer and James V. Staros, the UMass Provost at the time. Director Schafer was a strong supporter of OER (he was on the 2011 SPARC phone call) and convinced Staros to commit some discretionary funds toward the project if the library would match it. Staros was a former faculty member himself and was familiar with the burden placed on students. Billings, with the help of a resident librarian (a program for early career scholarly communication librarians), managed the mechanics of the grant. She also enlisted departmental librarians to announce the grant to their faculty and provide support once the projects began. Her vision was to integrate OER work into the existing workflows of academic support units within the library.

To ensure that grants were selected by a cross-section of campus support staff, an advisory group was created to help choose successful recipients for the grant. The group had representation from Academic Computing, the Center for Teaching and Office of Faculty Development, and the Academic Information Technology Program. Collaboration was a central tenet of the OEI and reflected the library as the hub of campus support for open access projects and student success. What distinguished the UMass and Temple effort from earlier OER projects was the fact that it was led by the library rather than educational technologists, distance learning course designers, or international education groups, such as had been done by previous early-to-mid aughts OER projects (Smith & Casserly, 2006).

An initial funding amount of $10,000 was settled on for the inaugural round. $5,000 came from the Provost's Office and $5,000 from the library. Compared to large, administratively-led, foundation-sponsored, campus-wide open education efforts such as MIT's OpenCourseWare project, the UMass plan was decidedly humble (Abelson, 2008). An information session was held for prospective applicants where various aspects of OER were discussed, such as available library and openly licensed material, copyright, technology, and pedagogy. Representatives from the library, Center for Teaching, and Academic Computing all offered their support for prospective projects. Eight faculty members from the colleges of Education, Humanities & Fine Arts, Natural Sciences, and Social and Behavioral Sciences, as well as management, submitted proposals. In April of 2011, the first round of grant winners was announced.

Initially, the OEI was focused on textbook affordability, which resonated with students, faculty, and administrators. Because of that, there was not a strict emphasis on OER. Licensed commercial library materials and services such as ebooks, article databases, reserves, archival material, and interlibrary loan, were shared with grant applicants as well. When discussing library-licensed content with faculty, it is important to emphasize that these are distinct from OER in that they are *free* for everyone at the institution but not *open* and not free to the library. Many library materials do not pass David Wiley's 5R test for OER: retain, revise, remix, reuse, redistribute. Wiley himself believes that there is too much emphasis by libraries on affordability and not enough on the pedagogical and ownership freedoms that OER affords (Wiley, 2017). If an OER or affordability effort is led by a library, it is natural that library offerings would be discussed. The high cost of textbooks is an easy entry point to begin talking to faculty about the other tenets of OER such as creating, revising, and sharing openly licensed material in new conceptual ways. This can also segue nicely into larger discussions about open access research and scholarship.

The initial outreach strategy for the OEI was fairly simple. An information session was held for all prospective applicants, advertised through typical library channels such as posters around campus, a press release, and website placement. These events were aimed not only at faculty considering applying for our grant, but anyone on campus, including administrators, interested in the concept of OER. The workshops consisted of overviews of copyright, OER vs. licensed library content, technological and pedagogical support, and more. This was also an opportunity for the faculty to hear about each other's proposals and get ideas on how they might structure their own.

The core team then got together to review the applications. During this first round there were not more applications than there was funding, so the selection criteria did not need to be rigorous. However, as the program has become more recognized, this is no longer the case. For this first round, all eight instructors received $1,000 grants.

Among the first OEI cohort were instructors from across many academic areas of the university: education, women's studies, art, animal science, natural resource policy and administration, communication, sociology, and management. The initial round of projects included: adopting an OER Flat World accounting textbook, creating an open natural resource policy lab manual, authoring an introductory women's, gender, and sexuality studies textbook, utilizing library databases for a language arts course, and finding interdisciplinary OER case studies for a graduate-level communication course. The projects varied between adoption, adaptation, and creation of OER, non-OER, and library materials. We found that a majority of the projects were hybrid projects, meaning they used existing as well as newly created content.

The program was a hit and ended up saving students approximately $101,632 from 2011 to 2015 from an initial investment of $10,000. 2015 is the last year on record that any of the original eight faculty taught the class that used the material developed with OEI money. Of course many of these faculty have continued to use OER in their other classes and have convinced colleagues to do the same or apply for the OEI. The second round of grants was done in the fall of 2011. This time, the budget was increased to $15,000. The cost was again split between the library and the Provost's Office. For this round it was decided to offer more money for larger classes due to the fact that the $1,000 grants were only attracting small, upper-level classes. Based on the Provost Office's experience with other grant programs, it was decided that a larger amount of $2,500 might attract instructors from larger classes who felt that the higher amount was worth their time and risk.

The second round attracted 13 applicants from a diverse range of colleges and departments including: agriculture, civil and environmental engineering, public health, anthropology, chemistry, and geoscience. All 13 applicants were able to receive funding and, again, put forth a wide range of projects that have saved students $167,964 since 2012. Some of these courses continue to be taught; but it is often the case that an instructor will rotate out of teaching a class and we have not tracked whether the following instructor has continued to use the open/free materials. However, we have found that many of the faculty who participate in the OEI continue to seek out alternatives to high-cost textbooks in their other classes whenever possible.

In the ensuing six years, the library has orchestrated eight rounds of grants, saving students a total of $1.8 million dollars.[2] The schedule has been slightly erratic due to staffing variables and funding. Some years, we were able to offer two rounds, while others we only offered one.

Our grantees are required to do the following:

- Attend a kickoff meeting where we answer questions, discuss open licensing and copyright, and outline technological, pedagogical, and research support.
- Circulate a qualitative and quantitative survey to all of their students at the end of the first semester they utilize the materials.
- Provide a copy of the revised syllabus or course outline used for the class.

---

[2] This figure includes every instance of the class taught by the faculty who received the funds. So if a faculty member from 2012 has taught a class three times, we multiply the average new/used cost of the original book times the total number of students in each of the three classes. Other initiatives simply use an average of $100 for every book.

- Deposit any openly licensed material created into an appropriate open repository (e.g. UMass' ScholarWorks, Open Textbook Library, MERLOT (the Multimedia Educational Resource for Learning and Online Teaching), etc.)
- Write a final grant report that includes a narrative summarizing the challenges and accomplishments of their experience creating/finding/using the materials, the impact on their teaching, the impact on students and their performance, and lessons learned.
- Participate in long-term assessments of the Open Education Initiative.

Partnerships

Partnerships with other campus stakeholders are indispensable to any OER effort. As I have illustrated throughout this chapter, it is through these partnerships that we have been able to facilitate our initiative. There is another chapter in this book, which I contributed to, that goes into greater detail on campus partnerships, so I will give a cursory overview of the partners utilized here at UMass.

Instructional Innovation, formerly known as Academic Computing, is the office that bridges the gap between information technology and academics. Instructional Innovation offers hands-on technical help for any faculty wishing to utilize unfamiliar or cutting-edge technology in the implementation of their project. Instructional Innovation also participates in our workshop for grantees and helps select proposals.

The Center for Teaching Excellence and Faculty Development (TEFD) "supports the professional development of faculty across all career stages and disciplines with programs and resources focused on student-centered teaching, course and curriculum design, faculty mentoring, intercultural competency, scholarly writing, leadership, and more." ("About TEFD", n.d.) Among their many other offerings, TEFD aids faculty in transforming classes when the infrastructure provided by a traditional textbook is removed. TEFD also participates in our workshop for grantees and has a member on our selection team.

We partner with faculty by including one faculty member from the Academic Information Technology Program on our selection team. Having the perspective of faculty can help interpret ideas included in proposals. Faculty also collaborate with the library on OER forums and programs.

Throughout the history of our program we have had several panel discussions, presentations, and forums where past grant participants have discussed their projects. We have several OER "champions" on campus who share their OER experiences with colleagues. Faculty have also supported global OER efforts by attending an on-campus OER workshop led by the Open Textbook Network and authoring reviews of OER textbooks in the Open Textbook Library.

Students play a significant role at UMass Amherst. We are fortunate to have a very active PIRG (Public Interest Research Group) and student activists on the Student Government Association. Students help agitate administrators, faculty, and other students to advocate for the use of OER. Students in the MassPIRG chapter have met with the Provost to push for more institutional support for OER, staffed information tables around campus, and held public information sessions. They also held a rally in the library lobby about OER that was covered by local print media. The Student Government Association has passed resolutions in support of more OER adoption and given an "OER hero" award to an instructor who supported their students by utilizing OER. A possible next step could be for the Faculty Senate to adopt a similar resolution.

Obviously, the program could not prosper without the support of library and campus administrators. Funding and encouragement from administration has enabled our program to thrive for the past six years. With budgets always a concern, wider financial support from upper administration has been cautious. In the future, there may be opportunities to utilize student support funds for the development of OER as a driver of student retention, recruitment, and success.

Faculty support the OEI by participating in the program as well as by acting as ambassadors for OER to colleagues in their respective disciplines. Faculty at UMass Amherst have encouraged fellow instructors to apply for grants and have spoken at local and national events about their use or creation of OER. In our physics department, one faculty member began teaching an introductory physics course with the OpenStax College physics textbook. He then encouraged two additional faculty to apply to our initiative. They both moved to OpenStax and now the entire part 1 and 2 of introductory physics, featuring large, 150+ person classes, uses no textbook.

In addition to local on-campus partners, the library has partnered with national OER organizations that support our local work. These include the Open Textbook Network (OTN), Rebus Community, and OpenStax Institutional Partners. OTN is part of the Center for Open Education at the University of Minnesota and supports OER with three initiatives: the Open Textbook Library, Network, and Fellowship. UMass Amherst is a dues-paying member of the Network.

Being a member of the OTN has been beneficial for several reasons. In addition to a day-long workshop for librarians and faculty, we have participated in a pilot project to facilitate the development of open textbooks with Pressbooks and the Rebus Community. Pressbooks is a WordPress-based open source platform for presenting online texts in a "book-like" way. It also allows readers to download texts in multiple formats such as PDF, mobi, epub, XHTML, and more. The Rebus Community is a "non-profit organization developing a new, collaborative process for publishing open textbooks, and associated content. Rebus is building tools and resources to support open textbook publishing, and to bring together a community of faculty, librarians, students and others working with open textbooks around the world" (Rebus Community, 2017). It is through these local and national partnerships that we are able to provide high-quality support for OER initiatives.

Assessment

Although not at the top of everyone's planning list, assessment is a key element of any OER initiative. Data gathered through assessment can illustrate to library and campus administrators that an investment of resources in OER is a sound financial and pedagogical decision. Even if the resources aren't immediately available to process and analyze the data, it should be gathered at the beginning of any initiative for future examination. The more data collected, the more opportunities to illustrate the success of a program and share local results with national OER assessment efforts.

As the OEI developed over time, we amassed lots of qualitative and quantitative data. Initially, not much had been done to analyze it. This was mostly due to the constraints put on the project by the lack of a full-time position. Once that position was filled, we were able to look at the data and gather more. We instituted some of the principles of the COUP Framework. COUP stands for costs, outcomes, usage, and perception. The COUP Framework was conceived of by David Wiley, Lance Fischer, and John Hilton III of the Open Education Group. The COUP Framework is an "approach to studying the impact of open educational resource...in secondary and post-secondary education" (Open Education Group, n.d.). The COUP looks at the financial impact of OER on students, the learning impacts of OER, the use/reuse of OER by students and faculty, and student and faculty perceptions of OER. Although the framework is primarily intended to analyze OER, we use it to assess our hybrid OER/free/low-cost materials approach.

As part of the application process, we ask faculty to include the title and average new/used cost of the current class textbook and the approximate number of students that will be in the class. Following the completion of the first semester using the OER/low-cost materials, we acquire the precise number of enrolled students from the online course catalog and multiply that by the average cost of the textbook to determine the money potentially saved by students. We have calculated this for all of the classes we've funded since 2011. We also add in cumulative data for each class over time. So if a class stopped using a $140 textbook in 2014 and has been taught twice since then, we multiply $140 times the number of students in all three instances of the class taught by the funded instructor.

All funded faculty are required to write a final 1–3-page grant report following the completion of their first semester using the materials they used or created. This report allows us to gather qualitative information on how the faculty used the materials as well as their perceptions of the effectiveness, coverage, rigor, and format of OER. We continue to engage with faculty over time by periodically sending out electronic surveys to gather their longitudinal perceptions of OER and their sense of student engagement with the material. We ask them if they have continued to use the material developed with the grant, used OER in other classes, converted colleagues to OER, and more. This helps us measure whether opinions and perceptions of OER among our grantees change over time.

We also survey students in the classes that we fund. We gather data on student perceptions of the OER/free/low-cost materials used in the class. We ask what the students think about the quality of the materials and how they compare to traditional materials as well as their level of engagement in the course. We also ask the students about their general attitudes and behaviors around textbook purchasing such as what they do to avoid buying textbooks, how much they spend, and how the cost of textbooks has impacted their academic choices. We use this data mostly for advocacy with faculty and administrators.

We have compared results on the local Student Response To Instruction forms, which are filled out by students every semester, for classes before and after our initiative was introduced. Our data mostly mirrors data collected by the Open Education Group, which shows that students perform as well academically, if not better, in classes where access to the learning material is not hindered. In the future, we plan on doing more investigation into academic outcomes by comparing drop rates, graduation rates, and number of students receiving a C or better, in OER and non-OER classes.

Obstacles

As originally conceived, the UMass OEI was an experiment. It has essentially existed in beta form since 2011. This, of course, has positive as well as negative consequences. This next section attempts to address some of these, so one can potentially avoid some of the same pitfalls.

Staffing

Staffing can be one of the most challenging obstacles when managing a successful OER program in a library. Although elements of OER-related work can be found in many library areas like research support, reserves, acquisitions, archives and special collections, and scholarly communication, there are very few full-time staff devoted to OER. Here at UMass, the program was begun by the head of the Scholarly Communication department, who also managed the institutional repository, served on several internal and external committees, and was responsible for additional administrative tasks that did not allow the amount of time needed to administer an OER program. Luckily, the library had a resident librarian program, which funded recent graduates of library school to have real-world library experiences. These emerging professionals were enlisted to help with the administrative burden of managing the Open Education Initiative by tracking data, communication, arranging publicity and events, and supporting faculty once the projects were initiated.

We were fortunate to have the resident program, but the success of the initiative forced the library to commit to supporting it in a more substantive way with permanent staffing in the spring of 2015. At this point, my position in Special Collections and University Archives was temporary and the library had decided to make a stronger commitment to supporting OER work. I was asked to consider moving into a permanent position that would be dealing with all things OER, in addition to other scholarly communication-related work. I accepted the position of the Digital Project Manager, which became, in essence, an OER librarian.

The evolution from temporary to full-time staffing was due in no small part to the dogged advocacy efforts of Marilyn Billings and Library Director Jay Schafer. Without their belief in the centrality of the library's role in this emerging field, it may have not survived past the pilot phase.

It is true that we are born of our own circumstances and that not every academic library has the resources to do what we have done. However, our experience has shown that if at least one person in the library is passionate about starting an OER initiative, and can garner administrative support for a pilot, and is successful, the benefits of the program will become evident and illustrate the clear need for more institutional programmatic support.

Grant Administration, Faculty Awareness, and Accountability

With the improvisational nature of the UMass OEI comes a fair amount of experimentation with how to administer a grant. Questions about the timing of funds, what the funds can be used for, and accountability all need to be addressed. Having a partner in the library business office is a must. The library business office will often be the ones who disburse money and will need to know when to transfer the funds, to whom, and how. Budget cycles must also be considered when planning the timing of a grant. Being in communication with the business office, the dean of the library, and your department is the best way to keep everyone in sync.

Anticipating potential issues with grant proposals can help make faculty proposals a success. Although the majority of our projects have run to completion, a few have either not followed the original proposal in some way or have not happened at all. Out of the 60+ faculty who have participated in our initiative since 2011, only one received funds and did not complete their project. Faculty become very reliant on commercial textbooks to form the skeleton of their classes and sometimes don't anticipate the fallout of removing it. Some proposals fail or alter after negative student feedback during the implementation semester.

Sometimes, while preparing their proposal, faculty will do a cursory search of the available material and once they actually start working on the grant, find it challenging to find appropriate open or library material. We also find that faculty have not thought through, or are unaware of, the differences between fair use, the public domain, Creative Commons-licensed material, free web content, and "free" library content. They also don't necessarily know how copyright affects the 5 Rs.

One way to address these issues is to hold information sessions for applicants before the grant deadline or afterwards for grantees. Alternately, a one-on-one meeting can be held to tease out ambiguous language in proposals or explain misunderstandings. Asking the right questions on the proposal form is also important. We have oftentimes been able to meet with faculty in advance to help them shape their proposals. This always clears up misunderstandings and tempers expectations. The proposal process must force the faculty members to think through the consequences of their ideas clearly and cohesively.

Sustainability

Building a successful and sustainable OER program can mean different things to different institutions. What works for a statewide initiative with government funding will not work for a one-person program at a community college. Therefore, it is hard to define what a sustainable OER program looks like for everyone. Funding for our program has lasted six years so far, but could be cut at any point during an inevitable budget shortfall or financial crisis. Funding has fluctuated between the Provost's Office, donations from the Friends of the Library, the Center for Teaching and Faculty Development, and more recently, a dedicated line item in the yearly library budget. The initiative has been very successful with participants, students, and administrators, but that is no guarantee of longevity.

Other obstacles to sustainability facing innovative initiatives like OER include some of the antiquated support systems currently available on college campuses. Donna Desrochers of the RPK Group, an education consulting firm, has spoken about this issue. She finds that although open to innovation, many campuses lack the organizational structure to sustain it. Funding models in higher education are outdated and not designed to incentivize innovation. There is a general lack of appropriate data systems to track the impact of innovative projects. Desrochers recommends several strategies for combating some of these barriers:

- Ensure stakeholders understand that OER is not just a "grant" or short-term initiative, but another tool to support student success.
- Communicate timeframes for achieving success.
- Begin planning early on to fund ongoing cost of supporting OER. Perhaps institute a course fee.
- Identify opportunities to reallocate resources.
- Capture potential return on investment for students, the institution and other stakeholders (Desrochers, 2017).

Since the OER position was created in 2015, we have attempted to find ways to make the program more sustainable. In late 2016, we wrote a proposal outlining how the OEI could improve and grow. Writing that the program was in a state of permanent beta, we presented the following five recommendations to the Provost and library dean:

1. Increase funding

Many faculty on campus would happily create open textbooks for use by their students for free if they were given the technical and financial support that matched what a commercial publisher can provide. Estimates of the costs associated with producing a new textbook range from $10,000 to $1 million. Currently, with our funding structure, it is a rare faculty member who is able to produce an open textbook for the amounts we provide. We believe that if we were to offer one or two incentives per year of at least $10,000 for the development of an open textbook, there would be significant interest from faculty. The University Libraries have recently partnered with Rebus/Pressbooks and the Open Textbook Network to provide technical support for the development of open textbooks by faculty at UMass Amherst. However, this partnership does not account for the time that actually goes into the production of a textbook.

2. Provide faculty release time to produce open materials

According to the latest report from the Babson Survey Research Group on open textbooks, a significant obstacle to the adoption/creation of OER by faculty is time (Allen & Seaman, 2016). If faculty were given release time for the production of OER, it would eliminate this barrier. Another barrier for faculty is that work on original OER, and teaching activity in general, is minimized during the promotion and tenure process, especially at research institutions. If this were to change, we believe it would stimulate further work in the field. We acknowledge that this is more of a culture shift, but it is worth mentioning.

3. Develop a campus-wide advisory group

To reach the wider campus and increase its profile, the Open Education Initiative must create a campus-wide advisory group that consists of representatives from the student body, administration, the library, faculty, and University Press. This will not only highlight the support of the campus for the goals and mission of the OEI, but it will position us to broaden the initiative across the entire UMass system in the future. This will put us in line with other system-wide efforts such as Affordable Learning Georgia, California State University System, Open Oregon, and BCcampus in Vancouver, which according to a recent report from OpenStax are among the colleges that have saved their students the most during the 2015–16 academic school year (Ruth, 2016).

4. Change funding structure

To maximize the funds allotted to the OEI, we suggest offering four categories of grants based on the scope of the project. Typically, OER fall into three categories (adopt, adapt, or create). Adopt is simply the process of adopting an existing OER as is. Adapting is a hybrid approach in which one takes elements of multiple OER and constructs, or remixes, a cohesive corpus of material. Creation is the creation of OER from scratch. The fourth category is for projects that don't fit neatly within any of the other three categories.

- Category 1: Adopt—Redesign course to incorporate an existing open textbook or open course content: $500.

- Category 2: Adapt—Combine existing OER with new open content to bridge gaps in available resources: $1,500.
- Category 3: Create—Create a new open educational resource or open course when there are currently no sufficient OER available to meet learning objectives. Range: $2,500–$10,000+.
- Category 4: Other—Projects not covered in any of the above: $TBA.

Many of our prior grants utilized library subscription materials in conjunction with other materials like blogs, websites, podcasts, and maybe some OER. These types of projects are not always considered open by the standard 5R definition and usually can't be shared with others outside of the university. However, we have funded them because they are free or low cost and therefore fit within the larger goal of the OEI to reduce costs for students. Additionally, many faculty still require incentives to rework their syllabi. Although we should still fund these types of projects, we believe that these should fall within category 1. This then allows us to focus the funding on projects that are more fully "open." Projects that aim to simply use existing library databases and other purchased materials can be funneled into the existing support infrastructure in the library and forgo funding.

5. Target Gen Eds

During the spring 2013 and 2016 grant rounds, we sought to target general education classes as an experiment. This reduced the number of applicants, but, once the projects are implemented, will impact more students. Many of the general education classes at UMass Amherst are large introductory courses that are geared towards non-majors. These types of classes are more likely to have quality OER available to them. In a recent study of UMass Amherst Gen Ed classes, we found a majority (26%) used commercial textbooks. It makes sense to target these specific classes, where there is a higher chance of OER being available. We would encourage all Gen Ed faculty to adopt existing free library resources, but would focus our funds towards those that wanted to develop, remix, or use open materials.

Of the five recommendations, only two were implemented during the spring 2017 grant round. We were able to secure some additional funding from the Provost's Office in order to offer one $10,000 grant to a faculty member who wrote a proposal to author an open textbook on radical social theory and we changed the funding structure to an adopt, adapt, create model, to shift the focus towards OER and away from library material. We plan on continuing to advocate for the other three recommendations and have discussed the possibility of creating a UMass system-run program that would provide funding and facilitation for the Amherst, Worcester, Dartmouth, Boston, and Lowell campuses.

Another area of future exploration for us will be the creation of a campus-wide OER policy. An OER policy can be a key ingredient in institutionalizing and sustaining OER across campus. Similar to an open access policy, it can serve the dual purposes of acquiring buy-in from a large swath of instructors and administrators and open up an opportunity to promote and enshrine the culture of OER within campus departments, Faculty Senate, the board of trustees, and state legislators. Lumen Learning, the OER course development company, has created an OER policy development tool on their website that allows anyone to choose one of several policy templates to customize for your environment (Lumen Learning). For OER to grow, it must move out of the grassroots and into the firmly rooted peaks of campus administration.

Conclusion

Having the vantage point of six years allows the UMass Amherst Libraries to look back at the successes, missed opportunities, and unforeseen pitfalls of their OER/affordability initiative. The overriding philosophy has always been improvisational. An idea may start one way, but will often respond to feedback or the changing campus and industry environment. The people served by OER, faculty, students, and administrators, are always exploring new ways of teaching, learning, and "administering," so librarians must be prepared to respond. Whether one is planning an initiative for the first time, or is expanding an existing one, I hope the efforts of UMass Amherst will provide inspiration.

Although much of what libraries do is support students and faculty in their pursuit of knowledge, it is rare that they also help facilitate the creation of new materials that can be freely shared with the world, open new possibilities for teaching and learning, and remove a barrier for financially disadvantaged students. This is what makes the future of OER and libraries so exciting.

References

Abelson, Hal. (2008) The creation of OpenCourseWare at MIT. *Journal of Science Education and Technology*, 17(2), 164–174. http://dx.doi.org/10.1007/s10956-007-9060-8

About TEFD. (n.d.). Retrieved from http://www.umass.edu/tefd/about-tefd

Allen, I. E. & Seaman, J. (2016) *Opening the textbooks: Educational resources in U.S. higher education, 2015–16.* Babson Survey Research Group. Retrieved from https://www.onlinelearningsurvey.com/reports/openingthetextbook2016.pdf

Bell, S. (2007). The textbook affordability project at Temple Libraries: About the project. Retrieved from http://guides.temple.edu/c.php?g=229152&p=1520174

Desrochers, D. (2017). *Exploring the economic costs and benefits of OER and achieving sustainability* [PowerPoint slides]. Retrieved from https://drive.google.com/open?id=0B16ftZ0-z-SJTzdlS1gycm9PMkU

Goldrick-Rab, S. (2016). *Paying the price: College costs, financial aid, and the betrayal of the American dream.* Chicago, IL: The University of Chicago Press

Malenfant, K. (2008, December 16). ACRL and SPARC announce speakers for forum on open educational resources. *ACRL Insider.* Retrieved from http://www.acrl.ala.org/acrlinsider/archives/320

Open Education Group. (n.d.). *The COUP framework.* Retrieved from http://openedgroup.org/coup

Rebus Community. (2017). *FAQ.* Retrieved from https://about.rebus.community/faq/

Ruth, D. (2016, August 1). OpenStax ranks the colleges that save the most with free textbooks. *Rice University News and Media.* Retrieved from http://news.rice.edu/2016/08/01/openstax-ranks-the-colleges-that-save-the-most-with-free-textbooks/

Smith, M. S., & Casserly, C. M. (2006). The promise of open educational resources. *Change, 38*(5), 8–17. http://dx.doi.org/10.3200/CHNG.38.5.8-17

UNESCO. (2002). *Forum on the impact of open courseware for higher education in developing countries: Final report.* Retrieved from http://unesdoc.unesco.org/images/0012/001285/128515e.pdf

Wiley, D. (2017, June 30). The Sleight of Hand of "Free" vs "Affordable" [Blog post]. Retrieved from https://opencontent.org/blog/archives/5055

From Start-Up to Adolescence: University of Oklahoma's OER Efforts

Jen Waller, Cody Taylor, & Stacy Zemke

In February, 2013, University of Oklahoma (OU) president, David Boren, issued a letter to all OU faculty members highlighting the high cost of textbooks, expressing his strong "support for the move to open access materials in teaching and research," and a charge to carefully "evaluate whether our textbooks and course materials add value to the educational experience equal to their cost to our students." President Boren's letter also announced the imminent hiring of one of the nation's first full-time librarians dedicated solely to open educational resources (OER). Boren recognized, as did many academic administrators, that college affordability was becoming increasingly important to the university's efforts to attract and retain students. The cost of textbooks, in particular, had risen dramatically, and the OU community proved willing to rise to Boren's 2013 charge. This case study describes OU's OER initiatives that arose from President Boren's charge from 2013 to the present—with a specific focus on the Alternative Textbook Grant, which by August 2017 had saved OU students over $1,000,000 in textbook costs.

OER Program Development as a Start-Up Initiative

The University of Oklahoma Libraries senior administration created the position of OER Coordinator in 2013 and is believed to be the first academic institution in the United States to dedicate a full-time librarian solely to OER. The first coordinator was an instructor in the OU School of Library and Information Studies and had a background in the OER movement, having attended the annual Online Learning Consortium/MERLOT (Multimedia Educational Resource for Learning and Online Teaching) conference (Online Learning Consortium, 2017), as well as developing a learning object repository as a contractor for a textbook publisher.

This Coordinator developed a plan for the first year, which focused on researching current OER initiatives at other academic libraries and then building awareness of OER on OU's campus. At the time there were only a handful of OER initiatives across the country. Fortunately, they were well documented, and their organizers were willing to share their experiences. These initiatives included those at University of Massachusetts Amherst (Billings, Hutton, Schafer, Schweik, & Sheridan, 2012), Kansas State University (Kansas State University Center for the Advancement of Digital Scholarship, n.d.), and Open Textbook Network at the University of Minnesota (Center for Open Education, n.d.-b). SPARC was just beginning to develop OER as one of their three focus goals (Scholarly Publishing and Academic Resources Coalition [SPARC], 2007), but their support was still critical.

OU's Alternative Textbook Grant program was modeled after the successful initiatives at University of Massachusetts Amherst and Kansas State University, and the University of Oklahoma Libraries (and particularly the OER team) still owe a debt of gratitude to these programs today. These programs, and subsequently University of Oklahoma's program, were built with the goals of:

- supporting faculty in creating open content
- supporting faculty in adopting open content
- creating awareness of open materials on campus.

The OER Coordinator formed an OER Strategic Initiative Planning Committee to formalize the OER initiative in the OU Libraries planning process. This committee of six was comprised of librarians and library staff who defined the first year of initiatives and researched the most expensive and most used textbooks held in the Libraries' textbook reserve program. The committee determined OU Libraries purpose regarding OER would be:

> to support the use of OER and affordable learning solutions (ALS) to reduce student costs. This will include the adoption of OER/ALS by faculty to replace traditionally purchased materials and by students for study support.

The committee further developed the scope of the OER initiative: "This project will focus on piloting sustainable and scalable OER/ALS adoptions on campus. The project will focus on four implementation areas," namely:

- OU Libraries will support the development and use of OER and ALS to replace *textbooks* in the classroom, to save students money, and to give faculty more control over their educational content.
- OU Libraries will support the development and use of OER and ALS to replace *course packs* in the classroom, to save students money, and to give faculty more control over their educational content.
- OU Libraries will work with the University College (University of Oklahoma, 2016) to identify appropriate OER as study aids for students.
- OU Libraries will provide an appropriate platform to support the discovery, creation, reuse, revision, remixing, and redistribution of OER and other affordable learning materials for faculty and students.

The committee also developed corresponding project deliverables and established a timeline of spring 2014–spring 2015 for implementation.

Recognizing the need to support the OER Coordinator's quick-moving start-up effort, OU Libraries hired a student employee to assist the OER Coordinator. The timing was serendipitous; the hired student, an undergraduate electrical engineering major, had made contacts in the library while doing class research on "openness" and Creative Commons licensing. He was interested in technology to support open courseware and through his research had become knowledgeable about open licensing and the open landscape. His technical background, combined with this interest in open education, made him an excellent addition to OU Libraries and the OER effort. From January 2014 through October 2015 the OER team consisted of one full-time equivalent (FTE) (the OER Coordinator) and a 0.5 FTE (the OER Student Assistant) who were solely dedicated to OER.

One of the first identified issues was a lack of knowledge about open content on the OU campus. The OER Coordinator created connections on campus to increase awareness of the rising cost of educational materials, as well as present possible solutions using both openly licensed content and materials licensed through OU Libraries. Fortunately, the use of openly licensed content was beginning to take hold in several key strategic areas across the university: the Dean of OU's College of Arts and Sciences had recently adopted the open textbook *Introduction to Sociology* (Griffiths et al., 2015); OU's Center for Teaching Excellence (CTE) was working on a MOOC (massive open online course) platform, Janux (NextThought, 2017), and was encouraging the development and use of openly licensed materials; and the University of Oklahoma Regents had joined MERLOT as a Higher Education Partner (MERLOT, California State University, 1997) with a faculty member from OU's Department of Physics and Astronomy serving as the Project Director/Partner Liaison. Yet these were isolated uses of OER, and there was otherwise a lack of knowledge among the general faculty, including the library faculty, on OER and its related components: Creative Commons licensing, finding and evaluating OER, and "open" as a concept.

Believing that faculty members listen and learn from their colleagues, the OER Coordinator first began her awareness efforts by enlisting three faculty members who were already familiar with open textbooks to give a panel presentation at OU's annual Teaching Scholars Initiative in fall 2013, less than a month after she was hired. She also quickly partnered with OU's CTE to design and distribute a survey to all faculty members with the goal of identifying those who had been using open materials or who were interested in knowing more about reducing the cost of materials for teaching and learning. Additionally, she continued to partner with staff at CTE to support Janux (NextThought, 2017), by finding open materials for faculty planning to teach in the platform. When the Janux platform launched, many of the courses were taught using fully open materials that had been curated by CTE and the OER Coordinator.

During fall 2013, the OER Coordinator also began to build awareness among librarian faculty by working with the subject specialist librarians in group and individual instruction sessions covering Creative Commons licensing and the OER movement. During these sessions, each participating librarian was given a matrix of large OER repositories such as MERLOT (MERLOT, California State University, n.d.), OpenStax CNX platform (OpenStax, n.d.), OER Commons (Institute for the Study of Knowledge Management in Education [ISKME], 2007), and the Open Textbook Library (Center for Open Education, n.d.-a). In some cases, more specialized repositories, such as ComPADRE (ComPADRE Digital

Library, 2003) and the Noba Collection (Diener Education Fund, 2017) were provided. Librarians then filled out the matrix by evaluating the quality and coverage of their corresponding disciplinary resources in these OER repositories. This exercise achieved two goals: it enabled librarians to become more familiar with OER repositories and the specific disciplinary resources held in each, and it provided the seeds for building an OER-focused LibGuide to assist faculty and librarians in their selection of OER and alternative course materials.

In anticipation of the soon-to-be-introduced Alternative Textbook Grant, the OER Coordinator developed the OU Libraries OER LibGuide (Taylor, Waller, Zemke, & Biamah, 2017) and an accompanying blog (Taylor & Zemke, n.d.) with the goal of making it easier for interested faculty to find open textbooks and OER by subject and disciplinary area. The blog was used to document OER-related matters, such as detailing the LibGuide development process, recording searches and search strategies for OER, publishing liaison librarian reviews of OER repositories, and posting interviews with OU faculty members currently using an open solution for their courses. The latter strategy, specifically, was a popular and engaging format in which to share faculty members' experiences and illustrate the many achievable (and easy) ways to use open content. The blog also gave the OER Coordinator an opportunity to grow OU Libraries' OER program by further supporting the activities of these faculty members.

Additional outreach efforts during this early phase of the initiative included events held during Open Education Week (Open Education Consortium, n.d.):

- A "Waffles for Writers" event, which connected faculty with OER and OU's Writing Center
- Tabling events designed to raise student awareness of OER
- A Wikipedia Edit-a-Thon to improve Wikipedia content about women in the history of science. This event was a particular success, because of partnerships already established with the Writing Center and a faculty member in the Department of History of Science who provided extra credit to participating students.

Establishing the Alternative Textbook Grant

In spring 2014, the OER Coordinator introduced the Alternative Textbook Grant at OU's annual Academic Tech Expo. The primary purpose of the grant program was taken directly from the OER Strategic Initiative Planning Committee—*to reduce student costs*. The initial grant program was extremely flexible, and the OER Coordinator was willing to support projects as long as they saved students money. This included the use of OER and library-licensed materials such as databases, ebooks, and collections of items placed on reserve. The OER Coordinator relied heavily on personal relationships to recruit applicants, and she continued to reach out to those faculty members who had already indicated interest in using OER. For example, some of the recruitment targets had responded to the Center for Teaching Excellence survey that had been distributed in the fall; some had attended OER events; some were already active library users, and others had been involved in OU's Teaching Scholars Initiative. These faculty members were thought to be most interested in new approaches to teaching and learning, so it was thought they might also be most interested in transitioning from traditional course materials to OER.

The Alternative Textbook Grant was designed to support faculty members in finding and creating alternative course materials for their classes. The amounts awarded in this pilot phase were between $1,200 and $2,500 and were designed to compensate instructors for the time and effort it took to find, adopt, modify, or create new resources as well as time and effort required to create accompanying slide decks, tests, quizzes, handouts, and other ancillary materials. The initial cohort of grantees consisted of five faculty members who were awarded a total of $9,600. They projected that for one semester a total of 420 students would be impacted, saving those students $57,975 in displaced textbook costs. In actuality, $59,842 was saved the first semester of implementation. The terms of the grant required the alternative resource be used for two semesters (the semesters did not necessarily have to be sequential, acknowledging that not all courses are taught every semester), and the projected savings for two semesters for the initial $9,600 "investment" was nearly $116,000.

The Not-So-Terrible Twos

During the second year of the initiative, the OER team continued an awareness campaign—now about OER in general and the Alternative Textbook Grant specifically—and continued to look for additional strategies to save students money. The first year's outreach had focused on "likely candidates" and "low-hanging fruit," but it was now time to recruit instructors who may have never heard of OER.

Therefore, a key component of building awareness in the program's second-year initiative was to *go to* the faculty members, instead of relying on personal contacts. One successful outreach strategy was to meet individually with faculty members, in their office, as a traditional publisher's textbook representative might. Instead of representing a traditional publisher, the OER team members became the "Open Textbook Representatives." Prior to these meetings, the OER team would research existing open textbooks and other OER that were applicable to the discipline and the class taught by the faculty member with whom they were about to meet. They would then go to the faculty members' offices with a curated list of sources and perhaps a complimentary coffee.

The OER Coordinator, where possible, attended faculty meetings to discuss OER—even if it was for only five minutes. Developing, practicing, and memorizing an "elevator pitch" targeted to every campus constituency (faculty, administrators, students, etc.) in as many disciplines as possible became important to this effort, because it was often necessary to quickly relay the benefits of OER and open initiatives in very short conversations.

Staff in the OU Libraries Circulation Department were already receiving a textbook list from the university bookstore in order to purchase copies of highly used textbooks to place on reserve, a strategy that certainly saved students money. The OER team began using this textbook list for an additional purpose—identifying the top 30 courses requiring the most expensive textbooks. This exercise prepared the team for focused faculty recruiting in the classes that would demonstrate the highest cost savings for students if the expensive textbooks were replaced with OER. The textbook list also allowed the OER Coordinator to glean additional insight about assigned texts. For example, she could now easily determine which classes were using a traditional textbook authored by an OU faculty member or which classes were using "custom" books assembled by publishers. The OER team chose to forgo outreach to these faculty members, for these would perhaps be more difficult conversations with higher barriers. Instead, the OER team used the textbook list to focus on faculty members who were assigning expensive texts but who would likely have fewer objections and obstacles.

Additionally, the OER team identified the most expensive course packs (collections of articles printed and bound at a local copy shop), and analyzed them to determine if they included materials that were available through library databases. While other academic institutions may have had success with this strategy, the second-year OER team did not. Many of the articles were not available through OU Libraries subscriptions. Additionally, the resources necessary to disentangle associated copyright issues prevented the team from exploring this idea more fully until 2017 when OU Libraries purchased a subscription to Leganto powered by Proquest SIPX, formerly Stanford Intellectual Property Exchange (Ex Libris Ltd., 2017).

In the initiative's second year, the OER Coordinator made the decision to partner with two existing organizations and, along with a handful of other academic institutions, became early partners with OpenStax (Rice University, 1999) and the Open Textbook Network (Center for Open Education, n.d.-b). Membership in these two organizations provided OU's OER initiatives with the additional support and resources necessary to grow the OER program. For example, OpenStax provided a textbook rack and physical copies of several of their then-current textbooks. The OER Coordinator used this rolling display rack at outreach events as a way to increase awareness among students and as a way to demonstrate the quality of open textbooks. Using the OpenStax books in this way also clearly demonstrated that open textbooks were available in a physical format should students desire to purchase them.

The Open Textbook Network's initial support included an on-site workshop, which at the time was a half-day learning opportunity for faculty members and librarians. Staff from the Open Textbook Network presented the background and context for open textbooks, and they provided the structure and incentives for OU faculty members to review open textbooks on the Open Textbook Library platform. This activity was extremely successful. By allowing faculty members to judge the quality of open textbooks themselves, they confronted one of their preconceptions—that open textbooks were not rigorous enough for their classes. Of the 18 faculty members who attended the workshop and wrote reviews, 14 have gone on to adopt, modify, or create an open textbook for use in their classes.

The second year also brought the beginning of two important partnerships that continue today. As previously mentioned, OU's Dean of the College of Arts and Sciences (CAS) had already adopted the OpenStax book *Introduction to Sociology* (Griffiths et al., 2015) for his sociology classes, which had approximately 300 students per semester. Using the book over a number of semesters gave him the opportunity to compare the open textbook to the traditional textbook he had previously used, to learn how students used the open resource, and to determine if the open textbook provided the same or better learning outcomes for his classes (The University of Oklahoma, 2014). His experience and his students' experiences were positive, so he was sold on using OER in classes where it was possible. As the Dean of CAS, he could help advocate for the use of OER among CAS chairs, directors, and individual faculty members. Even better, he became the first dean at OU to provide matching grants for CAS faculty members who received an OU Libraries Alternative Textbook Grant. Doubling the amount of money available to grantees helped motivate CAS faculty members to apply for these grants. In the third year of the grant program, OU's Price College of Business joined in the partnership by contributing matching funds as well. Since 2015, the Alternative Textbook Grant program has had funds contributed from CAS, OU's Business College, or both.

The second year of the OER initiatives also saw a rise in the outreach and support the OER Coordinator gave to using Wikipedia in the classroom. Wikipedia allows students to contribute in a way that helps further worldwide knowledge, instead of writing a term paper or capstone paper that gets graded and sits on a shelf (or worse). Wikipedia for Education's tag line is, "The end of throwaway assignments and the beginning of real-world impact for student editors" ("Wikipedia," 2017), and Wikipedia has enhanced their educational resources and tools, making it much easier for faculty members and students to participate in a Wikipedia-guided and structured course. Supporting faculty members on Wikipedia projects had the added benefit of engaging subject specialist librarians in OER projects, which until then had been relatively challenging.

The second year of the Alternative Textbook Grant saw an increase in faculty grantees over the first year, with 17 participating faculty saving students $274,000 in the first semester alone.

OER Initiative and the Evolution of Understanding the Technology

When OU Libraries began its pursuit of increasing the use of OER on campus, there was always a question about the form in which OER should be delivered. Initially, most of the OER used on campus were created by a faculty member at another university, which, for delivery at OU, meant distributing open textbooks as PDFs. Yet from the first year of the program, OU faculty pushed the bounds of available OER formats.

In the first year of the Alternative Textbook Grant, one of the grantees—a faculty member in OU's College of Engineering (now Gallogly College of Engineering)—used his grant to continue developing a platform he had created for his undergraduate engineering classes. This web-based platform, *OU Engineering Media Lab eCourses* (Gramoll, n.d.), contained resources on thermodynamics, statics, dynamics, solid mechanics, and calculus. Through this platform he also delivered exams to his students—students entered their responses into a web form using specially configured tablet computers. This grantee used funds from his Alternative Textbook Grant to purchase additional tablet computers necessary to deliver these resources. Also as a condition of his award, the grantee faculty member added a previously absent Creative Commons license to the eCourses site.

Also in the first year of the Alternative Textbook Grant, another engineering professor was awarded funds to implement an open textbook in her thermodynamics class. She chose to modify existing thermodynamics content available under a Creative Commons license. Instead of delivering the content as a PDF, she wanted to host the content on a website of her own so that she could make immediate changes to it as she presented to her students. She used her Alternative Textbook Grant to hire an exceptional student who had recently taken her thermodynamics class: this student helped her edit the content of the openly licensed thermodynamics books so that it would better fit her class. Because the original text had been published on the web, it was copied as HTML, and it was in this format that her student did the content editing. Many faculty members may have an aesthetic in mind for their website; however, they often do not possess the know-how to create such a site. This case was no different. Neither the faculty member, the thermodynamics student, the OER Coordinator, nor the OER Student Assistant had solid experience building the website envisioned by this engineering faculty member. The OER Student Assistant set out learning how to do so, and built an adequate website that served the faculty member's needs and her students' needs. Even though the resulting website was not aesthetically appealing or responsive to mobile devices, the exercise taught two important lessons about OER delivery: 1) how to properly display equations on the web, and 2) creating websites from scratch to host open content was not sustainable.

Realizing that mobile responsiveness would be key to future OER projects, the OER Student Assistant began to learn about responsive frameworks and eventually applied Bootstrap, a popular responsive framework, to the second iteration of the open thermodynamics book. Though this made the content easier to read on mobile devices, implementing it on websites built from scratch required far more individual attention than could be given to a single project with the available resources. This proved to be problematic if OU's OER efforts were to scale as hoped.

Also in the first year of the Alternative Textbook Grant, a faculty member in OU's Department of Chemistry and Biochemistry received an award to make his biochemical methods lab manual more accessible. Prior to receiving a grant, he had hired a graduate student to create the lab manual, which was created using iBooks Author. This yielded an attractive result, but such a solution made it only accessible to students who owned Apple devices. Other students who were required to use the lab manual had to borrow an Apple device from the Libraries or print the content using an Apple computer. Those involved in the project determined that transforming the lab manual into a website would make it far more accessible. Because a Bootstrap layout had already been built for the thermodynamics book, it was decided to "simply" insert the lab manual content into that same framework. Although the process was easier the second time around, it was still too labor-intensive to continue providing this service with the available resources; yet, it was too complex a process to ask the grantees to do it themselves given the technical skills required.

Not long after building these sites, the OER team discovered *The American Yawp*, a "free and online, collaboratively built, open American history textbook designed for college-level history courses" ("The American Yawp," n.d.). The OER team was inspired by its appearance and interface. Until this point, they had only known WordPress to be used for creating blogs, but *The American Yawp* definitely did not take the same form as a blog. This led to an investigation of WordPress as a publishing platform for OER. Applying what was learned from the previous two projects, the OER Student Assistant made use of a MathJax plugin (MathJax Consortium, 2009) for rendering equations from LaTeX markup and applied a mobile responsive theme to a WordPress instance. Given its promise, this approach was recommended as the preferred and supported solution for the next Alternative Textbook Grant cycle.

During the second grant cycle, a faculty member in OU's Department of Biology was the first grantee to use WordPress as a publishing platform. While he worked on authoring his biology textbook in WordPress, the OER team continued experimenting with WordPress by converting the previous year's thermodynamics content and the biochemical methods lab manual into their own WordPress site. These three individual WordPress sites were maintained by a single WordPress multi-site instance managed by the OER team.

Using WordPress as an OER publishing tool put the OER team one step closer to an ideal solution. It allowed them to publish equations to the web in an easy way—a feature that has become a litmus test for determining if a publishing solution is worth pursuing. Publishing with WordPress also allowed them to create their own OU OER-branded, mobile-friendly theme and apply it to all the works they produced. Despite these features, it became apparent after one year's worth of effort that WordPress might not be an ideal solution after all. Clearly it was better than building websites from scratch, but modifying WordPress themes was difficult, and some of the relied-upon plug-ins did not work well together. Any change they wanted to make to a theme required wrestling with "child-themes" and large stylesheets. More importantly, using WordPress this way made the OER team the gatekeeper of content hosted on the multi-site WordPress instance. Even though grantee authors were given login information and all reasonable privileges to their respective sites, authors would still contact the OER team regarding issues such as adding contributing authors. While this problem sounds like a very small one (and it was), the OER team did not want authors to depend on them to access or otherwise manage their content. They felt strongly that continuing to operate in such a way was antithetical to the principles of OER and the 5R Permissions (Wiley, n.d.).

During the search for a better way to author and publish OER, the OER Student Assistant learned about a widely used authoring and publishing tool, Pressbooks ("Pressbooks for EDU & Open Textbooks," 2017). Because he was already experimenting with WordPress, investigating Pressbooks was a natural next step—Pressbooks is a WordPress-based publishing platform featuring the option to export its contents as a number of different file types. Its ability to export content in this way was attractive and would theoretically make content available and accessible to as many people as possible, technically speaking. The OER team believed Pressbooks might answer the question they had been asking themselves, "What format will we officially support for OU-generated OER?" With Pressbooks they believed they could support them all! The OER team installed an instance of Pressbooks and began running tests and evaluating the platform, including the litmus test mentioned earlier, "How well does it handle equations?" Because they had encountered math-heavy projects early in the OER initiative, they were attuned to the challenges equations pose and considered it good fortune to have faced these challenges so early. Aspirationally, they sought to incorporate the beauty and functionality of the equations in *The Feynman Lectures on Physics* (Feynman, Gottlieb, & Pfeiffer, 1963) to the projects on which they worked. Simply put, Pressbooks does not support the inclusion of equations in all of its output formats. Because the seamless inclusion of equations is foundational to OER, this did not bode well for the continued use of Pressbooks.

Aside from its difficulty displaying equations, Pressbooks operates differently than other WordPress plug-ins. For one, Pressbooks completely "takes over" the familiar WordPress interface. This, in and of itself, was not a problem; instead the OER team was more concerned with the difficulty this posed for our desire to modify its *front-end* interface. In particular, OU's OER team did not appreciate the skeuomorphism apparent in Pressbooks' front-end interface. There is little reason to force a web browser to behave like a book and appear "book-like" to a reader. This, in combination with its clumsy way of displaying equations and its too-imperfect pagination in other export formats, closed the team's investigation into Pressbooks as a publishing plat-form—at least for the time being.

Having determined that Pressbooks was not the right platform and still not entirely pleased with scaling WordPress implementations, the OER team continued its pursuit of a better publishing workflow and next explored Markdown (Gruber, n.d.), a simple markup language often used in conjunction with a tool called pandoc ("Pandoc - About pandoc," n.d.). Intended to be both easily read and easily written, Markdown's syntax corresponds to the most common HTML tags making its syntax concise and easy to learn. When composing documents in Markdown, the con-tent is by nature separated from the styling. In contrast, programs such as Microsoft Word require that authors compose and style documents simultaneously. Separating content from style allows content to exist in-dependently of any output format, which is well suited for OER. Again, publishing OER in as many formats as possible is what OU's OER team strives for. By composing their works in Markdown, OU's faculty au-thors are, in essence, composing structured data that can then be made to take the form of a website, a PDF, an epub, and many other formats.

Even better, Markdown is easy to edit. Markdown files are flat, plain text files which means they can be opened and edited in any text editor, many of which are freely available. This is in contrast to open textbooks distributed as PDFs, which can be difficult to modify. Because Mark-down can be converted to a variety of formats, it can be thought of as the "universal source code of open textbooks"—as long as an open textbook's Markdown files are available, anyone has the ability to very easily edit the textbook. Using Markdown to author OER allows the OER team and their grantees to stay true to the fundamental to the tenets of OER, the 5R Permissions (Wiley, n.d.).

Though it is easy enough to read during the authoring process, Markdown is a markup syntax, so it is not intended to be read by end users. In order to put Markdown into a more fitting form for readers it needs to be converted. The open source conversion tool, pandoc, is one of the most useful and extensible tools for converting Markdown to more useful formats. Pandoc can convert and export Markdown to all the same file formats that Pressbooks can—HTML, epub, mobi, DOCX, and PDF. A drawback of pandoc is that it must be used via the command line. This nearly made the OER team forgo using Markdown, as they knew their grantees would, in most cases, be unwilling to jump over this additional hurdle. Encouraging them to learn Markdown seemed daunting enough; requiring them to use the command line seemed insurmountable.

Instead, in order to make writing Markdown as easy as possible the team set out to create a better way for grantee authors to access and use pandoc. In late 2016, the OER team built what is currently called the *Markdown Converter* (Taylor, n.d.), a web interface to pandoc packaged with additional tools and style sheets that make it ideal for quickly and easily producing a variety of outputs from one uploaded folder. Authors upload a zipped folder—containing the Markdown flat files along with accompanying image files to be used in the open textbook—to the web-based Markdown Converter, choose one or more output formats, and select and preview a style sheet. The Markdown Converter then quickly produces the properly formatted result in as many output formats as selected. The OER team is piloting the use of the Markdown Converter with instructors who received an Alternative Textbook Grant in the 2017 cycle for the 2017–18 academic year.

Operationalizing the OER Initiative: Into Adolescence

The 2015–16 academic year brought changes to OU's OER initiatives. In October, the OER Coordinator decided to pursue another job opportunity. Because the OER program had now developed some legs of its own, and because of changes to other OU librarians' job responsibilities, the OER Coordinator position description was revised to encompass both OER responsibilities and Scholarly Communication responsibilities—a change that more closely aligned the role with similar job responsibilities across the country. The new position, now called "Open Educational Resources and Scholarly Communication Coordinator," was split 70 percent OER and 30 percent Scholarly Communication and was posted in early November 2015, around the same time the original OER Coordinator left. A new OER Coordinator was hired in March but was not able to begin working until late May 2016. This is especially remarkable because during these seven months between November and June, the OER program was run nearly entirely by the 0.5 FTE OER Student Assistant with support from the Associate Dean for Scholarly Resources and Services. While this undoubtedly slowed the program's forward momentum a bit, the OER Student Assistant did an outstanding job of keeping the Alternative Textbook Grant program running. In April 2016 OU Libraries awarded grants to 17 faculty members for 19 different OER projects. In early June, the program "restarted" with the new OER Coordinator and, by this time, the OER Student Assistant had proved to be such a valuable asset to the organization that he was hired full-time as one of OU Libraries Emerging Technologies Librarian, devoting 30 percent of his time to OER projects.

The first order of business for the new OER Coordinator was to personally meet with all 17 grantees in order to better understand their projects, their personalities, and the support the Libraries could provide to them. These meetings primarily took place during summer 2016. At the same time, she began working on providing more structure to the Alternative Textbook Grant. The program had done very well up to this point, but much of the grant program's expansion had taken place organically and without clear guidelines. The new OER Coordinator wanted to bring more standardization to the program, while still allowing it to be flexible enough to accommodate as many projects as possible. This included establishing a tiered service model that outlined the services the OER team and subject specialist librarians would provide based on the type of OER project undertaken by each grantee.

Formalizing the Alternative Textbook Grant

The OER team had always kept track of their grantee's projects, and the new OER Coordinator determined these projects most often fell into four general categories:

- *Library resources*: Those who used library resources to replace their existing, traditional textbook, often assembling a reading list or using an ebook with a multi-user license from OU Libraries collection.
- *Adoption*: Those who replaced their existing, traditional textbook by

adopting an existing open resource and using it as is, or using significant portions of it and requiring minimal editorial changes.

- *Modification*: Sometimes called "adaption" or "adaptation," this category included grantees who made more significant editorial changes to an openly licensed resource. This sometimes included combining chapters from several different sources or adding a small amount of original content to an existing open resource so that it was tailored to their particular class.
- *Creation*: Those who created an original resource from scratch, which sometimes included heavily modifying content from an already existing open resource.

The OER team decided to formalize these categories, with the understanding that some grantees may fall into more than one category. They then determined the suite of services that they could provide for grantees at each of the four levels. This enabled support services to be more focused, instead of attempting to support every project possible. It also provided clear guidelines and expectations for the grantees. Of course, grantees have the freedom to pursue whatever alternative textbook solution they prefer; however, the OER team could no longer guarantee that they could support any and every solution.

The services the OER team provided at each level acknowledged the range of efforts in transitioning from a traditional textbook to an alternative solution and were as follows:

Table 1. Services Offered by the OU OER Team

Library Provides	Category 1: Library Resources	Category 2: Adoption	Category 3: Modification	Category 4: Creation
Funding ($250–$2500)	X	X	X	X
Orientation workshop	X	X	X	X

Library Provides	Category 1: Library Resources	Category 2: Adoption	Category 3: Modification	Category 4: Creation
Creative Commons license support		X	X	X
Print-on-demand services		X	X	X
Copyright clearance assistance			X	X
Stable repository platform		X	X	X
Assistance modifying existing OER			X	X
Workflow for authoring and publishing				X
Cover design				X
Assigning a DOI			X	X
Assigning an ISBN				X
Services of a project manager			X	X
Services of a subject specialist librarian	X	X	X	X

The formalized service model also explicitly stated the terms to which the grantees would agree. While the original OER Coordinator had always required grantees to sign a memorandum of understanding (MOU), those terms were not always clear to faculty members before they received a grant. Beginning in 2017, recipients of the Alternative Textbook Grant agreed to the following:

Table 2. Terms Agreed to by Grantees

	Type of Textbook Replacement			
Grantee Agrees To	**Category 1: Library Resources**	**Category 2: Adoption**	**Category 3: Modification**	**Category 4: Creation**
Provide access to student feedback	X	X	X	X
Share experiences willingly	X	X	X	X
Attend an orientation workshop	X	X	X	X
Follow the terms of license on adopted materials		X	X	X
Apply a Creative Commons license of your choosing to the work			X	X
Upload to SHAREOK		X	X	X
Use the Libraries' publishing/ authoring workflow				X

To make these categories and services clear to potential grantees, the OER team revised the existing grant application and moved it from a Qualtrics-based survey to a Google Form for ease and access. The new application linked to a LibGuide (Waller, Taylor, & Biamah, n.d.) that detailed the new service model, and it asked participants to place themselves in at least one category. The revised application form requested, among other details, information about the applicant, the course, the resource being replaced, and the process by which the applicant intended to assess the effectiveness of the OER used.

Creating a formalized service model and asking grantees to place themselves into a category, combined with the updated grant application, also provided the OER team with an additional way to evaluate grant proposals. For the first several years of the program when fewer faculty members applied for grants, it was relatively easy to contact each applicant and discuss their project well before the submission deadline. Additionally, many of the previous grantees had come from personal connections. As the number of grant applications grew, it became more challenging to reach out to each applicant individually. This was also a partial drawback of the new grant application as a Google Form—when the grant application was in Qualtrics, the OER team was able to see who had started an application and how far along they were in the process. With the move to Google Forms, this was no longer possible. Therefore, the additional, clarifying questions on the grant application allowed the OER team to better understand applicants' projects, even when we had not heard about them prior to evaluating the application.

With a more formalized program in place, the OER Coordinator began a concerted marketing and outreach campaign. The 2017 grant cycle kicked off with a panel presentation at the Academic Tech Expo where the OER Coordinator moderated a session that included three previous grantees and the Emerging Technologies Librarian working on OER. This was the start of many presentations over the next several months while the grant application was open—presentations in faculty and departmental meetings, Deans and Directors meetings, Executive Committees of Colleges, and for other university committees. Each presentation was similar, but each slide deck was individually tailored for the particular audience. For example, the OER Coordinator used images specific to the audience, such as a photos of a department's home building when presenting to faculty in a departmental meeting. Further, each slide deck always contained general information about textbook costs, but they also contained costs specific to the textbooks used in the particular academic department.

General "drop-in" information sessions were also scheduled between the time the grant application opened and when it was due. These sessions were held at least once per week until a month prior to the grant due date; in that last month, they were held between two and four times per week. Drop-in sessions were held in the main OU library, branch libraries, and in departmental conference or meeting rooms across campus. The OER Coordinator worked with the subject specialist librarians to schedule the departmental sessions. None of the sessions drew large attendance, but most sessions drew enough interest to warrant continuing them, and all sessions resulted in making a personal contact with someone interested in OER and/or the Alternative Textbook Grant.

The Alternative Textbook Grant was advertised on a rotating header on the home page of OU Libraries website, in addition to digital signage throughout OU Libraries, especially in high-traffic areas. The OER Coordinator crafted emails that subject specialist librarians could send to their faculty members, either in whole or in part, and she ensured that subject specialist librarians had the tools they needed to advocate and promote the Alternative Textbook Grant. Information about the grant, including dates for the drop-in sessions, was also posted in OU Libraries monthly faculty newsletter and the OU Provost's weekly newsletter. The drop-in events were advertised on the OU Libraries website as well, and the OU Libraries Communication Coordinator used social media, primarily Twitter and Facebook, to further spread the word across campus.

One of the most successful outreach strategies was a direct email campaign, which consisted of three different target groups: 1) faculty members who taught classes that mapped closely with existing OpenStax textbooks, 2) faculty members who taught classes with the most expensive textbooks, and 3) faculty members who taught classes where transitioning to an open textbook would make a high financial impact—classes containing a large number of students combined with a relatively expensive textbook. Each email was tailored to a specific faculty member, addressing them by name and explicitly referring to the textbook they used. These three campaigns, sent over a period of three weeks, generated grant applicants, and—more importantly—generated an increased dialog between faculty members and the OER Coordinator. Faculty members were willing to discuss their thoughts and opinions about OER, which often gave the OER Coordinator an opportunity to provide accurate information and to clear up misconceptions about open content. Creating, tailoring, sending, and responding to these direct emails was time-consuming, but well worth it for the increased dialog and applicants that resulted from this tactic.

Grant applications were reviewed by the OER team, which consisted of the OER Coordinator, the Emerging Technologies Librarian working on OER, and a new OER Student Assistant, hired in January 2017. The Associate Dean for Scholarly Resources and Services also served as a final reviewer. In an effort to formalize the evaluation process, the OER team developed a rubric, which was later abandoned. The OER team determined that since the grant applicants hadn't seen the rubric prior to applying, it would not be fair to apply it to judge their submissions. Therefore, applications were reviewed, and grants were awarded based on:

- The potential for student savings, which was the product of the projected class enrollment and the cost of existing materials. OU's OER team calls this "impact," and higher impact classes receive more funding.
- The frequency of course offering, with more frequently taught courses receiving higher funding.
- The overall impact of the project on open education. For example, an applicant creating an OER, especially one where there was an existing gap in openly available material, received higher funding than an applicant using library-licensed resources.
- Scheduling: the course had to be scheduled for summer 2017, fall 2017, or spring 2018. Courses that occurred later than spring 2018 would be placed on the next grant cycle.
- Adoption date: with some exceptions, course material had to be created and/or adopted over the summer and fall of 2017.
- Applicants' agreement to the terms in the support/agreement chart.

Grants, including any matching or contributed funds from other colleges, are paid in two installments; the first half of the grant is paid in the summer, and the second half of the grant is paid in the fall. Members of the OER team work closely with each grantee throughout the year to ensure they are making good progress on their grant projects.

OU Libraries places no restrictions on how grant funds are spent. Examples of how previous grantees have spent their funds include: supplemental income, funding a student to help create open resources, purchasing technology to be used in the classroom, and airfare and lodging for colleagues to travel and collaborate on creating alternative resources.

The 2017–18 grant cycle was the largest grant cohort, with 18 grantees representing 19 different projects across five colleges. With this grantee cohort, OU has cumulatively saved their students $1,631,935 throughout the four-year existence of the Alternative Textbook Grant program.

Growth Toward Adulthood: Next Steps

The OER team at OU has much to celebrate, especially the $1,000,000 milestone. But the celebration will be short-lived as the team looks toward future growth of the program. Some of these plans include:

- *Formation of an OER Action Committee*: the original OER Strategic Initiative Planning Committee was an internal library group, and it disbanded after delivering on its original goals. Recognizing the need for additional collaboration, the OER team, with support from the Dean of Libraries, has formed an " OER Action Committee" comprised of stakeholders across the university. These committee members include representatives from the Center for Teaching Excellence, the College of Liberal Studies (which houses OU's online degree programs), the Provost's Office, the Disability Resource Center, Information Technology, the Office of Academic Assessment, the OU Bookstore, and OU Press. Additionally, the committee will have a faculty member representing STEM disciplines (science, technology, engineering, and math), a faculty member from the University Libraries Committee, a faculty member from social sciences or humanities, and undergraduate and graduate representatives from Associated Student Government. The OER Action Committee is charged with promoting the awareness, reach, and uptake of OER at OU and will begin meeting in fall 2017.

- *Enhancing access to OER used at OU*: The Alternative Textbook Grant program has enabled the use and creation of a great number of OER, and these resources have clearly saved OU students money. The OER team has stayed busy keeping OER initiatives running and enhancing its existing programs, which has meant it has been challenging to make OU-authored works available to learners across the globe. Too often grantees use their OER in the learning management system, but it is not shared more broadly. One of the OER team's highest priorities is to provide better access to these works through a dedicated collection in OU's institutional repository, SHAREOK.

- *Better promotion of our textbook on reserve program and ebook collections as alternative textbook solutions*: Purchasing hardcopy textbooks of the most popular classes and placing them on reserve is neither a sustainable nor sought-after solution, yet it still helps save money for students. Unfortunately, not enough students are aware that they can check out textbooks on reserve at the Libraries. Additionally, like many, OU librarians are purchasing more ebooks. When licensing terms allow, the OER team would like to better market these ebooks to faculty members as low/no-cost solutions for OU students. While neither of these solutions fit the strict definition of OER, they do help lower the amount students spend on their education.

- *Refining Markdown authoring/publishing workflow*: As the 2017–18 academic year is the pilot year for using Markdown for authoring and publishing, the OER team will be making adjustments and enhancements to the Markdown Converter and the ways in which they assist faculty members in its use.

In addition to these actionable items, the OER team has also been thinking more philosophically about how it supports and advocates for OER in the future. For example, the Alternative Textbook Grant gives preference to authors who create original OER. These are the grantees who, generally, receive the most money and support. But perhaps it would be wiser to prioritize the adoption of already existing OER, which requires less time and energy on everyone's part. Additionally, the team has begun to rethink the term "ROI" and how administration views a "return" on the amount of money used for Alternative Textbook Grants. A "return" on OER is best analyzed over the long term, instead of on a semester or even yearly basis, for they cumulatively build over semesters of use, which for OU's OER team is an apt metaphor for the value of OER in general.

References

Billings, M. S., Hutton, S. C., Schafer, J., Schweik, C. M., & Sheridan, M. (2012). *Open educational resources as learning materials: Prospects and strategies for university libraries* (Research Library Issues: A Quarterly Report from ARL, CNI, and SPARC, no. 280). Retrieved from http://publications.arl.org/rli280/

Center for Open Education. (n.d.-a). Open textbook library. Retrieved from https://open.umn.edu/opentextbooks/

Center for Open Education. (n.d.-b). Open textbook network. Retrieved from https://research.cehd.umn.edu/otn/

ComPADRE Digital Library. (2003, 2017). Compadre.org homepage [Collection]. Retrieved from http://www.compadre.org/

Diener Education Fund. (2017). NOBA Project. Retrieved from http://nobaproject.com/

Ex Libris Ltd. (2017). Leganto—Course resource list solution. Retrieved from http://www.exlibrisgroup.com/category/Leganto

Feynman, R., Gottlieb, M., & Pfeiffer, R. (1963 [2006, 2013]). The Feynman lectures on physics. Retrieved from http://www.feynmanlectures.caltech.edu/

Gramoll, K. (n.d.). OU engineering media lab eCourses. Retrieved from http://ecourses.ou.edu/

Griffiths, H., Keirns, N., Strayer, E., Cody-Rydzewski, S., Scaramuzzo, G., Sadler, T., … Jones, F. (2015). *Introduction to sociology 2e*. Houston, TX: OpenStax. Retrieved from https://openstax.org/details/books/introduction-sociology-2e

Gruber, J. (n.d.). Daring fireball: Markdown syntax documentation. Retrieved from https://daringfireball.net/projects/markdown/syntax

Institute for the Study of Knowledge Management in Education. (2007, 2017). OER commons. Retrieved from https://www.oercommons.org/

Kansas State University Center for the Advancement of Digital Scholarship. (n.d.). The open/alternative textbook initiative. Retrieved from http://www.lib.k-state.edu/open-textbook

MathJax Consortium. (2009, 2017). MathJax. Retrieved from http://www.mathjax.org/

MERLOT, California State University. (n.d.). MERLOT. Retrieved from https://www.merlot.org/merlot/index.htm?action=find

MERLOT, California State University. (1997, 2016). Partner Consortium. Retrieved from http://info.merlot.org/merlothelp/partner_benefits.htm

NextThought. (2017). Janux. Retrieved from https://janux.ou.edu/index.html

Online Learning Consortium. (2017). OLC innovate 2017. Retrieved from https://onlinelearningconsortium.org/innovate/2017-conference-highlights/

Open Education Consortium. (n.d.). Open education week. Retrieved from
    https://www.openeducationweek.org

OpenStax. (n.d.). OpenStax CNS library. Retrieved from https://cnx.org/browse

Pandoc—About pandoc. (n.d.). Retrieved from http://pandoc.org/

Pressbooks for EDU & Open Textbooks. (2017). Retrieved from https://pressbooks.com/
    for-academia/

Rice University. (1999, 2017). OpenStax. Retrieved from https://openstax.org

Scholarly Publishing and Academic Resources Coalition. (2007, 2017). Open education.
    Retrieved from https://sparcopen.org/open-education/

Taylor, C. (n.d.). Markdown converter. Retrieved from http://guides.ou.edu/OER/
    markdown_converter

Taylor, C., Waller, J., Zemke, S., & Biamah, B. (2017, May 31). Open educational
    resources: Home. Retrieved from http://guides.ou.edu/c.php?g=113934&p=739332

Taylor, C., & Zemke, S. (n.d.). Blog. Retrieved from http://ouopentextbooks.org/
    archive/

The American Yawp. (n.d.). Retrieved from http://www.americanyawp.com/

The University of Oklahoma. (2014). *Using free, online textbooks in the classroom* [Video].
    Retrieved from https://www.youtube.com/watch?v=p9AnhwZu4sg

University of Oklahoma. (2016). University College. Retrieved from http://www.ou.edu/
    univcoll.html

Waller, J., Taylor, C., & Biamah, B. (n.d.). Alternative textbooks: Grant instructions.
    Retrieved from http://guides.ou.edu/AlternativeTextbooks/GrantInstructions

Wikipedia:Education program. (2017, June 1). In *Wikipedia.* Retrieved from
    https://en.wikipedia.org/w/
    index.php?title=Wikipedia:Education_program&oldid=783250577

Wiley, D. (n.d.). Defining the "open" in open content and open educational resources.
    Retrieved from http://opencontent.org/definition/

Appendix A: OER Initiative Scope

This project will focus on piloting sustainable and scalable OER/ALS adoptions on campus.
    The project will focus on four implementation areas:

- OU Libraries will support the development and use of OER and ALS to replace
    textbooks in the classroom, to save students money, and to give faculty more control
    over their educational content.
- OU Libraries will support the development and use of OER and ALS to replace *course
    packs* in the classroom, to save students money, and to give faculty more control over
    their educational content.
- OU Libraries will work with the University College (University of Oklahoma, 2016)
    to identify appropriate OER as study aids for students.
- OU Libraries will provide an appropriate platform to support the discovery, creation,
    reuse, revision, remixing, and redistribution of OER and other affordable learning
    materials for faculty and students.

Appendix B: OER Repository Evaluation Exercise

Site being evaluated:

Subject area evaluated:

General Questions:

1. Who are the main content authors and what are their affiliations/qualifications?

2. Who are the reviewers/curators for this site?

3. Is the site content actively updated?

4. What audience(s) is the content designed for (select all that apply)
   1. K-12

   2. Lower division undergrad

   3. Upper division undergrad

   4. Graduate

5. How easy is it to navigate and find resources on this site?
   1. Very easy

   2. Somewhat easy

   3. Easy

   4. Difficult

   5. Very difficult

6. Are the materials represented:
   1. Primary sources (images, graphs, drawings, recordings with little educational content)

   2. Secondary sources (instructor created lectures, presentations, videos, audio)

   3. Both

7. What types of media are represented on the site (select all that apply)
   1. Text

   2. Video

   3. Audio

   4. Simulations/interactive

   5. Textbooks

   6. Links to other web pages

8. Content can be exported from this site as (select all that apply)
   1. HTML files

   2. PDF files

   3. EPUB2 files

   4. EPUB3 files

   5. Can only link to content; cannot export

9. Use restrictions for content on this site:
   1. CC licensing

   2. Fair use

   3. Copyrighted to the owner (but content can be linked to for educational use)

   4. Varies by individual item

10. This collection is strongest in (select all that apply)
    1. Complete courses

    2. Textbooks

    3. Individual lessons

    4. Audio/visual

    5. Simulations

11. Site recommended for subject area?
    1. Yes (why?)

    2. No (why not?)

12. General comments or suggestions for using this site and content area by faculty.

Appendix C: Alternative Textbook Grant Application Questions

- **Basic Information**
  - Name
  - Email address
  - Position/rank
  - College
  - Department
- **Course information**
  - Class prefix and number (e.g. MATH1113)
  - Title of the class

- Catalog description
- First semester your alternative textbook solution will be implemented
- Number of sections you will be teaching
- Number of sections of the course taught by others
  - Will any of them be using this textbook alternative?
  - If so, please include these instructors' names
- Is the course taught every semester?
- Course enrollment – maximum and expected
- Is this a new course?
- **Resource(s) being replaced**
  - Title(s)
  - Author(s)
  - ISBN(s)
  - Retail cost (from Amazon)
  - Link to item on Amazon.com
- **Granting category in which you fall (see for additional information):**
  - Creation
  - Modification
  - Adoption
  - Library Resources

- **Alternative(s) to be implemented**: Discuss the materials you are planning to use to replace a traditional textbook (if you would like a consultation on available materials, please contact Jen Waller, Cody Taylor, or your liaison librarian).
- **Project Details**: How will students access the alternative content? If delivering content via the web, what hosting platform do you plan to use?
- **Concerns:** What are your greatest concerns about adopting an alternative textbook solution (both for yourself and or your students)?
- **Assessment:** How will the effectiveness of the new course materials be assessed? Check all that apply
  - Using a supplemental end of semester student evaluation
  - Using a survey I create
  - By comparing assignment grades and/or test scores
  - By comparing grade distributions to previous semesters
  - Using another method, described below
- How did you hear about this initiative?

A Grassroots Approach to OER Adoption: The University of Saskatchewan Experience

Heather M. Ross, Shannon Lucky, & David Francis

Introduction

During the 2017–18 academic year, approximately 3,500 students at the University of Saskatchewan (U of S) were assigned open textbooks for their classes, replacing commercial textbooks. This represented a more than 10-fold increase since our first major adoption in early 2015 and was a landmark in the increasing use of open educational resources (OER) at the university. This rapid growth is the result of individual efforts by our faculty, educational developers, and librarians, working with the students' union to champion the use of OER across campus. This rapid growth suggests a desire for OER in our classrooms. Supply has stoked demand from students and faculty for alternatives to commercial textbooks and we must be ready to meet this demand and the expectations of our community.

The U of S has a long history of grassroots innovations in research, teaching, and learning exemplified by OER adoption at the institution. We define our grassroots approach as one that emphasizes people-driven initiatives for change that are not fully reliant on the administrative structure of the university. The U of S is a medical/doctoral university in Western Canada and a member of the U15 group of research-intensive Canadian universities (akin to a Carnegie R classification). The University Library is a member of the Association of Research Libraries (ARL) and the Canadian Association of Research Libraries (CARL), with 145 full-time equivalent (FTE) librarian faculty and staff serving over 27,000 faculty, staff, and students, with a 2017 FTE student count of approximately 17,000 undergraduate students and approximately 3,000 graduate students (University of Saskatchewan Website, n.d.).

This chapter examines how we have encouraged the adoption of OER at the U of S from a grassroots effort as opposed to a top-down administrative directive. We illustrate the benefits and challenges of this approach along with the obstacles remaining to fully realize the potential of OER for teaching and learning institution-wide. We propose ways these obstacles could be surmounted through partnerships and collaborations between teams on campus. The library, teaching and learning center, distance education unit, administration, student government, faculty champions of OER, and other support units all have important roles to play in the highly integrated network of systems, services, and resources that will make the full-scale adoption of OER successful. The library is uniquely positioned to provide leadership for multiple aspects of OER adoption because of its ties to research, teaching, and learning at all levels on our campus.

The Role of the Academic Library

Academic libraries have the potential to lead in three areas that can encourage the adoption of OER on our campuses: *leadership in OA publishing*, *teaching and learning*, and *OER systems*. Although *leadership* is an ambiguous and oft-used piece of jargon in modern institutions for a range of initiatives, it is an apt term to describe the natural alignment between academic library advocacy and the advancement of institutional goals and the fact that libraries cannot do this work alone. Ferguson (2016) describes this collaborative model well in relation to the production and use of OER:

> As the faculty, and in some cases students, work to produce the content for their courses, libraries and librarians can play a key role in the production, adoption, and promotion of OERs, assisting with funding, research, copyright, and publishing options (p. 256).

Making a connection to the historical role of academic libraries, Clobridge (2015) draws a direct line from the library as information source to proponent for open access and OER. They argue that it is not beyond of the purview of academic libraries to become a leader for OER and that through "the auspices of an open access program or library publishing efforts, encouraging innovation in scholarly communication, or encouraging student success, libraries have ample opportunities to get involved in promoting and supporting open textbooks" (p. 68). There are many ways that academic libraries can support the culture change required to shift attitudes and actions on campus regarding the adoption of OER. The following sections explore three major areas where libraries can show leadership for OER initiatives that leverage their expertise and reputation and that we have considered in the context of OER use at the U of S.

Leadership in OA Publishing

Academic publishing at universities and colleges is, by virtue of the types of required inputs and outputs, a necessarily complex activity and the responsibility for it often resides across academic and support units, as it does at the U of S. Okamoto (2013) notes that libraries are in a strong strategic position to support, promote, or even create and distribute OER; however, with expanding mandates, libraries and library systems must be selective about the related services they wish to offer. This concept of "library publishing" (Howard, 2013) can partly address the rising costs of acquiring and maintaining collections by supporting the production of open and locally relevant publications for teaching and scholarship. Gaining skills in all aspects of OER publishing help librarians and library staff add value to an institution's open strategies by improving the usability, discoverability, and learner accessibility of OER materials (Ovadia, 2011). West (2017) notes that librarians are in a unique position to "help faculty find appropriate repositories or platforms to share their OER (textbooks and other resources)" (p. 43) and, we argue, to support faculty to develop their own OER.

Bell (2015) describes an example at Oregon State University where libraries collaborated with the university press on open textbook publishing. Under that model, faculty members supplied original or compiled works while the press offered editorial support, a peer review process, and an editorial board. Goodsett, Loomis, and Miles (2016) described a case where a university English professor had created curricular materials that were later converted to an electronic OER format by a team of library developers. The authors noted that success factors included an acknowledgment of the usefulness of project management, a need to respect the availability of staff and faculty time and using the diverse technical and information expertise of the library team (Goodsett et al., 2016). At the U of S, we currently do not have a library press, but we are exploring options for digital publishing services to meet growing demands on campus by mobilizing teams that can meet the complex challenges of digital publishing and long-term preservation and access.

One of the significant barriers to OER publishing is understanding copyright restrictions on the use and reuse of materials. Ferguson (2016) notes that bringing library expertise to OER development teams regarding copyright issues is an important factor of success. Given the changing landscape regarding copyright and acceptable use of educational materials—and the number of possible institutional areas where this responsibility may reside—leadership from the academic library is crucial when advancing OER throughout the institution.

Leadership in Teaching and Learning

An area where individual librarians can demonstrate the value of OER is in developing open curricular materials, teaching strategies, instructional designs, and assessments. Emphasizing the natural advantages of place and personnel of the academic library, Mitchell and Chu (2014) note that "librarians have a unique role as translators and mediators between content generators (faculty) and content users (students and other researchers). Libraries are positioned to provide guidance to faculty exploring alternative education materials" (p. 16). At the U of S we have seen examples of shared physical and virtual teaching spaces and relationships between librarians and instructors that have led to the adoption of OER for teaching on our campus. How these individual relationships have been a critical force in growing OER at the U of S is described in detail later in this chapter.

Academic libraries often act directly as teaching supports for faculty members. Hess, Nann, and Riddle (2016) report on an academic library that developed an online guide to OER, providing a basic introduction to the topic including best practices and design considerations. This approach could be easily adopted at the U of S and most other academic libraries that use online library guide systems (such as Springshare's LibGuides) and, in turn, could be produced as open teaching and learning materials. Other software systems (such as SelectedWorks) can be used within a university system to develop a shared understanding of faculty research and teaching interests, leading to an ongoing, portfolio-driven discussion between faculty and librarians in the area of support for teaching (Goodsett et al., 2016).

Libraries should consider themselves one academic support unit in a network of academic support units when considering taking a leadership role for OER support. Walz (2015) describes ways to use existing relationships with faculties and departments to better understand OER audiences. This helps librarians and library staff understand what educational resources are used, authored, or assigned and identifies faculty decision-making processes, values, and requirements in order to engage effectively (Walz, 2015, p. 27). It is not difficult to imagine the number of dependencies that exist between information technology staff, teaching and learning centers, faculty groups, continuing and distance units, and the university library. Ongoing, communicative partnerships with groups and units is key to ensuring support for OER teaching and learning.

The advancement of technology-based approaches to teaching and learning will continue to be an area where academic libraries can demonstrate leadership. Publishers continue to change their business models to adapt to the sharing economy, making significant adjustments to how virtual course packs, journals, and teaching texts are licensed and used. Very few professionals in a university or college setting outside of the library will have training and capacity to remain current and engaged with these emergent issues. This is a key area where academic libraries can bring their expertise and connections to bear on the challenge of communicating problems with scholarly publishing models and the benefits of OER for students and instructors.

Leadership for OER Systems

While there are large OER repositories that house resources from multiple institutions such as the Open Textbook Network (Salem Jr., 2017; West, 2016), OER Commons (Hess et al., 2016; Salem Jr., 2017), and California Open Online Network for Education (Ferguson, 2017), many post-secondary institutions have invested in locally hosted digital repositories that can be used to support OER. Maintaining a locally hosted repository offers many benefits, including being able to control new collections and metadata schemas (Mitchell & Chu, 2014), but it also brings significant challenges. Developing and maintaining digital infrastructure to support OER creation and use at a college or university demands significant investments of time and resources in technical systems and cultivating local expertise. These costs can be significantly reduced by partnering with libraries that already maintain infrastructure required for digital repositories (Ferguson, 2017; Walz, 2015).

Goodsett et al. (2016) demonstrate that established library systems and related services can be effectively leveraged to support OER. Search and discovery systems, data storage, metadata and indexing, digital preservation, and copyright expertise, long the domain of academic libraries, make hosting OER a logical extension for traditional library services (Walz, 2015). For example, stand-alone repositories tend to struggle with sustainability and suffer from short lifespans (Hess et al., 2016). Friesen (2009) found the average lifespan of non-government-funded repository projects to be less than three years, a lifespan closely correlated with project funding cycles. Academic libraries can provide a stable place to host and access OER, mitigating serious preservation challenges that come with short-term funding and leadership from temporary project teams. Expertise and experience in preservation and access of digital information is a major strength libraries bring to OER partnerships. Libraries often already have the digital systems infrastructure and expertise in place to support a successful OER project, providing solid, ready-made platforms on which to build projects upon (Ferguson, 2017).

A common example of existing digital library infrastructure that can be utilized to support OER are institutional repositories (IRs) which can serve as the primary access point for OER produced by faculty, staff, and students (Ferguson, 2017). Salem Jr. (2017) noted that libraries are often a leading partner in the development of OER repositories. While the traditional focus of IRs has been to host electronic theses and dissertations, journal articles, and conference proceedings (Goodsett et al., 2016), their functionality and the expertise gained by developing IR technology and services can be extended to include OER. For example, Goodsett et al. (2016) described a diverse set of collections in the Cleveland State University IR that included "more than 11,000 papers in over 680 disciplines, 200 books, thirteen conferences, six e-journals, image galleries, videos, music collections, and more" (p. 336). The ability for library-hosted systems to expand to accommodate new types of digital scholarly and teaching materials, including OER, make libraries a strong center of expertise to strategically grow OER across campus.

At the U of S, we have invested in two major library-owned systems to manage digital scholarly, research and teaching materials. We have an IR for digital theses and dissertations, pre-prints, open access articles, presentations, and posters. We also have a digital asset management system that allows us to build digital collections for researchers and instructors that students can contribute to and use as OER in the classroom. In addition to digital publishing platforms and traditional library systems for discovery and access of open textbooks, these systems allow our library to meet the growing demand for technical infrastructure that makes the creation and long-term maintenance of OER possible and affordable for instructors.

In addition to hosting systems, libraries can extend systems leadership in service areas they have expertise in. Ferguson (2017) mentions developing policies and systems support for multiple versions of resources as an area where libraries can contribute to OER projects. The modular nature of OER is highly desirable and can lead to multiple versions that must be carefully managed. Libraries are centers of expertise in creating descriptive metadata and using it to describe and provide access to complex materials. They also bring deep experience in dealing with technical challenges, such as providing concurrent user access to electronic resources, software and hardware conformity for digital platforms, and accessibility of locally developed and adopted OER (Billings, Hutton, Schafer, Schweik, & Sheridan, 2012). These are challenges libraries are accustomed to dealing with when providing licensed digital content and they have developed practices to provide technical support for students. Library frontline staff often first encounter students struggling with technology issues and, thus, they are in a good position to provide support to students when adopting OER (Billings et al., 2012). Hagel, Horn, Owen, and Currie (2012) wisely cautioned that OER project leaders must be cognizant of the various levels of digital literacy students have and work to meet the needs of those who may be disadvantaged by increasing reliance on online resources. The library is a natural place to both encounter and provide help for students struggling with OER technology.

How We Got Here

From the fall of 2014 to the spring of 2018 the number of students using OER in place of commercial textbooks at the U of S skyrocketed from fewer than 50 to more than 3,500, with a total estimated savings of more than CAD$625,000 during that four-year period. This increase was the result of workshops, partnerships, tenacity, and some serendipity. The success of OER adoption and the growth of support for open access (OA) initiatives generally have been the result of grassroots efforts from many directions on campus. One of the players in this area has been the University Library.

The adoption of OA practices and initiatives in the library has been driven by individual champions of OA. In 2010, a team of librarians developed the *University of Saskatchewan Librarians and Archivists Open Access Commitment* (University of Saskatchewan Librarians and Archivists, 2010) which affirms that librarians and archivists at the U of S would deposit the output of their scholarly activities in our local institutional repository (eCommons@USask, n.d.) and seek to publish in open access venues. To realize the commitment made by library faculty, the U of S Library expanded its use of the IR from hosting electronic theses and dissertations to include library faculty scholarly output. In 2016, in response to demand from the campus community and new OA requirements for federal Canadian research grant recipients, the library began a pilot project to expand the availability of the IR to other colleges and departments across campus. This leadership in assisting researchers at the U of S to deposit their work in the IR provides an opportunity to demonstrate the benefits of publishing resources that are freely accessible and provides the systems and support to do so.

The library has also been a proponent, although not the sole player, in OA publishing on campus, a theme that emerged in our review of the literature. One example is the *University of Saskatchewan Undergraduate Research Journal* (*USURJ*), an open access, faculty peer-reviewed journal featuring original work by undergraduate students at the U of S. *USURJ* is published through Student Learning Services in the University Library and is listed in the Directory of Open Access Journals (DOAJ) (University of Saskatchewan Undergraduate Student Research Journal, n.d.). The library has reinforced their commitment to support OA publications by including the DOAJ in the library catalog to increase the visibility of these publications to library users.

While the growth of OA support and services in the library has been the result of grassroots efforts, successes have led to increased institutional support. The U of S Library is a member of SPARC (the Scholarly Publishing and Academic Resources Coalition, https://sparcopen.org/) and has included initiatives to build OA expertise and service capacity in the library in the last two strategic plans. The library is also preparing to release a position statement on OA unequivocally stating the library's support. The OA expertise, resources, and campus-wide relationships that exist in the library make it a natural partner in the expansion of OER use on campus.

The U of S first engaged an OER approach in 2014, with what was termed a TOOC (Truly Open Online Course). The Gwenna Moss Center for Teaching and Learning (GMCTL), offered a face-to-face non-credit course for instructors and graduate students, *Introduction to Learning Technologies*, while simultaneously registering worldwide participants via a Google Form where they could provide the link for the blog they would use for assignments. They also could follow the course on Twitter, via a Facebook group, or via a Google Community. More than 300 participants signed up for this open course. All course resources carried Creative Commons licenses and were posted to a WordPress site. While this course progressed, the provincial governments of Saskatchewan, Alberta, and British Columbia signed a three-year memorandum of understanding agreeing to:

1. Through an efficient and effective process, facilitate cooperation between the Participants in the sharing and development of Open Education Resources;
2. Identify, share and encourage the use of best practices in Open Education Resources among the Participants; and
3. Through the best use of technology for students, faculty and administrators, foster greater collaboration and understanding of key issues and trends in Open Education Resources between and among post-secondary institutions in the Participant's jurisdictions. (Saskatchewan Government OER MOU, 2014)

The following year, the TOOC was offered again, but through the Canvas Network (all materials continued to carry Creative Commons licenses and the WordPress site was updated to align with the Canvas course) with more than 1,200 participants. Both offerings were supported by the Vice Provost Teaching and Learning (VPTL), whose portfolio includes the teaching and learning center. In early 2015, the university also launched a TOOC on *Circumpolar Innovation* through the International Centre for Northern Governance and Development in consultation with the GMCTL. This course received development funding from the U of S Curriculum Innovation Fund. However, as can happen with open courses, participation and interest in the open courses dropped off and the university decided that this was not the model to move open forward at the institution.

In 2014, the GMCTL began considering ways to encourage instructors to adopt open textbooks. The use of open textbooks to lower student costs had been part of the campaign platform of the president of the U of S Undergraduate Student Association, but no U of S courses were using these resources yet. During this time, much was being done with open textbooks in British Columbia, led by BCcampus, a province-wide agency that supports institutions of higher education in the areas of OER and open pedagogy, curriculum sharing and development, and learning technologies.[1] BCcampus had facilitated the creation of several new open textbooks and had pulled together a catalog of open textbooks available online. This work created an opportunity for the U of S to make use of these existing resources to the benefit of its students.

In the fall of 2014, a BCcampus poster describing open textbooks as an alternative to expensive commercial textbooks was placed outside of the GMCTL. This prompted a professor in the College of Agriculture and Bioresource to adopt the OpenStax *Principles of Economics* for one of his courses with roughly 270 students enrolled. Around this same time, DeDe Dawson (science librarian and OA proponent) was approached by a professor from the chemistry department who said that he could no longer, in good conscience, ask his students to pay more than CAD$250 for the required textbook, and sought an alternative. She recommended OER, and the next term he replaced the commercial book with the open *Analytical Chemistry 2.0*, which he found through the BCcampus website. This single adoption benefited more than 120 students that year and created an OER champion in that professor. The librarian, long a champion of OA in the

---

[1] For more information, see the BCcampus website: https://bccampus.ca/open-education

library, also became an advocate for instructors to consider OER and open pedagogy, a concept that will be discussed later in this chapter. Other librarians have since followed suit in an effort to improve both access to materials and pedagogy, thus demonstrating another theme from our review of the literature, leadership in teaching and learning.

An associate dean from the Edwards School of Business (ESB) heard about open textbooks and reached out to the GMCTL early in 2015 wondering if there might be an open resource to meet the needs of students in a course that served as an introduction to both university studies and ESB. Soon after, the associate dean and her co-instructor began adapting *College Success*, which was available through the Open Textbook Library through the University of Minnesota. They adapted the book as they taught the course to approximately 375 students, releasing their modified sections to students as they were completed. In the fall of 2016, their finished edition, *University Success*, was released publicly and soon added to the BCcampus open textbook directory. This project was supported through funding from the U of S and instructional design support from the distance education unit (DEU).

Late in 2015, the Saskatchewan government announced CAD$250,000 in funding to be shared equally between the three major post-secondary institutions in the province—the University of Saskatchewan, University of Regina, and Saskatchewan Polytechnic—to create open textbooks and other OER. At the U of S the VPTL was tasked with administering the funding. A small OER advisory group was formed consisting of the VPTL, the GMCTL director, and the educational developer who had thus far led the OER initiative. In addition, four faculty members, including the professors who had adopted open textbooks in agriculture and chemistry, and the associate dean from the ESB who had completed the adaptation, provided the instructor perspective as members of this group. The teaching and learning center was given the role of assisting faculty in completing applications and providing ongoing support while the professors made up the review committee.

The GMCTL, after conversations with educational developers working with OER at BCcampus, brought on board the DEU at the U of S to do ongoing work with faculty on the development of the open textbooks. The DEU provided instructional design expertise and were the initial hosts of the university's Pressbooks installation. The new textbooks were for specific topics that did not yet have existing open textbooks, such as engineering, economics, and human geography.

By the 2015–16 academic year approximately 900 U of S students were enrolled in courses using open textbooks. The provincial government announced a second year of funding and the GMCTL began offering regular workshops on the creation, adaptation, and integration of OER to raise awareness and encourage instructors to apply for funding. By the summer of 2016 five open textbooks were in production at the U of S, including books in geography, biology, and engineering economics. In addition, an instructor was provided with funding to create a test bank to facilitate her adoption of *Introduction to Sociology—2nd Canadian Edition* from BCcampus.

In the spirit of the memorandum of understanding signed by Saskatchewan, Alberta, and British Columbia, the Canada OER Group was formed. This community of educational developers and librarians working with OER in higher education in Canada began meeting virtually to share updates about current projects, opportunities for collaboration, and ideas about promotion and integration of OER. While it initially consisted of members in the three most western provinces, the group soon grew to include representatives from institutions across the country.

During the 2016–17 academic year the number of students enrolled in courses using open textbooks at the U of S grew to more than 2,700, with OER replacing commercial textbooks in 23 courses. The conversations at the institution around OER began to shift toward the idea of open pedagogy, using the flexibility of OER to engage students instead of simply replacing commercial textbooks with free textbooks. Instructional designers from the DEU and educational developers from the GMCTL shared ideas about this potential with instructors, including through the annual Course Design Institute, and we discovered several instructors were already doing it without knowing what it was called. For example, an instructor in astronomy had students post undergraduate research findings on an open WordPress site for future course participants and students at other institutions. Concurrently, a professor in the College of Law gave students the option of either writing a traditional paper or editing Wikipedia articles on topics covered in the course.

With the sizeable increase in the adoption of open textbooks for the 2016–17 academic year, the GMCTL began surveying students in courses using open textbooks to gather their opinions about the specific books being used. Those results are pending. In addition, they looked at one particular course where the instructor had previously taught sections without the open textbook. For that course, they compared student marks, which stayed the same compared to previous sections where the commercial textbook was used, while the percentage of students who completed the course increased.

In early 2017, the university appointed a new University Library Dean who arrived with experience working with and enthusiasm for OER. She joined the U of S OER advisory group just as that group was finalizing an institutional OER and open pedagogy strategy. Adaptations of two more textbooks on geology and physics went into production around the same time, and the GMCTL, library, and Information and Communications Technology (ICT) unit began planning for an institutional OER repository (the third theme from the literature review, leadership for OER systems). Finally, the educational developer leading the OER initiative also began having targeted conversations with subject area librarians in an effort to enable them to serve as advocates and supports for OER across the institution. We offer the following table as a means of summarizing the partnerships around the institution relating to OER:

Table 1. OER Functions with Responsible Units/Groups

Function	Unit/Group	
Leadership	Direction Decision making	Library GMCTL VPTL 4 Faculty instructors from 4 colleges
Advocacy	Connecting people/ groups Promoting OER Professional development	Library GMCTL VPTL DEU U of S Students' Union Bookstore

Function	Unit/Group	
Support	Discovery & access Licensing/Creative Commons Media/production Instructional design	Library GMCTL DEU Media Production
Platform	Institutional Repository Pressbooks Print-on-Demand	Library (IR) ICT (Pressbooks, IR) DEU (Pressbooks) Bookstore (Print-on-Demand)

What's Next at the University of Saskatchewan

Based upon our collective experience to date and the direction suggested by the university's planning documents, we see the future of library leadership for OER manifesting in the following ways:

- *Leadership in OA publishing*: Investigating how the library, instructional designers, and other educational developers could turn existing or future curated digital projects into OER (see example from Mitchell & Chu, 2014).
- *Leadership in teaching and learning*: Leveraging relationships between subject librarians and instructors to encourage the adoption of OER, Creative Commons licensing, and open pedagogy.
- *Leadership for OER systems:* Providing systems support (e.g., Islandora, DSpace, eCommons) and developing a service model to support locally developed OER and OA publishing and to ensure robust preservation and access for these materials.

In addition to the areas for leadership identified in our literature review, the OER advisory group and all proponents in the library and across campus can continue to grow the adoption of OER in the following ways:

- Continuing broad membership representation and activity on the OER advisory group.
- Providing targeted professional development training for librarians and other OER support groups on campus.

- Educating and helping students to advocate to their professors in support of OER.
- Widening overall institutional adoption by moving from strictly a grassroots approach to an approach where the integration of OER and open pedagogy increasingly gets on the agendas and planning cycles of academic and administrative university units.

Our Next Investment: Adaptations, Ancillary Resources and Open Pedagogy

There is a significant opportunity for the U of S to build upon the existing success of our OER initiative by focusing future efforts on not only adoption of existing OER, but also on adapting existing OER, including open textbooks, and creating needed ancillary resources (e.g. test bank questions, which are frequently provided by publishers when instructors require students to purchase a commercial textbook). These approaches are more cost-effective than creating entirely new open textbooks and allow the institution to stretch limited resources to benefit more students.

Increasing the number of adaptations and the utilization of open pedagogy will also allow for supporting other institutional priorities and building partnerships with the leaders of those initiatives across campus. For example, customizing an open textbook or having students conduct and openly share undergraduate research as part of the integration of indigenization and internationalization at the U of S would help meet demands for instructional resources needed for those priorities, while also improving the learning experience and outcomes for students.

Conclusion

The use of OER and open pedagogy improves student access to learning materials and allows for resources to be adapted to meet local needs and priorities. The monetary savings to students at the U of S in the past four years by using OER is considerable, while opportunities to improve pedagogy and build upon other university initiatives with these materials and learning methods is clear.

The OER initiative at the University of Saskatchewan has been successful in large part due to the partnerships across the institution between the library, teaching and learning center, distance education unit, media production, and ICT. The role of librarians, educational developers, instructional designers, and instructors as passionate champions has been key in raising awareness and supporting the development and adaptation of OER, as well as introducing the concept of open pedagogy at the U of S.

Librarians across the institution are now well positioned to take on a greater leadership position in the areas of OER publishing, teaching and learning, and systems to move the OER and open pedagogy initiative forward.

References

Bell, S. (2015). Start a textbook revolution, continued: Librarians lead the way with open educational resources. *Library Issues, 35*(5), 1–4.

Billings, M. S., Hutton, S. C., Schafer, J., Schweik, C. M., & Sheridan, M. (2012). Open educational resources as learning materials: Prospects and strategies for university libraries. (Research Library Issues: A Quarterly Report from ARL, CNI, and SPARC, no. 280). Retrieved from http://publications.arl.org/rli280/

Clobridge, A. (2015). The open road: Libraries, meet open textbooks. *Online Searcher, 39*(3), 68–70.

eCommons@USask (n.d.). https://ecommons.usask.ca

Ferguson, C. L. (2017). Open educational resources and institutional repositories. *Serials Review, 43*(1), 34–38. https://doi.org/10.1080/00987913.2016.1274219

Ferguson, C. L. (2016). Textbooks in academic libraries. *Serials Review, 42*(3), 252–258. https://doi.org/10.1080/00987913.2016.1207480

Friesen, N. (2009). Open educational resources: New possibilities for change and sustainability. *The International Review of Research in Open and Distributed Learning, 10*(5). doi: 10.19173/irrodl.v10i5.664

Goodsett, M., Loomis, B., & Miles, M. (2016). Leading campus OER initiatives through library–faculty collaboration. *College & Undergraduate Libraries, 23*(3), 335–342. doi: 10.1080/10691316.2016.1206328

Hagel, P., Horn, A., Owen, S., & Currie, M. (2012). "How can we help?" The contribution of university libraries to student retention. *Australian Academic and Research Libraries, 43*(3), 214–230. doi: 10.1080/00048623.2012.10722278

Hess, I., Nann, A.J., & Riddle, K. E. (2016). Navigating OER: The library's role in bringing OER to campus. *Serials Librarian, 70*(1–4), 128–134. doi: 10.1080/0361526X.2016.1153326

Howard, J. (2013, February 4). For new ideas in scholarly publishing, look to the library. *The Chronicle of Higher Education.* Retrieved from http://chronicle.com/article/Hot-Off-the-Library-Press/136973

Mitchell, C., & Chu, M. (2014). Open education resources: The new paradigm in academic libraries. *Journal of Library Innovation, 5*(1), 13–29.

Okamoto, K. (2013). Making higher education more affordable, one course reading at a time: Academic libraries as key advocates for open access textbooks and educational resources, *Public Services Quarterly, 9*(4), 267–283. doi: 10.1080/15228959.2013.842397

Ovadia, S. (2011). Open-access electronic textbooks: An overview. *Behavioral & Social Sciences Librarian, 30*(1), 52–56. doi: 10.1080/01639269.2011.546767

Salem Jr., J. A. (2017). Open pathways to student success: Academic library partnerships for open educational resource and affordable course content creation and adoption. *The Journal of Academic Librarianship, 43*(1), 34–38. doi: 10.1016/j.acalib.2016.10.003

Saskatchewan Government OER MOU (2014). Memorandum of understanding: Open educational resources. Retrieved from: https://oerknowledgecloud.org/content/memorandum-understanding-open-educational-resources

University of Saskatchewan Librarians and Archivists. (2010). University of Saskatchewan librarians and archivists open access commitment. Retrieved from http://lgdata.s3-website-us-east-1.amazonaws.com/docs/1198/403877/OA_Commitment.pdf

University of Saskatchewan Undergraduate Research Journal. (n.d.). retrieved from http://www.usask.ca/urj/

University of Saskatchewan website. (n.d.). Retrieved from http://www.usask.ca

Walz, A. R. (2015). Open and editable: Exploring library engagement in open educational resource adoption, adaptation and authoring. *Virginia Libraries, 61*(1), 23–31. https://ejournals.lib.vt.edu/valib/article/view/1326/1797

West, Q. (2016). Librarians and the open educational resource movement. *CHOICE: Current Reviews for Academic Libraries, 53*(10).

West, Q. (2017). Librarians in the pursuit of open practices. In R. S. Jhangiani, & R. Biswas-Diener (Eds.), *Open: The philosophy and practices that are revolutionizing education and science* (pp. 139–146). London: Ubiquity Press. doi: 10.5334/bbc.k.

Bringing OER to the Liberal Arts: An Innovative Grant Program[1]

Jonathan Miller

In this chapter I will describe the genesis of an open educational resources (OER) grant program; why we decided to support a grantee through three iterations of a course; and how and why we involved other experts from Instructional Design & Technology and from the Center for Teaching Effectiveness; outline our experience with the first three grantees; and finally relate this grant program to our strategic focus.

A common stereotype of liberal arts colleges is that they are elite institutions occupying a small niche in U.S. higher education, serving a small proportion of students whose families can afford to pay for small class sizes and personal attention from professors. Such a student population, and the professors who teach them, hardly seems like fertile ground for the growth of OER. This stereotype seems to be reflected in the professional literature. A combined search of the LISTA and ERIC databases for the terms "Open Education Resources or OER" and "liberal arts" retrieved one record, while and "Community colleges" retrieved 19, and "university" retrieved 359. An informal unpublished survey of the Oberlin Group of liberal arts college libraries conducted by Janis Bandelin of Furman University in late 2015 found that only 11 of the 80 member schools were supporting OER and most of those varied efforts were quite tentative (J. Bandelin, personal communication, November 15, 2015). A review

---

[1] Earlier versions of this work were presented at the Florida ACRL Fall Meeting Gainesville, October 16, 2015 and at the USAIN Pre-Conference, Gainesville, April 24th, 2016. The author acknowledges the work of his colleagues in the Olin Library, Instructional Technology & Design, and the Christian A. Johnson Center for Effective Teaching, and all those faculty who applied for OER grants.

of the membership of the Open Textbook Network shows that only two liberal arts colleges are individual members of the network, although others might support the network via consortial membership. Add to this liberal arts stereotype the very real phenomenon that personal attention from faculty means that many courses at liberal arts colleges are, in the best sense of the word, idiosyncratic, and do not make use of traditional, standardized, textbooks. With a small number of librarians to serve the diverse information needs of the community, why would one such liberal arts college library devote time and resources to an OER grant program?

Founded in 1885, Rollins College is the oldest institution of higher education in Florida. The total student body consists of approximately 3,000 full-time equivalent (FTE) students served by 235 full-time faculty and 93 adjunct and contingent faculty members. As of May 31, 2016, the endowment was worth $339,700,000 and the total annual tuition and room and board for a student in the College of Liberal Arts, before any financial aid, was $60,970 (Rollins College, 2016).

These figures would seem to confirm the liberal arts stereotype. But a closer look at the college shows that even in this admittedly privileged environment, the rising cost of required textbooks and course materials can be a burden for students. The college consists of three schools; the full-time undergraduate College of Liberal Arts, the Crummer School of Business, which provides a variety of MBA programs and a small DBA program, and the Hamilton Holt School, which provides both undergraduate and graduate degrees to non-residential students drawn from the Central Florida region, most of whom are part-time students who also work while pursuing their degrees. Holt School students pay by the course and are very often funding their own education. They are very sensitive to price, and textbook purchases, which are concentrated in the first week of the semester just as the students have managed to pay their tuition, can be especially hard on these students.

But it is not just Holt School students who are sensitive to textbook costs. In 2016, 87 percent of College of Liberal Arts students received financial aid (S. Booker, personal communication, June 19, 2017) and the vast majority of our students are digging deep into family resources to pay for college. Just like their colleagues in the Holt School, expensive textbook purchases at the beginning of the semester, right after the family has paid their tuition bill, can come as a very unwelcome shock.

All three schools are supported by a single library, the Olin Library, with 10 librarians and 12 staff members. The Library Director also oversees the Tutoring & Writing Center located in the Olin building, and the Information Technology (IT) Help Desk and Instructional Design & Technology staff are also housed in the Olin building. In the summer of 2017 we were joined in Olin by the Christian A. Johnson Center for Teaching Effectiveness and the Office of Accessibility Services.

The Rollins faculty and librarians have a long history of supporting open access (OA). College of Liberal Arts faculty passed an open access policy in early 2010 (Rollins College, Faculty of Arts & Sciences, 2010) and the library administers an open institutional repository that, among many other collections, makes accessible the scholarly publications subject to that policy. A more detailed account of Rollins faculty engagement with OA can be found in the author's 2011 guest column in *College & Research Libraries News* (Miller, 2011). In his role as the Library Director at Rollins and working through the ACRL (the Association of College and Research Libraries), the author has also been active in OA advocacy at the federal level, as have several other librarians at Rollins. In more recent years the librarians at Rollins have decided to move beyond advocacy to devote a portion of the collections budget to financially sustaining certain OA projects. Jonathan Harwell describes this effort in a 2016 *Against the Grain* column (Harwell, 2016).

All this interest in and activity around OA meant that the librarians followed developments in OER, but did not take any action until the College began to consider the future of the College bookstore. Rollins students, in a move common throughout American higher education, had begun to acquire more of their textbooks in ways other than simple purchase of the books in the college bookstore. In a 2016 report Nielsen found that only 34 percent of students used their college bookstore as a source for course materials (Nielsen Insights, 2016). The college bookstore was becoming more of a memorabilia store. As the college contemplated how to satisfy students' continuing need to acquire required texts we considered following the students and moving all (print and digital) textbook distribution online. Students would buy from outlets like Amazon and

Chegg and have the books delivered to the campus post office. To handle textbook adoption and the inevitable lag time, the college asked the library to investigate maintaining a reserve textbook collection for students. As many librarians who have maintained such collections have found, this would be expensive (Beck, 2012), both to initially collect and then to maintain. Encouraging the use of OER on campus was one way to help lower this cost, both to students and to the library. Eventually, as with so many such projects in higher education, the transformation of the bookstore was downgraded to a simple move, but the library decided to continue to the develop the idea of encouraging OER on campus.

The OER Grant Program[2]

Rollins has a popular grant program on campus that we thought could form the basis for such a plan. For many years the College's IT department has provided Faculty Instructional Technology Initiative (FITI) grants to faculty to encourage them to incorporate technology into their teaching and the classroom. These grants last for one year, provide a small stipend to the faculty member, and fund the acquisition of the necessary technology. Each grant costs the College approximately $2,500.

The most important part of the FITI grant, however, was based on the model provided by Hamilton College HILLGroup.[3] In that model, a faculty member seeking to incorporate technology into the classroom worked with a team of both instructional technologists and librarians. At Rollins, IT took that model and incorporated it into the FITI grants, providing each grantee with a team consisting of an instructional technologist, a librarian, and the Director of the Center for Teaching Effectiveness to work with for the duration of the grant. This team model was popular with faculty, well understood, and brought with it collateral benefits such as deepening relationships between teaching faculty and a variety of academic support professionals.

---

[2] More information on our OER program and the Wufoo online application form can be found at: http://www.rollins.edu/library/services/oer.html

[3] The HILLGroup has since been superseded at Hamilton where the library and IT operations are now fully merged. For more details see: https://www.hamilton.edu/offices/lits/research-instructional-design

Using the same team approach, we developed a set of three goals for an OER grant program:

1. Significantly lower the cost of textbooks to students.
2. Maintain or improve student learning outcomes.
3. Contribute to the growing body of OER.

We decided that the program should be open to all faculty members at Rollins. Unlike many grants, which are focused on full-time or tenure-track faculty, this one explicitly includes adjuncts, so that the program would be open to the many adjuncts teaching in the Holt School, where we hoped we might be able to have an impact on students who were financing their own education. We also decided that the grant would last for three iterations of a course. At Rollins, courses can be taught as frequently as every semester, so that three iterations would last for about a year and a half, or as infrequently as once every two years, so that three iterations would last for six years. We created this three-iteration structure because of what we had noticed about FITI grants: faculty members with FITI grants put significant effort into incorporating technology into a course and this tends to change the whole course. This is an enormous amount of effort on the faculty member's part and, of course, not all technologies succeed in the classroom. It is not uncommon to find that the effort is too much and the faculty member reverts to the way the course has been taught in the past. By basing the grants on three iterations of the course, discussed in more detail below, we hoped that the use of OER would 'stick' and we would also have more reliable assessment of the impact of the OER. The three iterations are structured as follows. As a small institution we can deviate from the standard structure if necessary.

1st *Iteration*

Teach the traditional course.

Assess the impact of the traditional textbook.

Select, or create, and organize OER materials for the course.

Begin to develop an assessment mechanism for measuring the impact of the OER.

2nd *Iteration*

Teach the course using OER materials.

Assess the impact of the OER.

Compare that impact to the first year.

3rd *Iteration*

Make any revisions and teach the course using OER materials.

Assess the impact of the OER and compare to first- and second-year assessments.

Publicize the results of the grant on campus and to a wider audience.

File a report on the outcome of the grant with the Academic Dean.

Upload any OER to the Digital Orange Grove or a comparable open repository

To keep the incentive for applicants in the same ballpark as FITI grants, we decided we would award a $1,000 stipend to the successful faculty applicant per course iteration, received after all work within that iteration is complete. Thus, each applicant receives a total of $3,000 over the course of the grant. Unlike the FITI grants, we decided to only award one new grant per academic year. This would limit our financial exposure to $3,000 per year, and more importantly, limit the workload for members of their team: their liaison librarian, an instructional technologist, and the Director of the Christian A. Johnson Center for Teaching Effectiveness.

The obvious shortcoming of limiting the program to a single award per year is that it would take us centuries to convert the whole faculty to OER. But we do not expect OER to be appropriate for all faculty members or all courses at Rollins. The grant program has a multiplier effect by raising awareness of OER. This happens in several ways. First, some faculty who have been using openly available resources (although not all always meeting the strict definition of OER) in their courses come to realize that they are inadvertently part of a wider movement. Secondly, some faculty who apply but are not awarded the OER grant continue to explore the use of OER in their courses, and finally the requirement that the successful grantee present in a faculty forum on their project spreads the word about OER, as does the normal everyday faculty and departmental conversation about teaching on campus. In these ways, the small OER grant is a catalyst for wider action and discussion.

Review Criteria

We based our review criteria on a common set of criteria for grants on campus and added some that are specific to OER. Each application is reviewed on the following criteria.

- The completeness of the application. Applicants are encouraged to consult with librarians, instructional technologists, and the pedagogy expert in the Center for Teaching Effectiveness early and often while drafting their application.
- The total cost to each student of the traditional textbook(s) in the course.
- The average enrollment in the course and the frequency with which it is taught. The multiplication of these three criteria (textbook cost, enrollment, and frequency) equals the total costs saved in that course, if we can entirely replace the textbook(s). The larger the number, the greater weight the reviewers give to the application.
- The availability of suitable OER in major repositories, such as: MERLOT (the Multimedia Educational Resource for Learning and Online Teaching),[4] Florida's Digital Orange Grove,[5] OER Commons,[6] etc. Note that this is not an exclusive list. Interested faculty are encouraged to search these and other sources of existing OER. Interested faculty are also encouraged to work with a librarian to search for existing OER prior to submitting their application. The list also needs to be regularly updated.
- The likelihood that the applicant can and will complete the work. This is a somewhat subjective criterion. But Rollins is a small campus and librarians and instructional technologists have close relationships with teaching faculty. The $1,000 annual stipend is tempting and we are investing a lot in providing a team. We want to maximize the potential for success by also considering an applicant's previous track record in terms of grant project completion and using our experience and expertise to make a call on the feasibility of the project.

---

[4] For more information on MERLOT, see: https://www.merlot.org/merlot/index.htm

[5] For Florida's Digital Orange Grove, see: https://florida.theorangegrove.org/og/home.do

[6] For OER Commons, see: https://www.oercommons.org

Even though these grants are financed by the library's budget and involve considerable effort from team members in different departments, the formal review and awarding of the grants is administered by the Faculty Affairs Committee (FAC). This is a standing governance committee of the faculty and one of its duties is to award and oversee various grants to the faculty. Both OER and FITI grant applications first undergo an expert review by a group consisting of the Chief Information Officer, the Head of Instructional Design & Technology, the Library Director, and the Director of the CAJ Center for Teaching Effectiveness. This group recommends applicants to the FAC, which formally votes to accept, revise, or reject that recommendation. Although this cedes control to a faculty committee, it gives both grant programs the imprimatur of the faculty, uses existing shared governance procedures and thus increases the confidence of the faculty in the process, and raises the visibility of both grant programs.

Experience

As I write this, the FAC has just awarded our third OER grant. The first awardee, Dr. Mackenzie Moon Ryan of the Art & Art History Department, is beginning her third and final iteration of the course and the OER grant. The second awardee, Dr. Julia Maskivker of the Political Science Department, is beginning her second iteration of the course and the grant, and at the end of the spring semester we awarded our third OER grant to Dr. Whitney Coyle of the Physics Department. The remainder of this chapter will draw out specific lessons learned from the experience of each awardee.

Dr. Ryan applied to bring OER to her 200-level art history course, *Introduction to Global Art*. In an interview with the author she noted that she had felt obliged to adopt a textbook when teaching such a broad subject, but had also felt constrained by the textbook. It had an authoritative voice without argument or criticism. It did not encourage students to develop the habit of questioning where the information came from. She sought more flexibility in choosing the artworks to focus upon and in selecting differing voices. She was dissatisfied by both the cost of the books to her students, the quality of the production, and that the publisher released new editions every couple of years (Miller, 2015b). In her application she identified digital resources from the Metropolitan Museum of Art in New York and OER resources from the Digital Orange Grove and from Saylor Academy. She noted that she would need to:

> augment [OER] with case studies utilizing peer-reviewed articles from scholarly journals. Many open-access resources are very introductory and it is crucial that students are also introduced to the sustained arguments and depth of research in scholarly sources. It will take some time to locate, evaluate, and implement select scholarly sources so as not to overwhelm students but also to convey the utility and necessity of peer-reviewed sources. (M. Ryan, personal communication, May 12, 2015)

It was clear from her application that she would not be able to move completely to OER in this course. The Metropolitan Museum's (the Met) digital content is very high quality, but it is made available under a somewhat restrictive license (Metropolitan Museum of Art, n.d.) that would enable us to link to the content, but not download or create and publish derivative works from that content. Obviously, this means that any OER works we created including Met content would need to simply link to that content, which means that we cannot be confident that those links will always work over the long term. We would also be depending on the future direction of the Met, which is already changing (Pogrebin, 2017).

Further, the peer-reviewed sources that Dr. Ryan planned to use would largely come from the full-text licensed scholarly journals available to the Rollins community. These would be free to Rollins students, fulfilling our first goal of lowering the cost to students, but not our third of adding to the body of open resources. Again, we would have to simply cite articles that future non-Rollins users might, or might not, be able to access.

Despite these limitations we decided to award Dr. Ryan the grant. We were excited by her topic and knew her as a dependable and enthusiastic teacher. The traditional textbooks she had adopted were, in her words, "really expensive" (Miller, 2015b) and she taught this course annually. If we could not reduce to the cost to zero, we could replace much of the required course materials with more open resources. She was also excited to work with a team (Miller, 2015b).

We were probably too excited. As Dr. Ryan has progressed through two iterations of the course within the grant, her gallant efforts and those of her team have not resulted in the assembly or production of any OER that meet the strict definition of the term.[7] There is a reason why art history textbooks are so expensive; the rights management and reproduction of large numbers of high-quality images is expensive and difficult to manage, and the synthesis of complex and diverse scholarship into appropriately written prose is a specialist activity for which authors expect to be rewarded.

We have learned from the experience. Perhaps most importantly we have learned not to bite off more than we can chew, and this is reflected in subsequent grant awards. We also learned that researching and understanding the rights and permissions attached to any particular resource that a faculty member is considering is a complex workload in and of itself. During the development of the application, assuming the faculty member consults with the library (where copyright expertise resides at Rollins) and certainly at the point of expert review, we must take time to delve into the rights and permissions of ostensibly "open" resources and insert the findings into the review process.

Finally, we gained experience in assessment. Dr. Ryan worked with our then Director of the Center for Effective Teaching, Dr. James Zimmerman. As Dr. Zimmerman noted in an interview, it is very difficult to isolate the impact of a single variable, like a textbook, on student learning, "but all hope is not lost" (Miller, 2015a). In the assessment of the first two iterations of the course, the team decided to use group interviews with students conducted by Dr. Zimmerman during class times with Dr. Ryan not present. Dr. Zimmerman found that most students found the traditional textbook valuable. He found that, not surprisingly, the students preferred the online open resources for the course to be clearly organized and that students preferred a combination of text and image rather than podcast and image. Dr. Zimmerman also noted that his discussion

---

[7] UNESCO defines OER as, "teaching, learning and research materials in any medium that reside in the public domain and have been released under an open license that permits access, use, repurposing, reuse and redistribution by others with no or limited restrictions." (UNESCO, 2011, p. v).

with Dr. Ryan suggested that instructors needed to have taught the course multiple times before they embark on the OER grant and that the OER transformation will take at least three years.

In the second year of the grant program we took Dr. Ryan's experience to heart and selected what we hope to be a far less ambitious application: Dr. Julia Maskivker, of the Political Science Department, and her course *Problems in Political Thought*. This is a course in which students are introduced to some of the classics of western political philosophy: Plato, Hobbes, Locke, and Rousseau. The course is taught every semester to approximately 25 students, so the impact of introducing OER could be quite large even though the cost of textbooks for the course was relatively low. The cost of textbooks is low because editions and translations of these classic texts exist in the public domain and they can be purchased in inexpensive paperback editions. The public domain status of these works also meant that they had already been digitized in Project Gutenberg and released with a very liberal license (Project Gutenberg, 2014).

The interesting aspects of Dr. Maskivker's application were less about creating or organizing OER, since her team planned to create simple epub editions, and more about how students would use these ebooks in the course. Rollins does not require students to use a particular computer or operating system. We provide access to both Macs and PCs on campus and while the current generation of students tend to favor Macs, we have to plan on delivering content via a wide range of hardware and software. Studying how students navigate through open ebooks would inform the Library and Instructional Design & Technology's wider understanding of students' evolving use of ebooks.

Of even greater interest however, is Dr. Maskivker's intention to incorporate the ethics of intellectual property, and OER, into the course, as she wrote in her application:

> I will culminate the experiment with an invited lecturer that will speak to my class on issues of intellectual property law—its philosophical underpinnings and its policy implications. I believe this activity is a wonderful way to make the class more fun and interesting by linking issues of classical theory like private property and state power to a practical discussion on

the policy implications and every-day-consequences of intellectual property law. In a fascinating way, "open source" means that the traditional barriers of intellectual property law are (at least temporarily or with permission) brought down. However, the concept exists in the background of a whole legal and philosophical apparatus, and I want my students to get a quick panoramic view of what that is and where it is moving. (J. Maskivker, personal communication, March 2, 2016)

The first iteration of Dr. Maskivker's course was delayed to accommodate her sabbatical, so the team is currently working on assembling the OER versions of her readings and on developing assessment. Dr. Maskivker has required students to write responses to readings and her plan is to compare those responses from the traditional iteration of the course to those from the OER version of the course and to combine this assessment with measures of student satisfaction with the ebook experience.

The third grant was awarded to Dr. Whitney Coyle of the physics department. The physics department recently purchased a number of IO-Lab carts. These 'carts' (each about the size of a mobile phone) have, "built in sensors [that] measure force, acceleration, velocity, displacement, magnetic field, rotation, light, sound, temperature, pressure, and voltages ... Expansion connectors provide access to over a dozen user controllable digital and analog inputs and outputs" (IOLab, 2016).

According to Dr. Coyle, each of these devices replaces a shelf of equipment that students have used in introductory physics courses. They are a relatively recent innovation and the initial development was funded by a Kickstarter campaign. The manufacturers note that, "sophisticated open-source software controls the device, acquires and displays data in real time, and provides a suite of analysis and data manipulation features" (IOLab, 2016). The devices are so new that no one has developed lab manuals for introductory physics courses using the carts. This is what Dr. Coyle plans to do for the PHY130 and 131 courses with the help of her OER grant.

Dr. Coyle also wrote in her application that, "for many years the Physics faculty have mapped out a skills tree that details scaffolded, by year, goals for student learning—skills that we expect our students to learn in each lab course we teach" (W. Coyle, personal communication, February 24, 2017). Her plan is to write a full OER lab manual that guides students through a unified learning experience using the IOLab carts. The skills Rollins faculty teach in this introductory sequence of courses are common in American college-level physics curricula and we anticipate that writing this lab manual, based around the IOLab carts, will be of use to many other physics professors using the carts. It also builds upon the open way in which these devices have been developed, with crowd-sourced funding and open source software. Dr. Coyle has reached out to the device developers. They are not developing such lab manuals and are supportive of her doing so.

How Dr. Coyle and her team will assess the impact of the OER lab manual on student learning is yet to be determined, but she is interested in measuring student perceptions of their own skill level and on work with her colleagues in more advanced courses to see how the skills students develop in the course are exhibited in more advanced physics courses.

Conclusion

This innovative grant program has taught us that OER do have a place in liberal arts colleges. Our commitment to open scholarship and learning can go beyond advocacy and support for open access publishing. The focused and nuanced attention faculty at liberal arts colleges have always paid to the required readings and content they bring into the classroom and their courses is a good fit with the OER movement and with OER development. Selecting a traditional textbook can sometimes be a case of "take it or leave it." Developing OER requires carefully thinking about the details of what is included, or not, in the final resource. This fits well with the traditional care and attention faculty who are attracted to liberal arts education have always paid to the classroom experience.

These three very different projects have taught us a number of things. First, don't be too ambitious. Secondly, as we suspected, the impact of one variable (the textbook or required course materials) on something as complex as student learning is very difficult to assess, but staying focused on assessment is constructive anyway. Finally, that such relatively small project-based grants, especially when combined with a focused team of academic support professionals, can have an outsized impact on the strategic success of the library.

The current iteration of the library's strategic plan is to "become even more thoroughly integrated into the teaching and learning of the College. While continuing to provide solutions to information problems, the library staff and librarians go beyond this to be partners with faculty and students throughout the learning and research process" (Olin Library, 2014). This OER grant program enables librarians (and instructional technologists) to partner with faculty at a new point in the teaching cycle, at the point of creation and adoption of the textbook, or its OER equivalent. This is much earlier than has traditionally been the case and means we are working with faculty as they develop the course. We remain deeply connected to the course as it is taught over three iterations (and hopefully beyond). We can use these grants to build partnerships around a number of topics throughout the learning and teaching processes. Including issues of information literacy, intellectual property, and research data management. For instance, Dr. Ryan teaches her students to question where information comes from and saw her team as helping that process. Teams also help faculty understand the intellectual property (IP) landscape of textbooks and OER, and how they can make their own decisions about the copyright status of their own works, but also—as is the case in Dr. Maskivker's course—help students begin to understand the nuances of IP. Finally, Dr. Coyle's IOLab carts require students to collect and manage many more data points than would be the case in more traditional introductory physics courses, which raise issues of research data management.

We still have a long way to go, but all this is a very long way from where we began; wondering if we could sustain a collection of textbooks behind the circulation desk.

References

Beck, S. (2012). Queensborough community college: Textbook reserve collection. *Community & Junior College Libraries, 18*(3/4), 119–126.

Harwell, J. (2016). Being earnest with collections: Investing in open access at a small academic library. *Against the Grain, 27*(6). Retrieved from http://www.against-the-grain.com/2016/02/v27-6-being-earnest/

IOLab. (2016) IOLab wireless lab system. Retrieved from http://iolab.science/

Metropolitan Museum of Art. (n.d.). *Terms and conditions.* Retrieved from http://www.metmuseum.org/information/terms-and-conditions

Miller, J. (2011). Open access and liberal arts colleges: Looking beyond research institutions. *College & Research Libraries News, 72*(1), 16–19, 30. doi:10.5860/crln.72.1.8490

Miller, J. (Interviewer) (2015a). Clip 3 James Zimmerman on assessment and the Rollins OER Grant Program [Video]. Retrieved from https://youtu.be/0rSkXQP11Lo

Miller, J. (Interviewer) (2015b). Textbooks and OER Mackenzie Moon Ryan on the Rollins OER Grant Program [Video]. Retrieved from https://youtu.be/Y9A8ZWQUvUs

Nielsen Insights. (2016). Textbook trends: How U.S. college students source course materials. Retrieved from http://www.nielsen.com/us/en/insights/news/2016/textbook-trends-how-us-college-students-source-course-materials.html

Olin Library. (2014) Olin strategic plan: Focus 2014–17. Retrieved from https://sites.google.com/site/olinplan/home/focus

Pogrebin, R. (2017, February 28). Metropolitan Museum's director resigns under pressure. *The New York Times.* Retrieved from https://www.nytimes.com/2017/02/28/arts/design/met-museum-director-resigns-thomas-campbell.html

Project Gutenberg. (2014, August 15). The Project Gutenberg License. Retrieved from https://www.gutenberg.org/wiki/Gutenberg:The_Project_Gutenberg_License

Rollins College. (2016). *Rollins College Fact Book 2016–17.* Retrieved from https://rpublic.rollins.edu/sites/IR/_layouts/15/WopiFrame.aspx?sourcedoc=/sites/IR/Fact%20Brochures/fact-brochure-2016.pdf&action=default#https://rpublic.rollins.edu/sites/IR/Fact%20Brochures/fact-brochure-2016.pdf

Rollins College, Faculty of Arts & Sciences. (2010). Open access policy. Retrieved from https://scholarship.rollins.edu/open_access_policy.pdf

UNESCO. (2011). *Guidelines for open educational resources (OER) in higher education.* Retrieved from http://unesdoc.unesco.org/images/0021/002136/213605E.pdf

Transforming Publishing with a Little Help From Our Friends: Supporting an Open Textbook Pilot Project with Friends of the Libraries Grant Funding

Chelle Batchelor

Defining the Problem

Challenges abound to both the adoption of existing open textbooks and the creation of new open textbooks. Key challenges identified by faculty are issues of quality, availability of content, and the time it takes to adopt or create open educational resources (OER), particularly open textbooks. Solutions to these challenges are being explored through a collaborative pilot project involving the Open Textbook Network, the Rebus Foundation, and several universities. This case study describes how, with the support of a Friends of the Libraries Grant, staff and faculty at the University of Washington (UW) participated in an Open Textbook Pilot Project to create new open textbooks within the Rebus Community platform. Although this pilot is ongoing, it has already begun to address some of the challenges to OER creation and adoption.

Despite the continued increase in the availability of existing open educational materials and the growth of the open education movement, awareness of OER is still a challenge, with 58 percent of faculty reporting that they were "generally unaware of OER" in a recent national survey. In this survey, only 6.6 percent of faculty reported that they were "very aware" of OER, with around three times that many (19%) saying that they were "aware" (Allen & Seaman, 2016). The same study found that the barriers to adopting OER most often cited by faculty who *are* aware of the existence of OER are: "there are not enough resources for my subject" (49%), it is "too hard to find what I need" (48%) and "there is no comprehensive catalog of resources" (45%) (Allen & Seaman, 2016).

UW faculty primarily have concerns about quality of content and the amount of time it takes to convert a course from a commercial textbook to an open one. This is consistent with a finding by Martin, Belikov, Hilton, Wiley, and Fischer that "while an overwhelming majority (90%) of respondents were open to the notion of using open resources, it was contingent upon the OER being 'suitable', or at least equal in quality to what they were currently using" (Martin et al., 2017). The Babson survey similarly found that quality concerns were present among faculty members (28% in comparison with other barriers), and also found that faculty who are aware of OER are more concerned about the quality of OER offerings than those who were not aware of OER prior to taking the survey (Allen & Seaman, 2016). The question of what is 'suitable' for a course can depend on many factors, as is demonstrated by reading reviews in the Open Textbook Library, which include criteria such as accuracy, comprehensiveness, relevance/longevity, clarity, consistency, grammatical errors, cultural relevance, and others. In one example, a UW faculty member states that the OpenStax biology textbook is "unusable" due to "topic(s) completely missing or coverage is so poor" on several topics that she goes on to list (Doherty, 2016). In another example, a Bemidji State University faculty member notes that a lack of ancillary materials is the primary reason his department would not adopt a financial accounting text (Joyce, 2015).

One of the advantages of using open textbooks is the fact that their licenses allow for adaptation. In a case such as the OpenStax biology example above, an instructor could remix and revise the book, adding their own content or creating assignments that require students to create new content for the book. Alternately, an instructor could supplement the book with other open resources or library-licensed content. However, when the topic of adapting existing open textbooks has been discussed in OER meetings and workshops at UW, faculty attendees have consistently responded that they lack the time to do so. Time emerged as a major barrier in a report by Chae and Jenkins who found that "Lack of time for course redesign in current college employment contexts emerged clearly in our study as a primary barrier to performing the often time-intensive work of finding, adapting and creating OER" (Chae & Jenkins, 2015). Faculty reported in this study that they had gained time for this work via sabbaticals and course releases. In an institutional environment where those options are not offered, time can be an insurmountable barrier to

OER adoption or creation. Activities related to open textbook adoption, including creation of new content, creation of ancillary materials, course and assignment redesign and pedagogical innovation are time-consuming. Any program that offers support for OER adoption or creation must take these challenges into consideration.

UW Open Textbook Pilot Project Background

The genesis of the UW Open Textbook Pilot Project was contingent upon what seemed to be a fortuitous coming together of several elements: 1) the Open Textbook Network was hearing an increasing demand from its members for support for publishing new open textbooks, 2) the Rebus Foundation was forming, with the specific intent of providing support of that nature, 3) the UW Libraries, a new member of the Open Textbook Network, had formed an OER Steering Committee that was exploring ways to support OER and 4) the Friends of the UW Libraries was accepting grant proposals for the 2016–17 academic year.

Open Textbook Network

The Open Textbook Network (OTN) launched in April 2012 with the goal of increasing the use of open textbooks in higher education. The Open Textbook Library was created to address the barriers to OER adoption cited above, particularly the lack of a comprehensive catalog and concerns about quality. In April 2017, the Open Textbook Network announced that their catalog contained over 385 books in 14 broad subject areas and that they had recently uploaded their 1000th faculty review of a textbook. These faculty reviews serve two purposes—one is to address the quality issue through peer review, the other is to raise awareness of the textbooks themselves in the process of soliciting peer reviews. When an institution joins the OTN, experts from the Network visit the institution to provide workshops to faculty, librarians, and staff. The workshops build understanding of OER for all who attend, and faculty are invited to write a review of a textbook in the Open Textbook Library. Faculty are provided a small stipend in compensation for attending the workshop and writing a review. Since its formation, this model has proven successful. The OTN has reported $3.1 million in savings to students by nine early members.

Rebus Foundation

The Rebus Foundation was founded by Hugh McGuire, an innovator with a passion for equity of access to information. McGuire had previously worked on two projects that uniquely prepared him to conceptualize and implement Rebus. The first was LibriVox, an online community that began in 2005 with the objective "To make all books in the public domain available, for free, in audio format on the internet" ("Objective LibriVox", n.d.). Twelve years later, LibriVox is a massive online community with over 10,000 completed projects. The second was Pressbooks, an open source software product that supports creation of ebooks. Pressbooks provides a user-friendly interface and simple publishing templates that together make it relatively easy to create a book and publish it online in multiple formats, including epub, mobi, and PDF. The Rebus Foundation brings together the best of both former projects to support the creation of open textbooks in a community-based setting. Taking the forum structure from LibriVox and using Pressbooks as the publishing platform, Rebus provides all the tools needed for textbook authors and contributors to work together to create new open textbooks.

UW Open Educational Resources Steering Committee

The UW Open Educational Resources Steering Committee (UW OERSC) was formed in January 2016 by the UW Libraries. The committee is co-chaired by John Danneker, Director of Odegaard Library and Chelle Batchelor, Director of Access Services. The charge of the committee is to bring together stakeholders from the UW community to advocate for and support OER efforts. Membership includes representation from UW faculty, Associated Students of the University of Washington, UW Book Store, University Press, Libraries, Undergraduate Academic Affairs, Disability Resources for Students, Teaching and Learning Center, and UW-IT Learning Technologies. Chelle Batchelor led the UW Open Textbook Pilot Project and drew from the expertise of other committee members on several occasions.

UW Friends of the Libraries

The Friends of the Libraries is an organization that was established in 1991 to provide support to the university libraries by promoting awareness of the libraries within the community and by stimulating financial support for the UW Libraries (Friends of the Libraries, n.d.). Funding for innovative projects in the Libraries is provided by the Friends by awarding grants of up to $5,000 per project. Grants are proposed and awarded once per year, and any member of the Libraries staff can apply for a grant. Projects are evaluated on how well they support the Libraries' four key strategic visions of research and scholarship, teaching and learning, engagement, and sustainability. Projects are more likely to be accepted if they benefit the Libraries and their users through imaginative and useful approaches to practice, research, teaching, and learning, and if they reflect the Libraries' values of collaboration, diversity, excellence, innovation, integrity, and responsiveness.

Case Study: The UW Open Textbook Publishing Pilot

The UW Libraries joined the Open Textbook Network in May 2015 and subsequently hosted Sarah Cohen, David Ernst, and Rajiv Jhangiani for a series of Open Textbook Workshops that were held in January 2016. The outline of the day included a workshop for staff and librarians, a workshop for faculty, and a mid-day open discussion to which staff and faculty from all academic units were invited. The open discussion drew a diverse group of attendees, including faculty and staff from the Center for Teaching and Learning, University Press, UW Book Store, UW Libraries, and Disability Resources for Students. Seeing the level of interest and engagement in the topic of OER and the already established collaboration between academic units, Sarah Cohen from the OTN invited UW to join the Open Textbook Publishing Pilot as one of the first participating institutions.

The idea of participating in the Open Textbook Publishing Pilot was attractive because several UW faculty had expressed interest in creating and publishing their own open textbooks when UW OERSC members spoke with them during their OER advocacy efforts between May 2015 and January 2016. The pilot had the potential to fill a need for the faculty, and it seemed likely that participants were readily available. However, successful programs to encourage the adoption and creation of OER offer incentives to faculty for their participation. Seeking advice from Karen Brooks, the Manager of University Libraries Grant Services, UW OERSC co-chair Chelle Batchelor learned about the Friends of the Libraries Grant, which was approaching the beginning of its 2016 application cycle.

Reviewing past grant proposals, she found that they were very focused on library collections, with examples ranging from purchase of video games to digitization of rare audio materials. However, the Open Textbook Publishing Pilot did fit within the grant criteria, so she worked with her co-chair John Danneker and another UW Libraries staff member, Steve Weber, to apply. The Friends of the Libraries approved the proposal with maximum grant funding, providing $5,000 to offer three stipends of $1,500 per open textbook, plus an additional $5,00 to fund student employee hours to assist with the project.

After receiving the grant funding, Batchelor sent a call for interest in the project to all UW faculty who had expressed interest in OER in the past. This included all faculty who attended the OTN's Open Textbook Workshop as well as several others. Although this was a relatively small group of faculty, the call for interest elicited three responses. The projects proposed were an introductory text for the digital humanities, a financial management textbook, and an interactive introduction to neuro science textbook. After an initial project kickoff meeting with Hugh McGuire that included a demonstration of Pressbooks, two authors decided to move forward with their projects and one, the person who proposed the interactive textbook project, decided the platform would not support his needs. Going forward, the pilot project participants were Chelle Batchelor (UW project coordinator), Justin Marlowe (lead author), Sharon Kioko (contributor), Sarah Ketchley (lead author), and Emily Thompson (contributor).

As a next step, individual meetings were held between the OTN Director of Publishing and Collections Karen Lauristen, Rebus staff, and the authors for each project. Batchelor attended those meetings as the UW project coordinator. Rebus staff made it clear in these early meetings that the projects would need to be licensed under a CC-BY license, and the authors agreed. One author had originally intended to license her work as CC-BY-NC, but was convinced by the Rebus philosophy:

> CC-BY is the most open of the Creative Commons licenses, which means that society at large can build upon content licensed this way in the easiest, freest and most effective ways. We are trying to help build an open information ecosystem,

> where not only can any student get access to textbooks for free, but further, anyone—another professor, a university, an app maker, or an artist—can build new value, new content and new services on top of this base layer of "public good," the Open Textbook. ("Licensing", n.d.)

After establishing that the Pressbooks platform would meet their needs and determining that they would license their textbooks as CC-BY, the authors embarked on their projects. Batchelor joined a few more meetings between the authors and Rebus staff, but the authors soon began to work very independently, with minimal assistance from the Libraries. The student employee wages that were paid for by the Friends Grant were used to provide one author with assistance with entering content into Pressbooks. That student, Emily Thompson, became a volunteer collaborator on the textbook after the funding was expended. The other authors requested no support from the Libraries.

An open textbook project being supported by the Rebus Community will typically go through the following phases.

1. Lead author(s) identified;
2. Lead author submits project proposal to Rebus staff;
3. If accepted, Rebus staff post project proposal to the Rebus Community forum;
4. Content collaborators are identified (optional);
5. Content is created in, or imported into, Rebus Pressbooks;
6. Peer reviewers are identified by author(s);
7. Peer review is coordinated by Rebus staff;
8. Publishing is coordinated by Rebus staff;
9. Marketing takes place via multiple community channels (Rebus community, Rebus staff, peer reviewers, Open Textbook Network, etc.).

The UW Open Textbook Publishing Pilot authors entered the pilot in very different phases of textbook development. Marlowe and Kioko were about halfway finished with a draft version of their *Financial Strategy for Public Managers* textbook, with a large amount of content already written and compiled. These authors did not foresee needing any collaborators to create content—they would write the remaining content themselves.

Ketchley and Thompson had an outline for their textbook and a small amount of content was already written.

From July 2016, when the Friends Grant was received, until November 2016, the participating authors began to work on their textbooks in Pressbooks while the Rebus Foundation began hiring staff and working on software development for the Rebus Community and Rebus Pressbooks. In November 2016, Rebus launched. From that point on, Rebus staff took over the bulk of the project management for both textbooks and the authors began meeting with Rebus staff periodically as the projects evolved. By May 2017 (when this book chapter was being written), the *Planning and Implementing a Digital Humanities Project* textbook had a table of contents and chapter placeholders in Pressbooks, as well as some introductory content. The project was still being worked on by the authors, but was somewhat stalled because the UW course it was originally being created for had been cancelled and both authors had moved on to new positions at UW. The *Financial Strategy for Public Managers* textbook was complete and was being used in classes by Marlowe and Kioko, and Rebus staff had identified five people who were interested in providing peer review for the text.

Because the *Financial Strategy for Public Managers* textbook was one of the first in the Rebus platform to reach completion, it was a perfect candidate to be the test case for another goal of the Rebus Foundation—to develop good accessibility practices throughout the open textbook publishing process. Krista Greear, Assistant Director of UW Disability Resources for Students and UW OERSC member, joined a team of people who reviewed Marlowe and Kioko's text, collaborated with the authors to remediate any accessibility issues with it, and worked to create recommendations for building accessibility best practices into the authoring process.

Pilot Outcomes

As is well evidenced in the literature on OER as well as in other chapters of this book, financial savings to students is one of the most compelling outcomes of OER adoption. Justin Marlowe and Sharon Kioko have thus far used their book in three sections of PUBPOL 522, which enrolls 60 students per section and is the core budgeting and finance course that all

UW Masters of Public Administration students take in their first year. According to the OTN formula for counting savings to students, their book has already saved students $27,000. Each time this course is offered in the future, another $6,000 will be added to that figure. Therefore, this textbook has the potential to save UW students almost $100,000 over a five-year period. If faculty at other institutions decide to adopt this textbook, the total savings to students from this one book could grow exponentially.

However, savings to students is only one of the benefits of this open textbook. When Chelle Batchelor spoke with Justin Marlowe in their first meeting to explore Justin's possible participation in the pilot, he spoke of how the existing commercial textbooks were not a good fit for his course. Those textbooks looked at financial strategy through a different lens, more geared toward business and marketing than public policy. The number of programs that teach financial strategy from this lens is very small, so there likely is not a sufficient market for a commercial textbook to be successful. Therefore, creation of an open textbook was a perfect solution.

After they began to use the textbook in their course, Marlowe and Kioko discovered that they were able to adopt open pedagogical practices that were directly tied to the learning objectives for their course. For example, one assignment requires students to apply an analytical framework to a problem, and the authors have incorporated some of the students' analyses into the textbook as additional examples and practice problems. They have also asked students for feedback on an exercise in the book and have revised it based on that input. Although the authors did not embark on the project with any specific plans to start utilizing open pedagogical models, they have naturally begun to do so and have found it to be beneficial because it allows them "to respond, almost in real time, to students' concerns and interests" (J. Marlowe, personal communication, April 8, 2018).

Faculty who have involved their students in this type of open pedagogical practice have noted that the ability for students to contribute to the resource they are learning from is an advantage of OER over commercial textbooks. Robin DeRosa articulates this on her blog, stating that her students "immediately seemed invested in the project" to co-create a textbook with her and "seemed more connected to the textbook itself, more willing to engage with it." She concludes, "Open textbooks save money, which matters deeply to our students. But they can also create a new relationship between learners and course content, and if teachers choose to acknowledge and enable this, it can have a profound effect on the whole fabric of the course" (DeRosa, 2016). In their study of K–12 teachers' perceptions of the role of OER, de los Arcos, Farrow, Pitt, Weller, and McAndrew similarly report, "in response to how OER affect learning, teachers stress better engaged, more independent students" (2016). Marlowe has found this to be true in his own students' response to the *Financial Strategy for Public Managers* textbook. Because they have provided a combination of editorial input as well as case studies for inclusion in the text, Marlowe has found that they have been more engaged with the text knowing that their feedback will be used to improve it.

Another outcome that seems to be developing out of our Open Textbook Publishing Pilot and merits continuing investigation is the possible formation of a community of users of and contributors to the *Financial Strategy for Public Managers* textbook. Marlowe had an opportunity to speak with a group of colleagues about his textbook at a meeting he attended when it was in the first draft phase. Several of those colleagues expressed interest in the textbook because they too had struggled with the lack of a commercial textbook that met the needs of their courses. When Rebus staff sent a call for participation in the peer review process to the same group of colleagues, Rebus was overwhelmed by the positive response. They received more than twice as many volunteers as they expected, so they restructured their peer review process to include chapter reviewers as well as book reviewers. If these colleagues who are now reviewing the textbook subsequently adopt it and possibly adapt it or provide updated content for inclusion in future editions, we will be witnessing the genesis of a Rebus Community approach to creating textbooks that involves faculty and students across multiple institutions. This would be incredibly exciting, given the potential of such an approach to resolve issues around the sustainability of open textbooks over time.

One certain outcome of the pilot is that the process of soliciting and securing peer reviewers created a built-in opportunity for promoting the new open textbook. Several faculty in the discipline within which the textbook is being taught are now aware of it, and are probably more aware of OER and the opportunities open licensing presents than they were previously. This awareness-building occurred as a natural outgrowth of Marlowe's peer-to-peer networking, seeking input into the work he was creating, and exploring whether colleagues in his discipline would benefit from it. As was previously discussed in this chapter, awareness of OER is one of the significant barriers to adoption. This outcome of the UW Open Textbook Pilot Project has shown that the Rebus model has the potential to break down that barrier.

Another barrier that was discussed previously is the issue of open textbook quality and comprehensiveness. Because the *Financial Strategy for Public Managers* textbook is just entering the peer review phase, it remains to be seen whether this barrier will be addressed. However, the review process will provide an opportunity for the textbook to be critiqued and improved upon by five experts in the field, ensuring a high likelihood of success.

The barrier of time is still a major factor, and not one that has yet been solved by the UW Open Textbook Pilot Project. Creation, adaptation, and even adoption of open textbooks requires time and effort on the part of one or more faculty members, for whom time is a precious resource. Faculty have many demands on their time, so work in OER must present them with other benefits that will outweigh the cost of time. For some, the cost benefit to their students may be enough. For others, the benefits of open pedagogy might be the influencing factor. In this pilot, the Friends Grant, though small, proved to be an important incentive. When asked what role the grant played for them (i.e. funding for editing, proofreading, or other role), the textbook authors responded that it acted as an incentive for them to contribute their time as textbook authors.

Pilot Success Factors
In addition to the outcomes described above, the UW Open Textbook Publishing Pilot surfaced numerous success factors that will be considered in future iterations of the pilot.

Factor 1: Departmental Support
Of the two open textbook projects from the 2016–17 pilot, one textbook was at a much more advanced stage of development by the end of the

pilot period. This textbook was written by faculty who were teaching a course in a well-established program and who had full departmental support for their project. The other textbook was to be taught in a course that was grant-supported. When the grant funding for the course ran out, the department in which the course was being taught chose not to fund the continuation of the course. Therefore, the course the textbook was being developed for ceased to be taught. The authors will continue work on the textbook, but with no departmental support, any work they do on the book will be on their own time. Also, when completed, the textbook will not have a course at UW where it can be used, tested, revised, and enhanced.

Ensuring future success: request a statement of departmental support as part of the project proposal process.

Factor 2: Project Management

Project management is a key success factor in any open textbook project. One advantage of working with the Rebus Foundation has been the availability of Rebus staff to provide project management support. Once a textbook project is launched, Rebus staff will periodically check in with authors on their progress, particularly if a task has yet to be completed. In retrospect, it would also have been helpful to have an established timeline and benchmarks at the outset of the project. This would be particularly useful for projects for which content creation is part of the project. The Marlowe and Kioko textbook was successful despite the lack of an established project timeline, but the Ketchley and Thompson textbook was less successful and likely would have benefited from a more structured approach.

Ensuring future success: create a timeline and benchmarks during the project initiation phase. Check on progress periodically throughout the project.

Factor 3: Authorship Plan

Another way to increase success would be to establish clear expectations for authors at the outset of the project. In a Rebus Open Textbook project, authors can take on a variety of roles. For example, one project might have a lead author who creates an outline of their proposed textbook and coordinates co-authors to contribute content, while another project might have one or two primary authors who contribute all the content and only reach out to collaborators for peer review. Other models might require the authors to outsource other work such as graphic design or proof-reading, either through the Rebus Community or via other channels. By creating an authorship plan at the beginning of a project, one can ensure that authors understand what is expected of them and that the plan will fit within their own capacity to do the necessary work of the project within the established project timeline.

Ensuring future success: create an authorship plan during the project initiation phase.

Factor 4: Ready Content

Another factor that appeared to be a predictor of success in this iteration of the pilot was the existence of content that was already written and ready to load into Pressbooks. Marlowe and Koiko had at least half of the chapters written when they began their project, and all they needed was a publishing platform to make their open textbook concept a reality. For the Ketchley and Thompson project, very little content was already written and ready to input into Pressbooks when they began. This was certainly a factor in the more rapid completion of the Marlowe and Kioko project.

Ensuring future success: include a question on future application forms asking how much content has been written.

Factor 5: Platform Ease of Use

Pressbooks, the publishing platform being used by the Rebus Community, is so easy to use it almost became an "invisible" factor in the UW Open Textbook Publishing Pilot. The authors quickly adapted to Pressbooks, had very few questions about how to use it, and provided generally positive feedback on the platform. It is notable, however, that neither of these projects necessitated mathematical equations, embedded videos or interactive elements. Both projects were text-based: the Marlowe and Kioko project included graphs and images, while the Ketchley and Thompson project included hyperlinks that necessitated a plan for creating stable links to web content.

Ensuring future success: continue to use Rebus Pressbooks for text-based projects.

Factor 6: Network of Peers

Marlowe was easily able to identify peer reviewers for his open textbook and the Rebus project team was surprised by how many of his colleagues volunteered. If this had not been the case, the project could have stalled in the peer review phase. In embarking on future projects, it would be wise to identify a mechanism for finding peer reviewers at the outset of the project, if not the potential reviewers themselves.

Ensuring future success: add a question on future application forms asking how peer reviewers will be identified.

Factor 7: Incentive Grant

A goal of the Rebus Community is to support the entire publishing process, from writing and design to review and marketing of the open textbook. Therefore, any funding that is secured to support the open textbook project can be offered purely as an incentive to the author(s). Numerous grant-funded OER projects across the country have shown that even a relatively small grant can act as an incentive for faculty to engage in OER work, including open textbook creation. In our case, the Friends of the Libraries Grant of $1,500 per project was a successful incentive.

Ensuring future success: continue to offer incentive grants for open textbook projects.

Current and Future Directions

The UW Open Textbook Pilot entered a second phase in April 2018, after the pilot coordinators applied for and were awarded $10,000 from the UW Libraries Kenneth S. and Faye G. Allen Endowment to explore the role of open textbooks in library collections. A request for proposals to create or significantly adapt an open textbook went out to all faculty across the three UW campuses. Proposals will be reviewed in late April and award recipients will be notified in May. This second phase pilot will not require authors to participate in the Rebus Community, but will support participation if an appropriate project emerges.

At the same time, the Rebus Foundation is in the process of launching a new platform for the Rebus Community. The new platform is intended to "enable global open textbook creators to collaborate on open textbook projects" (Rebus Community, 2018). The launch is anticipated to occur in May of 2018, and individuals who are interested in continued developments are encouraged to explore the Rebus Community website and attend or view Rebus Office Hours. More information and opportunities to get involved in Rebus are available on the community website, https://about.rebus.community/.

Reflections on the UW Open Textbook Pilot Project

The UW Open Textbook Pilot Project scratched the surface of the exciting potential for the Rebus approach to textbook publishing to transform higher education. Imagine the future: an open textbook is created by a community of faculty who all teach similar classes across the world. The textbook creation project itself acts as a catalyst for faculty collaboration across institutions. The community of co-creators for each textbook is formed and stays connected through the Rebus Community. Open textbooks are hosted by institutional networks or library consortia that are connected into a larger Rebus Pressbooks network. Peer-reviewed, published editions are available for printing or download through multiple vendors and platforms. The publishing platform being developed by Rebus is free to use, so in order to make the Rebus staffing model sustainable, students might have to pay a small amount for access to a textbook (i.e. $10 to download; $35 to print). However, they will then have indefinite access to that edition, as well as free, open access to an online version. New models of teaching with textbooks emerge—faculty use open pedagogical practices to engage their students with the textbook, either adapting it to create new versions or iteratively updating the original textbook. In this way, student course output is used to further future student learning instead of going into disposable homework assignments. The textbook itself continues to evolve, drawing new content from the experts and learners who use it.

Academic librarians have an important role to play in this evolving open textbook ecosystem. In the current formative phase of the Rebus Community, librarians can be crucial catalysts and connectors. Advancement offices in academic libraries often have funds like the UW Friends of the Libraries Grant that can be leveraged to catalyze a new open textbook creation project. The support provided by Rebus staff removes much of the onus of project management from the librarian, making the project more feasible for a person who has many other competing responsibilities.

Librarians can also act as catalysts by providing general OER education and advocacy on their campuses, generating enthusiasm for and interest in OER among faculty and librarian colleagues. Also, liaison librarians are naturally connected to faculty in the subject areas they represent, so librarians are well positioned to reach out to potential project collaborators. Over time, open textbooks might gain a place in academic library collections that commercial textbooks traditionally have not had, given their disposable, multi-edition nature. What might it look like for an academic library to collect, or even publish, a textbook that is ever-evolving and openly available online? These questions and others will surface as more open textbooks are created and need to be curated, so academic librarians must continue to be engaged and involved in the open textbook movement as it progresses.

References

Allen, I. E., & Seaman, J. (2016). *Opening the textbook: Educational resources in U.S. higher education, 2015–16*. Babson Survey Research Group. Retrieved from https://www.onlinelearningsurvey.com/reports/openingthetextbook2016.pdf

Chae, B., & Jenkins, M. (2015). *A qualitative investigation of faculty open educational resource usage in the Washington community and technical college system: Models for support and implementation*. Retrieved from OpenWA Website: http://www.openwa.org/1483-2/

de los Arcos, B., Farrow, R., Pitt, R., Weller, M. & McAndrew, P. (2016). Adapting the curriculum: How K-12 teachers perceive the role of open educational resources. *Journal of Online Learning Research, 2*(1), 23–40.

DeRosa, R. (2016). My open textbook: Pedagogy and practice [Blog post]. Retrieved from http://umwdtlt.com/open-textbook-pedagogy-practice/

Doherty, J. (2016). *Biology 2e* [Review]. Open Textbook Library. Retrieved from https://open.umn.edu/opentextbooks/BookDetail.aspx?bookId=167

Friends of the Libraries. (n.d.). University of Washington libraries. Retrieved from http://www.lib.washington.edu/support/friends

Joyce, B. (2015). *Financial accounting* [Review]. Open Textbook Library. Retrieved from https://open.umn.edu/opentextbooks/BookDetail.aspx?bookId=4

Licensing. (n.d.). Rebus community. Retrieved from https://about.rebus.community/licensing/

Martin, M., Belikov, O., Hilton J., III, Wiley, D., & Fischer, L. (2017). Analysis of student and faculty perceptions of textbook costs in higher education. *Open Praxis, 9*(1), 79–91.

Objective LibriVox. (n.d.). Librivox. Retrieved from https://librivox.org/pages/about-librivox/

Rebus Community. (2018, May 16). Office hours launch: Rebus Community Projects. Retrieved from https://about.rebus.community/2018/03/ office-hours-launch-rebus-community-projects-may-16-12-p-m-pst-3-p-m-est/

Closing Reflections

Nicole Allen

It has been 10 years since a group of visionaries published the Cape Town Open Education Declaration, an international call to action that begins with the words, "We are on the cusp of a global revolution in teaching and learning."[1] The Declaration outlines a powerful vision of a world where everyone, everywhere, has access to a wealth of educational opportunities, and where teachers and learners work to shape knowledge together. Over the last decade, this vision has spread from a small group of innovators to a worldwide movement to make education better through open content and practices. In North American higher education, it is difficult to imagine what the movement would look like without the inspired, dedicated work of academic libraries.

Librarians as Leaders

Reflecting on this collection of case studies and my own decade-long experience as an open educational resources (OER) advocate, I'm struck by just how rapidly academic libraries have become a pillar in the open education movement. I first intersected with the library community in 2009, as a panelist at a SPARC (Scholarly Publishing and Academic Resources Coalition)/ACRL (Association of College and Research Libraries) forum on OER. I was leading a national student campaign at the time, and admittedly had not given any thought to the potential role libraries could play in open education. Based on the discussion at the forum, neither had most of the librarians in the room. While most seemed aware of the high cost

---

[1] For the full text of the Declaration, see:
http://www.capetowndeclaration.org/

of textbooks—students had been lining up at the reference desk seeking relief for years—textbooks were considered outside the domain of the library, and a tangent to open access in a research context.

This begun to change quickly. Seeds planted during these early discussions grew into some of the first prominent library-led OER initiatives, including those at Temple University and the University of Massachusetts Amherst, which were quickly replicated elsewhere (Allen, Bell, & Billings 2014). Concurrently, the explosion of interest in the idea of MOOCs (massive open online courses) and launch of e-textbook platforms by major publishers drew libraries—which had been navigating the issues surrounding digital content licensing for years—into institutional conversations about course materials in a significant way for the first time.

Library interest in OER seemed to hit an inflection point in 2014, when the Open Education Conference—the North American OER community's largest annual event—introduced a track focused on the role of libraries in advancing OER. Just a few short years later, academic libraries are now one of the primary forces driving the open education movement and lead some of the most vibrant, successful OER initiatives across North America. I often describe libraries as the "missing link" in that they have truly helped the rubber hit the road for open education on campus.

Building a Movement

As evidenced throughout this book, academic libraries interface with OER in myriad ways. As experts on finding and curating information resources, librarians help faculty and students locate high-quality OER that meet their needs. Academic technology and publishing divisions within the library provide support for publishing and adapting resources. Scholarly communication and copyright librarians help navigate open licensing and fair use. Repository specialists assist with archiving, version control, preservation, and delivery to students. Teaching and learning staff provide professional development support for faculty, including how to bring OER to life through open pedagogy.

Libraries also occupy a unique position at the crossroads of campus, and thus can serve as powerful conveners of campus-wide activities. They are the key point of intersection between academic departments and interface regularly with students, faculty, and staff alike. While the specific capacities and activities vary from institution to institution, academic libraries are increasingly the keystone to successful OER initiatives.

Multiple case studies presented in this book underscore the importance of cultivating allies among campus constituencies. Chief among them is faculty, where identifying champions and early adopters who can influence their peers is often the first critical step. OER grant programs in particular have proved an effective strategy for bringing in faculty, whether at a larger scale like the case of the University of Oklahoma or a smaller one as presented by Rollins College. Students too are essential allies as the ultimate beneficiaries of OER. Students can tell compelling personal stories that motivate faculty, as illustrated by the University of Texas San Antonio's use of student testimonials in OER workshops. Student leaders can also be influential partners in spreading the word and convincing decision-makers, as shown by the University of Saskatchewan's advocacy work. Other important stakeholders include the bookstore, academic technology, and disability services, each of which make vital contributions to a campus-wide movement.

Raising awareness of OER is another critical step. A number of chapters cite Allen and Seaman's 2016 finding that about a quarter of U.S. faculty are aware of OER. This tends to be presented from a glass half empty perspective—that most faculty remain unaware of OER—but it can also be viewed as a sign of considerable progress, given that the movement was built from the ground up and continues to grow. Yet, Geoffrey A. Moore's theory of the technology adoption life cycle reminds us that the most difficult part of scaling innovation is "crossing the chasm" between early adopters and the mainstream (Moore, 1999). The kinds of messages and incentives that brought in early adopters may not resonate with a broader audience the same way, so it is essential that OER efforts continue to adapt. Academic librarians can help make the case for OER to a mainstream audience by focusing on the important ends that OER achieves, whether that is better student outcomes, greater ownership over course content, or expanding access to knowledge.

Sustaining Progress

A common thread throughout this book is a sense of both having come a long way and also having a long way to go. Having achieved significant outcomes in terms of student savings and access to course materials, libraries are now grappling with next steps to sustain and scale these efforts long-term. Some challenges are more local, including access to funding and staff time, and some are more global, such as how to build—and govern—infrastructure to support collaboration, discovery, and sharing both within and across institutions.

Models for publishing and curating OER are a key area of focus as academic libraries look to the future. This book contains several examples of successful pilots, including the University of Washington's open textbook publishing program. While these efforts tend to be resource-intensive at first, there are potential efficiencies to be gained through cross-institutional collaboration, communities of practice, and support services. The Rebus Foundation and the community of practice discussed by Hare et al. take promising steps in this direction. OER creation ties into broader conversations around library publishing, institutional repositories, and changes to incentive structures to support open practices. Much can be learned from advances in the scholarly publishing space, although education publishing comes with its own unique set of challenges. For OER, important considerations for libraries will include accessibility, adaptation and version control, and the availability of ancillary materials.

Another frontier is how to institutionalize OER efforts on campus, starting within the library organization itself. Thus far, libraries have taken different pathways to incorporating open education into library staff responsibilities, whether it is adding it to the scope of scholarly communications, appointing an open education coordinator, or building open education into the duties of liaison and reference staff. There is also the question of what kind of training and professional development is needed to build this capacity. SPARC's own contribution to this space is our newly launched Open Education Leadership Program,[2] which recognizes that a large part of open education librarianship is becoming an advocate and convener. Many of the core skills and capacities needed to support open education already exist within the library and elsewhere on campus, and the key is establishing the library as a

---

[2] For more information see: https://sparcopen.org/our-work/open-education-leadership-program/

locus of expertise that can connect and guide the various pieces into a greater whole.

Evolving into the Future

Ten years ago the drafters of the Cape Town Declaration expressed a feeling of being on the cusp of radical change. Looking back, the process has been less of a *revolution* and more of an *evolution*—small experiments growing into larger ones that build on learning and best practices toward a more open future. To that end, we must remember that open is a process, not an endpoint. Openness is not an end in itself but rather a means to improve teaching and learning practices, to instill the values of inclusivity and access, and to achieve broader societal benefits that flow from advanced technology and an improved educational system. Libraries are well positioned to be the engine for this change within education and research institutions, moving toward systems that are open by default.

References

Allen, E. I., & Seaman J. (2016). Opening the textbook: Open education resources in U.S. higher education, 2015–16. Babson Survey Research Group. Retrieved from https://www.onlinelearningsurvey.com/reports/openingthetextbook2016.pdf

Allen, N., Bell, S., & Billings, M. (2014). Spreading the word, building a community: Vision for a national OER movement. *Against the Grain.* Available at: http://works.bepress.com/marilyn_billings/61/

Moore, G. A. (1999). *Crossing the chasm: Marketing and selling high-tech products to mainstream customers.* New York, NY: Harper.

About the Authors

Christy Allen is the Assistant Director for Discovery Services at Furman University in Greenville, South Carolina. Her career has focused on digital librarianship with an emphasis on digital collections and website design. Christy and Andrea Wright, Furman's Science and Outreach Librarian, cooperatively lead Furman's scholarly communications program including support for open educational resources (OER).

Nicole Allen is Director of Open Education for SPARC (the Scholarly Publishing and Academic Resources Coalition), an international alliance of academic and research libraries working to make open the default in research and education. Nicole is an internationally recognized advocate and thought leader in the Open Education movement, who has worked tirelessly to expand access and affordability of education in the digital age since her own days as a college student. Over the last decade, Nicole has given hundreds of talks and trainings in more than a dozen countries on Open Education, education policy, and grassroots organizing. Based in Washington, D.C., Nicole's portfolio at SPARC includes a robust state and federal policy program, a broad librarian community of practice, and a leadership program for OER librarians. Learn more at www.sparcopen.org.

Jean Amaral (MLIS, MA), an assistant professor and open knowledge librarian at Borough of Manhattan Community College, partners with faculty across disciplines to create active and engaging learning experiences for students. Her focus in the classroom is on student-centered teaching and authentic assessment. Amaral also works with faculty developing research projects in the scholarship of teaching and learning. She is currently engaged in several studies, including ones that address student and faculty information needs and seeking, use of OER, future libraries, student technology use, and servant leadership.

Dr. Alesha Baker is an Assistant Professor in the Educational Leadership department at Northeastern State University where she has worked in the Library Media and Information Technology program for the past two years. Alesha has written and presented on topics such as teacher professional development, but her main area of interest is OER. She has written and presented on using OER in both secondary and PK–12 environments examining both teacher and student perceptions and outcomes.

Chelle Batchelor is the Director of Access Services at the University of Washington Libraries. She has been involved in many activities related to OER over the past several years, including co-chairing the UW Libraries OER Steering Committee, attending the Open Textbook Network Summer Institute, securing grant funding for two Rebus Community open textbook projects, and co-leading the effort to create the Pacific Northwest OER Directory. Chelle is particularly interested in supporting faculty who want to create or adapt new open textbooks, and is excited about the potential of OER to change the landscape of higher education.

Sarah Beaubien is the Head of Collections & Scholarly Communications in the Grand Valley State University Libraries. She holds a Master of Library Science from Indiana University. She provides leadership and strategic oversight for the GVSU Libraries' collections and scholarly communications programs.

Geneen E. Clinkscales serves as the Systems Librarian at Johnson C. Smith University. She holds a Bachelor of Science in Computer Information Systems from Hampton University and a Master of Library Science from Wayne State University. Prior to this position, she served as a Media Specialist for Charlotte Mecklenburg Schools. In her role, she facilitates students' discovery of information, stimulates inquiry, and provides support for integration of information sources toward the development of critical perspectives. Her goal with OER is to increase academic freedom for faculty and improve student success while saving students money.

William Cross is the Director of the Copyright & Digital Scholarship Center at NC State University where he provides guidance and support for author rights, fair use, managing scholarly identity, and open pedagogy. Will's research focuses on ways that library expertise can be used to drive change in the scholarly communication life cycle. He currently serves as co-Principal Investigator on two Institute of Museum and Library Services planning grants focused on developing OER for teaching scholarly communication and on the development of an "Open Textbook Toolkit" that leverages library publishing services to support open pedagogy.

Rebel Cummings-Sauls is the director for the Center for the Advancement of Digital Scholarship at Kansas State University. She holds a Master of Library Information Science from Florida State University. She leads the center's initiatives that maximize the creation, dissemination, preservation, and impact of digital scholarship produced at the university.

Kirsten N. Dean is a librarian at Clemson University, where she teaches information literacy and advocates for open education. She holds a degree in writing studies from the University of Illinois and is currently working on her Master of Library Information Science at the University of Alabama. Kirsten is particularly interested in exploring questions related to disciplinarity, transfer, and the library's role in teaching and learning.

Carolyn Ellis, assistant dean for organizational effectiveness and strategy, oversees the University of Texas at San Antonio Libraries' project portfolio, strategic planning life cycle, and the direction of the web, communications, and user experience areas. She has over 15 years of experience in user-centered design, project management, change communications, and process improvement while working in libraries, information technology, and economic development organizations. Carolyn holds a Master of Library Science from the University of Texas at Austin, and a Bachelor of Arts from Trinity University.

David Francis is Dean of the School of Professional and Continuing Education at Fleming College in Peterborough, Ontario. This school is responsible for providing flexible delivery options for post-secondary programs, customized training for industry, and online programs. David holds a doctorate in Educational Administration from the University of Saskatchewan, and focuses his research on areas of efficiency and effectiveness in higher education

Emily Frank is the Coordinator of Scholarship and Open Access for Louisiana State University Libraries. She leads the library's affordable course materials projects, including an e-textbook initiative focused on aligning licensed ebooks with courses and the OER program. She coordinates local projects under the Affordable Learning LOUISiana initiative spearheaded by LOUIS, the statewide library consortium.

Teri Gallaway, Associate Commissioner of LOUIS, serves in the capacity of Executive Director for the statewide consortium as well as the project lead for the Affordable Learning LOUISiana initiative. She is currently pursuing a PhD in Higher Education Administration from Louisiana State University and her research explores the opportunities and outcomes of OER programs and their institutional impacts.

Arthur G. Green teaches geospatial science and environmental geography as a faculty member at Okanagan College in British Columbia, Canada. He is also an Affiliate Assistant Professor at the University of British Columbia and a former BCcampus Open Education Faculty Fellow and Hewlett Foundation Open Education Research Fellow. His research on property rights issues in Central Africa, Southeast Asia, and North America has been featured in several international conferences including the United Nations Conference on Sustainable Development (Rio+20). His current research program examines textbook costs, develops open education practices for geography, and creates virtual reality OERs for environmental education.

Sarah Hare (formerly Crissinger) is currently the Scholarly Communication Librarian at Indiana University, where she works on several open and library publishing initiatives. Sarah's research focuses on scholarly communication outreach to undergraduate students and OER. Prior to joining IU Libraries in 2017, Sarah served as Information Literacy Librarian at Davidson College, where she created open access programming and led two OER initiatives.

John Hilton III is an Associate Professor at Brigham Young University. He is the author or co-author of over 60 peer-reviewed publications. He has a variety of research interests including the processes of learning and teaching and the effect of OER. He has published in several journals including *Educational Researcher, Educational Policy Analysis Archives, Educa-*

tional Technology Research and Development, and *The International Review of Research in Open and Distributed Learning.* John and his wife Lani have six children; his favorite hobby is learning Chinese.

Cinthya Ippoliti is the Associate Dean for Research and Learning Services at Oklahoma State University where she has administrative leadership for graduate and undergraduate library services, reference and information services, liaison efforts with teaching and research faculty, and assessment of library services. Previously, she was Head of Teaching and Learning Services at the University of Maryland where she was in charge of the spaces, services, and programming offered by the Terrapin Learning Commons in addition to coordinating the libraries' first-year instruction program. Cinthya has written and presented on topics such as digital badges, assessing emerging technologies both in and out of the classroom, and developing technology partnerships.

DeeAnn Ivie, Open Education Coordinator, leads the Adopt a Free Textbook grant program and facilitates outreach to partners in support of the initiative. DeeAnn also provides research and teaching support for social sciences faculty, and tailors library sessions and tutorials for classes, integrating active learning, group work, and flipped instruction. DeeAnn earned her Master of Science in Library and Information Science from the University of North Texas.

Dr. Rajiv S. Jhangiani is a Special Advisor to the Provost on Open Education and a Psychology Instructor at Kwantlen Polytechnic University in Vancouver, Canada, where he conducts research in open education and the scholarship of teaching and learning. He also serves as an Associate Editor of Psychology Learning and Teaching and an Ambassador for the Center for Open Science. His most recent book is *Open: The Philosophy and Practices that are Revolutionizing Education and Science* (Ubiquity Press, 2017, CC-BY). You can find him online at @thatpsychprof or thatpsychprof.com.

Michael LaMagna is an Associate Professor, Reference Librarian serving as library liaison to the science, technology, engineering, and mathematics division, and Information Literacy Program and Library Services Coordinator at Delaware County Community College. Michael serves as the chair of the Alt Text Committee with the charge of integrating OER content into courses across the college. His research interests include OER adoption, digital badges, and synchronous online instruction. Michael received his EdD in Higher Education Administration from Northeastern University, Master of Library Science from St. John's University, Master of Arts in History from Villanova University, and Bachelor of Arts in History from Susquehanna University.

Anne Langley is the Dean, University of Connecticut Library. Throughout her career she has held a variety of library positions at Penn State University, Princeton, Duke, NC State University, and the University of Tennessee, Knoxville. She holds a master's degree in library science from the University of Tennessee and a bachelor's degree in creative writing from Georgia State University. She has worked on a variety of open access and scholarly communication projects, including serving in leadership roles for the Coalition of Open Access Policy Institutions and is an avid supporter of all things open.

Jonathan Lashley serves as Senior Instructional Technologist at Boise State University, where he also teaches for the first-year writing program. He is a PhD candidate in Learning Sciences at Clemson University and his dissertation research focuses on the role that instructor values and training play in decisions about open textbook adoption. Named one of the first OER Research Fellows for the Open Education Group, Jonathan was recently awarded a Designing with OER Fellowship for his work as an instructional designer.

Shannon Lucky is a faculty assistant librarian in the Library Systems and Information Technology unit of the University of Saskatchewan Library. Her research focuses on how open and usable technology can support the information practices of people and communities. She holds a master's degree in library and information studies and a master's degree in digital humanities from the University of Alberta.

Jonathan Miller was Library Director at Rollins College in Winter Park, Florida, from 2006 until 2017. He became Director of Libraries at Williams College in 2017. He received his Bachelor of Arts from Sheffield University (UK), his Master of Library Sciences from State University of New York, Buffalo, in 1992 and his PhD from the University of Pittsburgh in 2009. His dissertation concerned the role of the Association of Research

Libraries (ARL) in the development of the 1976 Copyright Act. More information can be found at https://library.williams.edu/profile/jm30/.

Carla Myers serves as Assistant Professor and Coordinator of Scholarly Communications for the Miami University Libraries. Her professional presentations and publications focus on fair use, copyright in the classroom, and library copyright issues.

Julie Reed is currently an E-Learning Librarian at Central Piedmont Community College (CPCC) in Charlotte, NC. Previously, she was the Instructional Electronic Resources Librarian at Johnson C. Smith University (JCSU). Prior to JCSU, she was a news researcher with the Associated Press for over 10 years and public librarian with the Brooklyn Public Library. Her current research interests focus on OER and how to make the college experience more affordable and approachable for first-generation and adult learners as well as traditional students.

Michelle Reed is an Associate Librarian at the University of Texas at Arlington (UTA) Libraries. As Open Education Librarian, she leads efforts to support the adoption, adaptation, and creation of OER and advocates for experiential learning opportunities that foster collaboration, increase engagement, and empower students as content creators. She is a presenter for the Open Textbook Network, a recipient of the American Library Association's Carroll Preston Baber Research Grant, and an OER Research Fellow with the Open Education Group. Her research interests include librarianship at the intersections of information literacy and scholarly communication, the impact of OER, and undergraduate perceptions of open principles.

Lillian Rigling is the Program Coordinator at eCampus Ontario, a not-for-profit organization supporting equitable access to technology-enabled learning at 45 colleges and universities in Ontario. Lillian has a background in Scholarly Communications librarianship and holds a Master of Information from the University of Toronto. She writes and teaches about developing and sustaining open education work within unique organizational contexts.

Heather M. Ross is an educational developer at the University of Saskatchewan where she is a leader in advancing and supporting the integration of OER and open pedagogy across the institution. Her research interests include student and instructor views on the benefits and barriers to the use, adaptation, and creation of OER, and the integration of open pedagogy. She is an emeritus OER Research Fellow with the Open Education Group.

Matthew Ruen is the Scholarly Communications Outreach Coordinator in the Grand Valley State University (GVSU) Libraries. He holds a Master of Library and Information Studies and a Master of Archival Studies from the University of British Columbia. He is the GVSU Libraries' copyright and fair use specialist, institutional repository administrator, and subject matter expert on open access, OER, and other issues in scholarly communications.

Jeremy Smith is the Digital Projects Manager in Scholarly Communication and the Communication Department Liaison at the University of Massachusetts Amherst Libraries. His previous position was as the manager of a grant-funded project to digitize the W.E.B. Du Bois manuscript collection, housed in the UMass Library Special Collections and University Archives. Prior to acquiring his Master in Library Science in 2009, he was a staff producer and editor for the Media Education Foundation, a Northampton, MA-based nonprofit video production company founded by UMass Communication Professor Sut Jhally.

Cody Taylor works as the Open Education Coordinator for the University of Oklahoma Libraries where he manages the Libraries Alternative Textbook Grant and advocates for and supports the use of open educational resources. His interests are especially focused on addressing the technical hurdles of working with OER. Cody formerly worked as one of the Libraries Emerging Tech Librarians where he focused on makerspaces, electrical engineering, and programming.

Ciara Turner is a graduate of the University of Texas at Arlington, where she studied English and Disability Studies. She led the open textbook accessibility evaluation project during her internship with UTA Libraries in Spring 2017. Ciara currently teaches English at a high school in Houston, Texas. This is her first publication.

Jen Waller works as the University of Oklahoma Libraries' Director of Open Initiatives and Scholarly Communication. In this role she oversees the Libraries' OER initiatives, including the Alternative Textbook

Grant, and she coordinates the Libraries' scholarly communication products, programs, and services, including the institutional repository, journal publishing, and new forms of information dissemination and scholarly publishing. Prior to her career as a librarian she worked in the corporate world as a marketing communications manager, a project manager, and a professional chef. When not in the library, you may find Jen remodeling her home, cooking Thai food, or hiking with her dog, Travis.

Anita Walz is the Open Education, Copyright, and Scholarly Communication Librarian at Virginia Tech. She holds a Master of Library and Information Science from the University of Illinois at Champaign-Urbana, and an undergraduate degree in economics from Wheaton College. Her work experience includes over 15 years in international, government, and academic libraries. She has managed development of several open textbooks, designed and administers an open education grants program for faculty at her institution, and frequently teaches and moderates discussions on open licensing, Creative Commons, OER, and open educational practices. She serves in state and national advisory groups regarding open educational practices, is a frequent conference presenter, has been featured as a speaker on SPARC, ACRL (the Association of College and Research Libraries) and Rebus webinars, and is the author of both practical and academic publications including curated event recordings, an open textbook adaptation guide, an ARL SPEC Kit, guest blog posts, conference and journal articles, and book chapters. She served as a Fulbright Specialist on OER in Kyrgyzstan in April 2017.

Andrew Wesolek currently serves as the Director of Digital Scholarship and Scholarly Communications at Vanderbilt University. Previously, he served as Clemson University's first Head of Digital Scholarship. In this role he launched and developed a robust institutional repository, served as the copyright officer for the library, partnered with Clemson University Press to publish several open access journals, oversaw the digitization of cultural heritage items from the Upstate of South Carolina, and managed several Open Education initiatives on campus. His research and professional interests focus on library support for new forms of scholarship, with an emphasis on open initiatives and infrastructure. Wesolek also serves a founding co-editor of the *Journal of Copyright in Education and Librarianship*. His previous co-edited book, *Making Institutional Repositories Work* was published in 2015.

Andrea Wright brings her enthusiasm for library services and dedication to campus communities to the University of Southern Indiana as the Assistant Director and Head of Public Services for the Library. Her work revolves around increasing effective student and faculty engagement with information via instruction and support throughout the scholarly communication ecosystem. Previously, Andrea served as Science Outreach Librarian and University Copyright Officer at Furman University, where she cooperatively lead the scholarly communications program including support for open educational resources with Christy Allen, Furman's Assistant Directory for Discovery Services.

Brady Yano was the Assistant Director of Open Education at SPARC. In this role he supported SPARC's Open Education program through leading special projects like Connect OER, contributing to the OER Digest, and supporting the OpenCon conference and community.

Stacy Zemke works at the TEL Library as Chief Technology Officer, where she supports the development of open educational content for the college general education curriculum. She has previously worked as an OER Coordinator, instructional designer, and instructor in library and information studies. Outside of work, she wrangles her cat and would rather just be on the beach with her husband or watching the Giro d'Italia.

Index

3D printing 133, 203, 204
5 Rs 2–3, 64, 96, 143, 363
  and copyright 345
  failure to meet 35, 336
  restrictions on 21

AAUP Statement of Principles on Academic Freedom and Tenure 171
academic freedom 122, 171, 262
academic librarians *see* librarians
access 73, 383, 437
  and open pedagogy 395
  to education 433
  to textbooks 19, 21, 194
access codes 20, 62, 130, 197
accessibility 96, 108
  accessibility best practices 422
  accessibility considerations 34
  accessibility problems 97, 105–109
  accessibility standards 96, 98, 105–108
accessible design 34, 93; *see also* universal design
  resources 97
accounting 119, 337, 416
Achieving the Dream 24, 35, 59, 62, 214
ACRL (Association of College & Research Libraries) 185, 241, 333, 433
  Assessment in Action project 77
  Intersections paper 73; *see also Intersections of Scholarly Communication and Information Literacy*
activism 175, 340
adaptation 156, 337, 367, 395, 416

adaptive learning 67
administrators 25, 32, 54, 60
  and students 175, 177, 340
  partnerships with 180
  and OER 83, 155, 340
adoption 32, 67, 173, 219–222, 337, 366
  encouraging 217, 313, 384, 394
  motivation 388
  rate of 240
advocacy 188, 275, 303, 393
  advocates 125
  and OER movement 28
  by students 25, 175, 196, 261
  through professional development 280, 284
advocacy training 206
affordability 176, 336
  education 166, 351
  initiatives 245, 349
  textbooks 25, 52, 55, 299
Affordable College Textbook Act 22
Affordable Learning Georgia 215, 294, 347
affordable learning solutions (ALS) 352
ALL (Affordable Learning LOUISiana) 291, 296, 302
Allen, Christy 309, 439
Allen, Nicole 433, 439
allies 187, 255, 435
  bookstores as 182
  collaboration with 169
  department heads as 174
  faculty as 170

faculty support offices as 179
Alt Text Committee 281, 282
Alternate Textbook Project *see* text readability analysis: textbooks: Textbook Affordability Program
Alternative Textbook Grant 351, 357–360, 360
  development 351–355
  establishment 356
  formalization 366–373
Alt-Textbook 194–195, 207, 312
Amaral, Jean 51, 439
Amazon 182, 183, 278, 282, 401; *see also* Kindle
American Library Association (ALA) 28
ancillary materials 67, 221, 223, 395, 416
assistive technology 99, 100, 104, 105
authors 123, 135, 421, 426
automatic purchasing programs 20, 22
awareness 256, 353
  and advocacy 154
  awareness-raising activities 28, 55, 253
  low levels of 29, 81, 261, 324, 435
  maintaining 58
  of accessibility problems 97
  role of libraries 276
  through grants 404

Baker, Alesha 239, 440
barriers to adoption or use 19, 32, 109, 219–222, 384
Batchelor, Chelle 415, 440
BCcampus 27, 156, 347, 390, 391
  BCcampus Open Education Accessibility Toolkit 97
  OER evaluation rubric 322
  open textbook directory 391
  success of collections 29, 86
  Zed Cred 35
Beaubien, Sarah 165, 440
best practice 96–98, 280
Bill and Melinda Gates Foundation 24, 67, 293
blogs 127, 318, 348, 355, 389
BMCC (Borough of Manhattan Community College) 439

BMCC faculty 54
BMCC Learning Academy 58
BMCC library 55, 57
Board of Regents 301, 303, 305
  and LOUIS 291, 295
  consortium creation 293
Boise State University 444
bookstores 181–184, 401
  ancillary materials 221
  and libraries 193, 245, 298
  and students 208
  relationship with 133, 224
Boston Library Consortium 300
Brigham Young University 145, 442
Bronx Community College 59
budgets 334, 345
  and grants 344
  state budget cuts 295
  library budgets 55, 167
bundling of learning resources 20, 55; *see also* Amazon: ancillary materials

California Digital Library eScholarship Program 81
California State University 26, 220, 347
campus culture 132, 178, 266
Canada OER Group 392
Canadian Association of Research Libraries (CARL) 381
Cape Town Open Education Declaration 433
Center for Open Education 294, 341
Central Piedmont Community College 445
CETLS (Center for Excellence in Teaching, Learning and Scholarship) 56, 57
challenges 60, 415
change 1, 74, 87
  cultural 264, 265, 266, 268
change to 163, 383
classroom 86, 141, 241, 402
Clemson University 254–258, 441; *see also* courses: course material evaluation: CUSG (Clemson Undergraduate Student Government)
  timeline of OER adoption process

258–260
clickers 127, 128, 130, 133, 197
Clinkscales, Geneen E. 309, 440
collaboration 336
  between departments 4, 63
  collaborative planning 84
  inter-institutional 86, 142, 310, 429
  with bookstores 184
  with libraries 74, 88, 194, 276
College Textbook Affordability Act of
  2015 292
Committee on Higher Education 53
committees 202, 250, 267
  CAS Professional Development Com-
    mittee 277
  course material selection 122, 222
  CUNY Textbook Savings Committee 53
  LLA Legislative Committee 303
  New York City Council Committee on
    Higher Education 53
  OSU Textbook Affordability Committee
    245
  OU OER Action Committee 373
  OU OER Strategic Initiative Planning
    Committee 352, 356
  UW Open Educational Resources Steer-
    ing Committee 418
Common Ground at the Nexus of Infor-
  mation Literacy and Scholarly
  Communication 74
communication 166, 222–224, 265–266,
  337
community 152–154, 328, 429; see also Re-
  bus Community
  librarians 142, 302
  campus community 225
  developing 262
  users 424
Community College Consortium for
  Open Educational Resources (CC-
  COER) 65, 185
community college 17, 35, 52, 59, 185
Connecticut 293
Connexions see OpenStax
consortium 147, 294, 298, 303
  LOUIS 295

Connecticut open textbook consortium
  293
  Open Textbook Network 313
content 131, 360
  faculty produced 282
  of OER 42, 427
  student produced 2
copyright 326
  faculty knowledge of 81, 345
  librarian knowledge of 51, 73
  workshops on 64, 204, 336, 337
cost increase (textbooks) 215
COUP (costs, outcomes, usage, and perception) 227, 229, 342
courses 63, 67, 348
  course materials 115, 118, 130, 261, 400
    cost of course materials 120
    Handbook for Evaluating and Selecting
      Curriculum Materials 123
    incentives 128–131
    novel 133–136
    role in courses 125–128
    selection 121–123
    valued for 119–121
  course material evaluation 116, 121–123,
    132, 137
  creation 337, 360–365, 367, 419, 429
    co-creation 144, 243
    funding of 33, 374
    library support of 349, 353
  Creative Commons (CC) 3, 389, 420
    and William and Flora Hewlett
      Foundation 24
    Creative Commons licensing 42, 60,
      96, 136, 319, 394
    certification program 36
    Noba Student Video Award projects
      148
    student familiarity with 201, 210
    training in 354
  Crissinger, Sarah see Hare, Sarah
  Cross, William 193, 440
  Cummings-Sauls, Rebel 165, 441
  CUNY (City University of New York)
    36, 51, 53–56
  CUNY Office of Library Services 54,

57, 59, 67
curriculum design 115, 118
CUSG (Clemson Undergraduate Student Government) 257, 258, 260, 267

Data & GIS Librarian 150
data sources 149, 183
database subscription 159
Davidson College 309, 310, 318, 326
Dean, Kirsten N. 253, 441
Delaware County Community College 276, 443
department heads 173–175, 222
Department of Education 179, 186
digital divide 33, 126
Digital 20–21
digital learning environments 127
digital literacy 387
Digital Orange Grove 405
Directory of Open Access Journals (DOAJ) 388
disability 34, 108
disability studies 110
discoverability 155, 224, 355, 383
Duke Endowment 309, 317; see also TDEL (the Duke Endowment Libraries)
Duke University 309, 310, 317, 318, 327

ebooks 127, 418
accessibility 99, 108
library use of 66, 297, 336
purchasing 297, 298
student use of 409
eCampus Ontario 27, 445
economics 122, 245, 390, 392
economics of information 76; see also information literacy
Ellis, Carolyn 213, 441
engagement with students and faculty 195, 196, 208, 326–327
enrollment 32, 405
high-enrollment courses 223, 242, 249, 268
Environmental Science Bites 146
environmental science 147

e-portfolios 43, 44
evaluation 98–105, 115, 125
experiential learning 93, 109
expertise 187, 298
importance of 137, 312, 386
in copyright 87
in scholarly communication 167
of librarians 84, 148, 150, 153, 156, 284
of faculty 172
educational technology 126, 128, 134–135, 402

Facebook 64, 197, 371, 389
faculty 63–65, 169–172, 316–317, 319, 326–327
and librarians 434
and students 208
professional development (faculty) 280, 283, 300
course material selectors (faculty 55, 338
OER review program (faculty) 313
perception of OER 29, 415
reliance on commercial textbooks 345
outreach activities (faculty) 354, 357, 371
use of technology 402
faculty support offices 178–180
fair use 64, 345
Family Educational Rights and Privacy Act of 1974 177
financial support 24, 33, 86, 310, 356, 418
first-generation students 193, 213
Flat World Knowledge 334
Fleming College 441
flexibility 329, 356, 406
Flexible Learning for Open Education (Floe) 98
flipping (classroom) 127
Follet (bookstore) 183, 221
Framework for Information Literacy for Higher Education 75, 85, 241; see also Intersections of Scholarly Communication and Information Literacy
Francis, David 381, 441
Frank, Emily 291, 442
funding 57, 310, 314; see also grants
community contributions 282

cuts to 305
funding model 68, 304
funding structure 347
government funding 391
grant funding 174, 426
increases in 188
internal funding 195, 345
state funding 61, 293, 296
sustainability of 303
Furman University 439, 448
and OER 311, 326
OER faculty review program 318

Gallaway, Teri 291, 442
Geographic Information Science 149
Georgia State University 214
GitHub 195, 210
Google Docs 314
Google Form 315, 370, 389
government initiatives 22, 292–295, 389
grants 25, 217–219, 344; *see also* Alternative Textbook Grant, text readability analysis: textbooks: Textbook Transformation Grants
Department of Education grants 179
LCTCS eLearning grant fund 304
micro-retention grants 214
OER grant program (Rollins College) 402–406
OER support grants 215, 282, 292
OU Alternative Textbook Grant 371–373
student grants 207, 226
UW Friends of the Libraries grant program 420
grassroots action 266, 381
preferred over administrative action 253, 256, 262
SGA partnership 176
Green, Arthur G. 141, 442
GVSU (Grand Valley State University) 166, 440, 446
campus bookstore 182, 183
library publishing program 169
OER adoption 172, 187
OER promotion 174

OpenStax adoption 171
student government association 176

Hare, Sarah 309, 442
Harvard University 42
higher education 126, 176, 295, 429
expense of 17, 84, 217, 273
rising cost of 1, 256
Higher Education Opportunity Act 2008 209
Hilton, John III 22, 41, 342, 442
homework 67, 117, 130, 264, 429
Hostos Community College 59

incentive programs 167, 175, 428
incentives 54, 200, 266, 404
inclusive access 20, 209
Indiana University 442
information literacy 73, 74–77, 78, 84–85, 88
educating students in 147, 255
infrastructure 297, 302, 304, 436; *see also* repositories
communications infrastructure 296
course design infrastructure 339
digital infrastructure 385
physical infrastructure 148, 156
innovation 88, 346, 435
in-service 277, 280–281
Institute for Museum and Library Services (IMLS) 168
institutional repositories *see* repositories
instructional design 117, 132
instructor expertise 117, 125–128, 132
instructors 55, 125, 333
course material selection 19, 115, 172
perceptions of OER 30
intellectual property 82, 326, 409, 412; *see also* copyright
interactive 123, 133, 293, 420
interinstitutional collaboration 309, 311, 328
common documentation 314–315
customization 318–319
participant requirements 316–318
review board 315

Intersections of Scholarly Communication and Information Literacy 73, 76; *see also Framework for Information Literacy for Higher Education*
investment 57, 188, 303, 304, 341, 385
Ippoliti, Cinthya 239, 443
ISKME (Institute for the Study of Knowledge Management in Education) 24, 26
Ivie, DeeAnn 213, 443

Jhangiani, Rajiv S. 141, 443
Johnson C. Smith University 311, 319, 326, 440

Kenneth S. and Faye G. Allen Endowment 428
Kindle 280, 282
K-State (Kansas State University) 166, 187, 352, 441
  accessibility 169
  OER adoption 171, 172, 173, 181
  student government association 175
Kwantlen Polytechnic University 443

LaMagna, Michael 273, 443
Langley, Anne 1, 444
Lashley, Jonathan 1, 444
LaTeX 362
Laura and John Arnold Foundation 24
leadership 163, 211, 276, 382–387, 393
learner-centered teaching 150
learning 248, 384, 411
  learning experience 82, 240
  learning opportunities 78, 80, 82
  learning outcomes 22, 42, 46, 77, 131
  learning processes 240, 241
legislation 23, 86, 292–295, 292
liberal arts colleges 399, 411
liberal arts 59, 326
LibGuides 223, 319, 370
  course-specific 154
  OER discoverability 155, 258, 280, 355
  training in 64
librarians 37, 69, 343, 429
  and Creative Commons certification 36
  and discovery 4

  and faculty 412, 434
  as advocates 154, 274, 382
  as OER champions 28
  consultation 316, 318, 327
  information access 12, 331
  open pedagogy 141
  specialist 87, 359
librarians as teachers 77–80
  teaching support 217
    Library Publishing Coalition 185
    Library Services and Technology Act 282
    LibreText 327
    LibriVox 418
    licensing 3, 51, 297
    listservs 65, 257, 296, 318
    LOUIS 291, 295–299, 300–302, 442
    Louisiana Community and Technical College System (LCTCS) 304
    Louisiana State University 295, 297, 442
    Lower, Brian 146
    Loyola University 297
    Lucky, Shannon 381, 444
    Lumen Courses 221
    Lumen Learning 27, 67, 186, 349
      partnership with Follett 36, 183

Maricopa Community Colleges 264
Markdown 364–365, 374
Meinke 85, 156
MERLOT (Multimedia Educational Resource for Learning and Online Teaching) 65, 220, 294, 339, 405
  MERLOT conference 351
  size of 26
  training in 312
Miami University 445
Miller, Jonathan 399, 444
Minnesota Open Textbook Library 42
minority student populations 215
MIT (Massachusetts Institute of Technology) 24, 167, 336
MOOCs (massive open online courses) 327, 354, 434
Moore, Geoffrey A. 435

motivation *see also* incentives
  faculty 158, 262, 263
  learners 240
  partnerships 166, 187
Myers, Carla 17, 445

National Endowment for the Humanities
  (NEH) 168
National Institutes of Health 334
natural resource policy and administration
  337
NCSU Libraries 193, 195, 207
NCSU (North Carolina State University)
  193, 440
New York City College of Technology 45
New York Public Interest Research Group
  54
niche publishing 171
Noba Project 148, 355
no-cost materials 54, 56
Northeastern State University 440
Northern Virginia Community College 44

OEI (Open Education Initiative) 333
  assessment 341–343
  background 333–335
  challenges 343–345
  implementation 335–339
  partnerships 339–341
  sustainability 345–349
OER champions 66, 136, 176, 340
OER Commons 26, 312, 354, 385, 405
OER community 37, 53–58, 57, 110,
  184–186
OER Coordinator (University of Oklahoma) 351, 353, 357, 361, 365
OER Degree Initiative 24, 35, 59, 61, 66
OER Faculty Review Program 313, 315,
  319
OER fellowship programs 26
OER Grant Program (Rollins College)
  402–406
OER librarian positions 29, 168, 344
OER (open educational resources) 2
  definition 2–3
OER repositories 26, 220, 339, 354, 393

Pressbooks as repository 156
OER Resource Specialist 293
OER review 311, 340, 416, 417
OER State Policy Tracker 87, 292
Ohio State University 42
Okanagan College 442
open access 167, 388, 401, 434
open access publications 310, 383, 388,
  411
Open Access Week 198–201, 244, 245,
  258
Open Course Library 293
open culture 53, 58, 198, 205
open education 82–88, 117, 118, 415, 439
  and information literacy 74, 77
  practices 131
  promotion of 253
Open Education Conference 185, 258, 434
Open Education Leadership Program 436
Open Education Librarian 95
Open Education Week 205, 259, 355
Open Education Working Group
  (OEWG) 152
Open Educational Resources and Scholarly Communication Coordinator 365
open knowledge librarian 57
open license 33, 137, 145, 149
  awareness of 425
  training in 146, 206
Open Oregon 347
open pedagogy 241, 243–246, 391, 395,
  434; *see also* pedagogy
  adoption of 423
  definition 87, 142–144
  examples 144–152
  open pedagogy grants 208
  origins of 30
  within institutions 152–158
open science 149
open source 201, 202, 411, 418
open textbook evaluation 93, 153, 283,
  322
Open Textbook Library 27, 322, 339, 354,
  391
  Center for Open Education 294, 341
  OER discoverability 301

reviews 95, 184, 340
rubric used 119
Open Textbook Network 24, 300–302,
    341, 352, 385
Center for Open Education 294
partnerships with 346, 358, 415
membership 95, 225, 259, 400
success of 313
support for OER 37, 184, 417
workshops 171, 267, 312, 340
Open Textbook Project (BCcampus) 27
Open Textbook Project (eCampus On-
    tario) 27
Open Textbook Publishing Pilot 415, 417,
    419–429, 436
open textbooks 358, 390–393, 428
accessibility of 96
adoption of 381, 417
awareness of 29
faculty creation of 346, 415
publishing 383
Open Washington 185
Open/Alternative Textbook Initiative (K-
    State) 170, 174, 181
Open/Alternative Textbook Program
    (BMCC) 51, 55, 58–60, 62, 66, 68
Open courseware 167, 336
OpenStax 171, 185, 218, 347, 354
adoption of OpenStax textbooks 183,
    340, 390
quality of OpenStax textbooks 44, 45
founder of 333
partnership with 219, 225, 358
print textbooks 182, 245
success of 27, 29
workshops on 312
OpenStax Tutor Beta 27, 221
Oregon 86, 293
Oregon State University 383
OSU Libraries ePress 242
OSU (Oklahoma State University) 242,
    443
outreach 82, 95, 202–207, 260–263, 370
techniques 318
to bookstores 183
faculty 87, 174, 330

within libraries 83
open courseware 24, 353; see also UN-
    ESCO Forum on the Impact of Open
    Courseware for Higher Education in
    Developing Countries

partnerships 165, 187, 339–341, 393
building relationships 167, 179, 224
utilizing existing relationships 29, 86,
    356, 385
pedagogy 37, 52, 62–66, 129, 336; see also
    open pedagogy
peer review 76, 146, 243, 424, 428
Peer Review Working Group 36
Pressbooks 186, 363–365, 392, 420, 429
as open textbook repository 156
publishing 145, 147, 341, 418, 427
partnership with 346
principal–agent problem 130, 157
print format 34, 182, 245, 358
print on demand 153, 245
privacy 127, 314, 315, 327, 329
professional development 187, 274, 299,
    394, 436
priorities 277
programming 296
required 273, 277
programming 249, 250, 255
Project Management for Instructional Design-
    ers 2, 145
promotion 275, 370, 374, 383
public domain 2, 319, 409
Public Interest Research Group (PIRG)
    176
publishers 19–22, 135, 171, 298, 346
Elsevier 186
open textbook publishers 29, 185
publishing 419, 429, 436; see also Open
    Textbook Publishing Pilot, Pressbooks
library publishing 169, 383
platforms 418, 427
Purdue University 42

quality 44, 46, 95
concerns about 172, 228, 415, 425
perceptions of 42

Rebus Community 341
  open textbook project 415, 421, 424, 429
  Peer Review Working Group 36
Rebus Foundation 415, 417, 418, 428, 436
  Creative Commons licensing 420
  project management 422, 426
Reed, Julie 309, 445
Reed, Michelle 73, 93, 445
repositories 65, 159
  and OER discoverability 151
  awareness of 81
  lifespan of 386
  management of 343
  OER platforms 148, 169, 374, 386, 394,
    401
reuse 60, 336, 342, 353
  definition 3
  UNESCO Forum definition of OER 41
rhetorical approach 260, 266
Rice University 27, 185
Rigling, Lillian 193, 445
Rollins College 400, 435, 444
Ross, Heather M. 381, 445
Ruen, Matthew 165, 446

Salt Lake Community College 44
Saskatchewan Polytechnic 391
savings 62, 144, 268
  and other OER benefits 62, 157, 395, 422
  as return on investment 227
  BCcampus estimate of student savings
    86
  Borough of Manhattan Community Col-
    lege estimate of student savings 56
  Kansas State University estimate of stu-
    dent savings 173
  North Carolina State University estimate
    of student savings 194, 195
  University of Massachussetts Amherst
    estimate of student savings 337, 342
  University of Oklahoma estimate of stu-
    dent savings 356
  University of Saskatchewan estimate of
    student savings 388
  University of Texas at San Antonio esti-
    mate of student savings 229

scholarly communication 74–77, 439
  faculty understanding of 81
  librarians 73, 78, 84
  open access publishing 167
screen readers 100, 107
Shuttleworth Foundation 24
Smith, Jeremy 165, 333, 446
SMOG (Simple Measure of Gobbledygook) 124
social justice 158
  access to education 55, 65
  disabilities 108
  information literacy 76
  open pedagogy 141
social media 196, 197, 218, 257, 371
SPARC (Scholarly Publishing and Academic Resources Coalition) 24, 333, 439,
  448
  Connect OER 36
  listservs 65
  Meeting on Openness in Research and
    Education 225
  membership 254, 389
  mythbusting 222
  OER State Policy Tracker 87, 292
  support for OER 37, 185, 205, 352, 433
staffing 168, 335, 343–344, 365, 436
stakeholders 12, 32, 37, 298, 305
  identifying 4, 256
state initiatives 295, 302, 304, 345
STEM (science, technology, engineering,
  mathematics) 193, 373
  ancillary materials 66
  textbook accessibility 106, 107
stipends 259; see also OEI (Open Education Initiative)
  for OER reviews 95, 313
  funding 56
  to incentivize OER adoption 68, 253,
    262, 263, 333
  to incentivize workshop attendance 54,
    63
  to incorporate technology 402
student government association (SGA)
  175–177, 340
  collaboration with 165, 227, 244, 373

students 175–178, 226
  and textbooks 62
  student groups 25, 249
  benefits of OER 31, 435
  course material preferences 279
  impact of education costs 41, 52, 335
  student survivalism 197, 201, 209, 215
  student senate 206
  Student PIRGs (Public Interest Research
    Groups) 25, 56, 61, 196, 227, 340
  student learning 135, 179, 411, 429
  student engagement 239–242, 248–250,
    261, 424
  student debt 32, 94, 131, 176, 334
success 227–229, 263–265, 283, 425–428
  raising graduation rates 214
  role of libraries in 298
SUNY (State University of New York) 36,
  61
sustainability 215, 266–268, 299, 345–349

Taylor, Cody 351, 446
TDEL (the Duke Endowment Libraries)
  309–311
TEL Library 448
Temple University 334, 434
tenure 222, 403
  as OER adoption concern 67, 68, 173
  teaching and tenure divide 123
Texas A&M University 176
text readability analysis 124
  textbooks 2, 19–24
    cost of 18, 41, 400
    eTextbooks 20–22
    impact on students 19, 62
    limitations 406
    market 19–20, 182, 197
    reliance on 345
    selection processes 121, 177
    Textbook Affordability Program 334
    textbook evaluation processes 133
    textbook exchange 197
    textbook lending 193, 196
    textbook reserves 52, 159, 216
      awareness of 374
      funding 53, 55, 402

student survivalism 62
Textbook Transformation Grants 294
The American Yawp 362
Tidewater Community College 35, 43,
  185, 214
training 297; see also workshops
  for faculty 54, 56, 137
  for library staff 96, 394
  offered by libraries 142
train-the-trainer 300, 302
  Train the Trainer Workshop 311–313,
    328
Turner, Ciara 93, 446
Twitter 84, 133, 259, 371, 389
tenure-track and adjunct 126
textbook culture 194

University of Saskatchewan (U of S)
  387–393, 435, 444
UMass Amherst (University of Massachu-
  setts Amherst) 166, 176, 352, 446; see
  also OEI (Open Education Initiative)
  Amazon as campus bookstore 182, 183
  OER adoption 188, 333, 434
  training 169
UNESCO Forum on the Impact of Open
  Courseware for Higher Education in
  Developing Countries 41, 335
universal design 97, 109, 159; see also ac-
  cessible design
University of British Columbia (UBC) 42,
  44, 149
University of Calgary 42
University of California 81, 147
University of Connecticut 293, 444
University of Georgia 45
University of Hawaii at Manoa 85, 156
University of Idaho 248
University of Illinois (Urbana-Cham-
  paign) 42
University of Michigan-Flint 256
University of Minnesota 27, 313, 341, 352,
  391
University of Oklahoma 352, 435, 446
University of Regina 391
University of South Carolina 313

University of Southern Indiana 448
University System of Georgia (USG) 215, 294
U.S. Government Accountability Office 18
University of Texas at Arlington (UTA) 94, 446
University of Texas at Arlington Libraries 93–95, 445
University of Texas at San Antonio (UTSA) 213, 215–217, 220–222, 435, 441
University of Washington (UW) 415, 436, 440
UW Friends of the Libraries 418
Friends of the Libraries Grant 419

Vanderbilt University 447
veterans 94, 226
video 102–103, 107, 133, 169, 242
Noba Student Videos 148
Project Management for Instructional Designers 145
Virginia Tech 447

Waller, Jen 351, 446
Walz, Anita 115, 447
WAVE Web Accessibility Evaluation Tool 98
Web Content Accessibility Guidelines (WCAG) 98
webinars 296, 300, 303
Wesolek, Andrew 1, 447

Wiki Education Foundation 147, 208
Wikipedia 133, 136, 147, 208, 392
Wikipedia Edit-a-Thon 355
Wikipedia for Education 359
Wiley, David 261, 333, 342
5 Rs 336
Project Management for Instructional Designers 2, 145
open pedagogy 30, 143
William and Flora Hewlett Foundation 24, 37, 188, 244
WordPress 362–364, 389
Pressbooks 341
publishing platform 146, 242
workshops on 64
workshops 63–65, 78, 417; *see also* text readability analysis: train-the-trainer
3D printing 203
and professional development 276, 283
Intersections 74
Open Textbook Network 267, 300, 419
open textbooks 171, 218, 244, 337, 392
Wright, Andrea 309, 448

Yano, Brady 17, 448

Z-degrees 35, 214
Zemke, Stacy 351, 448
ZTC (zero textbook cost) 56, 58, 60, 62, 67

CPSIA information can be obtained
at www.ICGtesting.com
Printed in the USA
FFHW011555151218
49851941-54411FF